THE APOSTLE PAUL AND HIS LETTERS

SERIES EDITORS

Pablo T. Gadenz
Mount St. Mary's University and Seminary, Maryland

Gregory Y. Glazov
Immaculate Conception Seminary School of Theology
Seton Hall University

Jeffrey L. Morrow
Immaculate Conception Seminary School of Theology
Seton Hall University

EDITORIAL BOARD

Joseph C. Atkinson
Pontifical John Paul II Institute for Studies
on Marriage and Family at The Catholic
University of America

Lewis Ayres
Durham University and
Australian Catholic University

John C. Cavadini
University of Notre Dame

Anthony Giambrone, OP
École biblique et archéologique
française de Jérusalem

Nina Sophie Heereman
St. Patrick's Seminary and University

Reinhard Hütter
The Catholic University of America

Matthew Levering
Mundelein Seminary

Francesca Aran Murphy
University of Notre Dame

Matthew Ramage
Benedictine College, Kansas

Brant Pitre
Augustine Institute
Graduate School of Theology

Steven C. Smith
Mundelein Seminary

Jody Vaccaro Lewis
Pontifical Faculty of the Immaculate
Conception at the Dominican House
of Studies, Washington, DC

William M. Wright IV
Duquesne University

Copyright © 2021
The Catholic University of America Press

All rights reserved

The paper used in this publication
meets the minimum requirements of
American National Standards for Information Science—
Permanence of Paper for Printed Library Materials,
ANSI Z39.48-1984.

Nihil Obstat:
Rev. Christopher Begg, S.T.D., Ph.D.
Censor Deputatus
Imprimatur:
Very Reverend Daniel B. Carson
Vicar General and Moderator of the Curia
Archdiocese of Washington
September 17, 2021

The *nihil obstat* and *imprimatur* are official declarations that a book or
pamphlet is free of doctrinal or moral error. There is no implication that
those who have granted the *nihil obstat* and the *imprimatur* agree with
the content, opinions or statements expressed therein.

Cataloging-in-Publication Data available from the Library of Congress

ISBN PAPERBACK: 978-0-8132-3512-7
ISBN EBOOK: 978-0-8132-3513-4

Printed in the United States.

Book design by Burt&Burt
Interior set with Minion Pro and Astoria

The Apostle Paul and His Letters

AN INTRODUCTION

JAMES B. PROTHRO

Foreword by Thomas D. Stegman, SJ

The Catholic University of America Press
Washington, D.C.
2021

For Sophia

May the God of hope
fill you with all joy and peace in believing,
so that you abound in hope by the power of the Holy Spirit.

(Romans 15:13)

Contents

Foreword

When I first learned that James Prothro was writing an introduction to St. Paul and his letters, I thought, "Do we really need another one?" Indeed, there are many such resources available, both old and more recent. Having worked my way through Prothro's manuscript, I am happy that he engaged in this project.

As I read through the book, what strikes me is that the author is passionate about what Paul teaches concerning life in the Spirit, the life empowered by the gift of the Holy Spirit whom the apostle describes as "the love of God … poured into our hearts" (Rom 5:5). This way of life is the imitation of Jesus' self-giving love, which Paul incarnated in his life and ministry (1 Cor 11:1). One reason for reading and studying Paul—I would contend, the *main* reason for doing so—is to learn from him and be inspired by him to lead more Christ-like lives. Moreover, the letters in question are regarded by the Church as divine revelation. This motivation and conviction lie close beneath the surface throughout the book, making it a worthy endeavor.

Prothro's work is in some ways a "throwback." Classic introductions to the New Testament (or to parts of it) set forth in great detail such critical issues as date, provenance, historical background and context, reasons for writing, etc. This is precisely what the author does in the present work. And he does so with thoroughness, even-handedness, and (best of all) clarity. His stated purpose is to *lead* interested readers *into* (the root meaning of "introduce") Paul's letters, to encounter them by first appreciating what the apostle was trying to accomplish by writing to churches and individuals. These are real letters, written to address specific issues and concerns. An intelligent contemporary appropriation should take those issues and concerns into account. Prothro helps the reader to do so in an accessible manner.

I experienced his style as *invitatory*, inviting the reader to engage both Paul and the author himself.

His introduction to Paul also brings fresh "newness." I offer two examples. The apostle's understanding of the Jewish law subsequent to his encounter with the risen Lord has been the subject of much scholarly discussion. It is also an important issue for the study of Paul and for contemporary Jewish-Christian relations. Prothro presents the best of contemporary scholarship on this critical issue. The same holds for the author's explanation of what Paul means when he discusses *faith*. Everyone agrees that faith—and its relationship to what God has done through Christ—is central to the apostle's thought. But what precisely he means by "faith" has been hotly debated. The author skillfully deals with the issue, taking into account current scholarship, as he leads his reader into the texts.

Paul is not the only one who writes from a context. So, too, does any scholar who treats the apostle and his writings. Prothro writes as a Roman Catholic, a commitment and perspective I share. That perspective, and the tradition behind it, will come through at certain points in the book. Not all will agree with his interpretation in some places, but his style and tone are conversational, inviting respectful engagement—especially with the texts themselves.

As has been observed for two millennia (starting with 2 Pet 3:16), Paul's letters are not easy to understand. However, given their status of communicating *God's* word, and given what they teach about the Spirit-empowered *imitatio Christi*, they are worth wrestling with. James Prothro has produced an admirably useful resource to assist such a noble undertaking.

Thomas D. Stegman, SJ
Dean and Professor Ordinarius
Boston College School of Theology and Ministry
May 31, 2021—Feast of the Visitation

Preface

I am thankful for this book, not merely for its publication, but also for how the writing process has humbled and shaped me as a teacher, thinker, and reader. This book took shape during a period in which my duties called me to transition from doing specialized research at a secluded desk to teaching biblical theology broadly to parishioners, undergraduates, and graduate students. Though I wanted to write something like this five years ago, it would hardly have been the same book. Any such improvements I owe to support and correction from my family, friends, and fellow scholars. Any errors are my own.

I am grateful to the editors at CUA Press who accepted this book for publication, to the Verbum Domini series editors, and particularly to John Martino, who has guided this book from proposal to print. I am thankful also to my anonymous peer reviewers. One reviewer in particular—whom I have since learned is one of this series's editors, Fr. Pablo Gadenz—supported the project by offering extensive comments that have improved the book's style and content immensely. He went above and beyond not just as a reviewer for the press but as a colleague to me. My thanks also to Fr. Thomas Stegman, SJ, whom I admire greatly as a scholar and as a churchman, for his willingness to take time out of a year already interrupted by work, service, and the coronavirus pandemic to look at this project and commend it with a foreword.

Many others helped in larger and smaller ways. Accordance Bible Software kindly sourced the template I used for the maps that appear throughout the book. Shannon Lee served as a wonderfully careful copy editor. Sarah DeVille and Abigail Starcher processed countless interlibrary loans when I prepared several of this book's chapters while teaching at Ave Maria University. My thinking about Paul's biography and theology has been helped by constant conversation over the past year with Fr. Gregory Tatum, OP, John Kincaid, and Ben Blackwell. Michael Barber, John Sehorn, Brant Pitre, and Mark Giszczak have offered special encouragement as I wrote, and all my coworkers at the Augustine Institute have contributed to my ability to complete this project joyfully (even those who didn't know what I was working on). The employers, colleagues, staff, and students with whom I work constitute a network of support and joy for the spiritual and intellectual life as well as for productivity.

Finally, I thank my family. My parents have supported my education and shaped me from a young age both for critical inquiry and hard work. Thanks are hardly enough for my wife, Ashley. You are my constant companion and support in prayer, work, and rest. And to my children—Sophia, Heidi, Elizabeth, and Charles—thank you for letting me be your dad. I dedicate this book to our firstborn, Sophia, who wants to understand, loves to pray, and is just now beginning to read. May you never stop.

James B. Prothro
Augustine Institute Graduate School of Theology
Greenwood Village, Colorado
February 2021

Abbreviations

AB	Anchor Bible
ABD	*Anchor Bible Dictionary.* Edited by David Noel Freedman. 6 vols. New York: Doubleday, 1992.
AcBib	Academia Biblica
AnBib	Analecta Biblica
ANTC	Abingdon New Testament Commentaries
BECNT	Baker Exegetical Commentary on the New Testament
Bib	*Biblica*
BNTC	Black's New Testament Commentaries
BZNW	Beihefte zur Zeitschrift für die neutestamentliche Wissenschaft
CBQ	*Catholic Biblical Quarterly*
CBQMS	Catholic Biblical Quarterly Monograph Series
CCC	*Catechism of the Catholic Church.* 2nd edition. Revised in accordance with the official Latin text promulgated by Pope John Paul II. Includes revision of paragraph no. 2267 promulgated by Pope Francis. Rome: Libreria Editrice Vaticana, 2019.
CCSS	Catholic Commentary on Sacred Scripture
ConcC	Concordia Commentary
CRINT	Compendia Rerum Iudaicarum ad Novum Testamentum

DNTB	*Dictionary of New Testament Background.* Edited by Craig A. Evans and Stanley E. Porter. Downers Grove, IL: InterVarsity, 2000.
DPL	*Dictionary of Paul and His Letters.* Edited by Gerald F. Hawthorne and Ralph P. Martin. Downers Grove, IL: InterVarsity, 1993.
ECC	Eerdmans Critical Commentary
ECL	Early Christianity and Its Literature
EstBib	*Estudios bíblicos*
ESV	English Standard Version
HTR	*Harvard Theological Review*
ICC	International Critical Commentary
JBL	*Journal of Biblical Literature*
JJT	*Josephinum Journal of Theology*
JSNT	*Journal for the Study of the New Testament*
JSNTSup	Journal for the Study of the New Testament Supplement Series
JSPL	*Journal for the Study of Paul and His Letters*
JTS	*Journal of Theological Studies*
KJV	King James Version
LNTS	The Library of New Testament Studies
LPS	Library of Pauline Studies
NABRE	New American Bible, Revised Edition
Neot	*Neotestamentica*
NICNT	New International Commentary on the New Testament
NIGTC	New International Greek Testament Commentary
NJB	New Jerusalem Bible
NovT	*Novum Testamentum*

NovTSup	Supplements to Novum Testamentum
NT	New Testament
NTL	New Testament Library
NTOA	Novum Testamentum et Orbis Antiquus
NTS	*New Testament Studies*
NRSV	New Revised Standard Version
OT	Old Testament
OTP	*Old Testament Pseudepigrapha.* Edited by James H. Charlesworth. 2 vols. New York: Doubleday, 1983, 1985.
PG	Patrologiae Cursus Completus: Series Graeca. Edited by Jacques-Paul Migne. 162 vols. Paris, 1857–1886.
RSV	Revised Standard Version
SBLDS	Society of Biblical Literature Dissertation Series
SBLSBS	Society of Biblical Literature Sources for Biblical Study
SBLStBL	Society of Biblical Literature Studies in Biblical Literature
SNTSMS	Society for New Testament Studies Monograph Series
SNTW	Studies of the New Testament and Its World
SP	Sacra Pagina
SymS	SBL Symposium Series
TDNT	*Theological Dictionary of the New Testament.* Edited by Gerhard Kittel and Gerhard Friedrich. Translated by Geoffrey W. Bromiley. 10 vols. Grand Rapids: Eerdmans, 1964–1976.
THKNT	Theologischer Handkommentar zum Neuen Testament
VC	*Vigiliae Christianae*

WBC	Word Biblical Commentary
WUNT	Wissenschaftliche Untersuchungen zum Neuen Testament
ZNW	*Zeitschrift für die neutestamentliche Wissenschaft und die Kunde der älteren Kirche*

THE APOSTLE PAUL AND HIS LETTERS

CHAPTER ONE

The Importance and Challenges of Paul

THE IMPORTANCE OF PAUL

The writings of the Apostle Paul are central witnesses both to the faith of Christianity and to the earliest history of that movement. Historically, 1 Thessalonians is likely the earliest document by a follower of Jesus that we have in complete form. Among biblical writers, Paul authored more individual books than any other. His letters give outstanding evidence of the structures, beliefs, and challenges faced by the first Christians and their spiritual leaders as this apostle (and others) took the gospel from Judea and Syria to Europe.

Theologically, Paul's letters are of especial value. Traditional Christianity holds these letters to be inspired by God to shape the faith and life of believers in Paul's day and ever since. Indeed, Paul's writings were recognized as authoritative quite early in the church. In about 95 CE, likely only about thirty years after Paul's death, Clement of Rome wrote to the church in Corinth: "Take up the epistle of the blessed Paul the Apostle" (*1 Clement* 47.1). In about 110, Ignatius of Antioch praised him as "Paul the sanctified, approved, most worthy of blessing—in whose footsteps I hope to be found when I attain to God" (*Ephesians* 12.2). The powerful preacher John Chrysostom (ca. 347–407) had a particularly fervent devotion to Paul: "I love all the saints, but most especially the blessed Paul, the vessel of election, the heavenly trumpet, the friend of Christ the bridegroom" (*Homily on 2 Corinthians* 11:1 [PG 51:301]). Paul's acclaim is owed to his teachings, which are attested for us in his letters, as well as to his exemplary imitation of Christ. Gregory of

Nyssa wrote of Paul: "More accurately than all others, he ascertained who Christ is and showed through his deeds what sort of person one who bears his name should be. So manifestly did he imitate him that he showed the Lord figured in himself, through imitating him most precisely, the image of his own soul having been changed into its Prototype, so that it no longer seemed to be Paul living and speaking but Christ himself living in him" (*On Perfection* [PG 46:253]).

The faith of the church has been nourished constantly by Paul's letters. In them we see a devoted apostle instructing believers in the truth of Christ, God's love and faithfulness throughout salvation history, and the gift of the Holy Spirit within the church. Though they are not the only places these truths are evident in scripture, many Christian doctrines—such as original sin, justification, baptism, the eucharist, the role of the Spirit, and the future return of Christ and resurrection of the dead—are shaped by explicit statements from Paul. Indeed, at several points in the history of Christianity, it has been to the letters of Paul that the church has turned to discern and defend the faith against opposition. Thomas Aquinas compared Paul's letters in the NT to the Psalms in the OT for the formative role they play in Christian thought, claiming that "in each of these writings is contained almost the whole teaching of theology" (*Commentary on Romans*, preface). Indeed, when figures in the ancient church—East or West—refer to "the Apostle" without specifying which apostle they mean, they are referring to Paul.

THE CHALLENGES OF PAUL

While of utmost importance, Paul's letters also furnish numerous challenges. Many of the doctrines the church formulated based on Paul's letters were responses to others who claimed Paul for an opposite teaching. In the second century, Marcion of Sinope read Paul's words about being freed from the Mosaic law as support for his dualistic view that the God of the OT was not the Father of Jesus Christ; orthodox Christians such as Tertullian had to walk through Paul's letters one by one to show that this was a grave misinterpretation. (One should note that, given what Paul actually wrote, this was a fairly easy thing for Tertullian or anyone to do.) In the fourth and early fifth centuries, theological giants such as Jerome and especially Augustine used Paul's letters to defend the doctrine of grace against Pelagianism, which downplayed original sin and taught that humans could be saved by their own power without God's transformative grace. Most have agreed that

Pelagianism and Paul are incompatible, yet Pelagius too saw his teaching as an interpretation of Paul, having produced his own commentaries on his letters. In the sixteenth century, both the Protestant Reformers and the Catholic Counter-Reformers defended their views with quotations from Paul.

The contested interpretation of Paul is evidenced even in the NT itself. In Romans 3:8, Paul himself acknowledges that some have misrepresented his gospel of God's grace as a license to sin. Also noteworthy is 2 Peter 3:15–16: "Consider the patience of our Lord as salvation, just as also our beloved brother Paul wrote you according to the wisdom given him, as he speaks in all his epistles about these things—in them there are things hard to understand, which the unlearned and unstable distort to their own destruction, as they do also with the other scriptures." Strikingly, the author includes Paul's letters together with the "scriptures," revering them alongside the OT, and yet also states openly that they are difficult and prone to misinterpretation. Paul's letters have occasioned contrary interpretations from his own day to ours.

One difficulty readers face is that Paul's letters are *occasional.* Though they deal with topics of doctrine and catechetical formation, none of his letters is written as a catechism or a systematic explication of a doctrine. They are not written to treat topics separately or encyclopedically. They are *epistles* (Greek ἐπιστολή, *epistolē*, "letter"), letters sent to instruct particular churches in faith and life in view of some current event or circumstance. Further, with only one or two exceptions (Romans, Colossians), these letters were all written to churches that Paul had already evangelized in person. This means that what Paul wrote in his letters is hardly everything he believed or knew even about the topics he discusses. He preached far more than he wrote, and we do not even have all Paul's letters (he mentions one lost letter in 1 Cor 5:9). When one reads these texts as definitive treatises that say everything possible about a topic, instead of reading them as occasional letters that try to make a point and influence a community's behavior in light of a particular situation, it can be easy to overread what Paul says in one place and then misunderstand his point. And what is true of studying Paul's letters is similarly true of studying his life: his letters do not tell us of all his travels or of other activities. Likewise the book of Acts, which does present many details of Paul's life and travels, hardly gives a comprehensive history. Acts certainly conveys historical data about Paul's life, but it is an occasioned document with particular goals for particular audiences.

It can thus become difficult to form a mental "picture" of Paul and his personality, to understand what "makes him tick." In his own day, Paul came under fire for the way he preached salvation in Christ to gentiles (people not ethnically Jewish): they had only to believe and follow Christ, but need not and indeed should not be circumcised (Gal 5:1–5). Some Jewish believers heard this and thought he meant Jews too should not only cease practicing circumcision but give up all their heritage (see Acts 21:17–21). Likewise, since circumcision was a statute of the Mosaic law just as the Ten Commandments were, others misheard this teaching as an invitation to libertinism. We have already mentioned Romans 3:8: "Some say that we say, 'Let's do evil that good may come!'—their condemnation is just!"

Indeed, Paul's statements about the law and scholarly speculation about whether Paul saw himself still as a Jew or as something else instead (a "Christian") have dominated controversy about the Apostle since. Most patristic and medieval readers emphasized that what was "new" in Paul's religion consisted primarily in the gift of the Holy Spirit, perfect atonement (surpassing animal sacrifice) and eternal life in Christ, and the "new law" that no longer required observances such as circumcision or kosher dietary laws. But later interpreters drew up different divisions between Paul and Judaism. Luther, in his personal struggle to find a gracious God instead of the oppressive and wrathful God he sensed under God's commandments, recast Paul's gospel in existential terms: Paul's gospel opposed Jewish legalism and its demands for obedience with a promise of simple assurance of God's favor. In the twentieth century, the "New Perspective" on Paul emphasized the role of grace in Judaism and saw Paul opposing not Jewish legalism but Jewish ethnocentrism and arguing for the full equality of gentile believers within Christ's community. The scholarly attempt to profile Paul and his statements about Israel's law continues today as we learn to see Paul's preaching and mission for Christ not as a rejection of but, he believed, a part of his Judaism.

Other difficulties old and new come from questioning Paul's status or value within Christian tradition. Paul had been a persecutor of Jesus's followers until the Lord called him to faith and to his new apostolic task. Some "glorified God" because of this (Gal 1:24), and tradition upholds both Paul "the Apostle" and Peter as pillars of the church. But others in his day suspected him of being a proverbial snake in the grass, perverting what they believed was the original teaching of Jesus. In the last three hundred years or so it has become popular again to pit Paul against Jesus as "the first corrupter of the doctrines of Jesus," as Thomas Jefferson put it in an 1820 letter to his secretary.[1] Popular versions of this assertion state that Jesus taught

1 See Adams 1983, 391–94.

simple spirituality while Paul forced doctrine on us all by teaching about sin and atonement, or that Jesus only taught a revolutionary kind of love while Paul made the church into "status quo" conservatives by teaching about male headship in marriage or asking a slave to be reconciled to his master, Philemon. Though exaggerated, there is truth to the quip that "all Christian theology is merely a footnote to Paul"[2]—both theology that tries to follow in the Apostle's footsteps and theology that fights to erase them from the path.

THE AIMS OF THIS BOOK

Paul's letters and teachings are incredibly contested, and they are incredibly important. This body of biblical texts and the Apostle in whose name they are passed down form, in the words of Pope Benedict XVI, "an extraordinary spiritual heritage" that contributes to "the reinforcement of the Christian identity of each one of us and . . . the rejuvenation of the entire Church."[3]

This book is written to help readers read Paul's letters and to see him and his teachings through them. This is not a "Pauline theology" (a comprehensive account of what his letters show that he believed and taught) or a biography of Paul. It is not a commentary in which I treat every issue of each letter, and it is not a reference book simply giving brief reports of scholarly views. This is an *introduction*. We sometimes use the word "introductory" to mean something that merely gives basic information rather than provoking thought. Or, in biblical scholarship, books labeled "introduction" are sometimes simply academic reference books. This introduction will have much in common with both of these, but I intend the term here in its classical sense: I write this book to *lead* readers *into* (Latin, *intro* + *duco*, "I lead into") studying and appreciating the letters of Paul. This means that I aim to spend as much space guiding readers through *how to read and reason through* Paul's letters—what questions to ask, why scholars think this or that—as I do simply giving my interpretation. This book is focused on teaching Paul through his letters, as they are the primary source from which to make conclusions about Paul's person or about his doctrine. Naturally, I will take positions and make arguments in the book, and space prohibits discussing everything in each letter. But my aim is that those who follow me—as I indeed follow other scholars—will from this book develop good

2 Mullin 2014, 19.
3 Benedict XVI 2009, 128, 131.

habits of reading that propel continued study of what this book addresses as well as what it does not.

The opening chapters (chapters 2–5) orient readers to the study of Paul. They begin with a broad sketch of Paul's world and his life and identity within it. How was he formed? What cultural influences did he bear? What do we know of his biography? Next, within his life, how should we approach his letters? How did he write them, and what were they meant to do? Did he personally write all the letters that bear his name, or might some have been written by his associates or later followers? Most importantly for theological readers, how should we read these occasional letters to understand the Apostle's thought and hear his voice within the biblical canon? A further chapter will survey Paul's person and significance as presented in the book of Acts.

The remaining chapters treat the NT letters that claim Paul as their author.[4] Each chapter will address the letter's *background* and purposes, give a longhand *overview* of its contents, and then select certain *key features* highlighting theological themes and debated issues within the letter's argument. As we will see below in chapter 4, considering these issues of background, argument, and theology in each of the letters is important for understanding their historical and theological value. 1 Timothy, 2 Timothy, and Titus are treated together in one chapter because they share similar introductory issues, as are 1 and 2 Thessalonians. In those cases, background and key features may overlap, but each letter will receive its own overview within the chapter.

HOW TO USE THIS BOOK

To get the most out of this book, *it will serve readers best to read chapters 1–4 first before turning to the individual letter treatments.* The issues the first four chapters address—Paul's identity, letters, and how one approaches his

---

4 Hebrews was traditionally grouped with the Pauline letters, but the letter itself never names its author (contrast Rom 1:1; 1 Cor 1:1; etc.). Christians in the first four centuries or so disagreed about who wrote Hebrews, and today scholars across the ecumenical spectrum agree that Hebrews was not written by Paul, even if its author may have been connected to Paul's friends and successors (see Heb 13:23). The letter's placement in the canon acknowledges its disputed status by setting Hebrews outside the list of Pauline letters, situating it between Paul and James rather than after 2 Corinthians, where it would fall in the Pauline corpus as ordered by length.

theology—frame how one hears Paul's voice in his letters and how one reasons through certain aspects of the letters and Acts. After chapter 4, it is not necessary that each chapter be read in the order given in this book. When I teach the Pauline letters, I regularly teach them in the order in which I think they were written historically (beginning with 1 Thessalonians). However, as the chapters below illustrate, not all scholars agree on the historical order in which the letters were written. This book therefore presents the letters in canonical order, but the reader is not disadvantaged by skipping around. Chapter 5 treats Paul's portrait in Acts, and readers will benefit from reading the overall picture of Paul's life and ministry in Acts before diving into the letters, but reading Acts after the letters can be beneficial as well. However, a corollary to this flexibility—and the space constraints of this book—is that readers must *use the cross-references in the main text*, where a note such as "(see chapter 6)" or "(see chapter 1)" will direct readers to a pertinent discussion that they might not yet have read and that I will not repeat.

As an introduction, this book aims to be able to draw a wide swath of readers into reading and thinking with Paul. In part this means introducing readers to information in the text and pertinent works of scholarship that discuss or illuminate the text. Pauline studies is a massive field, and there are only so many topics and scholarly positions that can be addressed profitably in this book. My treatment of theological and historical topics is necessarily selective, not to deny the relevance of what is left unaddressed, but to introduce key information and interpretive questions that arise from and help illumine main features of the text. Interested readers will be able to further their study by diving into the footnotes and books listed as "Further Reading" at the end of each chapter, and hopefully they will be prepared to do so by using this book. I have tried to reference only scholarly literature accessible in English, but those who go on to read that literature (and a few of the footnotes in this book) will get a glimpse of the interpretive riches available only in other languages.

How does this book treat theological topics? Most readers who study Paul do so because they are interested in Christian theology, and Christian theology neither begins nor ends with Paul. As a Catholic, I am interested in hearing Paul's voice along with others in scripture in order to receive God's revelation through the whole biblical canon, a symphony of many voices through which God speaks the "one single Word" (*CCC* §102) of the Triune God's being and saving will. But hearing Paul's voice within the canon means, in part, appreciating his voice with all its distinctiveness, with his particularities of expression, and within his ancient contexts.[5] If God speaks by inspiring human communication, then hearing God's message requires attending to those elements of human communication. And, indeed, it is the human features and historical embeddedness of Paul's letters that often need the most explaining for theologically interested readers. So this book's primary goal is to help readers understand Paul's letters on their own terms, attending both to the words that Paul wrote and to the contexts in which he was inspired to write them. However, I will occasionally note the reception of Paul's words and ideas by ancient and modern church authorities. These notes, though not a main focus of this book, hope to nudge theological readers into the further work of biblical interpretation—to hear Paul's voice in symphony with the rest of scripture's authors and the living tradition that continues to play the tune.

One final bit of advice, autobiographically illustrated: *check the verse references in parentheses.* When I first became enamored of Pauline studies, I bought a book claiming to outline Paul's thought. It bored me at first. It seemed little more than summaries of doctrinal topics with proof-texts from Paul, showing me what the author thought Paul thought but little more. That changed when I started checking the author's parenthetical references. If the author said, "Paul believed X (cf. this verse and that verse)" or "Paul traveled to Galatia twice before he wrote this (see this verse)," I started checking those verses. Not only did this allow me to agree or disagree with the author more intelligently, but it forced me to retrace the author's thinking and interpretation of individual data points. And in doing so, I began to learn habits of noticing little details in Paul that I might otherwise have passed over, and I learned to use these little details to reason more clearly through Paul's letters and, through understanding the letters, to understand Paul. Interpretation is learned by apprenticeship, and there is always a lot hidden in parentheses. Following the reasoning behind the conclusions in this or other books is an important way of honing one's skill to read Paul with and beyond even the best books about him.

---

5 See Vatican Council II, Dogmatic Constitution *Dei Verbum* (November 18, 1965), §12: "Since God speaks in Sacred Scripture through men in human fashion, the interpreter of Sacred Scripture, in order to see what God wanted to communicate to us, should carefully investigate what meaning the sacred writers really intended, and what God wanted to manifest by means of their words."

A NOTE ON TRANSLATIONS AND VERSES

When translations of scripture or other ancient documents appear in this book, those translations are my own unless otherwise noted.

English Bible translations follow different versifications at certain points, mostly in the OT books. This book references biblical passages as they are numbered in the New American Bible—Revised Edition (NABRE). The NABRE follows editions of the Hebrew OT, in line with the *Nova Vulgata* (promulgated 1979), and so occasionally differs from English Bibles that follow the King James Version's numberings (such as the Revised Standard Version or English Standard Version). For readers who use such translations, I will signal the alternate versification in a footnote or as "KJV" in parentheses (e.g., Ps 51:3 [KJV 51:1]).

FURTHER READING

Benedict XVI (Pope). 2009. *Saint Paul: General Audiences July 2, 2008–February 4, 2009.* San Francisco: Ignatius.

Bird, Michael F., and Joseph R. Dodson, eds. 2011. *Paul and the Second Century.* LNTS 412. London: T&T Clark.

Chester, Stephen J. 2017. *Reading Paul with the Reformers: Reconciling Old and New Perspectives.* Grand Rapids: Eerdmans.

Dunn, James D. G. 2005. "The New Perspective on Paul: Whence, What and Whither?" In *The New Perspective on Paul: Collected Essays*, 1–197. Rev. ed. Grand Rapids: Eerdmans.

Gray, Patrick. 2016. *Paul as a Problem in History and Culture: The Apostle and His Critics through the Centuries.* Grand Rapids: Baker Academic.

Hafemann, Scott J. 2015. "Paul and His Interpreters since F. C. Baur." In *Paul's Message and Ministry in Covenant Perspective: Selected Essays*, 3–28. Eugene, OR: Cascade.

Levering, Matthew. 2014. *Paul in the Summa Theologiae.* Washington, DC: The Catholic University of America Press.

McKnight, Scott, and B. J. Oropeza, eds. 2020. *Perspectives on Paul: Five Views.* Grand Rapids: Baker Academic.

Mitchell, Margaret M. 2002. *The Heavenly Trumpet: John Chrysostom and the Art of Pauline Interpretation.* Louisville, KY: Westminster John Knox.

Nanos, Mark, and Magnus Zetterholm, eds. 2015. *Paul within Judaism: Restoring the First-Century Context to the Apostle.* Minneapolis: Fortress.

Wright, N. T. 2015. *Paul and His Recent Interpreters.* Minneapolis: Fortress.

Zetterholm, Magnus. 2009. *Approaches to Paul: A Student's Guide to Recent Scholarship.* Minneapolis: Fortress.

CHAPTER TWO

Paul's Life and Contexts

Before reading the letters, it is worth considering Paul's background and environment and getting a basic sketch of his ministry overall. The letters themselves make mention of Paul's own life as a testimony to God's work in him, and his formation and ongoing embeddedness in the world around him are important to consider as one reads his words.

A MAN OF TWO WORLDS

Paul is often referred to as a man of two (sometimes three) "worlds." Growing up he appears to have received considerable formation in *Judaism*.

> If anyone else thinks he has reason to put confidence in the flesh, I have more: circumcised on the eighth day, of the people of Israel, of the tribe of Benjamin, a Hebrew of Hebrews; as to the law, a Pharisee; as to zeal, a persecutor of the church; as to righteousness that is in the law, blameless. (Phil 3:4–6)

> For you have heard of my way of life in Judaism formerly, that I excessively persecuted the church of God and was overthrowing it, and I advanced in Judaism beyond many of my contemporaries among the people, being excessively zealous for the traditions of my fathers. (Gal 1:13–14)

Paul emphasizes his Jewish heritage and his great "zeal" as a Pharisee. His letters likewise show a great familiarity with Israel's scriptures. Though we do not find this claim in his letters, Acts holds that he received a rabbinic education under Gamaliel (Acts 22:3).

Yet, if Paul's identity was primarily defined and anchored in the faith, hope, and practice of Judaism, we should not imagine this means he was sheltered away in a ghetto uninfluenced by the *Greco-Roman* world. Jewish thinkers—even those who resisted it—had long been influenced by interaction and conversation with Greek culture or "Hellenism." One can see this already in Jewish works such as the book of Wisdom or the writings of Jewish philosopher Philo of Alexandria. And with Rome's takeover of Judea in 63 BCE and the spread of Rome's influence in the decades before Christ, Roman elements and the realities of life under the empire added to the cultural melting pot around the ancient Mediterranean. Paul's letters are written in fluid Greek and show some familiarity with Greco-Roman rhetoric (the art of persuasive speaking and writing) and philosophical concepts. According to Acts, Paul was born a Jew in Asia Minor, in the city of Tarsus, with the status of Roman citizenship (Acts 9:11; 21:39; 22:3, 27–28).

Paul's dual identity is in a way signaled by his double name reported in Acts—"Saul, who was also Paul" (Acts 13:9). What English Bibles render as "Saul" is a Semitic name, *Sha'ul*, one that befits his tribal heritage under the name of a famous Benjaminite, Israel's first king (see 1 Sam 9). Paulus, also spelled Paullus, is a Roman name (from the word meaning "little"). It has been popular to speak of Paul's name *changing* to reflect a change of identity, as a casting off of his heritage or as a new symbolic name from God—like Abram's renaming as Abraham ("Father of Many") or Jacob's as Israel ("God-wrestler")—but this is probably an invention. Acts is very interested to show continuity between God's work in the OT and the first Christians, but Acts never speaks of God or Paul changing Paul's name. Nor is there a clean break between his identities: Acts does not stop calling him Saul after he becomes a disciple of Christ. Rather, the phrasing of "Saul, who was also [ὁ καί, *ho kai*] Paul" (Acts 13:9) indicates merely a double name.[1] Many who had foreign names in the Roman Empire adopted an alternate name, especially if they were to advance or move freely in Greco-Roman society without coming off as aliens or outsiders. Often the new name had a similar sound or meaning to the original name.[2] That Greek speakers would find many foreign sounds hard to pronounce was a factor as well, though English translations of the Hebrew names obscure this. Just as one Yeshua was called Justus ("Jesus Justus," Col 4:11), Yochanan was called Marcus ("John Mark," Acts 12:12), and

---

1 Compare Kleodemus "who was also" (ὁ καί, *ho kai*) Malchus (Josephus, *Jewish Antiquities* 1.240). Some ancient manuscripts have the similar phrase "Saul who was *called* Paul" in Acts 12:25.

2 The same strategy was used in reverse early in the modern state of Israel, when the National Council called immigrants to Hebraize their names for public life (see Glinert 2017, 214).

Tyoma' (= Thomas) was called Didymus (both meaning "twin," John 20:24), so Sha'ul introduced himself to non-Jews as Paulus.

Rather than a radical change in identities, Paul's double name reflects the overlapping and admixed cultures in which he lived both before and after he became an apostle of Christ. His formation and ability to engage both worlds prepared him to be a formidable witness to and defender of his faith as a Jewish apostle of Jesus to the pagans. It prepared him to, as he says, "become all things to all people, that by all means I might save some" (1 Cor 9:22).

PAUL AND THE GRECO-ROMAN WORLD

In the late 300s BCE, Alexander the Great conquered much of the known world, from Asia Minor to northern Egypt, from Palestine to the edges of India. During and after his reign, Greek culture spread. His vision of a world united with one culture and under one emperor (himself) encouraged the amalgamation of many polytheistic religions, appending Greek names to the deities of conquered and incorporated cultures. The Greek language spread and became a lingua franca of business as well as philosophy and culture, influencing or even altering local customs and beliefs in non-Greek areas. Beginning in the 200s BCE, the Hebrew scriptures were translated into Greek, and some sacred writings began also to be written in Greek (forming what we know as the "Septuagint").

The Roman Empire was heir to these cultural influences as well as to its own peculiarities, and it spread to become in many ways as great as Alexander's empire. The rival consuls Julius Caesar and Pompey, respectively, campaigned west into Gaul (roughly, modern France) and sacked Jerusalem. And after their civil war Julius's heir Octavian became Augustus Caesar (27 BCE). Thus the Roman Empire was born. Rome's influence was felt structurally and in the spread of some Italian cultural elements, and naturally new fads, movements, and ideas emerged as well. The empire was seen as a household, with Caesar at the top as *paterfamilias*, his soldiers and government personnel like household servants under him, and others working and living in ways that ideally served the honor of the empire and emperor. Culturally, however, Caesar's empire did not lead to an undoing of the Hellenistic character of its lands. Many historians and philosophers continued to write in Greek, even as some cities showed their loyalty with Latin-language monuments and other signals of Roman identity. According to the Roman historian Suetonius, the emperor Claudius declared Greek the

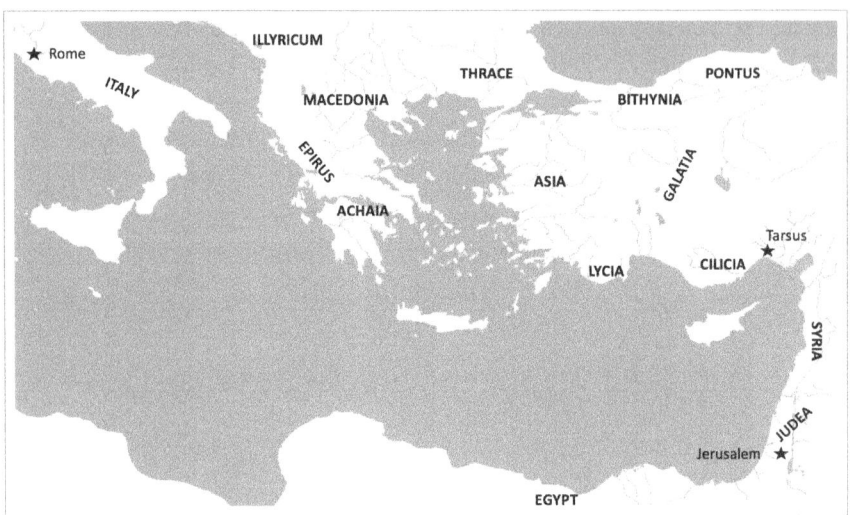

This map shows much of the Roman Empire in Paul's day. Provinces are given in capital letters. Cities are marked with stars.

"finest of all" languages and saw it as the heritage of his conquering empire, calling Greek and Latin together "our tongues" (*Claudius* 42.1).

We will see in later chapters how different aspects of Roman and Hellenistic culture in Paul's churches affected how he wrote to them and what problems he needed to address. We note for now that the empire and its cultural heritages connected these diverse places and facilitated Paul's international ministry. Paul's message was not hindered by writing in Greek even when addressing a Roman colony such as Philippi or the imperial capital in Rome. His missionary travels were helped significantly by major Roman roadways connecting the empire's provinces. And the spread of common philosophical ideas and categories allowed Paul to communicate the gospel in similar terms to persons of diverse local and national identities.

We should also note certain features of Greco-Roman religion and philosophy. Paul had much here to engage and appreciate, as well as much with which to contend as he aimed to "take every thought captive in obedience to Christ" (2 Cor 10:5). There was, on the one hand, what most readers will think of when considering Greek or Roman "religion," the standard religion of the state and its pantheon of gods such as Zeus (Roman Jupiter), Aphrodite (Venus), or Ares (Mars). Worship of these gods was everywhere, inscribed on buildings, written into civic ceremony and activity. There was no separation between religion and daily life. Many cities had specific patronal gods, families honored lesser ancestral gods, and devotion and even worship were beginning at this time to be extended to the emperors, who became seen as earthly "sons" of the gods bringing divine power and favor to the empire. These were realities with which Jews and new converts to Christianity had to live, from town festivals to imperial service to even the butchering of meats slaughtered in honor of gods—and those who refused to take part might be marginalized or persecuted for angering the gods. There were likewise "mystery religions," secret societies of devotion to a particular god such as Mithras or Demeter, with rituals of initiation believed to grant one (or unite one to) a god's power. Romans who knew anything of devotion to Jesus often saw it either as another mystery religion, as a "foreign" (and illegal) religion, or as an absurd movement worshipping a dead criminal.

Christianity also had analogues and competition from the philosophers. In general, philosophy was more interested in morality and consistent ethics than was the state religion, which appeased the gods more with sacrifice and civic duty.[3] Philosophers were interested less in the personalities and preferences of gods (when they believed in them) than in the ordering of the universe and in a way of life that accorded with it. *Stoicism* saw all realities as either finer or coarser forms of matter, originating from fire and set to return to it, with a principle called the Logos (λόγος) ordering all things and keeping them in balance. To live rightly in the cosmos was to align oneself with this reality, trusting a kind of providence or reasonable fate in the cosmic order and accepting anything beyond one's own control by governing one's passions with reason rather than being cast about by emotions or inordinate expectations. *Epicureanism* saw the highest good as "pleasure" and the absence of pain (physical or emotional). Theologically, Epicureans emphasized that any divine being could hardly be troubled by humans' daily existence; they also taught that the soul (which they, like the Stoics, believed to be material) perishes along with the body in death; hence, one should be untroubled by fear of the gods or concern for the afterlife.[4] A revival of *Pythagoreanism* sought mystical value in numbers and other

---

3 There were of course fears of miasma, when abominable acts brought blight or curses upon the land (see the opening of Sophocles, *Oedipus Rex*). But the criticism in Plato's *Euthyphro* proved generally true: polytheism allowed for little absolute conviction of what exactly was moral or god-pleasing, since the many gods had various and competing interests.

4 Compare the "Atheist Bus Campaign" in the 2000s in Great Britain, which placed ads in public transportation reading, "There's probably no God. So stop worrying and enjoy your life."

secrets of the universe and encouraged asceticism as the key to holiness and truth, blaming the body and physical life as the source of the soul's troubles. *Cynicism* emphasized the disjunction between natural good and social propriety, flouting cultural mores to live in accord with pure nature; by contrast, *Skepticism* argued the uncertainty of virtually anything and left ethics mainly to social convention. Plato's academy in Athens was a haven of Skepticism for a time, but by Paul's day it had become more eclectic and embraced a gradual rapprochement of Stoic ethics with Platonic and Aristotelian views of the immaterial, supreme mind that is god. Indeed, throughout the empire, followers of Plato were growing closer to Stoicism ("Middle Platonism") just as Stoics were drawn toward elements of Platonism.

The most popular of these philosophies in Paul's day was Stoicism, though we should not imagine most people were necessarily "strict" Stoics. Jewish thinkers (and the early Church Fathers), for one, were generally more at home in Platonic versions of Stoicism. Further, while there were those who "joined" a philosophical school to be tutored, many to whom Paul wrote and preached had probably only picked up bits from what they heard here and there and followed their own intuition or preference. As for Paul himself, his letters show him employing terms and ideas from the Stoicism and Platonism of his day, sometimes in disagreement and sometimes because he was influenced by them. But he probably did not belong to or join any of these "schools" as such. What he affirms of these philosophies is what was consonant with his faith as a Jew and as a follower of Jesus.

PAUL AND JUDAISM

If there was a diversity of worldviews and practices among Greco-Roman pagans and philosophers, Judaism in Paul's day was diverse as well. Several defining moments and influences had created disparities in what Jews believed God was up to and how they should be faithful in their new situation. Babylon had exiled Judah in 587 BCE, sending many to learn faithfulness toward God in foreign lands, which continued even after a few returned to rebuild Jerusalem under Persian rule. Should they be peaceful and wait faithfully (see Daniel, Tobit), or were there times to take up arms (see Judith, Esther)? One of Alexander's successors, Antiochus IV Epiphanes (ruled 175–163 BCE), tried to enforce the empire's "one world" vision by forcing Jews to abandon their customs: he sacked the sanctuary, mandated pagan offerings in Jerusalem, and punished new circumcisions with death (see 1

Macc 1:41–61). The Maccabees revolted and attempted to enforce obedience to the law, finally winning independence. But the new nation of Judah suffered its own troubles with internal conflicts and its new regime of priest-kings, who became a sort of aristocracy friendly to Rome after Jerusalem was sacked (63 BCE), and "Judea" became a province under Rome's thumb.

Under Rome, some were inclined toward nationalism and revolt, seeing Rome as the problem from which God desired to free them (or meant to help them free themselves). Had God not promised to restore the kingdom? Others were inclined simply to cooperate in the interest of survival, especially the Jewish ruling bodies in Jerusalem (see John 11:48). Others questioned the piety of their fellow Jews and doubted the legitimacy of the new non-Davidic "kings" such as Herod or of priestly lines that could not be traced back to Zadok (see 1 Kgs 2:27, 35; Ezek 40:46). Was not a renewal of legitimate priesthood needed? Was it not through a legitimate successor of David that God promised deliverance and prosperity (see 2 Sam 7:11–17; Isa 9:5–6 [KJV 9:6–7]; 11:1–10)? Religio-political sects formed. If the Sadducees and rulers in Jerusalem were satisfied enough with the status quo, other groups such as the sect at Qumran (who bequeathed the Dead Sea Scrolls to history) saw the temple and its priests as fatally compromised and withdrew to the wilderness to await God's promised new covenant and eschatological temple (see Jer 31:31–34; Ezek 34–48). Others sought piety in prayer and asceticism, with greater or lesser affinity toward the temple cult and its officiants. There was great variety according to conviction, and variety according to location as well, as those who lived in Jerusalem under the Sanhedrin and the city's elders were in a different situation than Jews in Galilee, Africa, or Asia Minor.

Paul's sect was that of the Pharisees (Phil 3:5; Acts 23:6; 26:5). The Pharisees sought fidelity toward God in personal purity and observance of the Mosaic law, for the laity as much as for priests or kings. In this they were heirs of Ezra the scribe, whose aim was to spread the Mosaic law among all the people (see Neh 8–10). They did not as a group forsake the temple, though they emphasized the need for personal piety beyond mere participation in the Jerusalem cult. They held strongly to their own interpretation of the law and to the traditions of their elders, which many believed came from Moses himself. Their hopes followed the promises of the prophets, that God would have mercy and deliver Israel through a new Davidic king (the Lord's "anointed," i.e., the messiah or, in Greek, "Christ") and raise the dead to eternal life.

Some readers will be familiar with the Pharisees only from certain one-dimensional depictions of them in the Gospels as Jesus's opponents. But we also see friendship and agreement between Jesus and some Pharisees and scribes (Mark 12:28–34; Luke 7:36; 11:37; 13:31–32; 14:1; John 3:1–2). There were different stripes of Pharisees, showing more or less rigidity in how they practiced their piety and how they taught others to do so.[5] Some were thus more receptive to Jesus even when they questioned his teaching about specific matters. The same was true after Christ's death and the beginnings of the church after Pentecost. In Acts, a Pharisee named Gamaliel recommends tolerating the Jesus movement with a docile attitude toward what God might be doing in it (Acts 5:33–40). Some Pharisees simply joined the church at the preaching of the apostles (Acts 15:5).

Other Pharisees, however, saw Jesus's teaching as a dangerous contagion spreading throughout the people and, after Jesus's death, rejected the apostles' claim that Jesus was the exalted messiah and Son of God. Paul, when he first heard this claim, "excessively persecuted the church of God" (Gal 1:13; cf. 1 Cor 15:9; Phil 3:5–6). Some have suggested that Paul persecuted the Church because he saw his fellow Jews, in the name of Jesus, welcoming gentiles (ethnic non-Jews) and thus rendering the nation impure. However, believers in Jesus were hardly the only Jews who were friendly or even welcoming toward gentiles (e.g., Luke 7:1–5), and there is no suggestion that Paul persecuted those groups with such ardor. Further, Christian evangelization of gentiles became public and widespread especially through the work of Paul, the "apostle to the gentiles" (Rom 11:13; Gal 2:7–9), and it is questionable whether there was even enough such outreach to inflame Paul's zeal before his own ministry began. Paul's zeal was likely inflamed against the church more for blasphemy than impurity. They proclaimed that Jesus, a man condemned for blasphemy by the Sanhedrin and hard-line Pharisees, not only had been innocent but was God's favored Son, raised and now exalted and ruling at the Father's right hand. This is the specific claim for which Jesus was condemned and Stephen martyred (Mark 14:61–64; Acts 7:54–58). And

---

5 The two main schools of thought in Pharisaism are often summarized under the names of two famous first-century rabbis, Shammai and Hillel, the former representing a stricter school of piety and the latter a more generous one. As an example, the Babylonian Talmud, tractate *Shabbat*, 31a, tells a story in which a pagan asked Shammai to convert him on the condition that Shammai teach him the whole Torah while the man stood on one foot. Shammai rebuffed him impatiently. But Hillel, when asked the same, responded: "What is hateful to you, do not do to your neighbor. That is the entire Torah, and the rest is commentary. Go learn it."

it makes sense that it was this claim for which Paul opposed Christians, since it was a vision communicating exactly this reality—that Jesus is the exalted Lord at the Father's right hand—that turned him quickly from persecutor to a preacher of the gospel (Acts 9).

Paul mentions his former life as a persecutor and the change brought about in him. He does not describe the event that caused the change in detail but claims to have seen the Lord in a vision near Damascus, to have been commissioned with his apostleship, and to have been "called" by Jesus to preach him to the world (1 Cor 9:1; 15:8–9; Gal 1:15–16). Acts presents it as a blinding light from heaven, by which the risen Jesus revealed himself to Paul as Lord and told him the mission he would undertake (Acts 9:1–9; 22:6–11; 26:12–20).

Scholars struggle to put a name to this event. To call it merely Paul's "call" to apostleship might suggest that he merely got a new job, but it is more radical than that. To call it Paul's "conversion" suggests, to many ears, that he left one religion behind for a different one.[6] But Paul continues to understand himself as a Jew not only ethnically (Rom 9:1–5) but, in Acts at least, religiously as well. When accused by the Sanhedrin for preaching Jesus as the Christ, Paul responds:

> "Gentlemen, I am a Pharisee, a son of Pharisees. It is because of our hope and the resurrection of the dead that I am being tried!" When he said this, an argument arose between the Pharisees and Sadducees, and the group was divided. For Sadducees say there is no resurrection, no angels or spirits, but the Pharisees confess them all. And there was a great uproar, and some of the scribes on the side of the Pharisees arose and argued saying, "We find no fault in this man. What if a spirit or angel spoke to him?" (Acts 23:6–9)

Paul says as much to Agrippa II as well—that he is on trial "because of hope in the promise God made to our fathers," specifically the hope his Pharisaic piety emphasized: the resurrection from the dead (Acts 26:6–8). Paul did not see believing in Jesus as casting off his Pharisaic heritage, but as doing what all who looked for the resurrection and the salvation of God *should* do when they realized that it had begun in Christ.

---

6 In Catholic (and, I understand, Orthodox) parlance, the term is less objectionable, as one uses the word "conversion" or "continued conversion" not only for switching religions but for all repentance and "turning to" (= *con* + *verto*) the Lord. Segal (1990) argues that Paul's conversion was more like switching from one sect of Judaism to another—still seeing himself within what one would call "Judaism," but with major consequences for his own faith and his opinion of others'.

Nevertheless, there was discontinuity in his religious outlook before and after this event, for his hopes as a Pharisee were now all located *in* the crucified and risen Lord Jesus, in whom God's promises are fulfilled (2 Cor 1:20). Paul came to view those who sought God but rejected Christ as uninformed in their "zeal" for God (Rom 10:2). Knowing Christ, and growing in knowledge of the mysteries of salvation, Paul read Israel's scriptures with new eyes, seeing how they prefigured Christ and his work in the church (Rom 4:1–25; 2 Cor 3:4–18; Gal 3:6–29; 4:21–31).[7] He saw himself in a new era of the history of God's work, as a "minister of the new covenant" that God had promised (2 Cor 3:6; cf. Jer 31:31–34). And as he sought to follow in the steps of the Lord who died to give life to sinners, Paul's values were reevaluated. He now set aside pride in the social esteem he enjoyed as a Pharisee: "I consider everything a loss" in order to "gain Christ," seeking the God of his fathers precisely in Christ Jesus, "to know him and the power of his resurrection and fellowship with his sufferings, being conformed to his death, so that I might somehow attain the resurrection from the dead" (Phil 3:8–11).

ACTS AND PAUL'S LETTERS: SKETCHING A LIFE

There are two principal sources for our knowledge of Paul's life. First and foremost are his own *letters*. Though primarily offering theological and ethical instruction, they give us a glimpse into the people and problems with which Paul was involved, as well as his travels, plans, and hopes. One also finds biographical details about the order of his travels, his being an "old man" when he wrote Philemon (Phlm 9), and so on. However, these occasional letters hardly offer a comprehensive depiction of Paul's life.

Supplementing the letters is the biblical *book of Acts*. The author of Acts, who also wrote the Gospel of Luke, purports to have been in close contact with Paul, speaking in the first person as one traveling alongside Paul at several points (Acts 16:10–17; 20:5–15; 21:1–18; 27:1–28:16). Acts tells of Paul's life from his part in the persecution and death of Stephen, the first Christian martyr (Acts 7), to Paul's turn to faith in Christ (Acts 9) and missionary travels, to his arrival as a prisoner in Rome waiting to defend the gospel before Caesar (Acts 28). Acts is helpful for giving an overall picture of Paul's ministry. Further, while Acts often speaks generally of "rulers" or "some days" in its

7 See Hays 1989.

account of Paul's travels, Acts occasionally provides specific names of rulers that offer more precise dates for some events, such as Paul's trial in Corinth before Gallio (51/52 CE) and his imprisonment in Caesarea under Felix and Festus (ca. 58–60 CE). Acts ends with Paul being transferred under guard to Rome for two years after his Caesarean imprisonment. Other ancient sources provide supplemental data and traditions, particularly the tradition that Paul was released from his first Roman imprisonment for a few more years of ministry before ultimately being martyred in Rome in the mid- to late 60s. This gives us a few dates for a basic sketch, but one can see that there is much left open.

5 BCE–10 CE (?)	Paul's birth
33–37 (?)	Call to apostleship near Damascus (Gal 1:17), followed by stays in Arabia, visits to Jerusalem, and missionary travels in especially Asia Minor and Greece
51 or 52	Tried in Corinth before Gallio (Acts 18:12–17), followed by further missionary travels
58–60	Imprisonment in Caesarea under Felix and Festus
60–61 or 62	Imprisonment in Rome (Acts 28:30–31), then released for further missions
62–68 (?)	Martyrdom

Of course, there is much more of Paul's life that is narrated in Acts or hinted at in the letters. The difficulties lie in determining a precise dating for each event and sometimes even determining the order in which they occurred. Paul's letters do not always relate where he is as he writes, which means it can be difficult to plot when his letters were written or exactly when the events mentioned in the letters occurred. Often the events and the letters can be fit within the narrative found in Acts. But Acts is not a biography of Paul. It is a theological history, a sequel to Luke, presenting God's work through the promised Holy Spirit (Luke 24:49; Acts 1:6–8) as Christianity grew from a small Jewish sect to an international way of faith and life. While it tells us much about Paul and Christian origins, it is not an account of everything Paul did or the exact order in which he did it. Comparing Acts and the letters, as well as noting how much Acts leaves out of its own narrative, makes this clear.

Overall, there is significant overlap between Acts and Paul's letters. In both, Paul was a Pharisee who saw the Lord Jesus and became an apostle. In both, Paul faced difficulties from Jewish groups and from pagans. Both attest that Paul faced imprisonments and beatings. Both agree generally on the places where Paul ministered and sometimes in the same order (Philippi–Thessalonica–Athens; cf. Acts 16–17 with 1 Thess 2:2; 3:1). Both even note the short story of his inglorious escape from Damascus in a basket (Acts 9:22–25; 2 Cor 11:32–33).

On the other hand, one also finds that Acts differs from the letters at certain points, both in its presentation of Paul's ministry overall and in some details. In Galatians, for example, Paul insists that after his initial vision of Christ he did not go to Jerusalem until three years later, staying in Arabia and Damascus in the meantime (Gal 1:16–18). Acts narrates a brief period ("for some days") in Damascus and presents Paul going to Jerusalem "many days" but not three years thereafter (Acts 9:19–30). Paul's letters state that an effort of major importance to his apostolate was his collection of funds for Jerusalem from his churches; it was the main purpose of his final trip to Jerusalem (see Rom 15:25–33; 1 Cor 16:1–4; 2 Cor 8–9). Acts presents this journey to Jerusalem and his subsequent imprisonment in Caesarea, but the collection is mentioned only later in passing (Acts 24:17). Further, while Acts highlights Paul's travels to the main cities to which he wrote and often gives great detail about Paul's travels between them, it appears to be very selective: Paul boasts in Romans 15:19 that he has already evangelized as far west as Illyricum (roughly Bosnia-Herzegovina today), while none of even the more detailed travel reports in Acts tells of Paul getting anywhere near Illyricum. Acts also tells of one imprisonment and no shipwrecks suffered before Paul delivered the collection, whereas Paul wrote of numerous imprisonments and shipwrecks already before the collection's delivery (see 2 Cor 6:5; 11:23–25).

This does not mean that Acts is untrustworthy as a historical source about Paul's life, still less about the importance of Paul in the Holy Spirit's work in the earliest church. It does mean that studying Paul's biography requires a reasoned use of both Paul's letters and Acts that recognizes what each source can and is meant to tell us. As first-person reports, Paul's letters provide us solid data, though we should remember that there is much that they are not interested to tell us and that, when he tells us of his life, he may omit things for the sake of his argument. Just because Acts reports something that Paul does not is no reason to jettison its testimony. With Acts, we need to adjust our expectations about what it is meant to tell us by considering how the author of Acts crafts theological history. Clearly much is left out. Acts 18:12–17 states that Paul stood before Gallio, proconsul of Achaia (southern Greece), in 51–52, and Acts 24:27 narrates the accession of Porcius Festus as procurator of Judea in 59. That means that almost a decade elapses between Acts 18 and 24. Further, if Jesus was crucified in 33 (the latest date usually hypothesized), then two decades elapse between Acts 1 and 18, in which Luke relates relatively few episodes and notes hardly any time intervals that would help readers piece together the chronology of the events reported. The omission of Paul's journey north to Illyricum also shows us that the framework of Paul's journeys in Acts has, at least at some points, been simplified and rearranged to link the narrative around the omissions.

This should not be surprising when one considers the other work by the author of Acts, the Gospel of Luke, when we compare its storytelling with the other biblical Gospels. Each Gospel communicates the life, teachings, and significance of Jesus, but each evangelist—even when borrowing from another—does so by rearranging or omitting material in order to highlight the aspects of Jesus's significance that they desire for their audience. They are not comprehensive (Luke follows Mark generally, yet passes over Mark 6:45–8:26); rather, they give paradigmatic episodes that represent the *kinds* of events that often occurred and that communicate or encapsulate something about Jesus. They even move events around chronologically in order to shape the narrative and its message: compare Jesus's anointing by the woman in Luke 7:36–50 (rather than during Holy Week as in Mark 14:1–9), Luke's and Matthew's different organizations of Jesus's beatitudes and new law (tightly woven together in the "Sermon on the Mount" in Matt 5–7, but spread across several chapters in Luke), and Luke's emphasis on Christ as the fulfillment of God's presence by framing his narrative to begin and end in the temple. This is in keeping with genre expectations of the time: while Greco-Roman readers expected to get the overall movements of someone's life from a biography or history, they focused on the main figure's character and significance, and chronology and ordering were flexible within that framework.[8] Luke and the other evangelists shape their narratives in different ways, collect and omit some material while expanding others in detail,

8 See Keener 2019a, 121–50, 303–27.

and rearrange or connect episodes for thematic effect as they aim to present the theological significance of the historical life of Christ. We should expect Luke to have done the same in presenting the significance of Paul within the Holy Spirit's work.

For Christians who hold that the Bible is human communication that God inspired in order to convey eternal truth, both Paul's letters and Acts are equally sacred and equally teach the truth about God, humanity, the church, and so on. When considering the historical order of Paul's travels, imprisonments, and details about Paul's life, we do not need to oppose the two, though one does need to reason between them carefully at each point of information. Paul probably went on more missionary "journeys" than the three neatly arranged for us in Acts, and we know Paul went to more places and was more often imprisoned and shipwrecked than Acts recounts. At the same time, Paul did go on missionary journeys to the areas mentioned in Acts, and we can trust that the stories in Acts give us a window into the kind of work that Paul did and the kinds of troubles and successes he faced. And there is usually little reason to doubt the few specific data about dates and rulers that Acts does give.

In this book, I will offer an independent overview of Paul in Acts in chapter 5. In the subsequent chapters, Acts will be compared when it furnishes information about the background of Paul's individual letters and the churches to which he ministered.

FURTHER READING

Becker, Jürgen. 1993. *Paul: Apostle to the Gentiles.* Louisville, KY: Westminster John Knox.

Campbell, Douglas A. 2014. *Framing Paul: An Epistolary Biography.* Grand Rapids: Eerdmans.

Cohen, Shaye J. D. 2014. *From the Maccabees to the Mishnah.* 3rd edition. Louisville, KY: Westminster John Knox Press.

Collins, John J., and Daniel C. Harlow, eds. 2012. *Early Judaism: A Comprehensive Overview.* Grand Rapids: Eerdmans.

Dodson, Joseph R., and David E. Briones, eds. 2019. *Paul and the Giants of Philosophy: Reading the Apostle in Greco-Roman Context.* Downers Grove, IL: InterVarsity.

Elliott, Neil, and Mark Reasoner. 2011. *Documents and Images for the Study of Paul*. Minneapolis: Fortress.

Ferguson, Everett. 2003. *Backgrounds of Early Christianity*. 3rd edition. Grand Rapids: Eerdmans.

Hengel, Martin. 1991. *The Pre-Christian Paul*. Philadelphia: Trinity Press International.

Inwood, Brad, and L. P. Gerson. 1997. *Hellenistic Philosophy: Introductory Readings*. 2nd edition. Indianapolis: Hackett.

Murphy-O'Connor, Jerome, OP. 1996. *Paul: A Critical Life*. New York: Oxford University Press.

Nickelsburg, George W. E., and Michael E. Stone. 1983. *Faith and Piety in Early Judaism: Texts and Documents*. Philadelphia: Fortress.

Penna, A. 1960. *St. Paul the Apostle*. Translated by K. C. Thompson. London: St. Paul Publications.

Phillips, Thomas E. 2009. *Paul, His Letters, and Acts*. LPS. Grand Rapids: Baker Academic.

Riesner, Rainer. 1998. *Paul's Early Period: Chronology, Mission Strategy, Theology*. Translated by Doug Scott. Grand Rapids: Eerdmans.

Segal, Alan F. 1990. *Paul the Convert: The Apostolate and Apostasy of Saul the Pharisee*. New Haven, CT: Yale University Press.

Tatum, Gregory, OP. 2006. *New Chapters in the Life of Paul: The Relative Chronology of His Career*. CBQMS 41. Washington, DC: Catholic Biblical Association of America.

Wischmeyer, Oda, ed. 2012. *Paul: Life, Setting, Work, Letters*. Translated by Helen S. Heron. Revisions by Dieter T. Roth. London: T&T Clark.

CHAPTER THREE

Approaching Paul's Letters

Continually, as I hear the epistles of the blessed Paul being read, twice each week and often three or four times, when we make remembrance of the holy martyrs, I rejoice taking pleasure in that spiritual trumpet; I am roused, and I am warmed with desire at the recognition of this voice I hold dear, and I seem to imagine him all but present and see him speaking to me. (John Chrysostom, *Homilies on Romans*, argument 1 [PG 60:391])

John Chrysostom opens his commentary on Romans by saying he is "warmed" as he hears Paul's "voice" when he reads. Chrysostom and readers like him are warmed in part because they read Paul's letters with faith in the message they proclaim, but also because they treat these letters as letters. Not merely doctrinal statements, they reflect an apostle who did not cast off his personality when writing; their words are filled with tenderness, love, and fiery zeal. Yet this can also make reading these letters difficult. One must not only understand what each letter is and is meant to do, but also hear all of Paul's letters together to synthesize and understand the mind of the apostle. The following chapter will discuss interpreting Paul's theology. The present chapter will consider what Paul's letters are, how they are put together, and how he would have envisioned them being received. Such elements are important to help shape our historical imagination about Paul's activity and what he and his audiences expected from a letter, which in turn helps us to interpret them today.

PAUL'S LETTERS AMONG ANCIENT LETTERS

Letters are a form of long-distance communication, a replacement for face-to-face interaction. Though today we often privilege the written word, many ancients preferred oral and personal communication. Written texts are one-sided, can be lost in transit, or may be damaged by weather or by a poor scribe. Papias of Hierapolis famously sought out the apostles' successors to learn about Jesus, "for I did not suppose that what came out of scrolls would help me as much as what was passed down through a living and surviving voice" (quoted in Eusebius, *Ecclesiastical History* 3.39.4). On the other hand, written texts had other values, especially coming from an authority figure. Written words could be crafted more deliberately, go through many drafts, and be practiced, and these more deliberately considered words then had a (fairly) fixed form that could be copied, reread, and circulated.[1]

As replacements for in-person communication, letters could have many purposes. Some ancient papyri show us letters of a single sentence inviting someone to a banquet. Most are brief correspondence between family or business relations. Others are more literary or didactic, not intended merely as brief correspondence with another person but as a vehicle for teaching philosophy to pupils, urging particular political actions, and so on. In most cases, letters aimed to persuade. They made a recommendation or request, however brief, and aimed to evoke a response.

Paul's letters are real letters. He mentions the persons to whom he is writing and appeals to their current situations or previous correspondence that has occasioned him to write (e.g., 1 Cor 5:1; 7:1; 1 Thess 3:6). His letters often update his audience on his own circumstances as well (e.g., Rom 15:23–33; 1 Cor 16:1–8). Reading them, one can see that what he writes—even if it is true in the abstract—is written to address his audience's particular concrete circumstances. These are not philosophical treatises with a mere epistolary veneer. However, they are also not the kind of casual correspondence we find in other letters. They are *apostolic letters*. Paul's letters are comparatively long—only Philemon (25 verses) is comparable in length to the average ancient letter. Paul's letters are filled with arguments, some drawn out at length, meant to influence and inform people's faith and life. Different from casual correspondence, Paul's letters were also expected to have religious value beyond their first addressees (Col 4:16). For, different from a son writing his mother, the authority and value of Paul's words were not understood to be based solely on his past relationship with his addressees (1 Thess 2:1–12) but also on his authority as an apostle commissioned by Christ for the church (cf. Rom 1:1–7; 11:13; 1 Cor 7:10–12; 2 Cor 13:10; 1 Thess 2:13).

---

1 The form is "fairly" fixed because reusing a letter usually required copying it by hand, a process that admitted accidental errors and sometimes intentional alterations by the copyist.

Letters came in different forms, but certain elements were fairly standard.[2] To illustrate, we may compare this second-century letter from Apion, an Egyptian writing to his father in Greek after joining the Roman navy.[3]

> Apion to Epimachos, his father and lord, very many greetings. Before all else I pray that you are well and that you may prosper in continual health, together with my sister and her daughter and my brother. I give thanks to the Lord Serapis, because when I was endangered at sea, he rescued me immediately. When I arrived at Misenum, I received a viaticum from Caesar of three gold pieces, and I am well.
>
> Therefore, I request that you, my lord father, write me a letter, first about your welfare, secondly about the welfare of my brothers [and sisters], thirdly in order that I may make obeisance before your handwriting, because you trained me well, and I hope by this means quickly to advance, the gods willing.
>
> Greet Kapiton much and my brothers [and sisters] and Serenilla and my friends. I sent my portrait to you by Euktemon. My name is "Antonius Maximus."
>
> I pray that you are well.
> Company: Athenonike.

Apion's letter appears quite different from those we know from Paul. But, as we approach Paul's letters, their commonalities are instructive.

The *opening address* is familiar from all the Pauline letters, stating the names of the sender and addressee and naming the relationship on which this correspondence is based. Apion writes his father as a son. Paul addresses believers as an apostle of Christ and characteristically greets them in the grace in which apostles and believers alike are grounded. "Grace to you and peace from God our Father and the Lord Jesus Christ" (Rom 1:7).

Apion continues with a wish of health and *thanksgiving*—in this case that the god Serapis delivered him at sea. There is likewise an update on his own status: upon arriving at the military harbor at Misenum, he received a stipend. Paul's letters usually open with a variation of this. Often he begins by

---

2 We are considering only basic features here. Ancient rhetoricians also classified various types of letter formats according to authors' goals and themes such as friendship, defense, advice for subordinates, etc. (see Klauck 2006). If Paul's education taught him the finer points of these formatting guides, he appears not to have followed them slavishly, and scholars debate how to classify each letter—debating, for instance, whether Philippians fits the form of a friendship letter, a consoling letter, or a letter of thanks, etc.

3 This example is borrowed from Klauck 2006, 9–14.

expressing his thanks to God for what God has worked through the churches to which he writes, either in general for their faith (Rom 1:8–14) or specifically in light of recent events (1 Thess 1:2–10).[4] The openings of Paul's letters sometimes narrate or describe his current circumstances, and this can be lengthy when Paul is defending his actions or making a point about God's work through Paul's situation (2 Cor 1–2; Phil 1:12–26). These sections of Paul's letters also often include a prayer for the addressees' spiritual health before turning to offer instruction (1 Thess 3:11–13).

Apion then makes his *argument*: a request to persuade his father to write to him. He wants news about his siblings, males and females, whom he collectively refers to with the masculine "brothers" (ἀδελφοί, *adelphoi*). He also wants a letter from his father so that, despite their physical distance, Apion can honor his father by paying homage to his handwriting in place of his person. Apion appeals to his father's relationship to his son, his own piety and love toward his father, and his own advancement and success to persuade his father to write back. We see a couple of features here paralleled in Paul. Paul too speaks often of his "brothers" in Christ (Rom 1:13, etc.), by which we should understand not only male believers but females too.[5] In terms of letter structure, Apion's brief "therefore" and request are parallel to Paul's arguments and exhortations. Paul's argumentation, however, is theologically developed for instruction, proof, and defense of what he wants his audiences to believe and do.

There were said to be three overall types of persuasive goals. *Deliberative* rhetoric aims to convince people to take certain courses of action. *Forensic* rhetoric focuses on defense or accusation, often recounting or shaping a narrative of events to assign or avoid blame. *Epideictic* rhetoric was the rhetoric of praise extolling virtue and building shared values. Paul's letters most often feature deliberative argument, trying to influence his people's behavior, sometimes using epideictic elements when he holds someone up as an example to follow. Forensic arguments also appear when he defends his actions or apostolate. Within any style of argument, the ancients generally spoke of three elements: *logos*, the logic of the argument; *pathos*, its appeal

---

4 At times this is expressed not by "thanking" but by "blessing" God, with a more Hebraic flair (2 Cor 1:3; Eph 1:3).

5 Some English translations translate "brothers and sisters" in these instances (e.g., NRSV); others translate "brothers" woodenly but add a note clarifying that it includes female believers (e.g., ESV). Greek and many other languages that use two grammatical genders for human beings regularly use the masculine for mixed-gender groups.

to or expression of emotion; and *ethos*, the character and reputation of the speaker or sometimes the audience. One can see, for example, Paul's *logos* as he offers reasons why denial of the resurrection undermines the entire Christian faith (1 Cor 15:12–19), *pathos* when he apologetically describes his emotional distress over writing a harsh letter to the Corinthians (2 Cor 2:4), and *ethos* when he reminds the Thessalonians of his character among them as a minister and caregiver (1 Thess 2:1–12). Paul combines these elements to persuade his audience to listen to him and remain in the gospel.

Apion's *letter closing* extends greetings through his father to other friends who live in the area. He also gives certain updates for future correspondence, giving the Roman name by which he is known in the military ("Antonius Maximus"), the name of the company to which his father should address the desired letter, and a notice about the delivery of a portrait of himself (perhaps in his uniform?) by Euktemon. Paul's letters also often conclude with greetings to individuals in or near the churches to which he writes (e.g., Phlm 23–24). Paul likewise will give notice of persons he is sending to his churches so that the leadership there will expect and welcome them (e.g., 1 Cor 4:17; 16:10). Paul, like Apion, concludes with a brief wish of well-being, again centered on the grace of God in Christ: "The grace of the Lord Jesus be with you. My love be with you all in Christ Jesus" (1 Cor 16:23–24).

WRITING PAUL'S LETTERS
Paul and His Team

Few people in the ancient Roman empire could read with any fluidity. Literacy rates were low. Paul's letters were sent with trusted emissaries or directed to particular leaders in his churches who would read the contents aloud to the assembled church. Note the abrupt charge in the closing of 1 Thessalonians 5:27: "I adjure you by the Lord that this letter be read to all the brothers [and sisters]."

If only a fraction of the population could read, even fewer could write. While literate people knew their letter shapes, it takes practice to write clearly with the end of a reed tipped with ink.[6] Likewise, papyrus was expensive,

---

6 Beneficiaries of modern education often learn reading and writing at the same time, but forming legible letters by hand is a separate skill from recognizing and interpreting them. To illustrate: all my students can read and can type well on a keyboard or smartphone, but computer use leaves many poorly practiced at legible handwriting, and almost none of them are adept at calligraphy.

and one had not only to write clearly with as few mistakes as possible but also to estimate the size of letters needed to fit the whole message into the space available.[7] Intelligence, skill in public speaking, and even the ability to read did not guarantee skill in the mechanics of writing. Developing writing skills involved supplies, funds, and opportunity to continue honing one's penmanship.

Renaissance art often depicts Paul writing alone with pen in hand. But, like most of his educated contemporaries, Paul appears to have used the services of scribes. Indications of this are evident in his letters. The most striking comes in Romans 16:22. Amid several greetings in the letter closing, we find this: "And I, Tertius, who wrote this letter, greet you in the Lord." While the opening address in Romans 1:1 names Paul alone, Paul is clearly not the one holding the pen. Paul has employed a Christian (note his greeting "in the Lord") scribe for Romans, and this appears to have been his standard practice. Funds to pay for letter production likely came from middle- or higher class believers who supported Paul's mission or hosted churches in sizeable homes (see Acts 16:14–15, 40; Rom 16:1–2). Paul did physically write parts of his letters, however. The conclusion of his letters was usually in his "own hand," as he often states, noting in Galatians that he writes with quite "large letters" (Gal 6:11–18; cf. 1 Cor 16:21–24; Col 4:18; 2 Thess 3:17–18). This was not uncommon: those who could write but could or would not write an entire letter employed scribes, but took up the pen themselves to append a conclusion. Though some have argued Paul's letters were "large" for emphasis or perhaps because his eyesight was poor, Paul's handwriting probably reflects that of a man who did not make a living practicing penmanship.[8]

If we should imagine Paul not alone but with a scribe, we should imagine others with him as well. Many authors wrote in collaboration with aides and associates in addition to the scribe, often without naming them in the letter. Paul appears to have done just this. Indeed, the opening lines of Paul's letters name trusted associates as cosenders or coauthors with Paul such as Timothy, Silvanus, or Sosthenes (1 Cor 1:1; 2 Cor 1:1; Phil 1:1; Col 1:1; 1 Thess 1:1; 2 Thess 1:1; Phlm 1). The letters also, though often speaking in Paul's first person "I" as the main authority addressing the audience, speak just as often

---

7 Richards (2004, 165–69) estimates from ancient evidence that Paul's shortest letter, Philemon, likely cost the equivalent of about $100 USD for supplies and scribal fees, while Romans would have cost more than $2,000.

8 See Reece 2017.

in the plural "we" referring to his coauthors. Paul is the lead authority and lead sender, and he bears responsibility for the letter sent out under his name. But in letter writing and in evangelization Paul was head of a team, sharing or delegating authority and responsibility with others. Paul regularly traveled with his compatriots, especially Timothy, and picked up new ones as he traveled. While new converts often served as leaders and contacts with Paul in their home churches (cf. Rom 16:9; Phil 2:25), they sometimes joined up with Paul, shadowing him, supporting or working with him, and serving as his emissaries (he often calls them his "coworkers" or fellow "slaves" of Christ; see Rom 1:1; 16:21; Phil 1:1; Col 1:7). Or he might invite a representative from the church to which he is writing and who knows that church's situation to join him in composing a letter.

How were Paul's letters prepared? Paul may have written or drafted some in transit, but he likely did most of his writing when he had arrived at a fairly stable location, with a Christian patron to pay for a scribe and supplies and more time to consider what should be written. Some scribes took dictation word for word or even syllable by syllable. Some took shorthand and smoothed it out later, while others were told the gist of what a letter should say and then put it into a standard format themselves. Paul and his team may have employed scribes in all of these ways at different points.[9] Depending on the letter's length, available funds, Paul's travel plans, and other constraints, Paul could have drafted some letters several times over. Others, however, may have been drafted all in one sitting and sent off quickly under tighter circumstances. As the authority and lead author, Paul would be responsible for the letter's content, in any case, and would have checked and approved the final draft when possible before having it dispatched.

Sending, Receiving, and Collecting Paul's Letters

As letters were sent in place of personal presence, Paul did not deliver his own letters. Occasionally he sent letters ahead of his arrival (Rom 15:23–33; 2 Cor 9:1–5) or sent letters ahead of emissaries who would come in Paul's place (Phil 2:19–24). At other times he sent them off with little or no expectation to visit the addressees. How were the letters sent? Paul seems to have used

---

9 Paul's quick self-correction in 1 Cor 1:14–17, naming several people he had baptized just after saying he had personally baptized only one Corinthian family, suggests that not all of Paul's letters went through thorough revision and that they were not all prepared with syllable-by-syllable accuracy before ink hit papyrus.

three main modes of delivery. First, he sent members of his traveling mission team to carry letters. Paul's coworkers might deliver the letter and leave soon to return to Paul or travel elsewhere. At other times Paul's coworkers delivered a letter and stayed to encourage and advise the faithful. Second, Paul would send letters back to a church with one of their own who had come from them to Paul (cf. Phil 2:25; 4:18). Third, he might send a letter through someone who, he knew, was heading toward the letter's destination (Rom 16:1–2). Letters written on papyrus scrolls were rolled up, with instructions for delivery written on the outside, where Paul may have been able to set down specific instructions for the letter carriers.

Once a carrier arrived, he or she would deliver it to a primary contact in the church. (This was especially important when Paul wrote to churches that had largely turned against him, as trusted allies or delegates could keep the message from being destroyed and could ensure that it gained a hearing.) These individuals would notify or assemble the church. In cases where the letter was delivered by one of Paul's team, the letter carrier may have been the one to read the letter publicly to the assembly. In other cases, Paul's primary contacts who received the letter first read and practiced it themselves before reading it aloud with rehearsed enunciation (1 Thess 5:27). The oral delivery of these letters is worth remembering as we interpret, for while exegetes are inclined to spend hours dissecting single words or sentences, Paul expected the letters to be heard in their entirety as a single exhortation. The details are important, but we can miss the intended effect if we interpret individual parts without the whole.

What did the churches do with these letters after they were received and read? And how were these letters, sent at different times to different cities, eventually collected and circulated so that they were known across the early church? We can look at this from two sides. From *Paul's* side, it was common for authors to employ a scribe to make two copies of a letter (at least, letters they considered important) before dispatch: one to send and another to be kept by the author. Given the vicissitudes of Paul's life, he may not have had funds or opportunity to do this for his every missive, but it is very plausible he did this for many of those we currently possess. From the *addressees'* side, in many cases someone in the congregation kept letters sent from Paul. As the network of churches grew, it may be also that they had copies made to share with other churches. Already in Colossians 4:16 we see an exchange of letter copies between two churches: "And whenever this letter is read among you, ensure that it is also read in the church of the Laodiceans and that you also read the letter from Laodicea." A few decades later, we can see clearly that Paul's letters were known at least in major bishoprics: Clement of Rome (95 CE) knows 1 Corinthians and expects the church in Corinth still to have a copy of that letter (*1 Clement* 47.1–2). Ignatius of Antioch (ca. 110 CE) mentions Ephesians to the Ephesians and Philippians to the Philippians (*Ephesians* 12.1; *Philippians* 3.2).

By the time 2 Peter was written, Paul's letters were known not singly by people who happened to have seen one or the other but as a collection ("all his letters," 2 Pet 3:16). How were the Pauline letters collected? And how did the collection become standardized to include the particular letters we know, even though Paul wrote other letters that, to our knowledge, none but their original readers ever saw (see 1 Cor 5:9)? Some suggest that it was only after Paul's death, when he was being revered and intentionally memorialized, that people first became interested to visit various churches and collect whatever remained of Paul's correspondence. Others argue that his letters were copied and shared from very early on, and various churches began to draw up their own edited collections, though not every collection would have had the same letters as another, and some of those were copied and circulated widely to become the letter collection that has been standard since the late second century. A final, quite plausible suggestion is that the collection began with Paul keeping copies of (most of) his own letters, preserved and published after Paul's death by his coworkers.

It is difficult to reconstruct exactly how the letters began to circulate. What is impressive, in any case, is how early these thirteen letters that bear Paul's name were used as an authority in theological argumentation and read in Christian liturgies on par with Israel's scriptures.[10] A plethora of papyrus manuscripts and comments from early bishops confirm that these letters were accepted and revered from Syria to Egypt to France as sacred and authoritative by 200 CE. The order of the letters was standardized later, differing slightly in different ancient manuscripts of the Pauline corpus. The standard ordering follows a combination of length and addressee. The letters are organized first with those whose canonical "title" bears the name of

---

10 In about 140 CE, the heretic Marcion developed a canonical list of Paul's writings, with all thirteen except the "Pastoral Epistles," 1–2 Timothy and Titus. One early papyrus containing Paul's letters also lacks the Pastorals, but Tertullian's attack on Marcion (*Against Marcion* V) affirms the Pastorals, and they are present in the other early manuscripts of the Pauline corpus. Hebrews was added to the collection in some locations in the second century, but not in all, since its authenticity was doubted.

a whole congregation, longest (Romans) to shortest (2 Thessalonians), and second with those titled by the name of an individual addressee, longest (1 Timothy) to shortest (Philemon).

Questioning Authorship

For especially the last two hundred years, many scholars have questioned whether everything collected in the Pauline letter collection is to be attributed to Paul's direct authorship. 2 Thessalonians 2:2 already countenanced the possibility that there may have been a letter falsely attributed to Paul in circulation. Is it possible that some canonical letters are "pseudonymous" or "pseudepigraphical"—that is, falsely attributed to Paul? Today, a large majority of scholars hold that Paul was not the author of 1 Timothy and Titus, and nearly as many doubt 2 Timothy and Ephesians. Colossians and 2 Thessalonians are more often held to be genuinely Pauline, at least in commentaries, but remain widely doubted. These six letters are commonly referred to as the "Disputed Paulines" (as opposed to the "undisputed" letters) or, in a phrase more strongly suggesting their inauthenticity, the "Deutero-Paulines" (as opposed to the "Proto-Paulines").

On what grounds are these epistles doubted? Every argument against Pauline authenticity is cumulative, and in each letter there are various smaller and larger elements that scholars debate.[11] In the main, however, there are three.

(a) *Style.* Perhaps the first and most basic reason people suspect a letter was not directly written by Paul is its style of language or argument. Indeed, when some received Hebrews as a Pauline letter in the early church, style was a main reason others doubted its Pauline authorship: it did not sound like Paul's other letters.[12] Many in the early church questioned the authenticity of 2 Peter for the same reason.[13] Modern scholar-

---

11 R. Collins 1988 presents the main arguments.

12 Eusebius, *Ecclesiastical History* 6.25.11–14, quoting Origen, says that to most readers the high "character of the diction" distinguished Hebrews from Paul, though its "thoughts" are not false to Paul; he suggests its author may have known or even taken notes from Paul's teachings.

13 Jerome notes this in a letter (*Letter* 120.11), suggesting that, while 2 Peter sounds different from 1 Peter, we should not deem one authentically Petrine and the other inauthentic; rather, we should see both as from Peter, but each prepared by a different scribe translating Peter's Aramaic thoughts into different Greek styles.

ship often notes differences in vocabulary: Why, for instance, is Paul's vocabulary so different in 1 Timothy from the other letters even when discussing the same issues? They also note syntactical and grammatical differences: Ephesians features wordy sentences that take up a page and uses the Greek genitive case frequently in ways uncommon in Paul's other letters. There are also questions of argumentative style. Scholars ask, for instance, why Colossians responds less clearly to its local heretical group than Galatians does.

(b) *Theology.* Scholars also see differences in the theological outlook of the disputed letters over against the undisputed letters. Paul clearly teaches that baptism joins one to Christ's death (Rom 6:3–10) and grants the hope of future resurrection. Colossians discusses baptism in almost the exact same words, except that it speaks of the baptized as already resurrected (Col 2:13). In 1 Thessalonians 4:15 Paul speaks of Christ's return as though he expects that he and many in his audience will still be alive, coming suddenly like a "thief" (1 Thess 5:2), so why does 2 Thess 2:1–12 insist that the same Thessalonians must *not* think Christ will return until several other events first take place? Paul says there is "neither male nor female" in Christ in Galatians 3:28, so why would he discourage women from holding the teaching office in 1 Timothy 2:11–15?

(c) *Place in Paul's Life.* Scholars also question whether some letters reflect real situations in Paul's lifetime. Some have suggested that talk of bishops and teaching offices in 1 Timothy and Titus reflects the growing ecclesiastical structure of the second century more than the first. Colossians and 2 Thessalonians are sometimes seen as offering competing answers to the problem of Christ's apparent "delay" to return and raise the dead—a problem more obvious after Paul's death than during his lifetime.

The possibility of pseudonymity in Paul's letters should be considered from two perspectives—historically and, for religious readers, theologically.

Approaching Authorship Historically

Historically, one should acknowledge that the discrepancies and questions raised above are legitimate. One should also be aware that determining pseudonymity is a complex affair and requires caution. It is one thing to observe that a letter sounds different or argues differently than others. It is another thing to conclude that, based on the undisputed letters, Paul *could* or *would* not have written what is written in another letter. Some arguments against authenticity are based on too rigid a view of Pauline style and theology. True, Paul does not state that believers are already "raised" in baptism in the undisputed letters, but he does describe the future hope of Christlike resurrection in the same way he speaks of his present participation in Christ—"living to God" (ζάω τῷ θεῷ, *zaō tō theō*: Gal 2:19; Rom 6:10). If we allow that Paul developed his own thinking and style of expression in the course of three decades of ministry, is present-tense "resurrection" language in Colossians 2:13 necessarily un-Pauline? Statements about male teaching authority in 1 Timothy 2:11–15 are unique to that letter, but when comparing them to the undisputed Paulines we should not overemphasize Galatians 3:28 and forget the statements about male "headship" and authority in 1 Corinthians 11:2–16. Likewise, while there is a different "feel" in the style and vocabulary of Ephesians, 1–2 Timothy, and Titus, technical analyses remind us that the undisputed letters are not uniform.[14] And it is possible that some letters feature distinctive style due to a change in Paul's situation, thinking, or something in his audience's situation to which he adapted his style.[15]

Differences in style and theology *can* be evidence that someone other than Paul formulated the words we are reading, but caution is in order when determining authorship based on them. Indeed, the various types of activity by authors, coauthors, scribes, and pseudepigraphers require us to qualify our definition of "authorship." For even if Paul was not responsible for the words in a letter that give us pause, our options are still not as simple as "Pauline or un-Pauline." Some differences in style or content may simply

---

14 For a technical study, see Van Nes 2018.

15 As an example: the undisputed letters usually refer to human "masters" or "lords" with the term κύριος (*kyrios*), while the other common word δεσπότης (*despotēs*) is found in 1 Tim 6:1–2; 2 Tim 2:21; Titus 2:9. Does this show that the author of Titus or 1–2 Timothy has a different default vocabulary from Paul? Or could the same Paul have switched to a different term when writing to Timothy or Titus because of his location, his mood, or perhaps for a shade of meaning he believes better fits his argument in those letters?

be attributable to the influence of Paul's coauthors. In some cases all of the style and wording may have come from a trusted scribe or representative whom Paul authorized and instructed to write in his name. Jerome Murphy-O'Connor cites these instructions from Cicero to his friend and scribe Tiro:[16]

> If there is anyone to whom you think a letter ought to be sent in my name, please write one and see that it is sent. (Cicero, *To Atticus* 3.15)

> Send letters in my name to any you think it right. You know my familiars. If they look for my [missing] seal or handwriting, say that I have avoided them because of the guards. (Cicero, *To Atticus* 11.2)

> I am so fearfully upset both in mind and body that I have not been able to write many letters; I have answered only those who have written to me. I should like you to write in my name to Basilius and to anyone else you like, even to Servilius, and say whatever you think fit. (Cicero, *To Atticus* 11.5)

Though some writers disparaged this practice, authorizing letters appears to have been a real option. Most readers would still deem such letters to bear the authority of the authorizer even if the scribe was responsible for the wording—just as ambassadors take seriously an invitation from the US president even if his signature was merely stamped on by a secretary.[17] In most cases, it was expected that the author would check the finished product to ensure that it accurately reflected his sentiments, which was surely Paul's usual practice after drafting letters with his team. However, the latter examples from Cicero above show that even authors protective of their message and reputation might authorize a trusted colleague to write in their name and dispatch it without a final check. And this is a possibility for some of the letters of Paul.

These possibilities, in addition to the likelihood that Paul's thought and vocabulary developed over time, mitigate the force of arguments that a letter must have been written after Paul's death because it differs in style or theology. Such arguments can still be correct, but they require other supports. The *strongest* indication that a letter might be pseudonymous is if it has no plausible setting within Paul's life and ministry. If a letter in Paul's name addresses theological problems or reflects political or ecclesial realities that did not exist until after his death, that should make us question its authen-

---

16 Murphy-O'Connor 1995, 15.
17 See Baum 2017.

ticity and its proximity to the historical Paul. Even here, though, we should carefully weigh the words and statements that we think reflect a post-Pauline situation to ensure that we are not simply reading later meanings into them. Some realities or problems prominent in later periods were growing already in Paul's day.

If a letter *was* written in Paul's name after his death, what is it meant to be? There was a convention already before Paul's time for philosophers and theologians to compose letters in the name of their predecessors or of great figures whose thoughts they followed.[18] These were homages to these figures intended to hand on their teaching or legacy to new readers. The letter form and personal details mentioned are decorative, part of this literary genre, imagined to fit with what was known of the figure to whom the letter was ascribed. Written after the death of the named "author," such letters were more intended to teach than to deceive, though naturally what such letters taught was their authors' interpretation of the "author's" teachings. They are, in that sense, something like didactic historical fiction. Many hold that pseudonymous Pauline letters fall into this category: while other successors of the apostles would write in their own name (e.g., Clement of Rome or Ignatius of Antioch), Paul's closest disciples passed on his teachings to perpetuate his legacy and theology in his name, handing on and packaging his teachings in new forms to churches that knew very well that Paul was dead.[19]

The other option for a letter attributed to Paul after his death is not so benign. Some suggest that the disputed letters were not only pseudonymous but forgeries intended to deceive. Theological disputes we see in them reflect conflict among early factions in the church, and one side put its views into a letter that they deceitfully circulated as a previously unknown letter of Paul. These letters are, in this reading, essentially power grabs intended to fabricate Paul's endorsement of later authors' positions and to ensure that people followed them.[20]

Approaching Authorship Theologically

Historically, the letters in the Pauline corpus might fall into any of the above categories. And this is significant when we are using the letters to understand the thought and life of the historical Paul. A letter one deter-

18 See Rosenmeyer 2001, 193–233.

19 See Beker 1992.

20 This is the perspective adopted in Ehrman 2013.

mines to be not merely coauthored or authorized but pseudonymous—and one should weigh all arguments carefully—offers less strong evidence about Paul's biography or what precisely *Paul* (as opposed to his followers) would have said about a given topic. The author may have known the real Paul or reliable information about him, but we should check the reliability of what a pseudonymous letter asserts against other sources before we use it to evaluate the historical Paul.

But a decision about the human authorship of a book, from the perspective of theological interpretation, is only a decision about human authorship. Paul's unique thought and autobiographical statements about his life are important, but they are not the only things religious readers should look for from a "Pauline" epistle. For those who believe in biblical inspiration, even pseudonymous letters furnish theological data. Historical questions are important for interpretation and thus for theological reading. Just as one should distinguish Jesus from Matthew and Matthew from Luke in order to hear the voice of each, it is worth distinguishing Paul from his followers in the case of a pseudonymous letter to hear and value the contribution of each within scripture. And, especially with letters, the real historical circumstances surrounding the author's words impact how we hear their theological message—whether 1 Timothy is private advice from Paul to Timothy or whether it is a pseudonymous letter instructing the whole church makes a difference in how we hear and apply its message.

But if these are inspired by the same God, then divine truth is to be heard not just by hearing Matthew or just by reading Paul, but by hearing the perspectives of all the authors through whom the Spirit speaks. We remember this when reading the OT and Gospels, but sometimes Paul's personality and authority as "the Apostle" whose voice we get to know through so many letters can have the effect of making us discount letters that we think should be but are not his.[21] But, as we have seen, even the Paul we hear in

---

21 Canonically, a pseudonymous book's "apostolicity" could be considered under the aegis of the apostle from whose *tradition* it stemmed rather than its actual writer. The *responsa* of the early Pontifical Biblical Commission on June 24, 1914—then quite conservative about authorship—affirmed that one could hold that Paul did not "plan" or "compose" Hebrews without denying its inspiration or its apostolicity (see Béchard 2002, 205). Tertullian defended the apostolicity of Luke's Gospel because Luke learned from Paul, and "what disciples promulgate is of their teachers" even though Paul was not the origin of the Gospel's words or stories (*Against Marcion* 4.5). To use an OT analogue: even Augustine knew that Wisdom of Solomon only spoke in Solomon's voice but was written much later. "Nevertheless," Augustine wrote, "the church, particularly in the West, has from ancient times accepted [it] as authoritative" (*City of God* 17.20).

the undisputed letters includes wordings and decisions owed to his coauthors. The Spirit's inspiration of texts is not restricted to the mind of a single author as though a letter not by Paul can suddenly become sub-canonical or sub-inspired. Theological interpretation calls us to hear the several inspired voices in the biblical canon together in symphony. If the author of Ephesians is not also the author of Romans, it makes as much difference as the fact that the author of Matthew is not the author of John. Knowing the difference in the authors' intentions and circumstances is important for interpreting the books' meaning and purposes. But both, along with all the other books of scripture, are inspired to communicate divine truth to the faithful.[22]

In this book, when dealing with the individual letters, I will mention different positions on authorship, usually briefly, referring back to this discussion. This book aims to introduce readers to the letters and their interpretation, while decisions about authorship depend on one already having interpreted the history and meaning of each letter against the others. It is hoped that what is offered here and in our treatments below will give a solid foundation upon which readers can build further historical and theological reasoning, including more nuanced positions on debates about authorship.

FURTHER READING

Aletti, Jean-Noël, SJ. 2011. "Rhetoric in the Letters of Paul." In *The Blackwell Companion to Paul*, edited by Stephen Westerholm, 232–47. Chichester, UK: Wiley-Blackwell.

Baum, Armin D. 2017. "Content and Form: Authorship Attribution and Pseudonymity in Ancient Speeches, Letters, Lectures, and Translations—A Rejoinder to Bart Ehrman." *JBL* 136 (2): 381–403.

Collins, Raymond F. 1988. *Letters That Paul Did Not Write: The Epistle to the Hebrews and the Pauline Pseudepigrapha*. Collegeville, MN: Michael Glazier.

Hughes, Frank W. 2010. "Pseudonymy as Rhetoric: A Prolegomenon to the Study of Pauline Pseudepigrapha." In *Rhetorics in the New Millennium: Promise and Fulfillment*, edited by James D. Hester and J. David

22 Regarding inspiration, interpretation, and historical-exegetical questions, compare the conclusion of the Pontifical Biblical Commission's *The Inspiration and Truth of Sacred Scripture* (2014), §137–50, and the excellent *The Interpretation of the Bible in the Church* (1993).

Hester, 216–34. Studies in Antiquity and Christianity. London: T&T Clark.

Kennedy, George A. 1984. *New Testament Interpretation through Rhetorical Criticism*. Chapel Hill: University of North Carolina Press.

Klauck, Hans-Josef. 2006. *Ancient Letters and the New Testament: A Guide to Context and Exegesis*. Translated and edited by Daniel P. Bailey. Waco, TX: Baylor University Press.

Murphy-O'Connor, Jerome. 1995. *Paul the Letter-Writer: His World, His Options, His Skills*. Good News Studies 41. Collegeville, MN: Michael Glazier.

Prior, Michael, CM. 1989. *Paul the Letter-Writer and the Second Letter to Timothy*. JSNTSup 23. Sheffield: Sheffield Academic.

Reece, Steve. 2017. *Paul's Large Letters: Paul's Autographic Subscriptions in the Light of Ancient Epistolary Conventions*. LNTS 561. London: Bloomsbury.

Richards, E. Randolph. 2004. *Paul and First-Century Letter Writing: Secretaries, Composition and Collection*. Downers Grove, IL: IVP Academic.

Rosenmeyer, Patricia A. 2001. *Ancient Epistolary Fictions: The Letter in Greek Literature*. Cambridge: Cambridge University Press.

CHAPTER FOUR

Approaching Paul's Theology

Understanding Paul's background, biography, and his letter writing is an important element of approaching Paul's "theology." What Paul believed and taught is to be discerned primarily from his letters, read against the background of his life and ministry to these churches.

Though Paul's letters are important sources for numerous Christian dogmas, they are not dogmatically or abstractly organized. They are responses to particular situations informed by what Paul already believes. "Pauline theology, then, is embedded in the pastoral responses that Paul gives when he encourages, rebukes, and counsels the communities to which he writes *in light of the gospel he has received.*"[1] Further, his letters clearly do not express everything he himself believed. Take the eucharist, for example. If the Corinthians had not misbehaved, we would hardly have evidence of what Paul thought of the sacrament (see 1 Cor 11:17–34). And even there, his discussion is not everything he felt was important to say on the matter: he concludes with a promise that he will "give instructions about the other matters when I come" (1 Cor 11:34). Earlier in the same letter, he insists that he teaches the deep and spiritual mysteries of the faith to the mature, but that he cannot yet teach these to the Corinthians because they are still immature (1 Cor 2:6–3:3). If the implication is that what Paul wrote in 1 Corinthians was theological baby's milk compared to the "solid food" he himself consumed, we may assume that none of his letters exhausts the heights of his own contemplation.

"Pauline theology," then, must be a limited exercise in reconstruction. We build from what Paul does say in his letters to adopt a coherent picture of how things made sense to Paul. This means we have to connect some dots

---

1 Matera 2012, 8, emphasis original.

speculatively if we hope to "think Paul's thoughts after him"[2] rather than merely to repeat his words. To do this, we need a framework to understand how Paul probably thought and drew his view of the world within which to understand how he expressed himself.

FRAMEWORKS FOR PAUL'S THOUGHT

One approach is to find a background against which to frame what Paul says, either focusing on the content of what he thought or identifying the primary "worldview" in which he made sense of Christ. Obviously, Paul's proclamation of the gospel comes from his encounters with Christ, but he understood these against the formation he had already received in the scriptures, Judaism, and the Greco-Roman world in which he lived. As William Wrede famously quipped, "Athene sprang armed in full power from the head of Zeus. The theology of Paul had no such origin."[3] Likewise, how Paul expresses his gospel in his letters is shaped not only by his thinking but also by his expectations about how his audiences thought, so we can also consider his audiences' contexts to understand his theological terms and argumentation.

Some approach Paul by locating him within Greco-Roman philosophical schools and frame his theology against this background, seeing his ministry as offering gentiles an alternative to popular philosophy.[4] Others hear his proclamation of Jesus's Lordship as primarily directed against the imperial powers and popular worship of Caesar as "Lord," reading his exhortations against the foil of Roman ideology.[5] Paul's talk of being "in Christ" and joined to his death and resurrection (see Gal 2:19–20; Rom 6:3–11) leads others to locate him primarily within Greco-Roman mystic cults and Jewish mysticism.[6]

Most seek frameworks from ancient Judaism, but Judaism in Paul's day was hardly monolithic, and scholars disagree about whether Paul is better compared with later rabbis, mystics, apocalyptic sectarians, or revolutionaries. Moreover, how were this Pharisee's convictions affected by his encounter

2 Wright 2005, x.

3 Wrede 1907, 137.

4 E.g., Engberg-Pedersen 2000.

5 E.g., Crossan and Reed 2004.

6 E.g., Schweitzer 1931; Ashton 2000.

with Christ? Did Paul see Jesus as a fulfillment—albeit surprising and world-changing—of what he through scripture and tradition had been taught to expect, the bringer of the promised new covenant?[7] Or does the revelation of God's justice in Christ (Rom 1:17) bring a radical newness that, though promised in the prophets, now breaks from or even opposes Jewish ways of thought?[8] And what keys might help us center our understanding of Paul against these backgrounds? Paul's own self-understanding as an apostle, specifically as an apostle for the gentiles (Rom 1:1–7), is a worthwhile starting point, as his letters are written out of that vocation and with that purpose.[9] Other approaches organize the search for his theology less around his mission and more around the content of the gospel he received, searching for a "center" to Paul's theology in Christology, in his view of salvation, in ethical transformation, and so on.

Different frameworks within which to understand Paul divide into different schools of scholarly thought. The "further readings" in this chapter represent various perspectives, and several provide discussions of how to evaluate Pauline theology.[10] The best approach will not ignore insights from any of the schools. Paul's mind was not walled off in a ghetto, and his understanding of the mysteries of Christ drove him back to his scriptures as well as to further contact with pagans, while simultaneously reconfiguring everything around the revelation of Christ. However, all of these perspectives must ultimately flow from and be judged by the sense they make not only of Paul's background but of the statements and arguments in his letters. It is from reading his letters, understanding his statements in each one, and comparing them all that we most reliably connect the dots.

PAUL'S THEOLOGY ACROSS THE PAULINE LETTERS

To form a paradigm for Paul's theological thought, one has to read his treatment of topics *across* the letters. We have seen that the letters hardly treat everything Paul believes; some topics are clearly important to him but

---

7 More "covenantal" approaches emphasize Paul's continuity with the OT and Judaism, e.g., Pitre, Barber, and Kincaid 2019.

8 Famously, Ernst Käsemann (1971) opposed any continuous concept of "salvation history" in Paul.

9 See, e.g., Fredriksen 2017.

10 See Matera 2012, 1–15; Donaldson 1997, 29–50; Dunn 1998, 1–26.

rarely appear in what remains of his literary career. On the other hand, when approaching Pauline theology one must also deal with the fact that some topics are discussed frequently and in apparently different ways.

In 1 Thessalonians 4:15, for instance, Paul seems to assume that he will be alive at the second coming of Christ ("we who are alive"), while in Philippians 1:21–26 he appears untroubled by the notion that he might die beforehand, and the statements in 2 Thessalonians 2:1–12 insist that there may be a good deal of time (how long is not specified) before Christ returns to judge. In 1 Corinthians Paul appeals to moral and other statutes from the Mosaic law for his churches to follow (see 1 Cor 5:8, 13; 9:9) and only lightly discourages gentiles from being circumcised, and in Romans he insists that "the law is spiritual" and its commandments are "holy, righteous, and good" (7:12–14). In Galatians, however, Paul seems to imply that the law is a curse from which to be freed, and he threatens gentiles who turn to circumcision with divine wrath (Gal 3:10, 23–24; 5:2–4). Or why does Paul insist that he "no longer" thinks of Christ "according to the flesh" in 2 Corinthians 5:16, but in Romans he treats Christ's Jewishness "according to the flesh" as perennially significant (Rom 1:3; 9:5; 15:8)? Readers of Pauline theology must read across these differing or apparently contradictory passages to understand Paul's thought on these topics.

Beyond such differences when treating the same topic, readers are confronted with the presence and absence of certain ideas from letter to letter. Why is "justification" present—even as a main theme in Paul's teaching about salvation—in some letters (Rom 3–8; Gal 2–5; Phil 3:4–11; cf. 1 Cor 6:11; 2 Cor 5:21) but not in the others? Why in 1–2 Thessalonians does he hardly mention his status as an apostle (only 1 Thess 2:7) but emphasize it strongly elsewhere? Why in 1 Thessalonians 4:16–17 does Paul say that Christ will raise the dead and all believers will "meet the Lord in the air," but there is no mention of this in his eschatological timetable in 1 Corinthians 15:20–28?

Apparent contradictions or the absence of an important theme might suggest that a letter is not historically Pauline. Those who reach this conclusion for this or that letter do not then need to account for their contents within the historical Paul's thought (though theologically they still need to be read in the canon alongside Paul, as discussed in chapter 3). However, removing disputed letters from Paul's "theology" can hardly resolve all the tensions one must deal with when trying to form a coherent account of his thought. As the examples above show, the same tensions exist across the undisputed letters.

So how does one account for these tensions or differences and evaluate Pauline theology from his occasional letters? In the main, there are three types of approaches.

Consistent vs. Inconsistent

Some respond to the diversity of Paul's expression across his letters on topics like the Mosaic law or eschatology simply by saying that he was not a consistent thinker.[11] Paul has things that he wants people to do, and he makes arguments and statements that he thinks will convince people to do them. But arriving at a consistent and systematic "Pauline theology" on one topic or other will be tenuous if not a dead end.

Others maintain instead that Paul *is* a consistent and systematic thinker. He always thinks the same thing about the same topics. The differences in his arguments are apparent to us only because of what we do not know or because we have overread one passage against others. If Paul says the law is "good" in Romans, there is no reason to think he would not have said the same thing at the time he wrote Galatians; we simply need to put the two letters together. The situation he faces might lead him, in his occasional letters, to emphasize his apostolic authority less in 1 Thessalonians than in other letters, but it is hardly because something changed in his self-understanding. Some anchor Paul's consistency in his biography, particularly in his vision of Christ near Damascus: he was already educated in philosophy and scripture, and when Christ revealed himself to him, Paul's doctrine of Christ, salvation, the law, and so on was sufficiently formed.[12]

On this view, Pauline theology's task is not to distinguish what Paul thinks about one topic "in 1 Corinthians" from what he thinks "in Romans," but to see what Paul thinks about the topic everywhere synthetically. Since he is always a consistent thinker, one can use what Paul says in any letter (no matter when or in what situation it was written) to temper or correct one's reading of what Paul says in another. Books on Pauline theology following this approach regularly proceed topic by topic—"God," "humanity," "sin," "salvation"—often following the succession of topics in Romans.[13]

11 See Räisänen 1983.
12 See Kim 1982.
13 E.g., Dunn 1998.

Coherence and Contingency

Another approach responds to the charge of inconsistency by emphasizing that "Paul was a coherent, but not systematic, thinker."[14] None of his letters develop a full "treatment" of any one topic, and even Romans cannot be used as a systematic reflection of how Paul organized his thought. Every letter is an expression of his theology in the sense that his words flow out of what he believes (see 2 Cor 4:13), but he only explains his beliefs insofar as he feels he needs to in building arguments to exhort his audience in faith and life.

This does not mean that "Pauline theology" is a mirage. Paul has basic and unchanging convictions within a theological framework out of which he responds with sometimes divergent arguments depending on how he is moved to address his audience's situation. Paul's own thinking is "coherent," but its expression is "contingent" on his situation and his audience.[15] Reconstructing an account of Paul's theology on certain topics, then, cannot simply focus on the statements he makes or simply add them up into a logical whole; rather, we need to see what he values and protects *in* the arguments and statements he makes, discerning the core convictions that sometimes are explicitly stated and sometimes lie beneath the surface. Paul has core convictions about Christ and the place of the law in God's plan, but he can speak in 2 Corinthians 3:6–18 of the law as the "old covenant" whose ministry is surpassed by the glory of Christ's "new covenant" and in Galatians 3:6–22 of Christ's as the older covenant, reaching back to Genesis, which the law given later by Moses cannot supersede. There is a core conviction about Christ and the law in salvation history behind these arguments, but we should not harmonize them into a single theory of "new" and "old."

This type of approach obviously needs to evaluate all Paul's letters individually before comparing them to distill his underlying aims and convictions. Individual letters are especially treated for their situations and for Paul's "aims in writing" in order to see the convictions that emerge differently across his letters.[16]

Development

Most agree that each letter must be appreciated for how Paul responds out of his convictions to certain situations. However, while Paul's argumen-

---

14 Sanders 1977, 518.

15 See Beker 1980.

16 Seifrid 1992, 183.

tation may differ because of changes in audience from letter to letter, many also emphasize that Paul's different arguments may result from changes in Paul himself. Paul's core convictions and ways of thinking can *develop* over time as he preaches, teaches, prays, and has new religious experiences of Christ (2 Cor 12:1–10). He is not an inconsistent thinker, but he is also not a static thinker. Paul may not yet have realized how spiritually dangerous circumcision could be for gentile Christians when he wrote 1 Corinthians, then may have seen it starkly in the events of the Galatian conflict and responded vigorously against believers adopting Mosaic customs, and then calmed to explain himself more cautiously in Romans. His experience of repeated reading of scripture, continuously contemplating Christ, or seeing more and more Christians dying may have revised his eschatological timetable and his way of counseling believers in hope between 1 Thessalonians and the other letters.

A great strength of this approach is its incorporation of Paul's biography and the recognition that Paul's study and experience continued to shape his convictions over time. On the same score, it is often critiqued because it requires us to know the order in which he wrote the letters and requires a sketch of Paul's biography from his letters and Acts, and there is no scholarly consensus on such things.[17] Likewise, when taking a developmental approach, one must acknowledge different types of "developments" over time that might be apparent across the letters.[18] Some differences across his letters may reflect a modification of Paul's *beliefs*, either because his actual conviction about something changed or because he grew in his understanding of its implications. However, they may also reflect only a development in his *argumentation*: Paul's belief about the topic did not change; his way of articulating it changed because he found a more persuasive way of saying the same thing. The most careful developmental approaches, then, must

---

17 For instance, perhaps Paul does not emphasize his apostolic status in 1–2 Thessalonians because he was not yet publicly recognized in "fellowship" with the apostles in Jerusalem (Gal 2:9), and Acts has simply moved the Jerusalem Council (Acts 15) before Paul's journey to Thessalonica (Acts 17) for the convenience of presenting Paul's whole "second journey" at once (Acts 16–18). This fits the chronology argued by Tatum 2006 and is possible given what one should expect of Acts (see chapter 2), but it is a conclusion that many would debate.

18 Probably the clearest articulation of this is only available in German (Hahn 1993). Sanders (2015, 172) helpfully encapsulates a cautious developmental perspective: "'Development' does not mean 'retraction.' On the contrary, I find no instance in which Paul retracts what he earlier thought, but rather a good deal of *movement* toward a richer, fuller description of the meaning of life in Christ Jesus" (emphasis original).

establish a chronological sequence of the letters within Paul's biography, evaluate each letter against its audience's situation, and then also trace Paul's convictions across the letters *and* across time to see where there is development and what type it is.[19]

READING THE LETTERS FOR CONTEXT AND THEOLOGY

The above paradigms all have merits. Our distance from Paul and our desire—especially for religious readers—to learn from the life and teachings of this apostle in whom Christ dwelt should bias us toward assuming that he makes coherent sense on his own terms. The question is *how* his thought is coherent, how his ideas fit together. Given the nature and purpose of his letters, we should not assume he would say things the same way to every audience. The thoroughly "consistent" approach is weakest in this regard. We must pay attention to the situations of Paul's own audiences to understand his response and discern the convictions out of which he writes. Likewise, the nature of Paul's life with Christ was one of service and relationship, and relationships and vocations deepen. Paul's Damascus experience did not upload a new detailed catechism into his brain, but it brought him to encounter a person and enter a new life filled and guided by the Spirit; we should hardly assume that his further experience and discernment in fellowship with Christ should not be reflected in his expression of the gospel across time.

In light of all this, I recommend four basic steps to reading and discerning Paul's theology when considering the letters individually and as a whole.

Author (What Is Paul's Situation?)

The first step is to ask what Paul's situation is in writing a letter, as it may affect how he addresses his audience. Compare, for instance, Galatians and Romans. In Galatians, he writes to a church that knows him (1:9; 4:12–20), but many of its members are now being swayed by a "different gospel" to switch their adherence from Paul to other missionaries (1:6). He also appears unable to visit them other than to send off this missive (4:20). In such a letter we should expect him not only to emphasize the legitimacy of his gospel and

---

19 Good examples are Schnelle 2005 and G. P. Anderson 2016.

his apostolic authority (1:11–17; 2:9–10), but also to write correctively and passionately—they know him and what he preached, and so he can assume that knowledge (e.g., 5:21) and argue forcefully rather than explain carefully, since it may be his last opportunity to persuade them. And this is precisely what we get in the passionate and less careful arguments of Galatians. In Romans, by contrast, Paul writes to a congregation he has not met and on which he has no claim other than that he is "apostle to the gentiles" (1:1–15), and he hopes that they will receive him well when he visits and support his travel to evangelize Spain (15:23–24, 28–29). Though he knows some in the area (16:3–16), he is aware that many or most of his audience know him only by rumors that his teaching of salvation apart from the Mosaic law is amoral and libertine (3:8). He is also anxious that people in Jerusalem, where he is visiting before Rome, are swayed by the same rumors and might reject him (15:25–27, 30–32). This gives his letter a somewhat defensive accent, and it makes sense of why he takes several chapters—often backtracking to clarify himself—to address questions of what he does and does not teach about the law and Israel and to show that his gospel promotes, rather than undermines, morality (Rom 2–11).

Paul's own situation can affect the themes that emerge in his writings, how he means to project or protect his own authority in a letter, and whether he argues forcefully or more carefully. It may also affect things that he thinks he needs to address. Interpreters are often surprised to find in Colossians and the later letters a list of duties for Christians in their household relationships—slaves and masters, husbands and wives, parents and children (Col 3:18–4:1). Such "household codes" are not found in the earlier letters. It may be because these letters are written at a later time in early Christianity by a disciple of Paul concerned with order in Christian homes. But it may be because they were written after something in Paul's life caused him to think he needed to start addressing this issue. Traditionally, Paul is understood to have written Colossians at the same time as he wrote Philemon, in which he intervenes to call a Christian master to forgive and be reconciled to his newly converted slave as a "brother" in Christ (Phlm 9–16). If this is true, it is easy to see why having to stick his nose into Philemon's household in the name of the gospel would cause him to begin treating such household relationships in later letters. He had just seen firsthand the way in-home relations and resentments might complicate life among believers and realized that churches would benefit from a thumbnail sketch of Christian household relations.

Audience (Who Is Paul Talking To?)

When reading Paul's theology from the letters, one must consider the situation of his audience. Communicators use words they assume people will understand, and good communicators estimate their audiences' capacities and needs consciously. If we consider Paul a good communicator as he and his team composed the letters, we should assume that what he expects his audience to understand or what he thinks they need to understand is part of how he shapes his message.

An obvious example is 1 Corinthians. The Corinthians have written Paul a letter raising questions about sex and marriage (1 Cor 7:1), and he has also received word about problems of division, sexual immorality, and disorder in the Corinthians' worship (1:11–12; 5:1; 11:17–22; 14:26–33). Paul's letter thus replies to these and other issues because of the Corinthians' situation. When we read, then, it is important to try to understand their own questions and, as far as we can, to imagine the reasons they might have had for their own behavior.[20] When we read Paul saying there is no difference between following his or Apollos's teaching (3:5–23), it makes a difference whether we think the Corinthians are competing over who is the more impressive minister or whether Apollos and Paul were teaching truly different doctrines. Is Paul saying it does not matter how impressive the person who baptized you is as long as you are baptized into Christ, or is he saying doctrinal divisions are fine as long as everyone gets along?

The audience's situation is also important for evaluating Paul's persuasive strategy, as the situation or location of his addressees can also shape the themes Paul employs as he evangelizes and exhorts. Philippians, as we will see, speaks of Christ and of the Christian life in ways that use and subvert particularly Roman conceptions of honor and shame. Philippi was a Roman colony that modeled itself on the imperial capital, and Paul expresses the truth in a way molded to the hearing and situation of his audience. Understanding these aspects of the audience's situation can help us understand what Paul is up to in the way he presents doctrines and how he hopes it will affect his churches.

---

20 More precisely, this includes imagining not just what they thought but what *Paul thought* they thought. It is Paul's understanding of his audience that directs his response, and he may not always have all the relevant information.

Argument (What Is Paul Saying?)

With an understanding of the situation, one needs to attend to Paul's *argument*. It is tempting to take a single sentence from Paul and contemplate it alone for its beauty or profundity. But Paul's sentences are not uttered separately for their own sake. Paul aims to use them to convince his audience to believe and act in a certain way in the name of the gospel as his arguments build throughout the letter. We need to keep reading, paying attention to what Paul is trying to get across to the audience and how his sentences and paragraphs build to prove it. For example, in 1 Corinthians 9:4–12 Paul lists a number of "rights" that he has as an apostle, including the right to marry and the right to be paid for his preaching. One might take either of these in isolation and systematize a list of rights that none should deny a priest or minister. But in the passage, Paul only emphasizes that these are legitimate "rights" to then show that his duty to serve Christ and others supersedes them—hence his celibacy and preference to support himself by manual labor (1 Cor 9:12–27). Moreover, Paul does not say all this about self-denial for the salvation of others merely for its own sake, but to offer himself as an example of how the Corinthians should let love for others supersede their own rights to eat meat butchered in sacrifice to idols, which may lead some of their brethren to sin. Paul raises the question of idol meat in 1 Corinthians 8:1, and it takes three chapters for him to finally answer it (1 Cor 8–10). But the apparent "detours" in between provide the proofs that support his answer, and we will miss it if we do not follow the way his argument builds.[21]

Once one has discerned Paul's individual arguments for their logic and against the letter's background, sketching Pauline theology calls for evaluating his arguments comparatively across the letters. When looking at two similar but differing arguments, what fundamental conviction do they both express in different contingencies? Are they logically consistent with each other, one argument simply saying less or the other saying more because of the situation? Looking at the chronology of Paul's life and letters, does Paul's treatment of the topic begin to change or develop to further heights after a certain point?

Assumptions and Tradition (What Does Paul Believe?)

One aspect of studying Pauline theology that is not always noted is the relevance of prior tradition in the convictions behind his arguments. But

21 See Aletti 2011, 241–43.

Paul's assumptions about what is true, even if they are not drawn out or developed in his arguments, evince his beliefs. Attending to them is one aspect of connecting the dots behind his arguments and of understanding his own thought.

Sometimes Paul's assumptions surface in his offhand remarks. Paul never develops a demonology in his arguments, for instance. However, he very clearly assumed that he lived in a world wherein demons were active and opposed the salvation of souls: at different points, Paul mentions Satan tempting believers and trying to thwart his ministry (Rom 16:20; 1 Cor 7:5; 2 Cor 11:3, 14–15; 1 Thess 2:18). We cannot develop a full Pauline demonology from these, of course, but they remind us not to exclude the demonic from our portrait of Paul or from our understanding of doctrines that he does develop. Paul did not see his world or his work separated from the angelic realm.

Another aspect of this task is to note what Paul does in addition to how he argues. Paul not only writes but also *acts* out of his basic convictions and expectations. Attention to Paul's practice is important, and it can sometimes help clarify what he thinks when his explicit arguments are unclear. Interpreters debate, for instance, about Paul's view of Christian perseverance and whether he thought one could genuinely convert and then fall away and lose salvation. Some of his statements suggest he did, others that he did not. His activity can bring some clarity, however. After he left Thessalonica, that church suffered persecution, and Paul was unable to return personally. He was anxious about their faith and perseverance. He later recounted that, during this time, he "could no longer take" the agony of being uncertain about their fate, and "for that reason" he sent Timothy "to ascertain your faith, lest perhaps the tempter tempted you and our [evangelistic] labor proved in vain" (1 Thess 3:1, 5). If he believed apostasy was impossible for people whom he says genuinely converted at his preaching (1 Thess 1:4–2:12), would he have experienced such anxiety or sent Timothy to ensure that they had not apostatized?

Finally, Paul's convictions are also evinced in his use of common Christian tradition and ritual. As mentioned above, Paul's letters rarely mention the eucharist. But in the only letter that discusses it, we learn not only that it was a regular part of the life of faith he handed on to his churches but also that he passed on Jesus's words of institution from early Christian tradition (1 Cor 11:23–26). We learn, then, that he hardly promoted religion without ritual. Likewise, some have argued that Paul, "taught" by Christ and led by the Spirit (Gal 1:11–12), was not interested in theology that did not come to him spontaneously. But Paul not only mentions that he received tradition from the other apostles (see 1 Cor 15:3) but also quotes and refers to traditional sayings and practices that he shared with the wider Christian movement.[22] He was a brilliant and inspired apostle, but he did not see himself as a lone wolf. And it may be that, while in his letters we see more words devoted to his own unique thinking in response to particular situations, the traditions he held in common with others lay at the heart of his convictions.

FURTHER READING

Anderson, Garwood P. 2016. *Paul's New Perspective: Charting a Soteriological Journey*. Downers Grove, IL: IVP Academic.

Beker, J. Christiaan. 1980. *Paul the Apostle: The Triumph of God in Life and Thought*. Edinburgh: T&T Clark.

de Boer, Martinus C. 2020. *Paul, Theologian of God's Apocalypse: Essays on Paul and Apocalyptic*. Eugene, OR: Cascade.

Donaldson, Terence L. 1997. *Paul and the Gentiles: Remapping the Apostle's Convictional World*. Minneapolis: Fortress.

Dunn, James D. G. 1998. *The Theology of Paul the Apostle*. Grand Rapids: Eerdmans.

Fredriksen, Paula. 2017. *Paul, the Pagans' Apostle*. New Haven, CT: Yale University Press.

Johnson, Luke Timothy. 2020. *Constructing Paul: The Canonical Paul*. Vol. 1. Grand Rapids: Eerdmans.

Matera, Frank J. 2012. *God's Saving Grace: A Pauline Theology*. Grand Rapids: Eerdmans.

Pitre, Brant, Michael P. Barber, and John A. Kincaid. 2019. *Paul, a New Covenant Jew: Rethinking Pauline Theology*. Grand Rapids: Eerdmans.

Plevnik, Joseph. 1989. "The Center of Pauline Theology." *CBQ* 51 (3): 461–78.

Sanders, E. P. 2015. *The Apostle's Life, Letters, and Thought*. Minneapolis: Fortress.

22 See Sumney 2017.

Schnelle, Udo. 2005. *Apostle Paul: His Life and Theology*. Translated by O. C. Dean Jr. Grand Rapids: Baker Academic.

Sumney, Jerry L. 2017. *Steward of God's Mysteries: Paul and Early Church Tradition*. Grand Rapids: Eerdmans.

Wolter, Michael. 2015. *Paul: An Outline of His Theology*. Translated by Robert L. Brawley. Waco, TX: Baylor University Press.

Wright, N. T. 2013. *Paul and the Faithfulness of God*. Christian Origins and the Question of God 4. Minneapolis: Fortress.

CHAPTER FIVE

The Portrait of Paul in Acts

The book of Acts is a major source for understanding Paul, his life, and his place within earliest Christianity. Acts tells of the earliest church after the resurrection and ascension of Christ, relating its story especially through the figures of Peter and Paul. Indeed, the last two-thirds of Acts follow Paul exclusively to the extent that the book is easily mistaken for a biography of Paul. Acts is certainly influenced by ancient Greco-Roman history and biography writing, and the author is interested to relate reliable information: its author also wrote the Gospel of Luke, where he tells us he was concerned to collect reliable traditions and eyewitness accounts to craft his narrative (Luke 1:1–4; cf. Acts 1:1–3). Indeed, he presents himself as an eyewitness to much of Paul's later ministry (Acts 16:10–17; 20:5–15; 21:1–18; 27:1–28:16), traditionally identified with the "Luke" present with Paul in Philemon 24 and Colossians 4:14.

However, Acts is neither history nor biography, simply speaking. It has a heavy focus on Peter and Paul, but is not simply a book "about" their lives. Peter drops out of the book almost completely after Acts 12; it tells us nothing of Paul's death, though most agree that it was written in the 80s long after Paul's martyrdom.[1] It is a history, but it does not merely relate the church's backstory to sate readers' curiosity. Acts is a *theological* history, telling the

---

1 Some date the book in the 60s before Paul's death, arguing that Luke, who is interested in portraying Christlike martyrdom, would have narrated Paul's death if it had already happened. But Luke is also interested to show the unity of Paul, Peter, and the Jerusalem church as well as the church's movement from Jerusalem to Rome, yet he does not mention that Peter was with Paul in Rome in the 60s as all (other) ancient reports attest. Luke also does not make much of Paul's collection, which Paul viewed as symbolic of the communion between Jerusalem and his gentile mission (see Rom 15:25–27). Luke mentions it only in passing in Acts 24:17. Other scholars date Acts much later, arguing that it evinces the theological perspective of the early second century, but this is probably unnecessarily late (see Holladay 2016, 4–7).

story of God's work to grow the church and spread the gospel from Jerusalem to Rome, the capital of the world. It focuses on Peter and Paul, not to give us an account of their lives, but to use their experiences and work as icons through which we see God's work to spread the gospel. Acts is not exhaustive, but it gives representative or paradigmatic episodes that epitomize the church's growth and struggles after Pentecost. Reading Paul in Acts, then, calls us to read beyond simply Paul's life to include Luke's perspective on the grand sweep of salvation history rooted in Jerusalem and stretching to all nations by the power of the Holy Spirit.

PAUL'S MINISTRY IN ACTS: OVERVIEW

Luke's Gospel began by highlighting the bridge between the Old and the New in salvation history, beginning with an angelic message in the temple and with miraculous births similar to those of Samuel or Isaac, and highlighting that Christ would bring the fulfillment and confirmation of God's promises to the patriarchs and to David (Luke 1:32–33, 54–55, 68–75; 2:30–32). Jesus will fulfill these promises as the son of David and Son of God to bring salvation to Jerusalem and the gentiles—but he will also cause the fall of many who reject and oppose him (Luke 2:32–34). These themes of scriptural fulfillment, rejection, and mission to Jerusalem and the gentiles recur in Jesus's commission to the disciples in Luke's Easter narrative. Scripture is fulfilled in Christ's death and resurrection, and now the disciples must fulfill the prophecies that "repentance for the forgiveness of sins would be preached in his name to all nations, beginning from Jerusalem" (Luke 24:47). They must wait in Jerusalem until the Holy Spirit is poured out on them, and the Spirit will empower their ministry to bring the gospel of repentance to all nations.

This is precisely the story Acts tells. It begins by reiterating this promise of Jesus: "you will receive power when the Holy Spirit comes upon you, and you will be my witnesses in Jerusalem, in all Judea and Samaria, and to the end of the earth" (1:8). The Holy Spirit comes, as promised, and converts thousands through Peter's preaching at Pentecost (2:38–41). Like Jesus, the believers (called "the Way," 9:2) face opposition from the ruling groups in Jerusalem. But some priests, Pharisees, and Samaritans also join the community (6:7; 8:5, 14, 25; 15:5). The ministry of Jesus continues and spreads through the work of the church, and in the course of Acts 1–8 the gospel has spread from Jerusalem to Judea and Samaria, as Jesus promised (see 9:31). The work of spreading the gospel "to the end of the earth" (1:8), however, is narrated especially through the ministry of Paul. Luke's account of Paul will highlight themes of continuity between the Old and the New in salvation history, mission and evangelization far beyond Jerusalem, and rejection.

Paul's Call

We first meet Paul in a moment of persecution, watching approvingly as Stephen, the first Christian martyr, is killed for his faith (7:58; 8:1). Stephen prays that God would forgive his killers (7:60), and in the aftermath of his martyrdom a great persecution causes the gospel to spread as believers flee Jerusalem and bring their faith to other environs (8:1–2; 11:19).

Paul's turn to faith in Christ comes while, as Acts characterizes it, he is "raging against the church" (8:3) and "breathing threat and murder against the Lord's disciples" (9:1). Traveling from Jerusalem to Damascus, he falls to the ground at the appearance of an intense heavenly light, from which he hears, "Saul, Saul, why are you persecuting me?" (9:4).[2] When he learns that it is Jesus who has spoken, he receives instructions to meet Ananias, a Christian in Damascus who will baptize him.

The episode encapsulates much. First, the specific way in which Jesus appears to Paul shows him the truth that he and others had murderously denied: that the crucified Jesus is the eternal Son, the Lord, risen and exalted at the Father's right hand (cf. 7:54–58; Mark 14:61–64). Paul receives the vision obediently (Acts 26:19), fasting and praying in consideration of the vision, and after being baptized he turns to preach its message that Jesus is the Christ and that in him the resurrection of the dead has begun (9:22; 13:30–37; 17:3, 18, 31–32; 18:5, 28). Second, the work of the gospel spreads through (and not merely despite) persecution. Stephen's intercession for his killers clearly was heard. Paul himself will now follow the martyr's path, no longer the figure in power approving of others' pain but one standing in Stephen's shoes and suffering in imitation of Christ (see 16:22; 21:30–32). Third, we see the divine providence that will be at work to spread the gospel through the hardships of Paul's life. Some of those who fled from Stephen's persecution (in which Paul had a hand) began evangelizing not just fellow Jews but also gentiles. This happened in the city of Antioch, in Syria, which became one of the first mixed communities of Jewish and gentile believers living and worshipping together. It was this community in Antioch that

2 Paul's heavenly vision is also told, with slight variations, in 22:1–21; 26:1–23.

would become Paul's "home base" for his missions (11:19–26) and in which he would begin to theologize about the place of gentiles in the church (15:1–5; cf. Gal 2:11–14). And divine providence through Paul's sufferings would lead him, ultimately, to an imprisonment that brought him to preach the gospel in the empire's capital (Acts 23:11).

"He is a chosen vessel of mine, to bear my name before gentiles and kings and the sons of Israel. For I will show him how much he must suffer for the sake of my name" (Acts 9:15–16). These words of Jesus serve both as summary and program for what happens in Paul's ministry in Acts. Persecution and evangelization are the immediate results of Paul's vision: Paul argues before his fellow Jews that Jesus is the messiah and gains some of his own "disciples" (9:25), but others respond to his message as he once did and plot to kill him. He flees Damascus for Jerusalem and is approved by the apostles, being especially commended by Barnabas, while others in Jerusalem plot to kill him and force him again to flee. Acts highlights this as a repeating pattern throughout Paul's journeys: at every point his evangelism will inspire faith in some but "threat and murder" from others, but even in his persecutions the gospel is spread.

Paul's Journeys and the Jerusalem Council

Barnabas brought Paul to Antioch after the mixed community there became known (11:25–26). After this, Acts organizes Paul's activity into three distinct "missionary journeys." On each, he leaves the community in Antioch, evangelizes and suffers in other lands, and returns to Antioch (see 14:26; 18:22). His third journey ends not in Antioch but in Jerusalem, where he is imprisoned (21:17). Between the first and second journeys, however, Paul leaves Antioch briefly for Jerusalem, where the apostles and elders settle disputes about whether gentiles need to be circumcised to join the church. The apostles' decision that circumcision is unnecessary then spurs Paul's further evangelistic work and eventual rejection in Jerusalem.

First Missionary Journey (13:1–14:28). Paul's first journey takes him into Asia Minor (modern Turkey). He sails to the isle of Cyprus and thereafter to towns in southern-central Asia Minor. Paul accompanies the more senior disciple Barnabas, yet proves himself to be the "chief speaker" as they evangelize (14:12; cf. 13:9, 16). He preaches to a ruling proconsul, to a synagogue where he is invited to speak, and to pagans who think he and Barnabas must be the gods Hermes and Zeus. The narrative highlights Paul's evangelistic scope, message, and strategy. As to scope, we see here his evangelization of "gentiles and kings and the sons of Israel" (9:15) already begun in preaching to Jews, gentiles, and a pagan ruler. Two speeches highlight his message and strategy. In the synagogue at Pisdian Antioch, Paul preaches much like Peter did at Pentecost, using proofs from the OT to show his fellow Jews (and gentiles who had already joined the synagogue) that Jesus is the messiah, raised from the dead (13:13–43). But with the pagans in Lystra, Paul instead uses proofs from nature to proclaim the one creator God (14:8–18). Paul and Barnabas again are met with both acceptance and violent rejection in the synagogues, and they conclude their journey by passing back through the towns they evangelized to encourage the believers and appoint presbyters to shepherd these nascent communities (14:21–23).

Jerusalem Council (15:1–35). When Paul and Barnabas return to Antioch, the church is troubled by some visitors from Judea who insist that gentiles cannot be saved without being circumcised and following Jewish customs. Paul and Barnabas, who by now have preached both to gentiles that already sympathized with Judaism (13:48) and to polytheists (14:8–18), oppose them publicly, and all parties agree to submit the matter to the Jerusalem apostles. Acts has already narrated God's revelation to Peter that the gift of the Holy Spirit communicates true purity and holiness to those who believe, so that gentile believers do not need to be circumcised to be considered pure and to participate fully in the church (chaps. 10–11). At the council, Peter reiterates that God "cleanses" the hearts of those who believe in Christ for salvation, regardless of their prior heritage or religion (15:8–11), and he invites Paul and Barnabas to tell of their work with gentiles. James, bishop of Jerusalem, agrees and cites the OT to prove that the gentiles would call on the Lord after the Davidic messiah comes. James formulates a policy that gentiles need not be circumcised or keep kosher diets, but should abstain from idolatry and impurities like eating blood and sexual immorality (15:13–21). The apostles send Silas and another representative from Jerusalem back to Antioch with Paul to confirm their support of Paul's work and to promulgate the decision reached by the council. As Acts presents it, this is a watershed moment affirming Paul and preparing for his further missions, yet the decision is also a source of trouble, as not all believers will support or understand this way of bringing gentiles into the people of the new covenant.

Second Missionary Journey (15:36–18:22). Paul and Barnabas have a falling-out over their choice of travel companions, and Paul begins his next journey now with Silas (called "Silvanus" in Paul's letters, 1 Thess 1:1) and soon Timothy as partners in mission. This journey begins much like the first, traveling through southern Asia Minor, but Paul is inspired in a dream to bring the gospel westward to Macedonia and then Achaia (roughly northern and southern Greece). Here we see Paul, Silas, and Timothy at work in many of the churches to which he would later write letters. In Philippi they evangelize a God-fearing gentile, convert their jailer during a brief imprisonment, and evangelize others as well. In a Thessalonian synagogue they have success with some but are rejected quickly by others, so they flee south to Berea. Paul continues on to Athens, where he addresses Stoic and Epicurean philosophers. Finally, he evangelizes Corinth and stays for more than eighteen months, strengthening the church and building his mission team (Acts 18:11). He supports himself by plying his trade as a leatherworker ("tentmaker," 18:3). On this journey, we see the gospel's acceptance and violent opposition continue. Acts also highlights that the church's scope increases not just *geographically* in Europe but also *socially*: Athenian philosophers and many women of industry and high society heed the gospel (17:4, 34). At the same time, Acts highlights the church's growing notoriety in the eyes of the government: Paul is jailed for disturbing commerce (by exorcising a fortune-telling demon) and accused of preaching a message subversive to both synagogue and empire (16:19–24; 17:6–9; 18:12–17).

Third Missionary Journey (18:23; 19:1–21:17). After his second journey, Paul passes again through Asia Minor to encourage his churches there. Thereafter he travels to Ephesus, a provincial capital along the west coast of Asia Minor. He remains there for the better part of three years (19:8, 10; 20:31), and the gospel spreads throughout the region through the efforts of Paul and his growing team of coworkers. Again, a disturbance prompts Paul's departure, this time a riot thrown by craftsmen whose sale of idols is being threatened by conversions to Christianity. From there, Paul returns to Macedonia and Greece with his team and sets sail for Jerusalem. This portion of the narrative is thick with a sense of foreboding: the Spirit "constrains" him to go to Jerusalem, and Paul follows, though he is warned repeatedly that this journey will end in suffering (20:22; 21:4, 9–13). As Luke's Gospel reinforces the necessity that Jesus suffer in Jerusalem for the sake of the world (see Luke 9:22; 13:33; 22:37; 24:26), Acts shows Paul under the Spirit's constraint to journey to Jerusalem and be rejected for Jesus's sake. For it is in Jerusalem that this journey will end and his long string of imprisonments for the gospel will begin.

Paul's Imprisonments

Jesus's pronouncement that Paul would bring the gospel before Jews, gentiles, and high rulers ("kings") and that he would "suffer for my name" (9:15–16) comes to a climax in the book's final chapters. Paul will defend himself and proclaim the gospel before all these groups again—and finally before an actual "king," Agrippa II (26:2)—preaching before Jews in Jerusalem and then, in his imprisonments, before gentiles in Caesarea and Rome.

Paul arrives in Jerusalem and is greeted by James and the ruling elders, and the report of his gentile missions in Asia Minor and Europe is received warmly.[3] But James tells Paul that his preaching has been misunderstood: many Christian Jews in Jerusalem have heard that he not only preaches that gentiles do not need to be circumcised but that Jews too should give up circumcision and their ancestral laws (21:20–21). To correct this, Paul follows James's suggestion to undergo ritual purification and have an offering presented in the temple, but some non-Christian Jews raise an outcry at his presence and spread a rumor (false, according to Acts) that Paul had brought a gentile into the temple (21:27–29). Paul is mobbed and arrested, but he is allowed briefly to defend himself to the people "in the Hebrew dialect," probably meaning Aramaic (21:40). His message is rejected, and he is readied for flogging. But then he appeals to his Roman citizenship. Citizenship bore certain obligations to the empire but also protected one against certain types of punishment and entitled one to appeal accusations and convictions before the emperor. Now on notice that they are dealing with a bona fide citizen, the guards quickly spirit Paul away from the mob into a holding cell.

Paul is held for a time and is told by Jesus that his work will not end in Jerusalem: "you must also testify at Rome" (23:11). Paul addresses the Sanhedrin, but when a plot on his life is discovered, the Roman tribune has Paul transferred to custody in Caesarea under the procurator Felix. Other than desiring carefully to honor his citizen's rights and being impressed by Paul's wisdom and virtue (24:24–26), the Romans are generally unconcerned with Paul's case. They see it mainly as another religious squabble between Jews (23:26–30; 25:18–19, 24–25). Indeed, Felix, realizing he would get no ransom money to free Paul, keeps Paul in prison for two years as a political favor for "the Jews" (24:26–27). Roughly two years into Paul's imprisonment,

---

3 Presumably we are to understand that they received the collection he mentions later (24:17), but we hear nothing of it here.

Felix is succeeded by Festus (59 CE), who hopes to ingratiate himself with Jerusalem's leaders by offering to let them try Paul again (25:9). But Paul, surely tired of this game, calls upon his rights as a citizen to appeal his case directly to Caesar in Rome. This appeal must be honored, and Festus's hands are tied. "To Caesar you have appealed; to Caesar you will go" (25:12).

The book's tone at this point is marked by notes of both hope and tragedy now that Paul's destination in Rome is fixed. While Paul awaits his transfer, he is allowed to address the Herodian king Agrippa II and his queen. He concludes with a wish that all would become followers of Jesus like himself, "except for these chains" (26:29). The king, who has authority to release Paul, responds solemnly that Paul is guiltless but cannot be freed: "This man could have been released, had he not appealed to Caesar" (26:32). Acts then narrates with not a little detail Paul's transfer by sea to Rome, with rough weather and shipwrecks that threaten the crew. Paul remains a blessed vessel for divine work here, too, not only for the preservation of the ship (27:21–38) but also in healing people on the island of Malta, on which they ran aground (28:1–10). Finally they come to Rome, where Paul summons the local Jews and presents his gospel to them, arguing from scripture that Jesus is the messiah. Some believe, others do not, and the book ends with Paul quoting God's words to Isaiah that God's own people would disbelieve the prophet's message. "Therefore," Paul concludes, "let it be known to you that God's salvation has been sent to the gentiles; they will listen!" (28:28). The book ends with Paul, under guard but free to receive visitors, preaching the gospel for two years as he awaits his audience with Caesar (ca. 60–62 CE). It is a note of hope for the gospel's spread to the "ends of the earth" and, for those who knew of Paul's ultimate suffering and martyrdom in Rome, a note of reassurance of God's wondrous providence to spread the gospel, not despite persecution, but through it.

PAUL'S PERSON AND SIGNIFICANCE IN ACTS

The book of Acts, as mentioned earlier, clearly does not intend to tell us everything about Paul. Comparison with Paul's letters indicates that Luke has omitted, simplified, and perhaps chronologically rearranged some events in Acts just as he has done in his Gospel (see chapter 2). But, as with the Gospels, we should ask what the author means to communicate by the way he shapes the narrative. What aspects of Paul's character and significance within earliest Christianity does Acts highlight? We will address three here.

First, Paul is *an apostolic figure, though not one of the Twelve.* In Paul's letters, he refers to himself frequently as an "apostle," particularly because he had "seen the Lord" after Easter (1 Cor 9:1). Luke-Acts almost always reserves the term "apostle" for the Twelve. When Matthias is divinely chosen to take this "office" in Judas's place, Peter indicates that twelve is a fixed number and that to be such an apostle requires having followed Jesus before his crucifixion (Acts 1:13–26; cf. Luke 6:13). Paul does not meet those criteria, and Acts distinguishes him from the Twelve, though Paul and Barnabas together are called "apostles" in 14:4, 14. However, Luke's narrative presents Paul as an equally formidable figure in God's work. Not only is Paul introduced to the Twelve by Barnabas as one who truly "had seen the Lord" (9:27) in his Damascus vision; Acts emphasizes that the Spirit of Jesus worked in the church through Paul as much as through the Twelve. Paul receives revelations from the Lord about his journeys (16:6; 23:11), by which Acts shows that Paul's ministry is endorsed and directed by God. Acts also parallels Paul with Peter as one in whom Jesus's miraculous power remained active in the world. Peter is freed from prison by an angel (12:7), heals the infirm (3:6–8; 9:33–34), kills infidels by God's power (5:1–11), raises the dead (9:40–41), and people are healed just by Peter's shadow passing over them (5:15–16). Paul is freed from prison by an earthquake (16:25–26), heals the infirm (14:9–10; 28:8–10), blinds a sorcerer and exorcises a demon (13:9–11; 16:18), raises the dead (20:10–12), and people are healed through contact with cloths that had touched him (19:11–12).

Luke's vocabulary and storytelling here suggest a kind of validation or defense of Paul. Paul called himself an apostle with others who had seen the Lord after Easter and claimed he had been given authority in Christ's name alongside the Twelve (1 Cor 15:5–8; Gal 2:6–9). And we know from his letters that Paul had to defend his apostleship against those who discredited him as a lesser minister (see Gal 1:11–12; 2:6–9). Luke's presentation, while distinguishing Paul from the Twelve, goes out of its way to highlight that Paul's ministry nonetheless bears God's unmistakable endorsement, authority, and power.

Second, in Acts, Paul's character and work embody Luke's theme of the *continuity of the New and the Old in salvation history,* despite rejection from many in Israel. As in Luke's Gospel, Christ and the salvation he brings are glory for Israel and fulfill God's promises to the patriarchs, but many Israelites reject Jesus (Luke 1:54–55, 68–75; 2:32, 34; 13:34–35). At the Jerusalem council, James affirms that the inclusion of gentiles in God's people through the messiah was prophesied long ago (Acts 15:16–17; cf. Luke 24:44–47). Even before this, Paul quoted Isaiah that God's servant would be a "light to the gentiles" (Acts 13:47). Paul reiterates this both as a part of his missionary calling but also as a response to the rejection he meets from some in the synagogues; indeed, faced with this rejection, he often responds that he will now "turn to the gentiles" (13:46; 18:6; 28:28). However, Acts makes it clear that he did not reject his heritage. Paul preaches that Christ brings a freedom and forgiveness not given under the Mosaic law (13:37–38) and incorporates uncircumcised gentiles who believe (15:1–2), but Acts goes out of its way to show this did not utterly reject the customs or hopes of Israel. Paul made voluntary Levitical vows (18:18), made a purification offering before entering the temple (21:26), and did not in fact bring a gentile into the inner courts of the temple as some had alleged (21:27–29). Indeed, Acts presents Paul's gospel of Christ as a fulfillment—not rejection—of his identity as a faithful Pharisee (22:1–21; 23:6–8; 26:2–23). "I affirm this to you, that I worship the God or our fathers in the manner according to the Way, which they call a sect, and I believe everything that accords with the law and is written in the prophets, having a hope in God which these [Jews] also await, that there will be a resurrection of the just and the unjust" (24:14–15). Paul's faith and ministry are depicted as completely faithful to Judaism, though Acts willingly acknowledges that even Christian Jews misunderstood Paul (see 21:20–21) and that other Jews rejected and opposed the message as he once did (17:4–5, 11–13; 21:27).

Third, Acts puts Paul at the center of its depiction of the church's increasingly *international and urbane character*. Many have argued that Acts is, at least in part, an attempt to legitimate Christianity for pagan and imperial audiences. As with Jesus before the Sanhedrin and Pilate (Luke 23:2–4, 20, 47), Luke emphasizes that Paul, and thus Christianity, is innocent not only of blasphemy against God but also of sedition against Rome (Acts 17:5–7; 25:25; 26:31). Paul is also a somewhat urbane—though not tame—character. He is a Jew but is also a Roman citizen, one born with his citizenship (22:28).[4] The note in 13:9 that Paul began to preach with a particular hand motion

---

4 Some argue that Paul's Roman citizenship is an invention of Acts for this purpose, pointing out that, if he had citizen's privileges, Paul would not have received Roman beatings (2 Cor 11:25) or feared execution without appeal (2 Cor 1:8–9; Phil 1:20–23). Others respond that even in Acts Paul does not use these rights simply to avoid suffering; in Philippi he publicizes his citizenship after being beaten (16:22–23, 35–38), and his appeal to Caesar aims at evangelizing Rome rather than avoiding pain.

depicts him like an educated orator, using stereotypical arm motions that philosophers and statesmen rehearsed for rhetorical effect. He speaks in the Athenian agora quoting ancient poets in front of philosophers, addressing them as Socrates did, "O men of Athens" (ἄνδρες Ἀθηναῖοι, *andres Athēnaioi*; cf. 17:22 and Plato, *Apology*, 17a). If some saw Christianity as a disreputable sect for the uncultured and foreign, Acts highlights the gospel's acceptance and sympathy among magistrates, kings, and the more well-to-do through the figure of this worldly minister.

Acts is a book not simply "about" Paul, but about God's work through the gospel. Yet in its presentation of Paul we can see a picture of the church at large. In the faith of this Jewish Roman citizen who speaks Greek (21:37) and in his preaching in Jerusalem, Athens, and Rome, we see the then-known world coming to faith in the Jewish messiah who saves all nations. In Paul we see a church of the privileged and of the beaten and imprisoned, of those who consort with kings and philosophers as well as those who labor. More importantly, we see in Paul a figure of Christ, beaten yet innocent, faithful yet rejected by both Jews and Romans, in whom Christ's work to heal and save is continued on earth.

FURTHER READING

Crowe, Brandon D. 2020. *The Hope of Israel: The Resurrection of Christ in the Acts of the Apostles*. Grand Rapids: Baker Academic.

Fitzmyer, Joseph A., SJ. 1998. *The Acts of the Apostles: A New Translation with Introduction and Commentary*. AB 31. New York: Doubleday.

Holladay, Carl R. 2016. *Acts: A Commentary*. NTL. Louisville, KY: Westminster John Knox.

Johnson, Luke Timothy. 1992. *Acts*. SP 5. Collegeville, MN: Liturgical Press.

Keener, Craig S. 2012–15. *Acts: An Exegetical Commentary*. 4 vols. Grand Rapids: Baker Academic.

Kurz, William. 1993. *Reading Luke-Acts: Dynamics of Biblical Narrative*. Louisville, KY: Westminster John Knox.

Lentz, John Clayton, Jr. 1993. *Luke's Portrait of Paul*. SNTSMS 77. Cambridge: Cambridge University Press.

Marguerat, Daniel. 2013. *Paul in Acts and Paul in his Letters*. WUNT 310. Tübingen: Mohr Siebeck.

Meek, James A. 2008. *The Gentile Mission in Old Testament Citations in Acts: Text, Hermeneutic, and Purpose*. LNTS 385. London: T&T Clark.

Moessner, David Paul. 2016. *Luke the Historian of Israel's Legacy, Theologian of Israel's "Christ": A New Reading of the "Gospel Acts" of Luke*. BZNW 182. Berlin: de Gruyter.

Porter, Stanley E. 1999. *The Paul of Acts: Essays in Literary Criticism, Rhetoric, and Theology*. WUNT 115. Tübingen: Mohr Siebeck.

Reasoner, Mark. 1999b. "The Theme of Acts: Institutional History or Divine Necessity in History?" *JBL* 118 (4): 635–59.

Rosner, Brian S. 1993. "Acts and Biblical History." In *The Book of Acts in Its Ancient Literary Setting*, edited by Bruce W. Winter and Andrew D. Clarke, 65–82. Vol. 1 of *The Book of Acts in Its First Century Setting*. Grand Rapids: Eerdmans.

Rowe, C. Kavin. 2009. *World Upside Down: Reading Acts in the Graeco-Roman Age*. New York: Oxford University Press.

Smith, Daniel Lynwood, and Zachary Lundin Kostopoulos. 2017. "Biography, History and the Genre of Luke-Acts." *NTS* 63 (3):390–410.

Uytanlet, Samson. 2014. *Luke-Acts and Jewish Historiography: A Study on the Theology, Literature, and Ideology of Luke-Acts*. WUNT 2/366. Tübingen: Mohr Siebeck.

CHAPTER SIX

Romans

Paul's longest and probably most famous letter, Romans, introduces Paul to a church he did not found. In it he expounds his gospel of God's grace for sinners of every race and clarifies his teaching about the Mosaic law and the life of freedom and righteousness in the Holy Spirit. Here we see the Apostle, after years of work, looking toward a new stage in his ministry: he hopes this letter will gain him a warm reception in Rome and that, when he visits, the Romans will support him on an ambitious journey to Spain.

BACKGROUND
Paul and the Christians in Rome

Unlike most of his letters, Paul wrote Romans to a church that neither he nor any of his mission team evangelized, in a city it appears he had never visited.[1] The origins of Christianity in Rome are traditionally ascribed to the work of one of the Twelve, though its precise origin is unknown. The Roman historian Tacitus disparagingly noted the spread of Christianity after Christ's crucifixion as naturally joining all the other foreign "filth" drawn to Rome: "Though repressed for a moment, this deadly superstition broke out again not only in Judea—the origin of this evil—but also in the City [Rome], where from everywhere all atrocious and shameful things converge and are celebrated" (*Annals* 15.44).

Tacitus's negativity aside, one can agree that, once those who had embraced the message of Christ left Judea—whether traveling, fleeing per-

---

1 Paul did not personally evangelize Colossae, but someone connected with Paul's mission team did (see chapter 12 below).

secution, or as missionaries (see Acts 2:10; 11:19)—it was only a matter of time before the gospel reached the imperial capital. And it appears that was not much time: Paul states that, already before he wrote, the church in Rome was renowned "in all the world" (Rom 1:8). The city housed a significant Jewish population and several synagogues, in which the faith of Christ surely first grew in the years after Pentecost.[2] The movement clearly expanded by the time Paul wrote and, as in Corinth, probably was made up of several interconnected groups that met together for the eucharist (cf. 16:5; 1 Cor 1:10–12; 11:17–20).

Though Romans is listed canonically at the head of Paul's letters, chronologically it was written later in his ministry. Paul states that he had longed to visit the Romans for some time (1:9–15), but he had no reason to evangelize a city in which the faith was already thriving, and his other work kept him from traveling so far west (15:17–22). However, as he now writes, he is preparing for a new phase in his ministry. He has brought the gospel from Judea through Asia Minor, Greece, and even to Illyricum (around modern Croatia and Bosnia-Herzegovina), and his sights are now set to the far west in Spain.[3] His mission work in these regions is complete except for one final step: to deliver a collection from his churches for the poor believers in Jerusalem, which he has been gathering for years (see 2 Cor 8–9). As he writes, he has finally completed the collection in Macedonia and Achaia (Greece) and is preparing to depart for Jerusalem; once he has delivered the collection, he intends to travel westward to Spain via Rome (15:23–33). Rome was a fine stopping point between Jerusalem and Spain—and a strategic one, too, as Paul hopes the Romans will support his mission by sending him on to Spain (15:23–33).

Where and when did Paul write? He writes after completing the collection and before heading to Jerusalem. Paul says that he has completed the collection in Macedonia and Achaia, and 2 Corinthians 8–9 show that Corinth, in Achaia, was his final stop to complete the collection before delivering it. This suggests that Romans was written from Corinth, which is corroborated in Romans: Paul sends greetings to Rome from people associated with Corinth (16:23; cf. 1 Cor 1:14; 2 Tim 4:20) and sends the letter with Phoebe, a Christian leader from Corinth's eastern seaport, Cenchreae (Rom

---

2 See Jewett 2007, 55–61. For an in-depth discussion of background, see Longenecker 2011.

3 For an exploration of Paul's motivations for this westward mission, see Noblom 2016 (in Spanish).

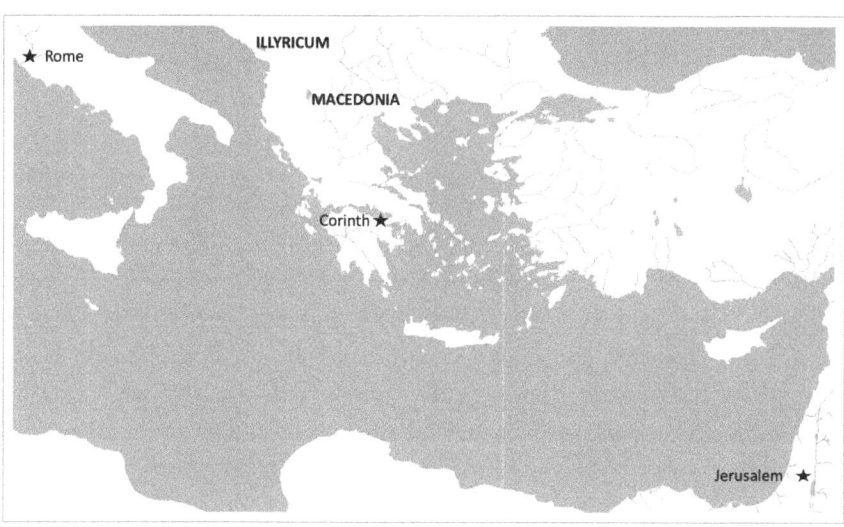

16:1–2). Most scholars date the letter around 57 CE. Following Acts, it could not have been written after 58: Acts reports that Paul was received poorly when he delivered the collection to Jerusalem, was jailed, and transferred to Caesarea about two years before Festus became procurator in 59 CE (Acts 24:27). Likewise, it must have been written after his ministry in Asia and after his writing 2 Corinthians in the mid-50s. Some also suggest that Paul's emphasis that Christians should pay "tax and tribute" to Rome (Rom 13:6–7) fits the social climate in Rome in 57–58, when there were riots and unrest about a new tribute demanded by the state.

Why Did Paul Write Romans?

The question of why Paul *wrote* Romans is answered easily if we consider his situation. He is on the cusp of completing his ministry around the eastern Mediterranean and looking to begin a new phase of his career in the west. Rome provides a place to make new connections with Christians in an important city and is a strategic launching pad on the way to Spain. He hopes to be "refreshed" by them (15:32), share his ministerial "charism" with them as apostle to the gentiles and be encouraged by them (1:11–12), and receive their (financial) support for his journey (15:24). This letter serves, in a way, as a personal introduction of himself and his gospel and serves to prepare them to receive him when he arrives.

However, if this explains why he *wrote* Romans, it does not explain why he wrote Romans *the way he did*. This is hardly a mere missionary-support letter introducing oneself and asking for support. Nor does it hone in on issues we might otherwise think would be germane to Christians in a city marked by elitism, the highest politicking, the Coliseum's grisly displays, and buildings and statuary that proclaimed the conquest of Caesar and Rome's gods over all. The letter reflects awareness of these issues—denouncing idolatry, addressing relations with the government, and calling for respect across status divides (see 1:18–32; 12:9–16; 13:1–7)—but its content is not shaped around them. Rather, the letter revolves around God's gospel of salvation from sin for Jews and gentiles in Christ, frequently with clarifications about what Paul teaches about ethics and the Mosaic law (chaps. 2–3, 7), matters of piety that were divisive among Jews and gentiles (chaps. 14–15), and the place of the nation of Israel in God's ongoing work of grace (chaps. 9–11).

Paul's writing is always affected both by his own situation and by the situation of his addressees (or what he knows about it). However, discerning how the occasion of this letter shapes its content is debated among scholars.[4] On one hand, he does not know the Roman church; on the other, he knows some Christians who were or now are in Rome (16:3–15). On one hand, he is cautious not to seem domineering to a church he did not found (1:11–15; 15:14–24; cf. 2 Cor 10:12–18); on the other, he writes "quite boldly in part" out of his charism as apostle to the gentiles (Rom 15:15–16). And indeed he is bold. After condemning idolatry, he condemns those who break the law but "call" themselves Jews in order to relativize any confidence in the worth of merely physical circumcision (2:17–29). When treating the question of Israel's salvation despite many Jews' rejecting Christ, he commands gentiles specifically not to be presumptuous but to be thankful that they share in the blessings of Israel's messiah (11:13–24). How do Paul's situation and his understanding of his audience's situation affect how he wrote?

Paul grounds what he says specifically in his vocation as "apostle of the gentiles" (1:5, 13; 11:13; 15:16; cf. Gal 2:7–9). Indeed, though he does send greetings to many Jews such as Prisca and Aquila (Rom 16:3; cf. Acts 18:1–2) and others he calls his "kinsmen" (Rom 16:7, 11; cf. 9:3), he seems to write with an eye toward Jew-gentile relations, with a focused edge toward the gentiles. To be sure, Paul addresses his message to "all those beloved of God who are in Rome" (1:7), not just to one group. And his theological arguments

---

4 See the essays in Donfried 1991.

proclaim judgment for sin and God's mercy in Christ for all, Jew and gentile alike (e.g., 2:6–11; 3:9; 10:12–13). Nevertheless, the theology presented here repeatedly hits ethnic nerves, from Paul's defense of uncircumcised gentiles being justified by faith (chaps. 2–4) to his defense of Israel's place in God's economy (chaps. 9–11) and of Christian Jews' dietary and calendric piety (chaps. 14–15).[5]

Many suggest a historical detail may lie behind this aspect of Romans: the expulsion and return of Roman Jews in the years prior to Paul's epistle. Though Judaism was recognized as a legal religion and attracted some converts, Jews had a rocky relationship with the empire. Many hated Jews for their distinctive practices, such as food laws and circumcision (see chapter 9 below), seeing Judaism as a foreign element to be suppressed for its opposition to some Roman morals and polytheism. When Jews were at the center of civil disturbance in the capital, emperors sometimes ensured peace by temporarily banishing Jews from the city.[6] One such expulsion occurred under Claudius in 49 CE, after perhaps a decade of the church's growth in the city.[7] Though perhaps some were able to remain, Jews *en masse* were banished and only returned when Claudius died in 54 CE. We see this reflected in the NT: the Jew Aquila and his wife, Prisca (in Acts "Priscilla"), reportedly came to Corinth because they had been expelled from Rome (Acts 18:1–2); after traveling with Paul in the early to mid-50s (see 1 Cor 16:19), the couple returned to Rome by the time Paul wrote Romans (Rom 16:3–5a).

It is important to imagine how Claudius's expulsion could have affected Roman Christianity, particularly regarding the ethnic tensions that stand out in this letter. If the first believers in Rome had been raised in the synagogue (or converted to Judaism as adults), this would have shaped the church's leadership, customs, and sympathies with non-Christian Jews. In Rome, as in Jerusalem, their lives would have been centered around Jewish festivals,

---

5 Some also argue that Romans 2 is more a rebuke for gentiles than for Jews, specifically for Roman gentiles who undergo circumcision and submit to Moses's law (see Rodríguez and Thiessen 2016; Rodríguez 2014). Paul's rebuke against one who "calls" himself a Jew in 2:17 is, on this reading, addressing not Jews who boast in the law against gentiles but gentile Christians who boast that they have gone "all the way," so to speak, against other gentiles who merely believe.

6 See Rutgers 1994.

7 Suetonius reports that they were expelled because of "disturbances at the instigation of one 'Chrestus'" (*Claudius* 25.4). Many believe this "Chrestus" is Suetonius's misspelling of *Christus*, "Christ," and the disturbances were due to conflicts between Christian Jews and their non-Christian kin. Some date this event instead to 41 CE, but see Riesner 1998, 157–201.

the food laws would not have been cast off, and most male members would have been circumcised. The church's leaders would have been catechized in scripture and God's law, even as less-informed pagans began to convert and join the community. But what happened when the ethnic Jews were banished? The church's leadership would have fallen to some gentiles who had already been circumcised and catechized before turning to Christ, but likely also to others who had less expertise in scripture, perhaps even newer converts who harbored a Roman contempt for Jewish practices. In the intervening years, the latter group would only have grown, and even those who desired to keep good relations with Jews would have had little occasion to let it shape their church's habits and culture. But what happened after 54 CE when Jews (Christian and non-Christian) returned? Would Jewish leaders have expected their positions back from these newcomers? Would they have insisted on Jewish standards of purity, whether out of zeal for God's law or for the sake of not offending their non-Christian kin? Would the converted pagans have seen the Jews as a strange historical hangover in the church, whose scrupulous policies threatened to make their newfound religion loathsome to their pagan friends? Would Roman converts of higher status have looked down on Jews—a conquered people, in Rome's eyes—as weak and in need of respectable leadership and education?[8]

Paul does not know every detail of the situation, but he has himself survived the theological conflicts and practical difficulty of integrating the lives of Jews and gentiles in Christ. Paul surely wrote with knowledge of the expulsion and could expect such conflicts. This historical detail might help explain why he, as apostle to the gentiles, both defends the place of the uncircumcised as full members of Christ (chaps. 1–4) and, against them, defends the historic and ongoing importance of Israel (chaps. 9–11) and even the distinctive piety of Jewish believers (chaps. 14–15).

We should also note the role Paul's own situation plays in how he writes this letter. As Paul prepares to deliver the collection, he expresses apprehension that "the disobedient in Judea" may cause him to be received poorly (15:30–31). According to Acts, Jerusalem housed a contingent of Christian Jews who were not happy with the Apostle's gospel of salvation without circumcision for gentiles, and rumors spread that his proclamation of "freedom from the law" amounted to hedonism and a rejection of Israel's

---

8 Note the language of "strong" and "weak"—probably not Paul's own terms—who "despise" and "judge" each other in chaps. 14–15. See Reasoner 1999a.

heritage (Acts 21:17–36). Paul mentions and rejects such rumors explicitly in Romans 3:8, which suggests he thought these rumors had reached Rome as well. The reputation of his gospel is clearly on his mind as he prepares to visit Jerusalem. It is also in his interest to quell any such rumors about him in Rome, as he hopes to present himself as a faithful apostle and ask the Romans' support for his mission. In addition to social tensions in the Roman church, this may help explain why Romans does not merely argue the unity of Jew and gentile but also dives more deeply into the relation between grace, sin, and the law (esp. chaps. 5–8). It also helps explain Paul's repeated use of "diatribe" to make his points, where Paul mimics false inferences one might draw from his words and then refutes them with further explanation (see 3:1, 9; 6:1, 15; 7:7, 13; 9:19; 11:1). He is clarifying carefully what his preaching of God's grace for sinners apart from the Mosaic law does and does not mean. All this makes Romans, to borrow Peter Stuhlmacher's words, "a didactic and hortatory document with an apologetic accent."[9]

OVERVIEW

I. **Letter Opening (1:1–17)**
  A. Paul, apostle of the messiah, with his authority to evangelize the gentiles, to all God's beloved in Rome (1:1–7).
  B. I thank God for your faith, and have long desired to visit you with the gospel I preach to all (1:8–15).
  C. I am not ashamed of the gospel. It reveals God's saving righteousness, as the prophets foretold, for all who believe, Jew first and also gentile (1:16–17).

II. **The Gospel of Salvation for Jew and Gentile (1:18–5:11)**
  A. For God's wrath is against all impiety and unrighteousness (1:18).
    1. Though the created order demonstrates God's power and divinity, humanity worshipped creatures instead of thanking the creator. Such crass sin only results in more ungodliness and incurs God's wrath (1:19–32).
    2. Those who judge such people are not exempt, either. If you know God's truth and condemnation of sin, you must know

9 In Donfried 1991, 236.

that you too will be judged by whether you heed God—not by self-righteous posturing. God shows no partiality: both his judgment and promise are for Jew and gentile (2:1–11).

    a. Whether they have the law or not, those who do what God commands are righteous in God's sight, and those who sin perish (2:12–16).

    b. So if you call yourself a Jew and boast in having the law, these do not absolve you of God's judgment (2:17–29).

        i. There is much benefit to the Jew—not least that Israel received the scriptures—even if some have disbelieved (3:1–4a). But even David, when guilty, does not boast but humbly submits to God's judgment (3:4b-8).

        ii. We have proclaimed that all—Jews and gentiles—are under sin. And scripture itself bears witness against the sin of all, so that all may stand silent before God's judgment (3:9–20).

B. All have sinned, Jew and gentile. But now God's righteousness, as scripture foretold, is revealed in Christ for all who believe, Jew and gentile. It is his gift of redemption and atonement, the grace of the righteous God to justify all through faith in Christ (3:21–26).

    1. This gift is given and received through faith, apart from the law (otherwise God would be God only of the Jews!), so any boast in having the law is ruled out (3:27–31).

    2. Indeed, scripture says as much. Look to Abraham. He was forgiven and justified when he trusted God's promise, even before he was circumcised. God's promise that his offspring would inherit the world is received by all—Jew or gentile—who follow him in faith (3:31–4:25).

    3. Our justification through faith in Christ brings us into friendship with God and gives us hope for eternal glory, because God's love is shown on the cross and poured into our hearts by the Spirit. Through Christ we boast not in ourselves but in God our savior (5:1–11).

III. **Death in Sin and New Life in Christ and the Spirit (5:12–8:39)**
   A. Thus, as Adam's transgression brought sin and death to all humanity, Christ has won justification and life for all by his righteous obedience. As much as sin increased, and as much as the law tallied sins up for condemnation, God's grace for salvation abounds all the more in Christ (5:12–21).
   B. This hardly means we should keep sinning to receive more grace! Our baptism unites us to Christ's death and resurrection. We have died to sin, freed from its grip on Adam's children and joined to Christ's new life. Act like it (6:1–11)!
      1. We are neither under sin nor law, but under God's grace through Christ and the Spirit. This is God's gift, and the reward it promises is eternal life. So serve God by following the Spirit, fighting against sin rather than serving it (6:12–7:6).
      2. Freedom from sin and the law does not mean the law is evil. The law is good, showing and condemning sin by its commands. But sin lures us to break the commandments and brings us under the law's condemnation. The weakness of Adam's children leaves us without hope for righteousness in ourselves, crying out for deliverance in Christ (7:7–25).
   C. In Christ, the Holy Spirit frees us from the law's condemnation and brings about what the law could not: by the Spirit's leading and power, God's righteous commands are fulfilled in us. The Spirit dwells in us to give life, to lead us in obedience, and to make us God's children by joining us to Christ the Son. And, if we suffer with him now, we will be raised with him in the end (8:1–17).
      1. Suffering in this life hardly compares to this glorious hope of resurrection. Adam's sin brought death and decay, but through Christ God is at work to renew creation, even our very bodies, at the last day. This is the hope for which we were saved, and the Spirit is constantly at work to bring us to this salvation (8:18–30).
      2. God is for us, loves us, and has given his only Son to make us his own. What grace! What confidence we have in God's goodwill! Even in greatest suffering, God leads us to life and victory (8:31–39).

IV. The Mystery of God's Mercy for Israel and the Gentiles (9:1–11:36)

A. I have great sorrow and love for my fellow Israelites who have not embraced Christ. God's covenants and even Christ himself belong first to them (9:1–5).

1. The disobedience of many does not mean God has failed. Israel is not merely defined by ethnicity but by God's promise. Even in the beginning, only one of Abraham's or Isaac's children bore God's promise (9:6–13).

   a. There is no injustice in this. As scripture says, God raises up and even hardens both for glory and for dishonor, always for his own purpose of showing his glory (9:14–23).

   b. For us, God's glorious purpose is to call not only Jews but also gentiles to himself. The prophets proclaimed that God would make outsiders his people; they also remind us that Israel, due to her sins, was only preserved by God's mercy (9:24–29).

2. In Christ, God's righteousness is revealed, and those who believe in him will be saved. But while many gentiles have converted to Christ, many Israelites—whose salvation I desire!—are scandalized. They seek God in the law, but do not submit to God's righteousness in Christ (9:30–10:3).

   a. Christ is the end of the law and justifies those who cling to him in faith. Moses also testified to the righteousness of faith, which takes root in the heart. This is the righteousness by which God saves Jews and gentiles who call upon Christ (10:4–13).

   b. This faith requires hearing God's message. And it has been heard. Scripture attests that God spreads his name abroad to call other nations, though it speaks also of Israel's disobedience (10:14–21).

B. Has God rejected his people? Of course not! I am one of them, and not rejected. God preserves a remnant of his people even when most disobey—by grace and not because of their prior merits (11:1–6).

1. God thus keeps Israel's remnant in the grace many rejected. But, as David prayed, God has allowed the rebellious to be hardened (11:7–10).

2. Is this situation permanent? No! Israel's stumbling has been purposed for salvation, for the gentiles and also for Israel (11:11–12).

   a. If Israel's temporary transgression meant salvation for many nations, Israel's restoration can mean nothing less than life for the world (11:11–16).

   b. Therefore, you gentiles, do not boast against Israel! God has not forsaken his people for you, but has grafted you into the blessings of Israel through faith. You can be cut off for unbelief just as many of them have, and they can be brought back through faith just as you were (11:17–24).

3. Only a part of Israel has been hardened, and temporarily, until the gentiles' salvation is complete. The messiah will accomplish the salvation of all Israel in this way, as scripture foretold (11:25–27).

   a. God's election of Israel is irrevocable; if now they disobey God's revelation in Christ, God's purpose is to restore them by his mercy, just as he purposed mercy for you gentiles (11:28–32).

   b. How wonderful and incomprehensible are God's ways! Glory to the creator now and forever (11:33–36)!

V. **Living Together by God's Mercy in Christ (12:1–15:33)**

   A. In light of all this, make your lives a pleasing offering to God, clinging to him and being transformed in obedience (12:1–2).

   B. Serve God in humility and love toward one another.

   1. As members of one body, we are joined together with different gifts and functions, and each should pursue his gifts with excellence (12:3–8).

   2. Love must be without pretense. Be steadfast in prayer and endurance, serving the Lord. To each other, be zealous to show honor, charity, sympathy, and humility (12:9–16).

      a. Do not give in to evil when oppressed by outsiders. And do not refuse taxes to the authorities. God institutes government for social order, and they are owed honor (12:17–13:7). But what you owe one another is love. Love fulfills God's commands, for it does no wrong to a neighbor (13:8–10).

b. The day of salvation draws near! Cast off wicked behavior and clothe yourself with Christ's love and sanctity (13:11–14)!

3. The "weak" in faith are not to be despised, but honored in love (14:1).

a. Some eat everything and some abstain; some observe many feasts and some observe each day equally. Neither should despise or judge the other. All must seek to honor the Lord in their piety, for it is before his judgment that we all will stand. Food is hardly worth harming our neighbor's conscience or damaging God's work to sanctify them (14:1–23).

b. Imitate Christ, who sought to please and honor God rather than seek his own prerogatives or advantage. He became a servant to bring salvation to the Jew first that he might call gentiles as well. Receive one another as Christ receives you (15:1–12).

c. May God strengthen you in faith and hope by his Spirit (15:13).

VI. **Letter Closing (15:14–16:27)**

A. I have no doubts about you, but I write—boldly in part—out of my apostolate to bring the gentiles to obey God. I have brought the gospel from Jerusalem to Illyricum, and now I hope to visit you and to have your support for the mission to Spain (15:14–24).

1. But first, I am bringing the collection to Jerusalem, after which I will come to Rome (15:25–29).

2. Pray that my offering will be received well, and that I will be delivered from opponents in Judea. God be with you (15:30–33).

B. Receive and support Phoebe, a servant of Christ (16:1–2). Greet all whom we know and who know us in Rome (16:3–16).

C. Watch out for those who incite division and would lead you astray. Pursue what is good and avoid evil; God will crush Satan under our feet (16:17–20).

D. Greetings from those with Paul (16:21–23).

E. Glory forevermore be to God our savior (16:25–27).

KEY FEATURES

Romans offers a breadth of theological insight and touches on several important topics. We will focus on three: the human condition apart from grace, God's work to justify sinners in Christ, and Paul's hope for Israel. Other major topics in Romans receive treatment elsewhere in this book—the Mosaic law (chapter 9), the work of the Spirit (chapters 7 and 9), and baptism (chapter 12).

The Human Condition

Writing to a church he does not know, Paul does not name and rebuke specific instances of sin in Rome as in, say, 1 Corinthians. Yet as Paul calls all to cease boasting against each other in the church—Jew over gentile or gentile over Jew—his argument illumines the reality of sin theologically and socially as he argues that "all" are under sin and that "all" sin incurs God's judgment.[10] Paul opens his rebuke in 1:18: "For the wrath of God is revealed from heaven against all impiety and injustice of men, who suppress the truth by injustice" (1:18). Apart from grace and repentance, sin sets one in opposition or "enmity" toward God (5:10; cf. Col 1:21; Jas 4:4).

Paul's opening chapters give instances of such impiety (wrong relation or activity toward God) and of injustice (wrong activity toward others) from different angles, calling all to repent and not to boast of any advantage before God against others (see Rom 3:9). Echoing Wisdom 13–15, Paul begins with the fundamental sin of idolatry and the litany of transgressions that flow from living under idols rather than living for God. Though creation itself testifies to the power of one transcendent God, humans did not honor God as the giver of all things, but instead made gods of their own desire (Rom

---

10 "All" (πᾶς, *pas*) is a keyword in Romans, demonstrating the unity of all before God and, apart from grace, the unity of all under sin. See 1:16, 18; 2:1, 9–10; 3:9, 19–20, 22–23; 4:16; 5:12, 18; 8:32; 10:4, 12–13; 11:32; 14:10.

1:19–23). And so they were "given over" to those desires, which in turn drew them only further away from God's truth in their relations toward others (1:24–31). Paul avers that they are "without excuse" (1:20) and that the consequence for turning from God, the source of life, is death (1:32).

Paul's condemnation of crass idolatry and immorality might be one with which many Christians in Rome would readily have agreed. The sins Paul lists were ones against which Jews and early Christians characteristically spoke out, and his audience in Rome probably would have heard this and thought of "those people," immoral idolaters they saw throughout the pagan capital. Yet he turns in 2:1 to rebuke not merely "those" crass sinners but any of "you"— Roman Christians—who boast in their knowledge of God or moral superiority.[11] Paul illustrates this by negatively depicting a pair of "yous" who posture themselves against other sinners and yet still transgress God (2:1, 17). The "you" of 2:1–5 is a picture of judgmental hypocrisy, committing sins himself, yet condemning only the sins of others as though he will thereby escape God's wrath. The "you" of 2:17–29 boasts in having God's law and circumcision, yet also transgresses and so also dishonors God. Directed toward the Roman church, Paul's depictions reach out inclusively to put all types of sinners under God's judgment—embracing those who had been (or in Christ have now become) moral gentiles as well as those who observe the law of Moses. With these "yous" Paul is not stereotyping people groups, but critiquing behaviors by caricature. Pagans who do not know the Mosaic law can observe it by seeking the creator (2:14–15), and Paul is quick to clarify that the historic heritage of Israel is of distinct worth, especially in knowing God's scriptures (3:1–3). But all knowledge of God's goodness is meant to bring repentance and therefore leaves the unrepentant without excuse (see 2:4; 3:19–20).[12] God's judgment against sin is for all who sin—Jew or gentile—as is his promise of life for those who seek him (2:5–13). For God does

---

11 Many have seen in this passage Paul's sly critique only of Jews, luring them to join Paul in condemning stereotypical gentile sins and then rebuking them for judging. But gentiles who had converted from crass paganism or who had already belonged to moral philosophical groups would surely have endorsed the condemnation in 1:18–32 as well. They are equally addressed by Paul's rebuke.

12 Knowledge of God's law through scripture or nature, which Paul says leaves sinners "without excuse," is an important component of one's guilt in the NT (cf. 1:20; 2:14–15; 3:19–20; 4:15; 5:13; 7:7–10; John 15:22; 1 Tim 1:13; Jas 4:17). Hence knowledge, along with willfulness and intent (e.g., Num 15:27–31), are important in the Catholic understanding of culpability for actual sins (*CCC*, §1854–64).

not judge by one's posturing or appearance but by behavior and the truth of one's heart (2:11; cf. Wis 6:7; Sir 35:15–16 [KJV 35:12–13]; Col 3:25; 1 Pet 1:17).

One can see the ultimate end of Paul's opening arguments: "We have already charged that all, both Jews and Greeks, are under sin" (Rom 3:9); "all have sinned and lack the glory of God" (3:23). While some may have slight external advantages, they are of no real consequence before God's judgment. Thus there is truly "no distinction" (3:23; 10:12) between Jew and gentile, and there can be no boasting of one against the other. Without grace, all are beggars before the cross of Christ. These arguments prepare the way for Paul's proclamation of justification by God's grace to all who believe, Jews and gentiles.

In chapters 1–3, Paul draws "all," both Jews and gentiles, under God's judgment and mercy by focusing on their behavior. In chapters 5–8, Paul looks at sin from another angle to show the fundamental problem of sin at work in all fallen humanity, the *power* sin holds in the fallen world. Beginning in 5:12, he focuses on Adam's first rejection of God for his own desires, as well as on its effects: "through one man sin entered the world and, through sin, death" (5:12). Humanity after Adam is characterized by the "reign" of death and sin over the heirs of Adam: death "reigned" through Adam's transgression (5:14, 17), and sin "reigned" in bringing humanity under the condemnation of death (5:21; cf. 1:32; 5:18–19; 6:23; 8:13).

Adam's descendants follow him in sinning—even those who did not transgress an explicit command as he did (5:14)—and are born into a cosmos occupied by disorder and decay (8:19–21). And this condition is reinforced on all sides, from without by the corrupted realities and examples around us, and also from within.[13] Sin and death wound and weaken human nature (a state Paul often calls "the flesh"). Paul depicts sin as a kind of slave-master over humanity (see 6:18, 22; 7:14) and as a power "dwelling within," inclining us to act against God—even against our own reason—regardless of how well we know God's law (7:9–11, 17, 20, 22–23).[14] In contrast to the "yous" of chapter 2, in 7:7–25 Paul gives voice to this human condition in the first-person "I" to illustrate the powerlessness of the law to overcome sin's internal effects (7:7–25).[15] The law is good—he emphasizes that he does not teach

---

13 See Eastman 2017, 109–25.

14 The term in Western theology for this inclination is "concupiscence" (*CCC*, §1426, 2515).

15 Paul's despairing "I" is likely not simple autobiography: contrast this depiction with his comment that he was "blameless" under the law (Phil 3:6) and his emphasis that in Christ believers are freed from such slavery to the law (Rom 6:6; 8:1–2; Gal 5:16). Yet the paradigmatic

otherwise—but the law cannot stop the sinful inclination. In fact, because of sin, the law's good commandments become sin's tools to tempt humans and, when sin is committed, the law leaves the knowing transgressor under its condemnation (7:7–13; cf. 1 Cor 15:56). Even when the "I" desires to obey God's law, he finds a different "law" within that leads against what he desires and takes him "captive" to serve sin (Rom 7:23; cf. Gal 5:17).

Choosing to transgress God's commands incurs guilt. Yet chapters 5–8 show that the problem of sin lies not merely in human choice, as though knowing the law better would fix it, but in the internal sinful inclination of Adam's descendants (cf. also Mark 7:21–23). Victory over sin requires something the law itself cannot accomplish. Righteousness and life in the inward person is brought about not by the law, but by Christ and the work of God's Spirit (Rom 8:1–10).

Justification and New Life in Christ

The fallen "I" under sin cries out, "Miserable man that I am! Who will deliver me from this body of death?" (7:24). Paul answers with the exclamation: "But thanks be to God through Jesus Christ our Lord!" (7:25). In Christ's death and resurrection, sin is conquered and death is dealt a fatal blow, and those joined to Christ participate in Christ's victory (cf. 1 Cor 15:57). They receive atonement for sin and are reconciled into friendship with God. They receive Christ's life and righteousness through the Spirit, who strengthens them in their weakness and sanctifies them that they may become heirs of eternal life.

Christ's victory over sin and the way in which humans participate in it are expressed with numerous metaphors in the NT that highlight different aspects of God's saving work—ransom, liberation, healing, purification, and so on. Several appear in Romans. Paul, like other early Christians, saw Christ's death as a new Passover and as a sacrifice like, though surpassing, those of the Levitical system (e.g., 1 Cor 5:7–8; Matt 26:28; Heb 8:1–2; 1 John 4:10). In Romans, he employs OT images of priestly atonement. Christ

---

experience here is surely not foreign to any whose concupiscence—even in Christ—utilizes God's commands as an occasion for temptation and condemnation (Rom 7:7–10). Modern scholars debate whether this "I" speaks with the voice of Adam in the garden or Israel after the golden calf, or reflects Paul's own experience (see the commentaries). Chrysostom, commenting on 7:12, notes similar disagreements among the ancients: some saw the "law" here as the natural law (e.g., Origen) or the command to Adam, while Chrysostom and others saw the Mosaic law (*Homilies on Romans* 11).

became for us a "sin offering" (8:3).[16] He makes atonement, expiating sin's guilt and purifying the people to restore them to communion with God. Paul evokes the great Day of Atonement when he refers to Christ and his blood as a ἱλαστήριον (*hilastērion*), a reference to the "Mercy Seat," the cover of the ark of the covenant where the blood of the sacrifice and the presence of God himself met and made purification for Israel's sins (see Lev 16).[17]

Not unlike these sacrifices, the atoning benefit of Christ's death is received through identification with the Victim, whereby his life and death are made one's own. For Paul, this type of union is mediated in baptism and endures in one's living faith and loyalty to God (on "faith," see chapter 9 below). The baptized are put to death with Christ and joined to his new life by the Holy Spirit (Rom 6:3–11; cf. 1 Cor 12:13; Gal 3:27; Col 2:11–15). Christ's life becomes the life of baptized believers, and his death becomes their death. The resurrected Lord sends his Spirit upon believers and so lives in them, drawing them up into who he is, that they may be conformed to his image as the holy children of God (Rom 4:25; 5:10; 8:12–17, 29–30).

Those joined to Christ's death and life are "justified" and "reconciled" to God. To be "justified" (δικαιόω, *dikaioō*) generally means to be considered "righteous" or "just."[18] Though this word has been used theologically as an umbrella term for all of God's saving work, in Paul it is only one of many metaphors. The word is at home especially in contexts of conflict and law-courts, meaning to consider someone righteous or "acquit" them of a charge, to "vindicate" someone; its opposite is condemnation (e.g., Matt 12:37; Luke

16 The purificatory sin offering is often referred to with the phrase "concerning sin" (περὶ ἁμαρτίας, *peri hamartias*) in the Greek OT, which Paul uses in 8:3 of Christ (see Lev 4:1–5:13). A sin offering could sometimes simply be called a "sin" for short, and Christ's "becoming [a] sin for us" in 2 Cor 5:21 may also evoke this sacrificial context.

17 On these and other images, see Finlan 2004.

18 Compare the noun δικαιοσύνη (*dikaiosynē*), "righteousness/justice," and the adjective δίκαιος (*dikaios*), "righteous/just." English borrows from both Latin and Germanic roots and so, unfortunately, does not always show their etymological connection. For consistency, some scholars use only the Latinate "just, justify, justice" or the Germanic "right, rectify, rectitude." A good deal of debate across ecumenical lines has been caused by the fact that, since Augustine especially, the word "justify" has in the West been used as an umbrella term for all of salvation. So both Luther and the Catholic Counter-Reformers sometimes packed all of salvation into the single term, with Luther insisting (because the language indicates acquittal) that salvation is primarily or only forgiveness, while others responded that it must refer to God "making" someone habitually righteous and transforming them (because Paul describes these realities in the process of salvation). For a history of the debates, see McGrath 2020. For an in-depth study of the biblical language of justification, see Prothro 2018.

7:29; 16:15; Rom 2:13; 5:16–19; 8:33–34). The word is borrowed especially from OT lawcourt imagery depicting God and his people in conflict. When people stand in sin against God, God is just or "in the right" over against them (see Neh 9:33; Ps 51:6 [KJV 51:4], cited in Rom 3:4; Ps 143:2, cited in Rom 3:20; Dan 9:7, 14). Yet in mercy and love, God desires to justify his people, to absolve their sin and reconcile them to himself, putting them "in the right" with him once more. Isaiah 53:10–12 prophesied that the Suffering Servant would offer himself for the people's sins and justify them, and Paul describes this occurring to sinners in Christ. Those who stood against God as "enemies" (Rom 5:10) are forgiven and reconciled to friendship with God. Though in Adam they were sinners heading for condemnation, in Christ they are put "in the right" in God's judgment and led on the path to eternal life (5:12–21).

In this biblical legal metaphor, God's holding sinners to be "in the right" and restoring them to friendship usually refers to the beginning of one's life with God. Paul sets "justification" alongside forgiveness, atonement, reconciliation, and being freed from sin (3:24–25; 4:4–8; 5:1–10; 1 Cor 6:11; 2 Cor 5:17–21; cf. Acts 13:38–39; Jas 2:23).[19] But Paul's vision of salvation from sin and union with God does not stop there. By faith and baptism one is united to Christ and receives Christ's Spirit within them (note the connections in Rom 5–8; Gal 2:15–3:9; 2 Cor 3:4–18). This brings about not merely a new status of being "in the right" but also a new reality, for God's holding them in the right "corresponds to an internal transformation" already taking hold from the first moment of grace.[20] "So if anyone is in Christ, they are a new creation. The old has passed away; behold, the new has come" (2 Cor 5:17). The justified "participate" in Christ. They are made part of the reality of who Christ is as God's truly righteous Son, and by the Spirit working in them they are "conformed to the image of [God's] Son" (Rom 8:29) in suffering and acts of love. In baptism they die to sin "with" Christ and are freed from the stranglehold of sin and the flesh (6:3–23), becoming "obedient from the heart" to serve God in righteousness (6:17–18). Though the law did not have the power to bring wounded and sinful hearts to righteousness, the Spirit strengthens and moves those in Christ so that they now "please God" and

---

19 Since Paul often uses biblical "justification" language when arguing about the law, some suggest the language primarily comes from his opponents (Martyn 1997, 141–56). Others see "justification" having primary reference to membership in the covenant community (Wright 2009). Seifrid 2000 develops justification out of God's self-disclosure as righteous and God's power as creator to set his creation right.

20 Aletti 2015, 32.

eagerly await the hope of glory that God promises his children (5:2; 7:4–6; 8:5–7, 30–39; 2 Cor 3:18).

The "justification of the ungodly" (Rom 4:5) occurs within this broader activity of God's grace to transform sinners and bring them to share Christ's inheritance as God's sons and daughters (8:12–17).[21] And, indeed, Paul's thinking about justification keeps this end in mind.[22] For Paul can also use the term "justification" of God's *final* judgment over a person, not at the beginning of their life of faith but at the end. "The doers of the law shall be justified" (2:13; similarly Matt 12:37). This final approval as "righteous" is received by those who have persevered in faith and love with God (Rom 2:7–8; 6:20–23; 8:13).[23] So Paul calls those joined to Christ to live more deeply into the reality of their justification, to follow the Spirit as he completes the work of sanctification that began at baptism (see Phil 1:6; 2:12–13). With Christ they have died to sin and now must "put to death" their sinful desires (Rom 8:12–13; Gal 5:24; 6:8) with Christlike love and endurance (Rom 5:3–5; 8:17). God has reconciled sinners who once stood against him (5:10), and they now use their bodies as weapons of righteousness for God against sin (6:12–23), loving each other and encouraging each other in repentance (12:9–21; 13:8–10; Gal 6:2; Col 3:12–14). Joined to Christ's eternal sacrifice, they present their very selves as offerings to God in mind and action (Rom 12:1–2). This is the life in which the Spirit leads them in holiness, and its "end" or purpose is "eternal life" (6:22), while those who return to sin without repentance will instead find condemnation (2:4–11; 8:13; 1 Cor 6:9–10; Gal 6:7–9). Paul's eschatological perspective keeps in view the coming judgment (Rom 2:5–10; 5:9; 14:10–12), God's final crushing of Satan (16:20), and the final revealing

---

21 This broader vision in Paul and throughout scripture is why the Council of Trent, Session VI, 7, concluded that justification "is not only the remission of sins but also the sanctification and renewal of the inward person by a willing acceptance of the grace and gifts whereby a person from being unjust becomes just, from being an enemy a friend, so that he is an heir in hope of eternal life." Salvation is a "process" that is ordered toward eternal life, owed to God's work of mercy and Christ's merit, but it involves the life of the believer in the faith, hope, and love that the Spirit works and prompts in them. For several essays in which Catholics and Protestants reflect on these issues together, see Aune 2006.

22 See Byrne 2021.

23 Some read 2:13 as merely hypothetical, given Paul's argument that the law makes no one righteous before God (3:19–20). However, because the Spirit pours out divine love into the heart and leads believers in righteousness, "there actually *are* Spirit-empowered law keepers" (Stegman 2018, 1245) who fulfill the law's commands through love whether they are physically circumcised or not (5:5; 8:4–10; 13:8–10).

of those who are truly God's daughters and sons (8:19–24). And so Paul calls the justified to live into this promised future and cling to Christ with faith, love, and hope. "Let us not grow weary in doing good, for at the proper time we will reap a harvest if we do not give up" (Gal 6:9).

To endure in God's righteousness is to cling to Christ and allow the Spirit to shape one's life in Christlike suffering and love (Phil 3:9–11). This is all the gift of God, his work of grace in Christ given through the Holy Spirit (Rom 5:15–19; cf. Eph 2:8–10). It is inescapably owed to God's initiative to act out of sheer love and mercy for those who were and would have remained opposed to him (Rom 5:6–10). It is gift. But this gift does not leave sinners mired in their wretchedness; God forgives *and* transforms, calling sinners upward to become worthy or "fit" recipients of the gift they freely received.[24] God is operative from the first inkling of faith, in the sanctifying waters, and all the way to one's final breath, drawing and inviting believers to receive and live in the life of the righteous Son, that they might finally receive the inheritance promised to God's children.

Israel and the Gentiles

Chapters 9–11 have sometimes been taken as an inconsequential excursus within the letter. However, they are integral to Paul's purposes. Just as, earlier in the letter, the Apostle frequently steps back to clarify what he does and does not teach about the Mosaic law, here he clarifies what his teaching about salvation for Jews and gentiles in Christ means about the many in Israel who now oppose the gospel.

Paul's argument in chapters 9–11 is complex, dealing with many aspects of salvation history and the situation of non-Christian Jews. We can approach the argument by considering two of its goals: (1) *explaining the present*, how and why so many Jews have not embraced the messiah sent to them; and (2) *estimating the future*, how God will achieve the final salvation of "all Israel" (11:26), and telling the gentiles how they should regard non-Christian Jews in the meantime. Here we see Paul look back on scripture and Israel's past to understand what God is up to in the present, finally pointing to a "mystery" (11:25) revealed to him about God's plans for his people Israel.

As Paul weaves through the attendant issues, he builds on a few basic convictions. First, he assumes *a distinct ethnic and salvation-historical iden-*

---

24 See Barclay 2020.

tity to "Israel." Paul's theology clearly includes Christian gentiles alongside Jews in the offspring of Abraham; there is no distinction in their need for grace or their way of receiving it—by faith (3:23–24, 29–31; 4:1–12; Gal 3:28). Yet there remains an ethnic and historical distinction. Jews who put their faith in Christ do not thereby become non-Jews. Paul offers himself as one such instance, calling himself an "Israelite" in the present tense (Rom 11:1; cf. 2 Cor 11:22; Gal 2:15; Phil 3:5).[25] Gentile Christians are "ingrafted" among the natural branches of Israel's tree and nourished by its root, yet they remain "gentiles" distinct from ethnic Israel (Rom 11:13), wild shoots that are grafted in among the tree's "natural" branches but do not replace them (11:17–24).[26] Throughout Romans, Paul retains an ethnic and historical distinction between Jews who possess the Mosaic law and the gentiles who are not "by nature" under the law (e.g., 1:16; 2:12–15; 3:1–3; 9:1–5; 11:11–26, 30–32). Israel also has a distinct identity in salvation history: they received the "oracles of God" (3:2), the covenants, the worship of God, and to them belong the patriarchs and, ethnically, Christ himself (9:4–5). Even Christ's gospel of justification is historically "first to the Jew and also the Greek" (1:16; 2:9; cf. Acts 3:26). Of course, many individual Israelites have turned away from God, and many gentiles have turned to God in Christ, but this priority and dignity for Israel as a nation remains even if some were unfaithful (Rom 3:3–4; 11:28). Indeed, as Paul's argument progresses, one finds an ongoing place for even currently unbelieving Israel in the salvation of the world (11:12–16, 28–32).

Second, the fact that a large contingent of Jews have not embraced Christ *does not imply that God's election of Israel failed or that God is unjust.* Paul opens the argument by expressing his sorrow for Israel (9:1–5), without naming the source of grief, and continues by insisting, "It is not as though God's word has failed" (9:6). The unstated source of grief, clear later, is that many (though not all) have rejected Christ even while gentiles are converting (see 9:30–10:3; 11:1). Paul prays for "their salvation" (10:1). Those who oppose the gospel do so out of zeal for God, but it is misdirected; for, rather than receive God's righteousness manifested through Christ, they continue to

---

25 If Paul sometimes speaks of "the Jews" as though he is outside their number, it is little different from one of Israel's prophets calling Israel "this people" to critique the majority (e.g., Isa 28:14; Jer 14:10) while still being of the people themselves.

26 See Gadenz 2009, 269–70. Paul's Greek "grafted in among them" (ἐνεκεντρίσθης ἐν αὐτοῖς, *enekentristhēs en autois*) in 11:17 is sometimes unfortunately translated as "in their place" (so NABRE, RSV), potentially giving readers the impression that gentile Christians simply replace Israel.

pursue a faulty source of life in the Mosaic law (9:31–32; 10:2–4; cf. 3:21). But if one might think this means God's word has failed, Paul insists it has not. He turns to scripture to make his point.[27] Being among God's people has always been a matter of promise rather than mere bloodline—God passed the line of the covenant through only one of Abraham's sons, Isaac, and through only one of Isaac's sons, Jacob (9:6–13). Nor is God unjust to raise up some rather than others apart from their prior merit (9:14–24). True, God has let many in Israel fall despite the nation's election and let many gentiles convert. But Paul cites biblical texts showing that God had promised to call gentiles as his children and that great disobedience by most Israelites in the past did not negate the nation's election, for God preserved a faithful remnant in his mercy (9:25–29; 10:18–21; 11:1–7; cf. Deut 9:4–6; Isa 1:9). In Christ God calls Jews and gentiles to salvation (Rom 9:24; 10:12), but within Israel there is division between those who follow God's anointed messiah and those who oppose him and are allowed to be hardened (as the anointed king David prayed regarding those Israelites who opposed him, 11:7–10).[28]

But if many have experienced a hardening and not recognized "the time of their visitation" (as Luke 19:44 puts it), this must not mean God's election of Israel has failed. God must be up to something in all this. This is buttressed by a third conviction: *God's distinct election of Israel is irrevocable* (Rom 11:29). There is no sense in which Israel as a unique people has served its purpose and is now to be replaced. By their unbelief, many appear to have been cast off, but God has not cast off his people or become unfaithful in response (3:3; 11:1). Proof of this in the present time is Paul and other Israelites who have embraced Christ's lordship, a faithful "remnant" whom God has preserved for Israel by grace (11:1–10). But even those who now are enemies of the gospel remain "beloved for the sake of the patriarchs" (11:28;

---

27 Notably, Romans is the Pauline letter most packed with citations from the OT, largely owing to his constant use of scripture in chaps. 9–11.

28 The language of election and "hardening" has given rise to much debate even within orthodox traditions. Noteworthy here is that election in these passages is regularly corporate: a hardening has come upon a part of Israel, yet all Israel is elect, even while this "election" only preserves certain individuals from hardening in Paul's day (see 11:7, 25, 28). Even individuals such as Pharaoh and Jacob (9:11, 15–21) are used as representatives of larger groups. When it comes to individuals, Paul ascribes their salvation to faith and their reprobation to unbelief (11:19–24), just as the Gospels can ascribe "election" to those who persevere in fidelity but not to those who reject their election (Matt 22:14). The passage unreservedly emphasizes the necessity of divine initiative and grace in salvation, yet here too one cannot escape the reality of human agency in receiving or responding positively to grace.

cf. Deut 7:6-8).[29] Therefore, Paul reasons, the present hardening—partial and not over all Israelites even now—must be temporary and to a purpose (Rom 11:11-16). Paul relies in part on the prophecy that, when Israel strayed from God, God would "provoke" Israel by welcoming "a non-people" (10:19; cf. 11:11, Deut 32:21), and Paul sees his own gentile mission as instrumental to save some Israelites in the present (11:14).[30] Looking to the future, Paul sees a divine mystery revealed: formerly hardened gentiles have received mercy in Christ in the wake of so many Jews rejecting him, and just so will the Jews who are now hardened receive mercy when the "fullness of the gentiles comes in" (11:25; cf. 11:12, 30-31). And in this way "all Israel will be saved" (11:26).

The exact nature of Paul's future hope for "all Israel's" salvation is debated. The comprehensive, singular πᾶς Ἰσραήλ (pas Israēl) indicates Israel as a whole, though not necessarily every individual Israelite. It is unlikely that Paul envisions this salvation including historic villains such as Jeroboam or Ahab.[31] He also does not likely mean to say that Israelites have a separate way of salvation without Christ: his anxiety over their "salvation" shows the stakes involved (10:2; cf. 9:1-3), and when he speaks of individuals (Jew or gentile) being cut off or restored it remains in the context of their "faith" (11:16-24).[32] Yet Paul's entire discussion would be superfluous if he merely envisioned the current situation to continue (with only a small remnant of Jews believing in Christ). Some suggest that "all Israel" will be saved when the gentiles are brought in because the ancient northern kingdom (the ten tribes of "Israel" as opposed to "Judah"), which split from David's line (1 Kgs 11-12), had assimilated fully with the gentiles abroad.[33] On this reading, descendants of the historic kingdom of "Israel" are saved through

---

29 Paul's defining of Israel according to election and promise in 9:6 cannot therefore remove all reference to ethnic Israel in the promises of 11:25-32. See Kaminsky and Reasoner 2019.

30 Paul's term παραζηλόω (parazēloō) is often translated "provoke to jealousy," but its place in the salvation of some by the gentile mission in these verses is debated. Does Paul mean unbelieving Jews will see gentiles convert and want to join, or that God provokes them to wrath in return for their forsaking Christ? The verb is usually used of provocation to anger or indignation (Deut 32:21; 1 Kgs 14:22; Ps 37:8 [KJV 37:7]; 78:58; 1 Cor 10:22), less often of mere jealousy (Sir 30:3). See Jewett 2007, 645-47.

31 When early rabbis asserted that "all Israel has a share in the world to come," they quickly name these and other people as exceptions (Mishnah, tractate Sanhedrin 10.1-2).

32 See Donaldson 2006.

33 See Staples 2011.

the gentile mission because they *are* gentiles in Paul's day, so "all" twelve tribes will be represented in the church by the conversion of some Jews and Israelite-gentiles. This view accords well with prophecies that all the tribes would be restored (Ezek 37:15–22; cf. Rev 7:4–8). On the other hand, Paul's future verbs in Romans 11:25–31 speak of the future salvation of the part of Israel currently "hardened" against the gospel as its "enemies," which seems quite distinct from his talk about unhardened gentiles presently converting. Indeed, gentile converts are commanded not to boast that they have been joined to the "natural branches" of Israel, which seems odd if Paul views at least some of them *as* genealogically natural descendants of Abraham. Paul's emphasis that this hardening is temporary and will be taken away for their salvation suggests to many scholars that Paul envisions a future event that is not simply identical to the gentile mission. Many thus believe Paul expected that Jews *en masse* would turn to Christ at his second coming or just before.[34] Another possibility focuses on the biblical texts Paul cites to illustrate his hope, particularly his citations in 11:27 of prophecies that the redeemer would remove Israel's guilt after a time of disobedience (Isa 59:20; Jer 31:33–34).[35] That is, those who have rejected Christ as part of God's plan to bring in the gentiles will recognize their redeemer and be forgiven when Christ returns.

Exegetically, it is challenging to pin down exactly the turn of events that Paul glimpsed as he wrote. Hermeneutically, however, readers are invited to hope with Paul and to share the basic convictions on which he based that hope. God's word does not fail. The story will not end with God's word being broken—not to Israel, not at all. This passage invites readers to share Paul's sense of awe as he marvels at God's plan and Paul's respect and love for Abraham's physical descendants in history and today. And Gentile readers in today's church must heed the commands of the passage—not despite but precisely because of the intervening millennia—not to boast over the natural branches among whom they have been "grafted in," but rather to recognize that they are supported by the root.[36]

---

34 See Goodrich 2016.

35 Intriguingly, the prophecies Paul cites here are of the new covenant, which is generally spoken of with respect to Christ's first advent and the outpouring of the Spirit (Luke 22:20; 2 Cor 3:6; Heb 8:13), but here is appealed to in a still-future context for the people of Israel at Christ's second coming.

36 Paul is helpfully echoed in the Pontifical Biblical Commission's *The Jewish People and Their Sacred Scriptures in the Christian Bible* (2002), §84–87.

FURTHER READING

Aletti, Jean-Noël, SJ. 2015. *Justification by Faith in the Letters of Saint Paul: Keys to Interpretation.* Translated by Peggy Manning Meyer. AnBib Studia 5. Rome: Gregorian and Biblical Press.

Barclay, John M. G. 2020. *Paul and the Power of Grace.* Grand Rapids: Eerdmans.

Byrne, Brendan, SJ. 1996. *Romans.* SP 6. Collegeville, MN: Liturgical Press.

Donfried, Karl P., ed. 1991. *The Romans Debate.* Expanded edition. Peabody, MA: Hendrickson.

Dunn, James D. G. 1988. *Romans.* WBC 38. Nashville: Thomas Nelson.

Eastman, Susan Grove. 2017. *Paul and the Person: Reframing Paul's Anthropology.* Grand Rapids: Eerdmans.

Fitzmyer, Joseph A., SJ. 1993. *Romans: A New Translation with Introduction and Commentary.* AB 33. New York: Doubleday.

Gadenz, Pablo T. 2009. *Called from the Jews and from the Gentiles: Pauline Ecclesiology in Romans 9–11.* WUNT 2/267. Tübingen: Mohr Siebeck.

Gaventa, Beverly Roberts. 2016. *When in Romans: An Invitation to Linger with the Gospel according to Paul.* Grand Rapids: Baker Academic.

Gorman, Michael J. 2009. *Inhabiting the Cruciform God: Kenosis, Justification, and Theosis in Paul's Narrative Soteriology.* Grand Rapids: Eerdmans.

Jewett, Robert. 2007. *Romans.* Hermeneia. Minneapolis: Fortress.

Matera, Frank J. 2010. *Romans.* Paideia Commentaries on the New Testament. Grand Rapids: Baker Academic.

Oakes, Peter. 2009. *Reading Romans in Pompeii: Paul's Letter at Ground Level.* Minneapolis: Fortress.

Perkins, Pheme. 2011. "Adam and Christ in the Pauline Epistles." In *Celebrating Paul: Festschrift in Honor of Jerome Murphy-O'Connor, OP, and Joseph A. Fitzmyer, SJ,* edited by Peter Spitaler, 128–51. CBQMS 48. Washington, DC: Catholic Biblical Association of America.

Prothro, James B. 2018. *Both Judge and Justifier: Biblical Legal Language and the Act of Justifying in Paul.* WUNT 2/461. Tübingen: Mohr Siebeck.

Reasoner, Mark. 2005. *Romans in Full Circle: A History of Interpretation.* Louisville, KY: Westminster John Knox.

Rodríguez, Rafael. 2014. *If You Call Yourself a Jew: Reappraising Paul's Letter to the Romans.* Eugene, OR: Cascade.

Schnelle, Udo. *The Human Condition: Anthropology in the Teachings of Jesus, Paul, and John.* Translated by O. C. Dean Jr. Edinburgh: T&T Clark, 1991.

Tobin, Thomas H., SJ. 2004. *Paul's Rhetoric in Its Contexts: The Argument of Romans.* Peabody, MA: Hendrickson.

CHAPTER SEVEN

1 Corinthians

First Corinthians addresses several problems plaguing the Corinthian church. They competed with each other, engaged in sexual immorality, and at times treated the church like any other Greco-Roman social club. Paul calls them to recognize the unity of Christ's church, to serve others in self-giving love, and to cultivate holiness through the Holy Spirit they received in baptism.

BACKGROUND

Paul and the Corinthian Christians

Corinth was one of the most important cities in the Roman empire. Once a prominent Greek city, it had been largely destroyed in the mid-second century BCE and refounded as a Roman colony by Julius Caesar in 44 BCE. Roman Corinth became the capital of the province of Achaia (southern Greece) and grew quickly in population and prominence. It was a port city, a center for trade and travel, and hosted the popular Isthmian Games. The city's denizens came from across the economic spectrum and from many ethnicities, from Egyptian to Jewish to Greek and beyond. This cultural "melting pot" was home to many different customs, philosophical ideas, and religious pieties.

According to Acts, Paul brought the gospel to the Greek region of Macedonia (Philippi, Thessalonica) and arrived in Corinth after a very brief stint in Athens (Acts 16–18). Paul's letters match well with this overall sequence (1 Thess 2:2; 3:1). According to Acts, Paul met in Corinth a Jew named Aquila and his wife, Prisca (in Acts, "Priscilla"), with whom he plied his trade as a "tentmaker" or leather-worker to support himself while he evangelized (Acts 18:2–3; cf. 1 Cor 4:12; 9:1–18).[1] As usual, his preaching encountered opposition, and he was arraigned as a rabble-rouser before the proconsul Gallio—a charge that was dismissed (Acts 18:12–17). Nevertheless, his preaching was effective, and a variety of people—Jews and Greeks, slaves and free, rich and poor—were baptized by Paul or his coworkers (1 Cor 1:14–17, 26; 7:18–22; 11:22; cf. Acts 18:4–8).

With a fruitful mission and a stable connections for manual labor, Paul stayed in Corinth some time, leaving only after an eighteen-month stay according to Acts 18:11, 18. Some time after he left, an impressive preacher named Apollos arrived to minister in Corinth (1 Cor 3:6; cf. Acts 18:24–19:1). At the hands of Apollos and others, the Corinthian church continued to grow in Paul's absence. But its growth was plagued by trouble, and Paul kept in regular contact with the community. The prevailing culture of Corinth was difficult for many converts to reject, particularly its competitive factionalism and immorality. Before writing 1 Corinthians, Paul wrote one letter now lost to us (see 1 Cor 5:9–10) and, after writing 1 Corinthians, at least two other letters dealing with similar issues (see 2 Cor 2:3–4; 7:8, 12; 12:21).[2] We see in this correspondence Paul's own "anxiety for the churches" (2 Cor 11:28). As a spiritual "father" (1 Cor 4:14–15) tending a rebellious child, Paul kept in constant contact with Corinth, writing, sending, and receiving emissaries and addressing them with tears, encouragement, and sometimes "tough love."

Where and When Did Paul Write 1 Corinthians?

Relating his travel plans in the letter's closing, Paul states that he is currently in Ephesus, and he intends to remain there "until Pentecost" (16:8), a springtime Jewish feast. He planned to leave Ephesus, spend time in Macedonia (16:5), and thereafter spend a longer time, perhaps the whole winter (when travel was difficult), in Corinth (16:1–7; cf. 11:34). His plans ultimately changed, which caused some controversy (2 Cor 1:15–2:11).

Can we be more precise about the year? Most date Paul's stay in Corinth between 49 and 52 CE. The bookend dates for this come from Acts. On the front end, Prisca and Aquila are said to have come to Corinth in the

---

1 Acts describes them as σκηνοποιοί (*skēnopoioi*), literally "tentmakers." But the term appears to include work with leather and similar materials.

2 Later, too, in about 95 CE Clement of Rome addressed disunity in Corinth again (*1 Clement* 47).

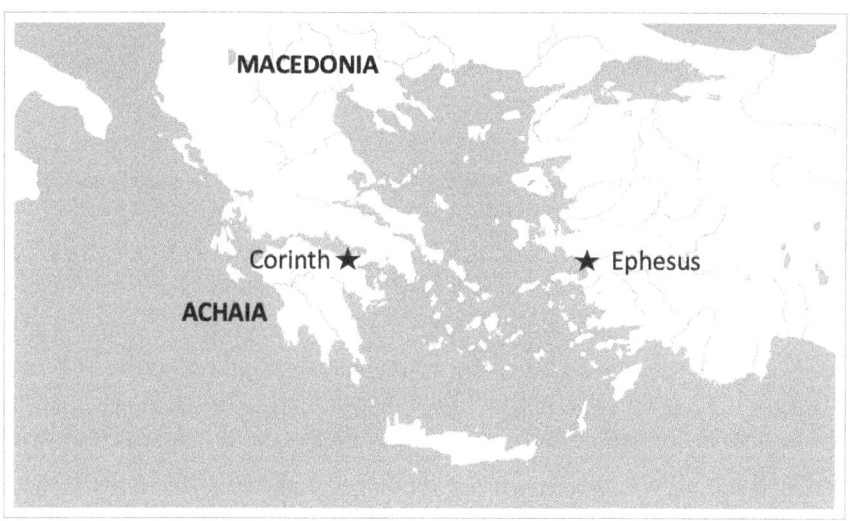

wake of Claudius Caesar's expulsion of Jews from Rome in 49 (Acts 18:2; cf. Suetonius, *Claudius* 25.4).[3] On the back end, Acts 18:11–17 has Paul accused before the proconsul Gallio, who served from summer of 51 to summer of 52.[4] If we assume these dates, we can posit that Paul left Corinth in 52. How long between his departure and the writing of 1 Corinthians? Several things must have happened in the meantime. Apollos has come, had an influential ministry in Paul's absence, and left (1 Cor 3:6; 16:12). Paul at least needs to have written them a short letter (5:9), heard reports from travelers (1:11), and received Sosthenes and other delegates with the Corinthians' letter before he wrote (1:1; 7:1; 16:17). Paul was an industrious man, but we can guess all this took at least a year. This fits with the detail in 16:19 that there are plural "churches in Asia" while Paul writes from Asia's capital, Ephesus: he has been there long enough to have established several congregations. Accommodating this time frame, an estimate of 53/54 works well for the date of this letter.

Why Did Paul Write 1 Corinthians?

The occasion for 1 Corinthians comes especially from information Paul has received about the church. Since his previous (now lost) letter, he has

---

3 Some have argued instead that this occurred in 41 CE. See, however, Riesner 1998, 157–201.

4 See Haacker 1992. Some, however, revise Gallio's dates slightly to 52–53, adding a year to our dates for this and other letters.

received reports from people associated with Chloe (1:11)—perhaps a merchant?—and has been visited by emissaries from Corinth (16:17). Among them was Sosthenes, presumably a leader in the Corinthian church (a "synagogue official" according to Acts 18:17). These brought Paul not only their own reports and concerns, but also a letter from Corinth to Paul (1 Cor 7:1). With Sosthenes (1:1), Paul writes to address several issues.

Competition and Faction. Roman culture was very concerned with honor and social advancement. Those who had honor and money wanted to keep it, and those who did not wanted to get it. For those on the lower end of the social ladder, a main way to advance was by being tied to someone more successful. Economically, even selling oneself into slavery could be a move up the ladder by becoming the slave of a wealthy and respected person. Being attached to a prominent person could elevate one's own social standing.[5] The same logic applied to other aspects of society in which one's name was tied to someone else's, such as politics, religion, and schools of rhetoric. Students would boost their own profile by making sure that everyone thought *their* teacher was the best, and they would discredit or jeer other teachers as worse.[6] If *my teacher* is better than yours, then by extension *I* am better than you—and the louder I shout it, the more everyone knows it.

This social logic encouraged disunity and competition. And the Corinthians seem to have applied it within the church to the ministers who baptized them or whose patronage they claimed. Some claimed to belong to Paul, the founder of their church and apostle of God, while others claimed to belong to Apollos, the eloquent and well-educated preacher who came after Paul (3:3–4; cf. Acts 18:24–28).[7] Others claimed Cephas/Peter over these, either merely because of his apostolic reputation or because he had visited Corinth himself (1 Cor 1:10–12; 3:22).[8] Urbane Corinthians who possessed or desired higher status may have taken to the preaching of Apollos and been baptized by him, and they surely stood to gain—by this social logic—from boasting in Apollos at the expense of Paul, who himself admits his public

5 For this social structure, see Wolf 1966.

6 See B. Winter 2001, 31–43.

7 In 1:12 there appears to be a fourth group claiming, "I am of Christ," but this was likely not a distinct faction (surely none would have denied being "of Christ"). It may be Paul's own phrase added to show where their true allegiance should lie.

8 See Witetschek 2018. If Peter did not visit Corinth, Paul's mentions of Peter indicate that his significance as an apostle of Christ was known well enough that people might have claimed him even if he did not baptize them (see 9:5; 15:5; Gal 1–2).

speaking was unimpressive (2 Cor 10:10). Having claimed their allegiance to these ministers, they then used them in competition against each other. If *my apostle* is better than yours, then by extension I am better than you in this church community. They are "boasting in men" and becoming "puffed up" against each other (1 Cor 3:21; 4:6). Paul spends the better part of four chapters calling them to unity and to reevaluate how the world works by spiritual wisdom (1:10–4:21).

This competitive spirit appears to have overflowed into many Corinthians' treatment of charismatic gifts. Some are inspired by the Spirit to speak in tongues, prophesy, and perform miracles. Paul's insistence that, within the body of Christ, all are equally needed and all possess the same Spirit by baptism (12:4–31) suggests that some Corinthians let these charisms also become occasions for boasting: "I have a better gift, so I must be closer to God." Paul spends three chapters calling them to an ethic of charity, unity, and edification, to use their charisms for the common good rather than personal glory (12:1–14:40).

Sexual Misconduct. The old Greek city of Corinth was so well known for prostitution, often connected with pagan worship, that the verb κορινθιάζο-μαι (*korinthiazomai*, "to act Corinthian") meant "fornicate," and "Corinthian lady" was a euphemism for "prostitute" (e.g., Plato, *Republic* 3.404d). The new Roman Corinth of Paul's day differed in many ways, but the port city surely retained much of its old sexual culture, and this proved a constant problem in the church. It was a main topic in Paul's first, lost letter to Corinth (1 Cor 5:9–10). When Paul wrote 1 Corinthians, he addressed the same issues again, even a case in which a believer bedded his father's wife and was applauded for it (5:1, 11; 6:9–11, 15–20; 10:8). On the other hand, others thought it was better to avoid sex altogether—even within marriage—and wrote Paul for clarification (see 7:1–5).[9] This view could have originated in pious Corinthians' desire to emulate Paul's celibacy, a philosophical disdain for the body (see below), or perhaps merely an overreaction to the immorality around them. In any case, sexual issues were significant, divisive, and recurring problems in Paul's Corinth.

---

9 Most modern commentaries and translations (e.g., NABRE, ESV) put "It is good for a man not to touch a woman" (7:1) in quotation marks to indicate that this represents what the Corinthians wrote to Paul. Such Corinthian "slogans," which Paul repeats and then addresses, appear often (e.g., 1:12; 6:12–13). Others interpret the statement as Paul's own, reading it as a summary of his comments later in the chapter that celibacy is preferable or "better" (e.g., RSV, NJB).

Idol-Food. In cities, most meat available to buy had been slaughtered in sacrifice to pagan gods and was usually sold through their temples. Those who did not own or slaughter their own flocks had little other affordable access to meat. Indeed, those on the lower end of the economic spectrum may have primarily eaten meat only at pagan feasts and civic events.[10] This caused tensions in the church. Jewish believers reared on the stories of Daniel or the Maccabean martyrs, who heroically refused to pollute themselves with unclean food, may have shunned most or all available meat as implicitly idolatrous (see Dan 1:1–21; 2 Macc 7:1–42; Rom 14:2). The apostolic council in Jerusalem and the book of Revelation took a negative view of eating idol meat (Acts 15:29; 21:25; Rev 2:14, 20). Some pagan converts associated meat with their former life, which they had renounced for Christ, and shunned idol-meat lest they be tempted to return to idolatry (note 1 Cor 8:7). Others, however, held that no harm could come of eating idol-meat. These other gods do not really exist, they reasoned, so what difference does it make what building I visit to buy meat or what "god" some pagan fool thinks I am pleasing by eating it? Prominent Corinthians faced social pressures as well: if they were to shun all idol-meat, their absence from civic events or abstinence at dinner parties might lose them business and status. Paul takes the better part of three chapters to argue that love and respect of others' consciences should take precedence in their actions and that, while it is true that there are no other gods, there are demons, and flirting with idolatry invites danger (8:1–10:22).

The Resurrection. A final issue, though one "of first importance" (15:3), is that of the resurrection. Some Corinthians apparently denied the resurrection of the dead (15:12). Paul's response suggests that they were primarily skeptical about the "general resurrection" of all the dead on the last day (15:13, 16, 21–22), though some may also have held modified views of Jesus's own resurrection. It is easy to imagine how popular philosophical ideas may have influenced these Corinthians.[11] Philosophers borrowing from Plato chimed that the body was the soul's "prison," and they would hardly have seen dead souls being raised with eternal bodies as something to *hope* for.[12]

---

10 See Blue 1993, 309; Theissen 1982, 125–29.

11 See Wright 2003, 32–84.

12 In Plato, for example, Socrates lauds the god Hades for refusing to associate with humans until death, when the soul becomes "pure from all the evils and desires associated with the body" (Plato, *Cratylus* 403e–404a). Indeed, souls who in their earthly life serve or love their bodies will not commune with the divine after death, but become ghosts stuck on earth or pass into baser animals (Plato, *Phaedo* 81a–83e).

Epicureanism, on the other hand, encouraged people not to fear death by arguing that souls were mortal and disintegrate with the body, thus making postmortem life (and any worry about postmortem judgment) ridiculous.[13] Paul spends a long chapter (15:1–58) defending and clarifying the Christian hope of bodily resurrection.

OVERVIEW

I. **Letter Opening (1:1–9)**

  A. Paul and Sosthenes to the Corinthians, who have been called to be holy together with all the churches (1:1–3)

  B. Thanks be to God that he has given you his gifts and called you to fellowship in Christ (1:4–9).

II. **Call to Unity (1:10–4:21)**

  A. I hear you are dividing over which minister you belong to! You belong to Christ, into whom you were baptized (1:10–17)!

  B. God's economy of grace overturns the world's categories and expectations. God chose to save the world through a crucifixion and chooses unimpressive people to be vessels of his power (1:18–2:5).

  C. There is wisdom in God's ways, but it is known by those who heed God's Spirit (2:6–16). Your divisions show you are still thinking in worldly ways. We apostles are God's servants for your sake, and you are God's temple. And God will judge each by how they have served him (3:1–17).

  E. If you want to be wise, become a fool by human standards and learn God's wisdom, for in God all things are yours—Paul, Apollos, and Cephas included—and you belong to God (3:18–23).

  F. So stop boasting against each other and judging God's apostles. Otherwise, I may have to correct your worldliness with God's power when I come (4:1–20).

III. **Call to Purity in Unity (5:1–7:40)**

  A. The church of God is to be pure!

   1. How can anyone boast about a man bedding his father's wife? This impurity must be cast out (5:1–8). Judging outsiders is

---

13 See Lucretius, *On the Nature of Things*, book 3.

God's business. Our business is to remove insiders who are openly and obstinately unrepentant (5:9–13).

2. How can some of you take disputes outside the church to pagan courts? God's people will judge the fallen world at the final judgment (6:1–3). Take your grievances to people who judge by the Spirit of God (6:4–8).

B. You were once impure, but you have been washed and made God's holy people in Christ and the Spirit (6:9–11).

1. The body is not for sexual immorality but for the Lord (6:12–15).

2. God has redeemed you—your body included—to be one with Christ, his holy temple. Do not pollute God's temple by impurity (6:16–20).

C. Relatedly, you asked about sex and marriage . . .

1. No, marital sex is not bad and can guard against temptations (7:1–5). Still, my own view is that it is better to remain single if that is one's gift from God (7:6–9).

2. If you are married, you should not divorce (if you do, do not marry another) (7:10–11). Even if you are married to a nonbeliever, you may leave if they insist on divorce, but it is better to stay and sanctify them (7:12–24).

3. Still, marriage brings many distractions from devotion to God's work. If you must, then marry and stay married until death parts you; if you can, choose celibacy in service to God (7:25–40).

IV. **Call to Love in Unity (8:1–14:40)**

A. Concerning food offered to idols, let love for others guide your choices, rather than your freedom or knowledge (8:1–3).

1. True, there are no other gods, but some think there are. No food is sinful in itself, but you sin against the church if you flaunt your liberty and scandalize others to think actual idolatry is permissible (8:4–13).

2. Take my example: I have many privileges as an apostle, but in the interest of Christ I lay them aside for the sake of others' salvation (9:1–27).

3. And never forget: idolatry is no small matter. The Israelites were redeemed by God's grace, but when they abandoned God for idols they were struck down (10:1–14). You are all joined to the Lord and to each other in the eucharist; do not join yourself to demons by eating from an idol's altar (10:15–22).

4. If you are buying meat or accepting a dinner invitation, you do not have to be scrupulous, but if someone makes a point that it is idol-food, abstain (10:23–30). Let faithfulness and love govern your decisions (10:31–11:1).

B. Regarding your worship together . . .

1. The distinction and union between man and woman in the Lord should be manifest in their dress at worship. Give no offense. Let men uncover their heads during prayer, and let women have their hair covered or neatly done up (11:2–16).

2. When you gather to celebrate the Lord's Supper, you must not treat it like a profane dinner party, divided by class or self-ishly filling yourselves while others go hungry. It is the Lord's Supper! I have handed it on to you as I received it. Approach it in repentance and purity (11:17–34).

3. Regarding spiritual gifts, you are all united by baptism in the one Spirit, who gives all differing gifts for the common good (12:1–13). In Christ, as in a body, there are many members with different gifts, but each is needed (12:14–26).

a. In the church, all gifts are ordered under the ministerial offices (12:27–31).

b. Everything is to be done in Christlike love, for it is love (not these impressive gifts) that endures to eternity (13:1–13).

c. Therefore, do not let your own interests or desire for prominence control how you use your gifts. Everything in the liturgical assembly should be done to build others up by the clear word of God, which means tongues (unless someone interprets them intelligibly) are secondary to preaching and prophecy (14:1–35).

d. Keep in line with the practice of all the churches, and do all things in good order (14:36–40).

V. **Call to Hope (15:1–58)**

A. I have handed down to you the gospel the whole church believes, that Christ was crucified, buried, and raised for us (15:1–11).

1. How can some of you deny that the dead are raised, if we believe Christ was raised and the dead will be raised in Christ? If Christ is not risen, we are not saved and have no hope (15:12–34).

2. Do not laugh at the idea of a resurrected body. At Christ's return, both the dead and the living will be transformed into immortal bodies. Like the risen Christ's body, they will be like our present bodies, but differing in glory and no longer subject to decay (15:35–49).

3. On that day, the Lord will defeat death by raising the dead and transforming us. This is our sure hope. Therefore, stand fast in faith and works, for your work is not in vain (15:50–58).

VI. **Letter Closing (16:1–24)**

A. Collect money for the saints in Jerusalem. I plan to visit you, hopefully the whole winter, and will bring it to Judea (16:1–9). In the meantime, honor your leaders, and receive Timothy or Apollos well if they come (16:10–18).

B. My companions greet you (16:19–20).

C. I, Paul, write this greeting. Come, Lord Jesus! Grace be with you (16:21–24).

KEY FEATURES

There is much of significance in this letter, especially in light of later doctrinal development. For example, Paul's call for the Corinthian assembly to be able to judge disputes rather than deferring to pagan courts (6:1–8) not only parallels the church with Israel (as in 10:1–22) but also anticipates the development of systems of ecclesiastical governance (cf. also Exod 18:13–26; Matt 18:15–20). Paul's comments about celibacy for the sake of serving God and endorsement of remarriage only after a spouse's death also anticipate later developments (along with texts like Matt 19:1–12).

But each of these fits within a greater theme found throughout the letter: the church's unity and, within it, its purity or holiness. Though the length of Paul's letter and the several topics treated may make some sections seem disjointed, one can see Paul's call to unity, purity, and charity throughout. Indeed, one can find here the marks of the church according to the Nicene Creed: *one, holy, catholic,* and *apostolic.*

One, Holy Catholic Church

Christ's One Body

The theme of unity touches virtually everything in the letter explicitly or implicitly. Obviously concerned that the factious Corinthians be united with each other, Paul also wants the Corinthians to walk in step with the universal church, emphasizing that they are co-members "together with all who call on the name of our Lord Jesus Christ in every place" (1:2). All must thus maintain the same doctrine and even some practices (see 4:17; 11:16; 14:33; 15:1–11). The unity of the church bespeaks its *catholicity.*

This one church in Christ is also necessarily *apostolic.* One sees this in other letters, wherein Paul warns of the dangers of willfully departing from him and the apostolic faith to ally with false teachers (2 Cor 11:2–6; Gal 1:6–9; 5:2–5). It is evident also in 1 Corinthians, when Paul speaks of the importance of traditions handed down by himself or other apostles (11:2, 23; 15:1–3, 11) and in his comments about the duties of God's "coworkers" who lay the foundation of Christ's church (3:5–11; 4:1–16; 9:1–2, 11–16).

Most especially, however, 1 Corinthians treats the congregation's internal *unity,* threatened by factionalism and competition. As discussed above, many are competing with one another by claiming allegiance to different apostolic figures—Paul, Apollos, and Cephas (Peter). Paul's response first appeals to their common baptism: in the very structure of how one enters the church, everyone is equal. No matter the minister, the baptized are baptized into *Christ,* and Christ is not divided—as though one can get baptized into a better part of Christ separate from others (1:13–15). Next, he contrasts human wisdom with the apparent "folly" of God's wisdom (1:18–3:4). This has often been understood as Paul's way of denigrating Apollos, since Apollos was reputedly educated and eloquent (see Acts 18:24). But Paul puts himself and Apollos on the same side together as "stewards of the mysteries of God" (1 Cor 4:1; cf. 3:5–9; 9:5; 16:12). The contrast between worldly wisdom and God's "folly" is probably not a jibe against Apollos but rather an emphasis that God

---

14 See Mihaila 2009.

and the world have entirely different ways of operating.[14] The Corinthians' self-promoting behavior is merely "human" (3:4), based on worldly values and expectations. The social logic of God's kingdom operates contrary to such thinking: in Jesus's words, "If anyone wishes to be first, he will be last of all and the servant of all" (Mark 9:35). The greatest proof of this is the *crucifixion*. That the "Lord of glory" (1 Cor 2:8) chose to be shamed on a cross, that God gave life to sinners by dying innocently, is pure "folly" and hardly intelligible within the expectations of worldly wisdom (1:18–31). There is certainly a speculative wisdom that Paul teaches, flowing from the revelation of God in Christ and the Spirit, but the Corinthians are not ready for it (2:1–3:4).[15] They need to let their minds be laid low and transformed by the unexpected and scandalous salvation into which they have been baptized. Then they will recognize their unity with one another and see their ministers as instruments of God rather than personalities over whom to divide (3:5–11).

This focus on God's work through different persons is mirrored in Paul's discussion of the Spirit's gifts—especially "speaking in tongues" (*glossolalia*), a kind of mystical communication from or with the Spirit that manifests in ecstatic speech.[16] Paul's treatment spans three chapters (12:1–14:40). All the baptized partake of the same Spirit (12:13), and this one Spirit gives different gifts to different people, but all for the "common good" of the church's edification and growth (12:4–11). Christ's church is a body with many members, each with a different place and different task, but even the weakest and least impressive contribute to the life of the body (12:12–26). And the virtue that must animate each member's use of their gift—whether prophecy, tongues, administration, charitable giving, or whatever (see the differing lists in 12:8–10; Rom 12:3–8)—is *love*. Love has no envy, no competition, no selfish ambition, but patient kindness and care for the good of others (1 Cor 13:1–13). Paul applies this to the use of tongues in the liturgy in chapter 14: tongues spoken in the public assembly need to be interpreted publicly (either by the speaker or by another with the gift of interpretation) so that all are edified

---

15 See Scott 2006.

16 Some argue that "speaking in tongues" refers merely to people speaking their mother tongues in a diverse assembly (Latin, Aramaic, etc.), hence the need for an "interpreter" (14:13, 27–28). But speaking non-Greek languages in a port city with a diverse populace would hardly be a strange "sign" to convict anyone of the Spirit's power (14:22–23). Moreover, Paul says that what is spoken "in tongues" is unintelligible not merely to bystanders but perhaps even to the *speaker* (14:2, 9, 13–15), hardly something Paul would say of someone speaking their mother tongue.

by the content of what is said, not merely impressed by one person's display (1 Cor 14:19, 27–28). Paul's point is not to disparage or prohibit tongues entirely (14:39). But even with real, Spirit-given goods, love calls all to put aside their prerogatives for the sake of others. And in the public assembly, every word should be ordered to teach, rebuke, and exhort the faithful (cf. 12:3, 27–31; 14:12, 24–25).[17]

The Spirit's Holy Temple

Related to Paul's vision of Christ's church being *one* is his insistence that it is and must be *holy*. Holiness has to do with God's distinct character, and here especially the distinction of God and what is God's from what is impure or evil. God commands Israel in Leviticus 19:2, "You shall be holy, for I the LORD your God am holy," and from there he calls them to distinct ways of life and worship proper to this holy God. This command is grounded also in Israel's redemption: God separated them out from the rest of the world to be his, so they must be his in every way (see Exod 20:2–3; Lev 20:26). Such holiness also has an evangelical function, that pagans living under gods of greed, sex, or warfare will see Israel's good and just society and glorify Israel's good and just God (Deut 4:5–8; cf. Matt 5:16).

Paul sees a deep typology—a pattern or correspondence within scripture—between Israel and the church, and it resurfaces often in 1 Corinthians. Those redeemed at Passover and brought through the Red Sea were called to be holy. So too are those redeemed by the paschal sacrifice of Christ. "For indeed, our Passover—Christ—has been sacrificed! Therefore, let us celebrate the feast not with the old leaven or with the leaven of wickedness or evil but with the unleavened bread of purity and truth" (5:7–8). This is their calling. God has washed Christ's people and made them holy through the work of the Holy Spirit (6:11; 12:13). The Spirit empowers them in holy and pure living by drawing them more intimately to God and renewing their minds in divine wisdom.[18]

Each individual must live in holiness, repenting and reproving themselves in penitence (11:27–32) and by walking in the Spirit (cf. Rom 6:12–23; 8:5–10). This means fleeing from idolatry and from sexual immorality

---

17 This emphasis is retained in the *Catechism*'s discussion of charismatic gifts (*CCC*, §799–801, 2003).

18 See Rabens 2010.

(chaps. 5–6) as well positively pursuing love toward others (chaps. 8–14). It also means that the church has a duty to reprove sin in its midst and encourage penitence (1 Cor 14:24–25; cf. Gal 6:1–2)—or, if a Christian is obstinately and openly unrepentant, the church may even expel them from fellowship until they are reconciled (1 Cor 5:1–13). This discipline has to do partially with effects such immorality can have on outsiders, since Christians' holiness can actually sanctify them (7:12–16), and partially with the good of the individual sinner who can be lost if not brought to repentance and reconciliation (3:16–17; 10:1–13). But it especially has to do with the *holiness of the Spirit that dwells in them.* The Spirit dwells in the community and in each individual as God's temple (3:16; 6:19). This is not just pious metaphor for Paul. If the body joined to the Lord is the Spirit's dwelling and "temple," then sexual immorality defiles that temple and can grieve the Spirit (6:15–20; cf. Eph 4:30; Jas 4:5). Indeed, sin in one can defile the whole community—"a little leaven leavens the whole lump" (1 Cor 5:6).

Paul warns the Corinthians against presumption and against flirting with idolatry, reminding them that those who were redeemed from Egypt but then turned to idols and immorality perished quickly and did not reach the promised land (10:1–22). And he constantly calls them back to the transforming power of God's grace. They who formerly were great sinners have been justified, made holy, and given the gifts of the Spirit (6:11; 12:2–13). They have been drawn into the life of God by a very real indwelling of God's Spirit, who is a pledge of final redemption for those who endure (2 Cor 1:22; 5:2; Eph 1:14). The Lord's power is present to aid them in every temptation (1 Cor 10:13). God mercifully cleanses and reconciles those who repent (cf. 11:31–32; Rom 2:4; 8:33–34; 2 Cor 2:5–11) and will purify the faithful of their sins to finally raise them to perfect communion with God (1 Cor 3:12–15; 15:20–28; 2 Cor 5:1–10).

The Eucharistic Body

1 Corinthians is the only Pauline letter in which the eucharist appears explicitly. And it is quite fitting that it appears in a letter emphasizing the church's catholic and apostolic unity, its internal unity and holiness, and indeed the hope of Christ's return. Paul grounds his exhortations on the eucharist and its reception in two passages (10:16–22; 11:17–34). His appeals place it at the intersection of the church's unity and holiness.

Paul's first mention of the sacrament comes within his argument against eating meat offered to idols. Paul concedes that false gods do not really exist, which to some meant that they were free to associate with pagan civic festivals and eat idol meat. But Paul cautions them against openly eating idol meat because it may scandalize others (chaps. 8–9). He also warns that participating in pagan sacrifices might court fellowship with demons and provoke the Lord's jealous wrath (10:21–23). To establish their unity with Christ's altar against those of the pagans, Paul appeals to the eucharist. "The cup of blessing which we bless, is it not a participation in the blood of Christ? The bread which we break, is it not a participation in the body of Christ? Because there is one bread, we though many are one body, for we all partake of the one bread" (10:16–17).

His appeal to their regularly shared eucharist exhorts them to *unity* and *holiness*. First, their unity—forged first in baptism (1:13; 12:12–13)—is continually reforged in their reception of the eucharist. They are one body "because" they partake of the one bread (10:17). Second, this unity in Christ grounds their *holiness*, here in their belonging exclusively to God and necessary separation from other altars. Paul compares the church around the eucharist to Israel's exclusive worship of and belonging to God (10:18). "You cannot partake at the Lord's table and the table of demons" (10:21; cf. Exod 20:2).[19] Third, the eucharist appears to ground their unity and holiness not just because of their communal eating but because of what they eat. Paul points first to what the elements are, a "participation" (κοινωνία, *koinōnia*) in the reality of Christ's body and blood (1 Cor 10:16). This is what forges their unity together as the one corporate "body" of Christ (10:17) and indeed is part of their continued union with Christ. If eating from idols' altars brings them into communion or makes them "participants" (κοινωνούς, *koinōnous*) with demons, partaking of the eucharist makes them commune with or participate in God. The bread, by being itself a participation in Christ's body, joins them to Christ as his holy, corporate "body."[20]

---

19 Paul does not explicitly speak of the eucharist itself as a sacrifice, whether a thank offering ("eucharist") or otherwise. He does compare it to Israel's sacrifices (10:18–22), and eucharistic overtones in the repeated "feast" of Christ "our Passover" (5:7–8) may also suggest a sacrificial conception. A sacrificial understanding is explicitly attested in the late first (*Didache* 14.1–3) and second centuries (Justin Martyr, *Dialogue with Trypho* 41; Irenaeus, *Against Heresies* 4.18.5).

20 Paul speaks especially of "bread" in 10:17, though he expects people to receive under both forms in 11:27–28. In the early second century, Ignatius of Antioch spoke of the blood with the same logic: "Hasten to celebrate one eucharist, for one is the flesh of our Lord Jesus Christ, and one is the cup to unite us to the blood of Christ" (*Philadelphians* 4.1).

Paul's second mention of the eucharist comes when he discusses their social disunity when they celebrate the meal. Their meetings for the eucharist and the communal meal that surrounded it are "for the worse" because of their disunity, resulting in a supper that is not truly the Lord's (11:17–20). Instead, each goes ahead with "his own supper," some indulging while others go hungry (11:21).[21] Paul's practical response is to call believers to wait for one another and, if one is hungry, to eat at home—perhaps anticipating the church's later separation of the communal banquet from the eucharistic liturgy proper (11:22, 33–34). But he first refocuses them on what the sacrament itself is and how one should approach it.

Paul moves from his description of their behavior to the nature of the eucharist itself, reiterating Jesus's words at the last supper, which he says he received from the Lord and handed on to the Corinthians:

> The Lord Jesus, on the night he was betrayed, took bread and, giving thanks, broke it and said, "This is my body which is for you. Do this in remembrance of me." Similarly also the cup, after supper, saying, "This cup is the new covenant in my blood. Do this, as often as you drink it, in remembrance of me." For as often as you eat this bread and drink this cup, you are proclaiming the Lord's death until he comes. (11:23–26)

Paul's tradition is strikingly similar to the form of the words in Luke. Matthew adds that Christ's blood is "for the forgiveness of sins," and Matthew and Mark both refer to it as "the blood of the covenant" (Matt 26:28; Mark 14:24), echoing the sacrifice of the Sinai covenant (Exod 24:8) and promises of messianic salvation (Zech 9:11). Luke identifies Christ's blood as that of "the new covenant," which Jeremiah 31:31–34 promised would bring intimate knowledge of God along with forgiveness of sins (Luke 22:20). Luke's version, like Paul's, also includes the declaration of benefit "for you" (Luke 22:19–20). All accounts include the declaration that the bread "is" Christ's body and the content of the cup "is" his blood. Jesus's action of "blessing" the bread in Mark and Matthew is described as "giving thanks" (εὐχαριστέω, eucharisteō) in Luke and Paul (cf. Matt 26:26; Mark 14:22; Luke 22:19). The

---

21 What is likely going on is that a middle- or upper-class home is being used for the celebration (what else could accommodate the Corinthian Christians?), and the host and attendees are treating it as though it is a regular social party, seating and serving first (and with more food) the higher-status attendees. This befits Paul's comments about disparity between the rich and poor (11:22). Paul's comments about "divisions" and "sects" (11:18–19), paralleling his comments about factions in 1:10, might suggest that the hosts are not necessarily privileging the wealthy but those who belong to the host's faction (see Lanuwabang 2016).

action of "breaking" the bread is consistent across the Gospels and Paul here and in 1 Corinthians 10:16.

Paul repeats the eucharistic words to remind the Corinthians what the meal is and follows with his interpretation of their significance for the community. The liturgical act both looks backward to commemorate Christ's death and simultaneously points forward to his return to judge and save (11:26). The Corinthians should not approach this as a convivial dinner party. Paul has stated already that God will judge those who destroy his church (3:17), whose unity in part is maintained in the eucharist (10:17). They must not divide Christ's corporate body when receiving the eucharistic body that unites them.[22] Rather, Paul calls them to approach in holiness and repentance in view of what the eucharist is. His immediate conclusion after repeating the words of Jesus is, "Therefore whoever eats the bread or drinks the Lord's cup in an unworthy way will be guilty of sin against the body and blood of the Lord. But let a person test himself and in this way let him eat from the bread and drink from the cup" (11:27–28). The paschal sacrifice in which this meal is a "participation" calls Christians to put away all wickedness just as Israel was commanded to put away all leaven to celebrate the Passover (see 5:7–8). Those who approach the eucharist should do so with self-examination and self-discipline in anticipation of Christ's return, lest they be guilty of sin not only against their brethren but specifically against Christ's own body and blood. The sign gives what it is and commemorates: an "ongoing redemptive participation in Christ's death."[23] Paul's warning and call to personal discipline then grounds his answer to the Corinthians' corporate disunity: celebrate this meal for what it is, a participation in Christ's body that unites believers as one body, so wait for one another and partake together and sate your hunger at home (11:33–34).

Paul's closing words on the topic indicate that he had more to say on the matter, but he preferred to say it in person (11:34). We would love to know what it was. But what he has said in these passages is significant and, indeed, beautifully sets the eucharist at the center of the marks of the church that we

---

22 As in 10:16–18, Paul's argument makes the identification of the bread and wine as Christ's body and blood inseparable from the unity of the church as the corporate "body of Christ." Though some argue that "body" language here *only* refers to ecclesial unity (as in 12:12–26), Paul never speaks of the church as Christ's "blood." That misuse of the eucharist is a sin not merely against unity but against Christ's "body and blood," and that Paul derives this directly from the words of institution ("this is my . . ."), indicates that he believes the elements share in and communicate this reality (see Lakey 2019, 145).

23 Lakey 2019, 143.

see in 1 Corinthians. The eucharist is a part of the church's catholicity under the apostles: Paul handed down to the Corinthians the eucharistic tradition that he received "from the Lord" (11:23) and that, as we saw, he shares with Christian tradition elsewhere. This meal likewise is part of and indeed maintains the church's unity as a participation in Christ. And we see the holiness that it calls for, both personal and corporate.

The Resurrection of the Dead

In the lengthy chapter 15, Paul proclaims and defends the promised resurrection to eternal, bodily life with God against those in Corinth who mock or reject this hope. Corinthian acceptance of the resurrection not only is important to Paul for doctrinal fidelity, but is a matter also of their *unity* in faith with all Christ's churches as well as their *holiness*, as Paul believes one's hope in the future resurrection affects one's present bodily conduct. At the letter's climax, then, Paul upholds—and somewhat clarifies—this hope to call the Corinthians to unity and steadfastness.

The Importance of the Resurrection

Resurrection from the dead was a controversial but important belief in the Judaism of Paul's day. Its earliest articulations in scripture come in prophetic literature before or during the exile (Isa 26:19; cf. Ezek 37:1–10), but it is especially in later periods that it flourished. After being exiled by Babylon and returning only to suffer under the thumbs of other empires, many Jews set their hope on God's restoration of his people, his reward for the martyrs, and his punishment for the wicked: God would raise the dead for judgment with the living, publicly vindicating the righteous and giving them eternal and glorified bodies (Dan 12:2; 2 Macc 7:7–38; 14:46). Innocent suffering and martyrdom will not go unrewarded, and the wicked will be called to account. God will restore his good creation, and death will be "swallowed" up forever (see Isa 25:6–12; 65:17–25). The dead therefore still had a future destiny and goal, such that piety demanded not merely burying them (Tob 1:17–18) but also offering prayer and sacrifice for them (2 Macc 12:39–45).

---

24 See Josephus's descriptions in *Jewish Antiquities* 18.16, *Jewish War* 2.164–65, and Jesus's refutation of the Sadducees in Mark 12:18–27 and parallels. According to early rabbis, those who deny the general resurrection will not enjoy a share in the world to come (Mishnah, tractate *Sanhedrin* 10.1).

Belief that God would raise the dead was not held universally among Jews; the Sadducees famously denied the resurrection (Acts 23:6–8).[24] However, the followers of Jesus—who was raised from the dead—saw this as fundamental to faith. The NT authors are in concert about the fact that belief in the resurrection—the resurrection of Jesus, and in him the resurrection of the faithful to glory—is a basic element of Christian doctrine (e.g., John 5:24–29; 20:19–29; Rom 10:9–10; 2 Pet 3:1–13). Nevertheless, this belief met opposition. The final judgment and resurrection were mocked by some, and even some Christian teachers spiritualized this bodily hope (2 Tim 2:16–18; 2 Pet 3:4).

In 1 Corinthians 15:1–34 Paul drives home the importance of the resurrection with two main arguments. First, Paul reminds them that the message that Christ died, was buried, and rose is a necessary part of the gospel and thus their salvation (15:1–11). Indeed, if Christ did not rise again, his saving work is incomplete and "you are still in your sins" (15:17). It is also a catholic and apostolic tenet, one proclaimed everywhere by every true servant of the church (15:11).

Second, Paul argues, there is no reason for hope if *we* are not going to be raised to new life with Christ. God's promise of future glory allows one to suffer, sacrifice, and labor steadfastly in the Lord, knowing there is hope on the other side of suffering (15:58; cf. Rom 5:2–5; 8:17–18; Gal 6:7–10). With this hope, all suffering in Christ and every act of love is a small investment in an "eternal weight of glory" (2 Cor 4:17). But without faith in the resurrection—Christ's and ours—hope is easily exchanged for cheap hedonism and self-seeking (1 Cor 15:30–34). Belief in the coming resurrection is essential not only for Christian doctrine but also for believers' lives of good works and holiness.

What Kind of Body?

Paul's insistence *that* there will be a resurrection is quite forceful. Indeed, we seem to have hit theological bedrock in Paul's thought: this must be believed (*de fide*). But Paul will also clarify how one should envision the resurrection. It is worth noting that in the frequent phrase "resurrection of/from the dead," the word translated "dead" is the word for "corpse" (νεκρός, *nekros*). Paul preached the resurrection of bodies. Some Corinthians may have mocked the resurrection because they imagined long-decayed corpses

---

25 Later, Gregory of Nyssa voiced and addressed many other objections in his dialogue *On the Soul and Resurrection.*

walking about in some kind of zombie paradise, raising questions about how the earth could hold them all again. They may also have imbibed philosophical ideas about bodies as the soul's unhappy prison (see above).[25] In any case, they balked. Paul mimes their objection: "What kind of body do they come with?" (15:35).

Paul rebukes the question brusquely and sketches a response (15:35–58). Two things can be the same thing but be different: all stars are of the same stuff (in the ancient conception), but are not all the same; the oak tree is contained in the acorn, but they differ in maturity and glory. So too the resurrected body will be a body, our own bodies, but different (15:35–44). All bodies, of the living and dead, will be "changed" (15:51). Paul describes them as "spiritual" ($\pi\nu\epsilon\upsilon\mu\alpha\tau\iota\kappa\acute{o}\varsigma$, *pneumatikos*) bodies (15:44–49). Scholars debate exactly what this means. It is unlikely that "spiritual" means immaterial. For many ancients, even "spirit" was material (air, when it blows, can knock down a tree), though a very different kind of material than "body."[26] So what are these "spiritual bodies"? Will they be *made* of "spirit" instead of flesh?[27] Or should we understand these as conventional bodies and interpret "spiritual" with a capital "S," meaning that the Holy Spirit will be their driving life force?[28]

Paul is adamant that what is corruptible, "flesh and blood," cannot inherit the kingdom of God (15:50). Further, Paul appears to say that resurrection bodies will differ in glory even from Adam's natural body (15:42–49). The discontinuity will be significant; these "spiritual bodies" do not appear merely to be undying versions of what humans now have. Yet Paul's hope is not for the casting off of the physical creation but its perfection, the "redemption of our bodies" from the curse of mortality and decay in which sin locked Adam's children (Rom 8:23; cf. 1 Cor 15:21–23). This redemption comes in being made like Christ, whose resurrected body is a body but different and more glorious than that of Adam (1 Cor 15:45–53; cf. Rom 6:3–11; Phil 3:21). The resurrection is neither a resuscitation of the same body nor the shunning

---

26 See D. Martin 1995, 1–15. We can see this belief in early theology: when Origen clarifies that the Godhead is immaterial, the statement "God is spirit" (John 4:24) was something he had to refute because it might imply that God was a corporeal being (*On First Principles* 1.1).

27 So Engberg-Pedersen 2010, 26–38.

28 So Wright 2003, 348–56.

29 See Augustine, *City of God* 20.16; 22.16, 21.

of all corporeality, but a "taking off" of all that is corruptible and a "putting on" of immortality (1 Cor 15:53–54; 2 Cor 5:2–4).[29]

What precisely a body with no possibility of corruption looks like remains difficult to imagine. In the words of 1 John 3:2, "What we will be has not yet been disclosed." But if Paul's words do not answer every speculation about the daily life of the resurrected, they do stress what the resurrection means. God has finally defeated sin and death (1 Cor 15:54–57). He has won the victory, and those who endure in faith will share that victory and reign under him in everlasting life (see Rom 5:17; 16:20). And every act of love and faith in this life, every suffering endured in the Lord, will not be in vain but will endure into the next age (1 Cor 15:58; cf. 3:11–14; 13:8–13).

FURTHER READING

Blue, Bradley B. 1993. "Food Offered to Idols and Jewish Food Laws." *DPL* 306–10.

Chow, John K. 1992. *Patronage and Power: A Study of Social Networks in Corinth.* JSNTSup 75. Sheffield: Sheffield Academic.

Collins, R. F. 1999. *First Corinthians.* SP 7. Collegeville, MN: Liturgical Press.

Engberg-Pedersen, Troels. 2010. *Cosmology and Self in the Apostle Paul: The Material Spirit.* Oxford: Oxford University Press.

Fee, Gordon D. 1996. *Paul, the Spirit, and the People of God.* Peabody, MA: Hendrickson.

Fitzmyer, Joseph A., SJ. 2000. *First Corinthians: A New Translation with Introduction and Commentary.* AB 32. New Haven, CT: Yale University Press.

Garland, David E. 2003. *1 Corinthians.* BECNT. Grand Rapids: Baker Academic.

Johnson, Luke Timothy. 2013. "The Body in Question: The Social Complexities of Resurrection in 1 Corinthians." In *Contested Issues in Christian Origins and the New Testament: Collected Essays,* 295–315. NovTSup 146. Leiden: Brill.

Lakey, Michael J. 2019. *The Ritual World of Paul the Apostle: Metaphysics, Community and Symbol in 1 Corinthians 10–11*. LNTS 602. London: Bloomsbury.

May, Alistair Scott. 2004. *"The Body for the Lord": Sex and Identity in 1 Corinthians 5–7*. JSNTSup 278. London: T&T Clark.

Mihaila, Corin. 2009. *The Paul–Apollos Relationship and Paul's Stance toward Greco-Roman Rhetoric: An Exegetical and Socio-historical Study of 1 Corinthians 1–4*. LNTS 402. London: T&T Clark.

Mitchell, Margaret M. 1991. *The Rhetoric of Reconciliation: An Exegetical Investigation of the Language and Composition of 1 Corinthians*. Louisville, KY: Westminster John Knox.

Stegman, Thomas D., SJ. 2017. "St. Paul on Holiness." *JJT* 24:60–73.

Theissen, Gerd. 1982. *The Social Setting of Pauline Christianity: Essays on Corinth*. Edited by J. H. Schütz. Minneapolis: Fortress.

Thiselton, Anthony C. 2000. *The First Epistle to the Corinthians: A Commentary on the Greek Text*. NIGTC. Grand Rapids: Eerdmans.

Ware, James. 2014. "Paul's Understanding of the Resurrection in 1 Corinthians 15:36–54." *JBL* 133 (4): 809–35.

Winter, Bruce W. 2001. *After Paul Left Corinth: The Influence of Secular Ethics and Social Change*. Grand Rapids: Eerdmans.

Wright, N. T. 2003. *The Resurrection of the Son of God*. Christian Origins and the Question of God 3. Minneapolis: Fortress.

CHAPTER EIGHT

2 Corinthians

Second Corinthians shows Paul's continued struggles with the Corinthians and a new threat to their unity by a group, ironically called "super-apostles" by Paul, whose impressive credentials tempt them to break from the apparently inglorious Paul. Paul defends the Christlike character of his suffering as an apostle and calls the Corinthians to renew their fidelity to him and to Christ by contributing to the collection for Jerusalem. Though in one way much of 2 Corinthians treats questions of Paul's apostleship, its focus remains throughout on the God whose grace exhibits his saving power through weakness.

BACKGROUND
After 1 Corinthians

More than other letters, 1 and 2 Corinthians give us a window into Paul's relations and regular correspondence with a church over a substantial period of time. After founding the congregation (ca. 50 CE), Paul wrote a letter calling them to abstain from sexual immorality (1 Cor 5:9–10). Problems with immorality continued, and Corinth's culture of competition also occasioned factionalism in the church, with groups finding ways to claim higher status because of the ministers they followed or their own charismatic gifts. Paul responded to these with the letter we call 1 Corinthians in about 53/54 CE (see chapter 7).

That letter was not unsuccessful, but in 2 Corinthians we see that Paul continued to struggle with the Corinthians. Strained relations with many Corinthians became exacerbated by the arrival of an interloping group that Paul calls false apostles or, ironically, "super-apostles" (11:13–15). These troubles impeded the Corinthians' preparation of the collection for Jerusalem previously commanded in 1 Corinthians 16:1–8. And it threatened the church's relationship with Paul's apostolate and, Paul feared, with Christ himself (2 Cor 11:2–4).

In 2 Corinthians Paul points to several events that transpired after he wrote 1 Corinthians, which are important for understanding this letter's context and the intent of Paul's words. As Paul tries to persuade them to be fully reconciled to his apostolate and to complete the collection, he argues from *pathos*, emotionally retelling the best and worst moments of their recent history.[1] He retells these events with a theological lens, emphasizing God's work of consolation and clarifying that he—even in his less popular moments—has been at work to build them up in faith (demonstrating his character or *ethos*). Such retellings make the argument beautiful and gripping, but they can make determining a precise chronology of these events challenging. Indeed, the emotional changes in tone and chronological difficulties lead many to see the letter as a composite of what were originally two (or more) letters. Below we will sketch the main events and then return to the letter's composition and purpose.

A Painful Visit and a Tearful Letter

In 1:12–2:13 Paul invites the Corinthians to recognize that his conduct toward them has always been upright and honest. Paul has been accused of inconsistency and deceptive, perhaps selfish, behavior because he changed his travel plans after a painful visit. He explains that he had intended to visit them and then pass on to Macedonia (1:15), but he chose not to return then to avoid exacerbating the situation (1:23–2:1). Instead, he wrote a letter "through many tears" (2:2–4).[2]

What was the situation? Paul's comments in 2:1–13 and 7:5–16 center around an individual who had "done wrong" and "caused grief." Paul clarifies that the Tearful Letter was written out of his apostolic vocation to test the Corinthians' obedience and give them an opportunity to repent in the case of this man (see 2:5, 9; 7:12). We later learn, likewise, that at this painful visit there were unresolved problems with sexual impurity, mentioning particular persons who "had sinned before" and not repented (12:21).

---

1 See Thompson 2001.

2 Some suggest that the Tearful Letter is in fact 1 Corinthians (see Campbell 2014, 61–98), but its tone and occasion do not match Paul's description of the Tearful Letter very well.

Some suggest the "painful visit" was an emergency visit: Paul had heard about the offender (perhaps from Timothy, whose coming was promised in 1 Cor 4:17; 16:10) and then made an emergency visit to deal with the problem. However, it is easier to imagine the visit being "painful" not because it was an emergency response to a problem but because something happened *during* the visit to make it painful.

Paul's second visit to Corinth presumably fulfilled his promise to visit in 1 Corinthians 16:1–8: to prepare and hopefully dispatch the collection for the poor saints in Jerusalem. Naturally the apostle would have preached as well. In fact, he states that on this second visit he rebuked some who had not fully repented of their immorality (2 Cor 12:21; 13:2).[3] One can imagine many scenarios in which a Corinthian might oppose Paul during such a visit. Perhaps the offender was a target of Paul's preaching, who then lashed out at Paul and enticed others to withhold contributions to the collection, perhaps accusing Paul of dishonesty. Paul's protestations that he himself was not truly the one injured at this visit suggest that attacks against his reputation contributed to the "pain" of this visit, and this befits Paul's defensiveness about his financial honesty (8:20–21; 12:16–18). On the other hand, the wrongdoer singled out here seems singular among those who had "sinned before" and not repented of sexual immorality, and traditionally this offender has been identified with the incestuous man of 1 Corinthians 5:1–5. This can make sense of Paul's emphasis that the church responded to his Tearful Letter with much "punishment" (2 Cor 7:11) and Paul's call for them now to forgive the man as he himself has (2:6–11): Paul had called them to excommunicate the incestuous man in 1 Corinthians 5:1–5, but they had not yet done so. During his visit he rebuked the man among others, the man lashed out and incited others against Paul, and after the Tearful Letter the "majority" responded by punishing the man. Hence Paul characterizes the Tearful Letter as successful: they demonstrated their obedience in this act (2 Cor 2:9; 7:8–13, 16), and Paul can affirm their show of obedience and counsel reconciliation now that the man has been sufficiently punished.[4]

---

3 Carlson 2016 notes that πάλιν (*palin*, "again") in 2:1 does not imply that grief was the *purpose* of the painful visit, though he does not see how the visit rebuking immorality and this painful visit can be identical.

4 Tertullian, after leaving the Catholic faith for the rigorous Montanist sect, argued that this could not be the incestuous man precisely because such a sin cannot be forgiven (*On Modesty* 13–15). Several modern scholars also argue against the traditional identification (though not

Whatever precisely the offense was, it caused Paul's collection to be interrupted and called for a response. When Paul left, though he promised to return and deal harshly with the Corinthians if they did not repent (13:2), he wrote the Tearful Letter instead. His change of travel plans would bring another charge of inconsistency and insincerity against Paul (1:15–16), but this would be only one of many charges against which Paul would have to respond.[5]

Titus's News and His Collection Visits

Paul's companion Titus is named nine times in 2 Corinthians, more than in all the rest of the NT (Gal 2:1–3; 2 Tim 4:10; Titus 1:4). Titus is involved in the delivery of the Tearful Letter and the current preparation of the collection, as well as probably a prior collection visit.

First, Titus brought Paul news of the Corinthians' reception of the Tearful Letter. Indeed, Titus was probably also the emissary who delivered it to Corinth. In 2:12–13, Paul says that after he had sent the Tearful Letter, he was ill at ease until he found Titus in Macedonia, anxious to know the Corinthians' response. When Paul mentions this event again in 7:5–16, we learn Titus's report of the letter's success: the Corinthians (or at least a "majority" of them) had repented and affirmed their allegiance to Paul, and Paul notes their rebuke of the offender as a clear sign of this (2:6; 7:5–13).

Second, we hear of Paul sending Titus to gather the collection for Jerusalem. They had been ready to begin this ministry "a year ago" but did not complete it (8:10; 9:2). After their favorable response to the Tearful Letter, Titus eagerly accepted Paul's assignment to return and gather the collection (7:13–15; 8:16–17). He was dispatched along with other "brothers" strategically chosen for their reputation, lest the Corinthians suspect any mismanagement of funds (8:6, 18–23).

Paul's description of Titus's collection visit in chapters 8–9 sounds like it is happening *now*, as Paul writes: they are to comply with Titus in prepara-

---

for the same reasons as Tertullian), seeing this offender as opposing Paul for other reasons or as perhaps under the influence of the super-apostles. However, Paul held out hope for the man's eventual salvation even when commanding the Corinthians to excommunicate him (1 Cor 5:5–13), and those rebuked at the painful visit were to be corrected by the congregation for continued sexual immorality (2 Cor 12:21; 13:2). Thus, the traditional identification fits the data in both letters plausibly.

5 Because the unfulfilled travel plans in 1:15–16 (Corinth, then Macedonia, then Judea) differ from the promised visit in 1 Cor 16:1–8 (Macedonia, then Corinth, then Judea), some have suggested that 1 Cor 16:1–8 actually reflects the revised itinerary that frustrated the Corinthians. But see Thrall 1994, 69–74.

tion for Paul's impending third visit (see 9:1–5). However, 12:16–18 clearly speaks of Titus's collection visit with "the brother" in the past ("Did Titus take advantage of you?"). For some, this is a sign that chapters 10–13 were written later than chapters 8–9 (see below). Many others posit, however, that this is simply a reference to an *earlier* visit by Titus. Titus himself was there for a previous collection visit, that time "a year ago" (8:10) when the Corinthians were initially ready to begin the collection. So two collection visits by Titus are mentioned in this letter: one on which Paul sends him *now* as Paul composes 2 Corinthians and prepares for his third and final visit, and one a year prior at which Titus "began" the collection in Corinth (8:6), probably after the painful visit. Paul rebuked many at the painful visit, with a threat that they must rebuke the immoral and comply with the collection before his return, and he sent Titus to exhort them to do so and report back to Paul.

The "Super-Apostles"

However, before Paul arrives for his third visit, the Corinthians' compliance is interrupted by a new problem: the arrival of the "super-apostles." In chapters 10–13, Paul mounts a passionate defense against an opposing group of missionaries who arrived and vied for the Corinthians' allegiance. They boast of their Jewish ancestry and, as evidence of their divine authority, impress the Corinthians with claims of superior spiritual powers and experiences (see 11:12, 21, 23; 12:1–13). They—and probably the Corinthians who favor them—claim that Paul conducts his ministry in a weaker and more "fleshly" way (10:2–3). Despite his strong letters, Paul is unimpressive as a person or preacher, hardly evidence of the great power of Christ that he claims to possess (11:6; 13:3). Paul probably correctly captures how these people presented themselves when he mockingly calls them "super-apostles" (11:5; 12:11).

Paul characterizes them as preaching a "different" gospel (11:4) and claiming to be ministers of Christ (10:7). This tells us they were Christian, but we know almost nothing about their actual doctrine. Some view them as the same group that troubled Paul's churches in Galatia by insisting that gentiles be circumcised (Gal 1:6–9; cf. Phil 3:2–7). Yet Paul's standard polemic against circumcision and works of the law is not present here or, at least, is surprisingly understated. Rather, Paul's response seems to depict them as self-aggrandizing pneumatics, touting their own spiritual experiences as proof of God's special approval.[6] In either case, Paul's arguments focus not

---

6 See the careful study of Sumney 1990.

on their doctrine but on their self-promoting manner of ministry and the claims by which they sway the Corinthians away from Paul.

One can imagine the fuel their arrival might throw on the still-glowing embers of Paul's recent conflicts with Corinth. Many were still on Paul's side after the painful visit, but those who had been targets of his rebukes may quickly have taken to these newcomers. Any pressure or intimidation they had felt from Paul's rebukes would have been relieved, and their friends within the church may have found an attractive way to keep their friends by changing apostolic loyalties. Added to this, already in 1 Corinthians we saw that some Corinthians were unhappy with Paul's refusal to accept personal payment for his preaching (1 Cor 9:1–18), and the super-apostles' accusations—and probably their willingness to accept pay—seem to have aggravated suspicions that Paul must be skimming off the collection (see 2 Cor 7:2; 8:20; 11:7–11; 12:13–18). We also saw in 1 Corinthians a competitive spirit that prized the most eloquent preachers and the most outwardly impressive miracles and spiritual gifts (see 1 Cor 1:10–4:21; 12:1–14:40), and any who had not yet fully imbibed Paul's theological response to these would have been easily enticed by the "super-apostles."

Aftermath and Date

Paul writes 2 Corinthians to defend his apparently inglorious apostolate and promises to come "a third time" (13:1), calling the Corinthians to be reconciled to him and to complete the collection before his arrival. We are not told exactly how it happened, but we learn in Romans 15:25–27 that Paul did arrive in Corinth and that the Corinthians received Paul and successfully completed the collection. It may be that these preachers were a fly-by-night sensation, stirring things up (and getting paid?) for several weeks and then departing of their own accord. Or perhaps the Corinthians were convinced to reject the super-apostles by the strength of Paul's letter or Titus's final visit.

Since Paul wrote Romans from Corinth after completing the collection, we can use Romans to reason back to the date of 2 Corinthians. Paul wrote Romans in about 57 CE after arriving in Corinth, and after staying there long enough to gather the collection and write that lengthy letter. And 2 Corinthians was written not long before he arrived in Corinth. Paul is writing from Macedonia when 2 Corinthians is dispatched and appears to be planning to come to Corinth with some urgency (9:1–5; cf. 2:13; 7:5; 8:1). This puts some time between the completion of 2 Corinthians and Romans, but not too much time. Likewise, Titus's prior collection visit "a year ago," after the painful visit, means that well over a year transpired between when Paul wrote 1 Corinthians in 53/54 and the completion of 2 Corinthians. A fair estimate, then, is that 2 Corinthians was completed in Macedonia in 55/56 CE, probably closer to 56. But is it possible some of it was written earlier?

The Letter's Unity and Purpose

One of the most intriguing questions for students of 2 Corinthians is that of its unity. A large contingent of scholars believes 2 Corinthians is in fact a compilation of at least two originally separate letters that Paul wrote the Corinthians, later put together in their canonical form by the Corinthians themselves or by those who arranged Paul's letter collection. Compilation theories focus especially on changes in tone and apparent changes in situation that suggest the chapters were not originally dispatched together:

(a) The tone of chapters 10–13 is markedly combative and emotional, an abrupt change from that of the preceding chapters. It reads as though the whole congregation is departing from Paul, but in chapters 1–9 Paul speaks of his joy at the Corinthians' repentance in the matter of the Tearful Letter (7:5–16). Likewise, chapters 10–13 speak in the singular "I," defending Paul particularly, while chapters 1–9 are more general and more often speak in the "we" of Paul's whole team. Perhaps these were originally separate letters.

(b) Chapters 8–9 are both about the collection, but chapter 8 includes several direct references to the Corinthians and Titus, whereas chapter 9 is more general. And one can be read without the other. Perhaps chapter 9, maybe also chapter 8, was originally an independent letter.

(c) Paul breaks off discussing his travels and search for Titus in 2:13 but resumes it in 7:5–16. Perhaps these were originally one letter together, but a later editor inserted another Pauline letter defending his apostolate (beginning 2:14) in between.

(d) The command to separate from evil in 6:14–7:1 sits oddly between two softer appeals asking the Corinthians to be open to Paul (6:11–13; 7:2–4). Perhaps it was originally part of Paul's lost first letter calling the Corinthians to avoid immorality (see 1 Cor 5:9–10) or is a non-Pauline text added by a later editor.

Following some or all these considerations, scholars divide the letter variously, and different theories naturally alter one's chronology of the events. For instance, one commentary divides 2 Corinthians into five original letters in this sequence: Paul wrote a first apology for his apostolate (mostly preserved in 2:14–6:13; 7:2–4); then he sent a second, harsher defense (preserved in 10:1–13:10); after Titus's visit and happy report, Paul and Timothy wrote 1:1–2:13; 7:5–16; 13:11–13 as a letter of reconciliation; then Paul sent Titus again with a general letter for the whole region of Achaia about the collection (chap. 9) and one especially to Corinth (chap. 8) that included their history with Paul.[7]

The majority of scholars, however, see at most one or two original letters present in our 2 Corinthians, with any division between chapters 1–9 and 10–13. All acknowledge 10–13 as an obvious unity, and there is insufficient reason to divide up chapters 1–9. Paul's mention of his anguish when he could not find Titus (2:13) is not a mere travelogue interrupted until 7:5–16. If Titus was the emissary the Corinthians dealt with when receiving the Tearful Letter, the audience would hear Paul's anxiety about finding Titus as his anxiety about their loyalty to his ministry, which is precisely what he reflects on in the intervening chapters before recalling Titus's good news and calling them to renew their commitment to the collection. Chapters 1–7 thus fit together as a whole. The discussion of the collection in chapter 8 presupposes this reflection on Titus's return, so there is no need to separate chapter 8 from what precedes. Chapter 9 is more general, but it builds on Paul's boast in the preceding chapters that the Corinthians would comply (cf. 7:14; 8:24; 9:1–3) and adds further encouragement to give generously.[8]

The relationship between chapters 1–9 and 10–13, however, is more difficult. The change in tone is undeniable, and it is possible to read chapters 1–9 independently without 10–13. Indeed, more than the change in tone, these two bodies of text seem to reflect different stages in the events sketched above. On one hand, both speak of Paul's painful, second visit to Corinth and promise a third visit soon (2:1; 9:3–4; 13:1–2). On the other, there is no mention of the Tearful Letter or of Titus's second collection visit (only the

---

7 Betz 1985, 129–44. By contrast, Thrall, who sees three original letters in our 2 Corinthians, concludes that they have been arranged in correct chronological order (1994, 77).

8 See Lambrecht 1998.

first) in chapters 10–13. Likewise, while chapters 1–9 certainly emphasize the glory of Christ in the weakness of his apostles, Paul's arguments seem less forceful, as if only aiming to heal some lingering wounds that remain after a conflict, while the passion and threats of chapters 10–13 sound like they are written in the thick of that conflict.

For those who see no reason to divide up chapters 1–9, there are three major possibilities: (1) we have two separate letters, chapters 1–9 written before 10–13; (2) we have two separate letters, chapters 10–13 written before 1–9; (3) we have one letter, with the change in tone either owed to Paul's rhetorical strategy or because Paul received new information while writing the letter.

Chapters 1–9 before Chapters 10–13: Separate but Chronological

This hypothesis reads the chronology of events largely as we have above, except that it delays the arrival of the super-apostles to after Titus has been sent with the brothers for Paul's final collection visit.[9] As above, after the painful visit, Paul wrote the Tearful Letter and sent it with Titus. Titus returned with good news of the church's warm response, and then Paul sent him back to prepare the collection with some other brothers and dispatched chapters 1–9 as a letter of exhortation, with hints of self-defense and reconciliation, calling them to prepare the collection before his third visit. However, when Titus arrived or during his time there, the super-apostles came. They accused Titus of mismanaging funds (12:16–18) and drew the Corinthians, who had only recently made a show of obedience, away from Paul. Titus returned and reported to Paul, and Paul wrote chapters 10–13 to defend himself and attack their attachment to these "ministers of Satan" (11:13–15). He still promises the same third arrival, now with the threat of discipline by the power of Christ (13:1–10).

On this view, Paul's reception upon arriving was anything but certain, but the completion of the collection in Romans indicates that things were straightened out after this somewhat-frantic near miss in Paul's relations with Corinth. Variations of this view have been defended by many. Yet others wonder why there are apparent reflections of the conflict with the super-apostles already in chapters 1–9—such as Paul's defense of his ministry or financial practices against greedy preachers who boastfully commend them-

---

9 For two defenses of this view, see Oropeza 2016, 2–15; Furnish 1984, 35–55.

selves (e.g., 1:12; 2:17–3:1; 5:12–13; 8:20–21)—or how a church that has just reconciled with Paul and heard his defense of his apparently "weak" ministry in chapters 1–9 would turn from him so quickly. Defenders can respond, however, that the super-apostles are not the only ministers Paul finds overly ambitious (see Phil 1:14–18), and Paul's apostolate was often challenged in Corinth and elsewhere. Likewise, the Corinthians have proved fickle enough for this sequence of events to be plausible.

Chapters 10–13 as the Tearful Letter

An attractive alternative posits that chapters 10–13 are in fact the Tearful Letter.[10] Though some emphasize these chapters' biting invective against the super-apostles, Paul's pleas to the Corinthians are clearly filled with emotion and could certainly have been written "through many tears" (see 11:1–11, 20–21; 12:14–20; 13:9–10). This view also follows the same basic sequence of events sketched above, except that it puts the arrival of the super-apostles *before* the Tearful Letter and Titus's report. Paul left the painful visit with a promise that he would discipline the immoral and seditious if the rest of the church did not do so before he returned (12:21; 13:2). He sent Titus on his first collection visit after the painful visit, but while Titus was there (or just before he arrived) the super-apostles came on the scene and exacerbated the Corinthians' strained relationship with Paul. Titus returned and Paul wrote the Tearful Letter (chaps. 10–13), especially defending his ministry but also keeping an eye to the still-promised third visit, calling them to repent now before he arrives. Titus delivered the letter and ministered to them, and the majority of the church heeded the letter, turning from the super-apostles and rebuking especially the immoral offender as a sign of their obedience. Titus reports the good news, and Paul writes chapters 1–9 in a more conciliatory tone to prepare for his arrival. Here Paul emphasizes the love out of which he wrote that harsh missive, encourages forgiveness of the punished offender, and offers theological reflection on Christ's work of reconciliation and consolation through his suffering apostles as he calls them to give generously to the collection.

A strength of this view is the data it accounts for and the sense it makes of the sequence of events. The primary issues are resolved before Paul arrives, and the lighter references to the challenge to Paul's apostolate by the super-

---

10 For two defenses of this view, see F. Watson 1984; Welborn 1995.

apostles in chapters 1–9 can be read as a past-tense reflection rather than as a polemic against a present threat. It can account for the changed travel plans: Paul promised to return when he left the painful visit (13:2), wrote the letter instead promising a potentially harsh third visit, but in hope and confidence (as he later characterizes his feelings) he waited until he heard Titus's report (see 1:23–2:3). The primary objection against this view is that the description of the Tearful Letter in chapters 2 and 7 seems to focus on the offender, while chapters 10–13 focus on the super-apostles. However, defenders can respond that Paul does not claim that the offender was the *only* thing addressed by that letter. Likewise, chapters 10–13 do not focus solely on the super-apostles but also warn the Corinthians that disobedience and still-unrepented immorality must be corrected before Paul arrives (10:6; 12:21–13:3). He discusses the offender because they responded to the Tearful Letter by punishing him, which encouraged Paul as far as their obedience goes (8:8–13), but this must be revisited for the sake of the now-penitent offender and to bar Satan's divisive wiles from gaining a foothold in the church (2:6–11).

Chapters 1–13 Dispatched as a Unity

Many scholars, however, argue that Paul dispatched the whole letter as we have it. Indeed, the fact that there is no known ancient evidence of this letter's parts circulating or being read separately suggests that objections to its unity are not insurmountable. Defenses of the letter's unity fall broadly into two different hypotheses, each of which has a different chronology and a different way of reading the intent of chapters 1–9.

One defense of unity maintains that the letter was dispatched as a literary whole, but not *composed* as a rhetorical whole. This view accepts that chapters 10–13 reflect a different situation than 1–9. However, rather than affirming that these were originally dispatched as separate letters, this explanation holds that the situation changed in the course of Paul's writing. The chronological sequence here is essentially the same as that of the first compilation theory above, except that Paul hears of the super-apostles *before* he has dispatched chapters 1–9. The Tearful Letter addressed only the matter of the "offender," Titus brought back good news of the church's repentance and goodwill, and then Paul wrote chapters 1–9 to reflect on these events and exhort them to prepare the collection. But before Paul dispatched chapters 1–9, word came back to Paul that the super-apostles had arrived and swayed the church against Paul. Rather than rewrite his whole missive, Paul simply added chapters 10–13 to address this new situation and dispatched the letter as a unity.

Alternatively, others do not see chapters 10–13 as reflecting a different situation than 1–9. The letter's beginning indicates that the majority, but not necessarily all, had repented after the Tearful Letter (2:6), and there Paul still exhorts them to be reconciled to God and not receive God's grace in vain (5:20; 6:1). If chapters 10–13 address more jarringly the problem of the super-apostles, those arguments are already anticipated subtly in chapters 1–9, so there is no need to posit that the lighter tone of chapters 1–9 indicates that the conflict had already been resolved or was not yet known. Rather, the arrangement of the letter is a display of Paul's rhetorical prowess at work to win back the wayward Corinthians.[11] Titus has returned with good news about their treatment of the offender after the Tearful Letter, but Paul has also received less happy news about the arrival of the super-apostles. In addressing this situation, then, Paul recounts the aftermath of the painful visit and Titus's good report in order to emphasize his consistency and love toward the Corinthians so that they will realize, even before reading the more jarring chapters 10–13, the error of breaking from Paul or accusing him of impropriety (12:14–18). Likewise, in the same way that his praise of their past eagerness to begin the collection is used to obligate them to complete it now (8:8, 24; 9:1–5), recounting these past events also presents a positive example of themselves to which they should aspire. When Paul praises them for their goodwill and obedience in the matter of the offender in chapters 2 and 7, he knows full well of the super-apostles' threat, but he draws them into the good relationship that he wants them to reengage. These earlier chapters, in which Paul clarifies (in an amiable tone) his suffering for them and the cruciform character of his ministry (chaps. 3–5), likewise prepare for his turn to address the problem of the vain super-apostles in chapters 10–13, where he calls them to return to the obedience that he has previously praised in them (2:9; 7:12–15; 8:8; 10:5–6; 13:5). Paul, not unique among other orators, builds to the greatest *pathos* and direct demands at the end of his letter in order to persuade them in every way to remain in Christ under his own apostolate.

11 A major study of this type is Vegge 2008. For an accessible, rhetorically sensitive commentary, see Stegman 2009.

Reading Chapters 1–13

The arguments for and against each of these views can become quite complex. The question is which view makes the best sense of the text and Paul's apostolic strategies and aims. Despite the historical complexity of the question, it should not be passed over. The sequence of events differs on each view above (even among those who take the letter as a unity), and one's view of that sequence affects what one thinks the text was meant to *do* to its audience, which is part of the meaning of the text. At the same time, however, how Paul meant his arguments to affect the Corinthians is not the whole of the text's meaning, and its substantial theological points about charity (in the collection) and about the character of Christian ministry remain in any case. This means that edifying and accurate theological reading can be done even if certain aspects of the context are uncertain. Whether Paul's defense of Christ's power through apostolic weakness in chapters 3–5 was written before or after the "super-apostles" came on the scene, we still learn his point about the cruciform nature of the church and the mediatory role of its ministers.

The outline below attempts to allow for one- and two-letter theories (with a break at 10:1). However, readers are reminded that each theory may summarize a turn of phrase or the point of an argument differently according to its own understanding of the situation.

OVERVIEW

I. **Letter Opening** (1:1–11)

A. Paul and Timothy to the Corinthians (1:1–2)

B. Blessed be God, who comforts us ministers in our affliction for the church, so that our comfort overflows to you, if you share in our sufferings (1:3–7).

   1. We suffered greatly in Asia, but the Lord delivered us, to his glory (1:8–10).

   2. And we hope God will deliver us in the future through your prayers (1:10–11).

II. **Receive Us as Your Servants for Christ's Sake** (1:12–7:16)

A. Our boast is that we have been sincere toward you. You recognize this, and I hope you will recognize it fully (1:12–14).

B. Yes, I had planned to visit you, but my absence is not because I was dishonest (1:15–22).

    1. It was to spare you, out of the joy and love we should share in Christ, that I did not come. I wrote you instead with great sorrow, to avoid causing grief (1:23–2:4).

        a. Your punishment of the offender is sufficient. Forgive him now, as I do (2:5–11).

        b. Myself, I went to Troas, but found little rest until I heard from Titus (2:12–13).

C. But in all things, God reveals his glory through us, even if many will not see it. His grace empowers us to behave and speak sincerely for Christ's sake (2:14–17).

    1. We do not say all this to commend ourselves again. Unlike others, we have no need to. You are our commendation from God: through us you received the Spirit in God's new covenant (3:1–6).

        a. The glory of the new covenant surpasses the old, as the ministry we have received surpasses even Moses's. For through our apostolate God grants life, righteousness, and the Holy Spirit (3:7–11).

        b. And this glory is revealed—unlike the veil that covered Moses's shining face. Through Christ and the Spirit, we behold God's glory and are transformed more and more into God's likeness (3:12–18).

        c. Therefore, we do not lose heart as ministers of Christ for your sake (4:1–6).

    2. Weak as we are, God's glory is revealed in our weakness, and Christ's life-giving power is at work for you even in our daily sufferings (4:7–15).

        a. So we do not lose heart, for our hope is in the unseen, the eternal glory promised after these present afflictions (4:16–18).

        b. Remembering God's promise and the goal of eternal life, we make every effort to please God and so be rewarded at the judgment (5:1–10).

3. With this knowledge, we call others to fear God. I hope that you can recognize this and boast in our sincerity and service (5:11–12).

   a. All we do is for you, because Christ's love compels us (5:13–15).

   b. So we strive to serve Christ and to know him truly, for all things flow from him. His death reconciles us all to God, and he has made us ambassadors of his reconciliation (5:16–19).

D. Therefore, as ambassadors through whom God speaks, we beg you to be reconciled to God; do not receive his grace in vain (5:20–6:2).

   1. We endure all to commend ourselves as God's ministers for your sake (6:3–10).

   2. We opened our mouths and our hearts to you. Be open to us (6:11–13).

   3. Do not stray from God and the fellowship of the church. God has promised us all adoption and calls us to holiness and the fear of God (6:14–7:1).

   4 Receive us in your hearts. You are in our hearts, and I abound with joy in our affliction for you (7:2–4).

   a. When we came to Macedonia, we suffered until we found Titus, who comforted us with news that our letter led you to repentance (7:5–11).

   b. You responded as I hoped, and your response brought joy to Titus as well. So I do not regret being bold toward you. I have complete confidence in you (7:8–16).

III. **Prepare for the Collection (8:1–9:15)**

A. We want you to know that the Macedonians, afflicted and in great poverty, begged for the gift of being able to give to the collection. We have asked Titus to invite you again to contribute (8:1–6).

   1. We hope that you will. I say this not as a command but to prove your love in Christ, whose poverty has made us rich in grace (8:7–9).

   2. You had begun to do this a year ago; complete it for the sake of equity and fellowship (8:10–15).

3. Titus is eager to give you this opportunity. We are sending him with highly approved companions (lest any should suspect mismanagement), that your contribution might demonstrate your love before all (8:16–24).

B. I send these brothers to prepare you, so that when I come to collect, you and I will not be shamed in front of the Macedonians, to whom I boasted of your readiness last year (9:1–5).

1. Remember: we reap what we sow, and that includes financial charity. Give joyfully, and know that God remembers and rewards such acts of righteousness (9:6–11).

2. Such giving is itself a thank-offering to God. It is pleasing to God and endears you to the poor saints, who in turn will pray for you. Such is God's wonderful grace in the church (9:12–15).

IV. **Call to Fellowship and Obedience (10:1–13:10)**

A. Now I, Paul myself, exhort you. I do hope that when I come I will not have to be bold against those who oppose us. We are Christ's apostles fighting a spiritual battle for your obedience, and we are ready to punish any disobedience by God's power and the authority Christ gave me (10:1–11).

1. These others who commend themselves boastfully are without understanding. We boast in God and keep within the bounds God appointed for our ministry, which includes you (10:12–18).

2. I betrothed you to Christ as a pure virgin and now see you going astray to defile yourself. I am jealous for you for Christ's sake. Put up with a little foolishness from me; you put up enough with others who draw you away with a false gospel (11:1–4).

a. I hardly think I am inferior to these "super-apostles." You know my character—unless you think I wronged you by refusing payment and trying not to burden you (11:5–11).

b. These false apostles are workers of Satan, masquerading as servants of Christ, and they will be judged (11:12–15).

B. Boasting would be foolish, but you put up with such foolishness from others who abuse and deceive you in their so-called strength (11:16–21a).

1. I can boast as they do. I too am an Israelite. If they are apostles, I am more of an apostle! For I have suffered more greatly in service to Christ's church (11:21b-29). If I must boast, I will boast of my weakness for Christ's sake (11:30–33).

2. I could boast in revelations from the Lord—I have been mysteriously caught up into paradise. But when Satan sent me a recurring torment, God refused to take it away. For he said, "My power is made perfect in weakness." So I am content with being a suffering apostle for Christ's sake (12:1–10).

3. I'm boasting foolishly, but you brought me to it. I am your apostle, and through me the signs and wonders of Christ were performed among you. You should commend me, not force me to commend myself (12:11–13)!

C. I am ready now to come to you a third time, not because I want your money—neither I nor Titus has taken advantage of you— but because I want you (12:14–18).

1. I am not trying to be defensive, but to build you up in truth. I fear that when I arrive I will be shamed by your divisions and will have to punish those who sinned beforehand and have not repented, as I warned you in my previous visit. If I do have to punish, it will be by the power of Christ, since you want proof that Christ is in me (12:19–13:4).

2. Test yourselves and prove you are still in the faith. We pray you will pass the test and do no evil, even if it means we will not display our strength in disciplining you. We rejoice in our weakness; we pray for your restoration (13:5–10).

V. Letter Closing (13:11–13)

A. Finally, rejoice, restore, and encourage each other in peace and unity, and God will be with you (13:11–12a).

B. Receive and pass on our greetings (13:12b).[12]

C. Grace be with you (13:13).

12 Some English versions (e.g., KJV, RSV, ESV) number "all the saints greet you" as 13:13 and the closing greeting as 13:14.

KEY FEATURES

Though sometimes overlooked amid debates about its unity, theological riches fill 2 Corinthians. The letter includes important statements about the final judgment and resurrection (5:1–10). Satan is mentioned here more than in any other Pauline letter, setting the Corinthians' struggles against the backdrop of the spiritual warfare (2:11; 4:4; 6:7, 15; 10:3–6; 11:2–3, 13–15; 12:7–10). Here we discuss two topics that relate to the main argument of the letter as well as to broader issues in Pauline theology.

Christ's Glory in Broken Vessels

In view of past and present controversy, Paul defends his apostolic charism and the legitimacy of his apparently inglorious mode of ministry. His arguments show a rich theology of ministerial suffering and the presence of Christ mediated by the church. Two substantial proofs of Paul's apostolate recur: the Spirit's work through Paul and his team to convert the Corinthians in the first place and Paul's ongoing Christlike suffering.

Paul hopes that the Corinthians will see more fully his sincerity and his use of Christ's authority for their good (1:12–14). Others (like the super-apostles) boast of their spiritual power and experiences. Paul can boast of the same, yet his use of the Spirit's power has been not for his own benefit but for the church's (5:13; 12:1–10). He performed the "signs of an apostle" with "wonders and mighty deeds," but all for the sake of their conversion and salvation (12:12; cf. Rom 15:18–19; Gal 3:1–5). In 2 Corinthians 3:1–18 he reflects on this in more depth. Unlike others, Paul has no need to produce letters of recommendation to prove the character of his apostolate. The Corinthians' own faith should be proof enough. For if "none can say 'Jesus is Lord' except by the Holy Spirit" (1 Cor 12:3), then the Spirit of God was powerfully present through Paul and his team to convert the Corinthians. They themselves *are* his letter of recommendation—from God, not men—"inscribed not with ink but in the Spirit of the living God, not on stone tablets but on tablets that are fleshy hearts" (2 Cor 3:3).

These last phrases recall Jeremiah 31:31–34 and the promised "new covenant" in which God would forgive his wayward people and transform them by inscribing knowledge of God and his law on their very hearts. Ezekiel 36:25–27 similarly promised that the people would be sprinkled and cleansed, be given a "heart of flesh" rather than stone, and receive God's

Spirit so that they might walk in his ways. Paul presents himself and his team as "ministers of the new covenant" (2 Cor 3:6), administering the gifts of forgiveness and regeneration in Christ through the Spirit in baptism and evangelization (cf. Rom 6:3–11; 1 Cor 2:4; 6:11; Col 2:11–15). Christ died to reconcile all things to God and has given his apostles the "ministry" of this reconciliation (2 Cor 5:18–21).

Paul's view of ministry in the Spirit comes to the fore in a comparison with the ministry of Moses. The covenant of law given through Moses was broken and brought condemnation (cf. Rom 3:20; 4:15; Gal 3:10). It was inscribed on mere stone tablets and could not itself transform persons (cf. Rom 7:7–12; 8:3–4; Gal 3:21). Yet it is glorious and was given with visible glory. Moses, the minister of that covenant, shone so radiantly after meeting God that his face had to be covered (2 Cor 3:7; see Exod 34:1–8, 29–35). How much more glorious, then, is Paul's ministry in the new covenant? Paul's comparison does not denigrate the law or Moses as such. Rather, Paul reasons from lesser to greater, from glorious to super-glorious.[13] Christ's covenant, mediated through his apostles, gives the gift of the Spirit and effects righteousness (2 Cor 3:8–9; cf. 5:21).[14] Moreover, the glory of this covenant is purposed to endure, whereas the old was always, Paul believes, meant to find its fulfillment in the new (3:10–11, 13; cf. Rom 10:4). And the ministry of this covenant, by the Spirit given through the apostles, requires no veil between the people and the glory, for God's glory in Christ transforms them more and more into the image of God (2 Cor 3:12–18).

The glory of Paul's ministry is an objective one, given by Christ, with the power to make alive and conform sinners to the image of God. Yet this glory is not apparent to those whose minds are darkened by sin and the world's wisdom (2:14–16; 4:3–4). Seeing glory in Paul's suffering is clear only when one considers the crucified "Lord of glory" (1 Cor 2:8) who reveals himself in Paul (2 Cor 3:12–18; 1 Cor 1:18–31). Paul has been entrusted with his apostolate to give life to sinners by conforming them to Christ. But that

---

13 See Stockhausen 1989. Numerous studies debate the precise nature of Paul's reading of Exodus in this passage and its social background (e.g., Cover 2015; Nathan 2020).

14 Augustine (*The Spirit and the Letter* 4.6–8.13) insists correctly that Paul's letter-Spirit contrast (2 Cor 3:6) is not merely a hermeneutical note on reading the OT figurally (as in, e.g., Origen, *On First Principles* 1.1.2; 3.5.1; Augustine, *Confessions* 6.4.6). The contrast emphasizes the power and agency of the Holy Spirit (2 Cor 3:3, 6, 8, 17–18) to mediate God's forgiveness and transform the heart, without which the law's commands ultimately condemn transgressors.

means that the glory of his ministry must be *lived and effected* in sacrificial, cruciform suffering rather than boastful displays of power. In Christ, life comes through death, and manifest glory follows obvious lowliness (2 Cor 5:14–15; 8:9; 13:4). Serving this Lord, the lives of Christ's true apostles are a "theater" (θέατρον, *theatron*, 1 Cor 4:9) in which this saving script is replayed again and again for the good of Christ's church (cf. also Col 1:24). Paul's sufferings hardly indicate that Christ has not blessed his ministry—it is precisely *because* Christ is at work in him for others that he is constantly "given over to death" (2 Cor 4:11)! The apostles are fragile "clay pots" through whose cracks Christ's power not only shines but also gives life to others (4:7). "Death is at work in us, but life in you" (4:12). Paul catalogues his own sufferings for Christ and the church, both those imposed upon him such as beatings or imprisonments and those he takes up voluntarily such as fasting, refusing pay, and the hard and humble work of preaching the gospel to all (4:7–12; 6:1–10; 11:7, 23–29; 1 Cor 9:1–23). Like Christ, all that he does is for their good (2 Cor 4:5, 15). Even if many cannot see it now, this life of service and suffering is a pleasing offering to God (2:15), one that will end in immeasurable—and obvious—glory (4:16–18). Paul rejoices in this, and so should all whom he serves.

Paul, the Collection, and God's Commerce of Grace

Possessing this ministry of renewing hearts in the righteousness of Christ, Paul suffers and exhorts the church at large. Reflecting on the glory wrought through their sufferings, Paul says he and his mission team press on in hope, with one eye toward the final judgment (4:16–5:10). They long to be finally clothed with immortality at the resurrection, and so they set it as their constant goal "to be pleasing to God" (5:9). For all must appear before the divine judge and receive recompense for what they have done, "whether good or bad" (5:10).

And, Paul continues, because apostles "know the fear of the Lord" themselves, they zealously encourage all to press toward God's final reward (5:11). Christ has brought forgiveness and reconciliation for sinners, transforming and re-creating them in the Spirit, and has made the apostles ambassadors of this reconciliation (5:16–21). As Christ's ambassador, then, Paul exhorts the Corinthians not to "receive God's grace in vain" but to live in continued friendship with God (5:20; 6:1–2). This means that those renewed by God's righteousness must live in allegiance to God and not join themselves to iniquity (6:14). It also means that those who have received Christ's wondrous gift of salvation must live in a manner that befits it, by being givers themselves. For charitable giving is itself an act of "righteousness" (9:9) mirroring the transformative grace they have received (5:21).[15]

This theology, in which believers are to be conformed to the character of their redeemer, deeply informs Paul's discussion of the collection. The collection is an embodiment of the gospel, and in more than one way. On a broad scale, it demonstrates the unity of the universal church. Christ has torn down the division between Jew and gentile and united both in God's saving plan; the gentiles in Christ have been adopted into God's family and share the blessings of the new covenant and God's promised inheritance (see Rom 4:1, 11–17; 11:11–32; Gal 3:28; 6:15; Eph 2:11–22). They are one body, one family, and family members take care of each other. Christian gentiles thus "owe" a debt of "equity" to support the poor saints in Jerusalem (2 Cor 8:12–15). "For if the gentiles share in their spiritual things, they owe it to serve them also in fleshly things" (Rom 15:27). The collection also serves God as a cultic offering of the gentiles through Paul, an act of the universal church's worship (Rom 15:16).

In another way, the gospel is embodied by the collection because such contributions mirror Christ's own grace. Paul grounds his discussion in the $\chi\acute{\alpha}\rho\iota\varsigma$ (charis, "grace" or "gift") of Christ: "For you know the gift of our Lord Jesus Christ, that he, though rich, became poor on your account, that you might become rich by his poverty" (2 Cor 8:9). Perhaps remarkably, Paul parallels and interconnects Christ's self-giving "grace" with giving to the collection, which Paul also calls a $\chi\acute{\alpha}\rho\iota\varsigma$ (8:1, 4, 6–7, 19; 1 Cor 16:3). Christ's gift of himself creates a pattern of gifting among his people, a communion of mutual generosity, shared benefits, and shared thanks. The Macedonians gave eagerly, beyond their means, for the good of the church. But Paul interprets their act not merely as a gift of cash but as a Christlike gift of "themselves" to God and to Paul's apostolate (2 Cor 8:5). In giving, especially giving beyond one's means, one entrusts oneself to God, actively confessing confidence in God's provision.[16] Such giving takes part in a fellowship of shared blessings within the church. The gentiles have received a share in the spiri-

---

15 It is noteworthy that, while in Greek-speaking Judaism alms were identified by the language of "mercy" ($\grave{\epsilon}\lambda\epsilon\eta\mu\omega\sigma\acute{\upsilon}\nu\eta$, eleēmosynē), in postbiblical Hebrew and Aramaic alms were called "righteousness/justice" (צְדָקָה, tsedaqah).

16 On charitable giving as a confession of one's worldview, see G. A. Anderson 2013.

tual resources of Israel and now share other resources in return. Paul also reminds the Corinthians of the benefit returned by the poor in Jerusalem—a gratitude given through prayer. The poor recipients of the collection will in turn love the Corinthians and pray for them (9:14). And through and beyond this swell of generosity and thanks in the church stands its faithful God, who regards such charity as a pleasing offering to him and will repay it handsomely (8:15; 9:6–10).[17]

Far from being a mere political overture to Judean Christians or a practical appeal to pay for ministerial expenses, the collection is an opportunity for the Corinthians to enact their "confession of the gospel of Christ" (9:12–13). It declares their solidarity with the whole apostolic church, an expression of union with Paul and with the saints in Jerusalem as well. As an ambassador of Christ, Paul exhorts them to complete the collection before he comes, testing and giving them an opportunity to renew and further their life of friendship with God (8:8; 9:13). It is part of his appeal that they not "receive God's grace in vain" (6:1).

FURTHER READING

Bowens, Lisa M. 2017. *An Apostle in Battle: Paul and Spiritual Warfare in 2 Corinthians 12:1–10.* WUNT 2/433. Tübingen: Mohr Siebeck.

Collins, Raymond F. 2013. *Second Corinthians.* Paideia Commentaries on the New Testament. Grand Rapids: Baker Academic.

Downs, David J. 2016. *The Offering of the Gentiles: Paul's Collection for Jerusalem in Its Chronological, Cultural, and Cultic Contexts.* Grand Rapids: Eerdmans.

Eubank, Nathan. 2015. "Justice Endures Forever: Paul's Grammar of Generosity." *JSPL* 5 (2): 169–87.

Furnish, Victor Paul. 1984. *II Corinthians: A New Translation with Introduction and Commentary.* AB 32A. New York: Doubleday.

Gorman, Michael J. 2015. *Becoming the Gospel: Paul, Participation, and Mission.* Grand Rapids: Eerdmans.

Guthrie, George H. 2015. *2 Corinthians.* BECNT. Grand Rapids: Baker Academic.

17 See Eubank 2015.

Hafemann, Scott J. 1990. *Suffering and Ministry in the Spirit: Paul's Defense of His Ministry in II Corinthians 2:14–3:3*. Grand Rapids: Eerdmans.

Lambrecht, Jan, SJ. 1999. *Second Corinthians*. SP 8. Collegeville, MN: Liturgical Press.

Matera, Frank J. 2003. *II Corinthians: A Commentary*. NTL. Louisville, KY: Westminster John Knox.

Stegman, Thomas D., SJ. 2005. *The Character of Jesus: The Linchpin to Paul's Argument in 2 Corinthians*. AnBib 158. Rome: Pontifical Biblical Institute.

_____. 2009. *Second Corinthians*. CCSS. Grand Rapids: Baker Academic.

Stockhausen, Carol Kern. 1989. *Moses's Veil and the Glory of the New Covenant: The Exegetical Substructure of II Cor. 3,1–4,6*. AnBib 116. Rome: Pontifical Biblical Institute.

Thompson, James W. 2001. "Paul's Argument from *Pathos* in 2 Corinthians." In *Paul and Pathos*, edited by Thomas H. Olbright and Jerry L. Sumney, 127–45. SymS 16. Atlanta: Society of Biblical Literature.

Vegge, Ivar. 2008. *2 Corinthians—A Letter about Reconciliation: A Psychagogical, Epistolographical, and Rhetorical Analysis*. WUNT 2/239. Tübingen: Mohr Siebeck.

CHAPTER NINE

Galatians

Paul's letter to Galatia is one of his most passionate. A group of Christians has come to Galatia compelling gentiles to be circumcised in accordance with the Mosaic law, against Paul's and the apostles' gospel. And many are beginning to follow them. Paul responds by defending his gospel and attacking such teaching. Drawing on Israel's scriptures, he shows that a universal Jew-and-gentile family in Christ has always been God's plan. Jews and gentiles are justified together in Christ by faith and the work of the Holy Spirit.

BACKGROUND

The story behind Galatians is a fascinating problem. It fascinates because of the passion of Paul's response to the crisis. A new group of missionaries has convinced the Galatian gentiles that they must keep Jewish observances, especially circumcision, in the name of the Mosaic law. Paul retorts with a fervent and apparently exasperated appeal that they must not. He opens with astonishment and curses (1:6–9) and ends with a curt command to trouble him no more (6:17), with vexed and caustic exclamations in between (e.g., 3:1; 4:20; 5:12).

The story behind Galatians is a problem because of all the uncertainties. Nearly every detail of the letter has been scrutinized and reinterpreted.[1] Who precisely are the Galatians? Who are these teachers, and how did they win people over? And what happened between the Galatians and Paul?

---

1 Several positions on key issues are represented in Nanos 2002.

Paul and the Galatians

Regarding the Galatians' past relations with Paul, a few basics emerge within the letter. Paul and his mission team evangelized them (1:8–9). Further, Paul explains his visit to Galatia as a kind of providential serendipity: "You know that it was because of a bodily weakness that I preached the gospel to you the first time" (4:13). What precisely this malady was is unclear, but the statement suggests that this visit was unintentional, that Paul stopped here on his way to somewhere else and ended up evangelizing the area and then its environs, the several "churches of Galatia" to which he now writes (1:2). The Galatians received him well and believed his message, receiving the Holy Spirit by faith (3:1–5; 4:14–15).

Who were these Galatians and when did Paul evangelize them? The Roman province "Galatia" encompassed a large swath of central Asia Minor (modern Turkey), running up almost to the northern coast and down almost

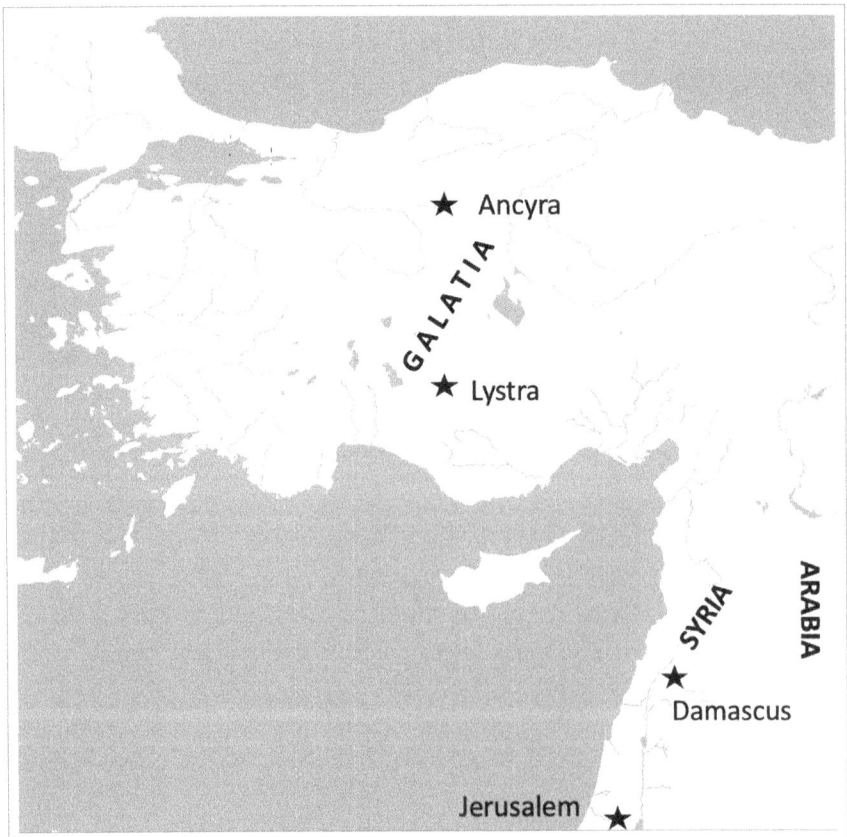

to the southern. The word "Galatian" was originally an ethnic designation for Celts or Gauls, many of whom had settled this region, though they did not necessarily make up a majority in any of its cities in Paul's day. The chief Galatian towns, with slightly more "Galatian" heritage, were in the north around Ancyra. Ancient and many modern interpreters believed Galatians was addressed to converts in this region. This fits Paul's reference to the audience as "Galatians" and as former pagans (3:1; 4:8–9). Acts mentions Paul in "Galatia" briefly in 16:6 and 18:23.

But the cities further south could also be called "Galatia," and Acts 13–14 narrates Paul evangelizing this region in his first missionary journey (the cities of Lystra, Derbe, Iconium, and Pisidian Antioch), regularly in synagogues. Recent scholarship, especially in the Anglo-American world, increasingly views this as the destination of our letter.[2] There were plenty of pagans in the south—in Lystra they tried to worship Paul and Barnabas as Greek gods (Acts 14:8–18). Some, mapping out Paul's travels from Acts, argue that the references to Galatia in Acts 16:6 and 18:23 also indicate the south, as the north would be too far off his route.[3]

The precise geography is not incredibly weighty, but it can affect one's view of the letter's date and Paul's situation—an early evangelization of Galatia could mean an early letter, which could affect views of Paul's theological development, for instance. It can also affect how we imagine the Galatians' culture, how they heard certain aspects of Paul's argument, and how regularly he visited them. The northern view is quite possible. Acts simply does not mention all Paul's travels and, as we have seen (see chapter 2), is free to rearrange some events, so mapping routes of travel exclusively from Acts is inadvisable. Some southern theorists argue that Galatians must have been written quite early (and thus that Paul must have evangelized "Galatia" quite early) because Paul mentions Barnabas in the letter (2:1, 9, 13), and Acts 15:36–39 presents Paul and Barnabas parting ways before Paul's second journey. But this is unnecessary: Paul thinks Barnabas is well-enough known to mention him as an example to the Corinthians, evangelized after Paul split from him in Acts (1 Cor 9:6). Nor does Galatians connect Barnabas

2 The northern hypothesis finds more frequent support from European scholars. See, e.g., the Italian commentary by Cardinal Vanhoye, now condensed and revised in English (Vanhoye and Williamson 2019, 19–22).

3 See DeSilva 2018, 41–43.

with Paul's evangelization of Galatia (Gal 4:12–20). If the southern theory is accepted, Paul's report that he evangelized these churches almost by accident, "because of" a bodily ailment (4:13), differs apparently from the more deliberate evangelization presented in Acts. One could reason that Acts presents a simpler narrative for convenience's sake. Alternatively, one could see this letter addressed to an area more southern than Ancyra (still "south" Galatia), but not in the exact southern cities mentioned in Acts 13–14, an area he perhaps evangelized on a later, broader journey in central Asia Minor in which a "bodily weakness" slowed or rerouted him (see Acts 16:6).

The Letter's Occasion

Paul had success evangelizing these communities, and Paul's mention of "the former time" in 4:13 suggests he returned once more after his founding visit. They were "running" their race of faith well, but then someone stopped their progress (5:7). The letter's opening expresses Paul's dismay: "I am amazed that you are so quickly deserting the one who called you by Christ's grace for a different gospel" (1:6). A group of preachers has arrived and insists that Christian gentiles must be circumcised (6:12–13) and follow distinctive observances of Judaism like calendric feasts (4:10) and probably kosher food laws (see 2:11–14). Paul characterizes these as "troubling" or "agitating" the Galatians (1:7; 5:10), and with selfish motives. They have an unhealthy desire for the Galatians' affections (4:17), Paul alleges, commanding circumcision because they themselves want to look good and avoid persecution (6:12–13).

The "Other" Gospel and Its Preachers

Who were these people and how did they make their case for circumcision? It is tempting to read Paul's arguments and guess that an opposite teaching by these preachers lies behind each, but Paul's words are probably not a point-by-point response.[4] We may begin with a few basic points of profile. They seem to have come into the Galatian church from outside as interlopers. That the Galatians are convinced "so quickly" (1:6) rather than by a slow process—in addition to Paul's surprise at the crisis—suggests that these preachers came on the scene suddenly and intentionally. "Preachers" or "teachers"—Paul calls them troublemakers or agitators—seems an apt description for what they

4 See Barclay 1987.

came to do. Paul casts their activity as evangelizing (εὐαγγελίζω, *euangelizō*), preaching a "gospel" different from his own (1:6–9).[5]

The core of their message that Paul opposes is this: they impose circumcision and other distinctive practices of the Mosaic law on Christian gentiles, contrary to Paul's teaching when he preached to them (1:8–9). This reflects a long-standing conflict in the earliest churches: how to incorporate gentiles into Christ in the most faithful way.[6] Indeed, it was debated among non-Christian Jews as well.[7] Fullest incorporation to the Jewish community involved faith and practice, including especially (for males) circumcision—though even then they remained "proselytes," not Jews.[8] Other gentiles sympathized with Jews and supported synagogues, and some adhered more closely to Jewish custom. The welcome these sympathizers received may have differed from one synagogue to another, but many Jews who followed Christ were of the stricter persuasion: gentiles who would receive salvation from Abraham's God and be united to the messiah's people must fully join that people by following the Mosaic law (see 2:4–5; Acts 10:28; 11:2–3; 15:1, 5). Some bore a bias against gentiles, due partly to persecutions suffered and partly to interpretations of the Davidic messiah as conquering the pagans, working "vengeance against the gentiles" (*Testament of Moses* 10.7; cf. Ps 18:43–51 [KJV 18:42–50]). But many also remembered the prophecies that gentiles would join the people when the messiah redeemed Israel.[9] When the messiah arrived, they were ready to bring them in but wanted to do it the right way.

The right way, for many, centered around the law of Moses. The law bore moral, social, and cultic significance. It bore political significance as well, particularly in distinctive "lifestyle" observances such as circumcision, diet, or refusal to work on the Sabbath. For a gentile to accept the commandment

---

5 They have often been referred to as "Judaizers," but this is imprecise. To "Judaize" (ἰουδα-ΐζω, *ioudaizō*) means for a gentile to act like or identify *himself* as a Jew (2:14; Esth 8:17), not make someone else act like a Jew.

6 Indeed, it continued far beyond the earliest church. In the fourth century, Chrysostom railed—sometimes uncharitably—against Judaism in an effort to convince his parishioners to stop adopting Jewish observances (*Discourses Against Judaizing Christians*, whose title was formerly translated "Against the Jews").

7 See Cohen 1989.

8 For instance, the Mishnah stipulates that full proselytes were not to utter the phrase "God of *our* fathers" in synagogue prayers (only "God of the fathers" or "your fathers"); a proselyte is still not ethnically of Abraham's line unless his mother is (Mishnah, tractate *Bikkurim* 1.4).

9 See Donaldson 2007.

against murder was hardly a sign that she or he had entered the Jewish community. But circumcision, the Sabbath, and food laws were distinctive observances that showed solidarity with God's people and obedience to God's word. Josephus recounts an illustrative episode in which a pagan king, Izates, was won over to Judaism and desired to convert fully through circumcision. His Jewish teacher Ananias discouraged it, since it might incite rebellion if his kingdom saw him joining "the Jews" over against his own people. He should follow the law without making such a show, and God would forgive his foreskin. But once, while Izates was reading the Mosaic law, "another Jew from Galilee" named Eleazar approached and exclaimed: "You gravely neglect the laws, O king, and thereby do injustice to God! For you must not only read them, but first do what is commanded by them. How long will you remain uncircumcised?" (Josephus, *Jewish Antiquities* 20.43–45). Circumcision is the "sign of the covenant" between God and Abraham (Gen 17:11).[10] Resting on Saturday, the Sabbath, was mandated in the commandments and grounded in creation itself (Exod 20:8–11). How could a gentile claim to be faithful without submitting to God's commands?[11] And, if even Jews who failed to maintain ritual purity needed cleansing, how could a gentile be a full participant in the community if he neglected the basics?

The apostles came to see that God's way to bring in gentiles was to give them the Holy Spirit. The narratives of Acts 10–15 encapsulate this, culminating in the decision reached by the council in Jerusalem. Peter states that he had held a conservative view that visiting gentiles made one unclean (Acts 10:28), but God revealed in a dream that if God now pronounces something clean, even if the law said otherwise, Peter must treat it as clean (retold twice in Acts 10–11). From there he is sent to preach to gentiles, and when they believe they receive the Holy Spirit. Relating this to the apostles and elders at the Jerusalem council, Peter interprets this to mean the Spirit has cleansed or "purified their hearts by faith" (Acts 15:9), so those who have received the Spirit are pure before God regardless of their diet or foreskin. God made "no distinction" between them and Jewish believers (Acts 10:47; 11:17; 15:8–11). In addition to this proof and reports of Paul's ministry among the gentiles, James offers biblical support as well. James cites a prophecy that, when

---

10 In the rabbinic *Genesis Rabbah* 46.10, Izates weeps and gets circumcised upon reading Gen 17:11.

11 Notably, some Jews spiritualized the *meaning* of circumcision, Sabbath, or foods, but most did not throw out the concrete observance. See *Letter of Aristeas* 142–50; Philo, *Migration of Abraham* 89–92.

David's line was rebuilt in the messiah, the gentiles would call on the Lord (Acts 15:15–18, using the Greek of Amos 9:11–12). The Mosaic law remains a source of moral instruction for gentiles, however: James commends that gentiles hear it. But concretely the council decides that it is sufficient that gentiles abstain from the impurities associated with idolatry and the sexual immorality pervading the empire (Acts 15:19–29).[12]

Paul's letters make the same arguments: he appeals to the fact that the Galatians have already received the Spirit to show that they do not now need Mosaic observances to be justified (3:1–5), and he cites scriptural passages indicating that gentiles would come to God in the messiah by faith, not circumcision (3:6–18). Yet Paul still appeals to the law of Moses as an authority for moral instruction, and like the council he prohibits sexual immorality and discourages eating meat offered to idols (see 1 Cor 5–10). However, some heard Paul's words about salvation apart from the law as a libertine call to immorality (Rom 3:8), and others misunderstood him as saying that not only gentiles but Jews too should reject Moses's statutes (Acts 21:17–26). Christian Jews in Judea continued worshipping in the temple (see Acts 2:46; 3:1–8; 5:42; 21:26), and impurity contracted from gentiles remained a concern, whatever they thought about the gentiles' salvation. Political loyalties played a role as well. Distinctive practices like dietary laws, Sabbath rest, and circumcision were things many Romans reviled (e.g., Tacitus, *Histories* 5.4–5) and, in biblical tales that formed Jewish self-understanding, were precisely what pagans attacked when they wanted to overthrow Judaism altogether (1 Macc 1:41–61; 2 Macc 6–7; cf. Tob 1:10–11; Esth 14:15–18; Dan 1:3–21). To devalue these was, for some, tantamount to betraying the church's own heritage—it certainly made relations with non-Christian Jews difficult.

The social practicalities of Jews and gentiles communing together were difficult to discern even for those who supported it (Paul gives an example in Gal 2:11–14). Others simply opposed the apostles' decision and, thus, Paul's ministry. A dissenting contingent in Jerusalem remained opposed to Paul, suspecting him of opposing not only gentile circumcision but all that the law of God stood for (cf. Acts 21:17–26; Rom 15:31). Acts attests that some actively traveled to Paul's churches to preach circumcision to the gentiles, claiming support from the authorities in Jerusalem—though both Paul and Acts maintain that these did not have the apostles' approval (Acts 15:1, 24).

---

12 Some argue that the few stipulations placed on gentiles in Acts are essentially the same as purity regulations regarding blood and sexuality that were given to foreigners sojourning in the land of Israel (Lev 17:10–18:30).

The interlopers in Galatia were likely part of this dissenting movement in Jerusalem or stirred up against Paul by its message. Paul's defensive assertions that the Jerusalem apostles agreed with him (not the interlopers) suggest that the interlopers at least claimed Jerusalem's authority. They surely used biblical arguments in their preaching. Paul's rejoinder that the interlopers were merely trying to avoid persecution might also indicate that they had motivations other than mere biblicism (Gal 6:12–13). With increasing tensions between Jews and the Roman regime—leading up to the revolt in the 60s CE—we can imagine some Christian Jews hoping to bolster and show their solidarity with non-Christian Jews, who might have seen their communion with gentiles as siding with the enemy. We can also imagine support for this movement from gentiles who had already renounced paganism, gotten circumcised, and joined the synagogue: as adults who had sacrificed much to join the Jewish community rather than being mere sympathizers, they would surely have been armed with arguments for circumcision and may have had little patience for other gentiles who now wanted God's blessing without following the same path.

Situation and Date

It is unclear how long the interlopers stayed in Galatia. It is clear that they persuaded many, and "quickly" (1:6). When Paul received word, he fired off this impassioned letter. But when did he do so? The letter itself reveals few details of where Paul is or who he is with when he writes. Paul does say that at least "three" and "then fourteen" years passed between becoming an apostle and his meeting with the Jerusalem apostles about his mission (1:15–18; 2:1), but he is not giving a detailed biography, and he does not say how many years have passed between that meeting and the crisis in Galatia. Different interpreters posit an early date (ca. 51–52 CE), a very early date (ca. 48 CE), and a later date (ca. 54–56 CE) for Galatians.

Cases for an earlier date usually coincide with arguments for a southern "Galatian" audience evangelized early with Barnabas according to Acts. Arguments are also made that Galatians cannot have been written after the Jerusalem council narrated in Acts 15. If the matter of gentile circumcision were already decided, and if the apostles promulgated a letter detailing their decree (Acts 15:22–31), why does Paul not simply quote the decree to settle the issue in Galatia? Likewise, Paul mentions two visits to Jerusalem in chapters 1–2, but in Acts the council is his third—the first after he left Damascus (Acts 9:19–26) and the second to bring aid in a famine at the time of Herod Agrippa's death in 44 CE (Acts 11:27–30). Proposals for early dates for Galatians thus see this letter as evidence of Paul's vehement protest against circumcising gentiles in a time when the rest of the church had not officially decided.

Later dates can fit with either a northern or southern destination, and a later date is more likely. First, an early date is chronologically difficult, especially for those who argue that Paul's second visit to Jerusalem (Gal 2:1–10) refers to his visit to Jerusalem after Agrippa's death in 44 CE, since Paul describes it as seventeen years after he came to believe in Christ.[13] That would put his conversion (and, before it, Christ's crucifixion) incredibly early. Second, 2:1–10 does in fact appear to describe a less grand but substantially consistent account of the council presented in Acts 15.[14] Paul visits Peter, James, and others in Jerusalem to present his gospel and is granted a hearing despite opposition from proponents of gentile circumcision, and the apostles agree that gentile Christians need not be circumcised and approve Paul's mission. Citing this story and the apostles' endorsement makes quoting the letter described in Acts 15 unnecessary. Indeed, Paul seems not to prefer such modes of arguing. That decree also prohibits food sacrificed to idols, but when treating this problem in 1 Corinthians 8–10 and Romans 14–15, Paul prefers to persuade by educating people in the heart of the issue rather than resorting to magisterial decree, which die-hard dissenters would not have accepted anyway.

Other factors suggest a later date as well. One is the similarity of the arguments in Galatians to those in Romans. Indeed, at points Romans reads like a longer, more cautious restatement of Galatians, particularly some of its hastier statements about the law and the value of circumcision for Jews, which could suggest that Paul wrote Galatians not long before Romans.[15]

---

13 Some object that "then after fourteen years" (2:1) might *include* the "three" mentioned in 1:18, thus requiring only fourteen years from his call to this letter. But the sequential ἔπειτα (*epeita*, "then/thereafter") makes this interpretation unlikely: "*Then* after three years I went up to Jerusalem.... *Then* I went.... *Then* after fourteen years I went up to Jerusalem again" (1:18, 21; 2:1).

14 See Keener 2019b: 7–13. There are differences in presentation between Acts and Galatians, but of little substance. In Galatians Paul met "privately with those of repute" (2:2), while many are present in Acts. But Paul's "private" meeting apparently did not keep out many "false brothers" who opposed him (2:3–4), and "those of repute" need not exclude the apostles and ruling elders present in Acts 15.

15 Cf. Gal 2:15–21; 3:10–13 with Rom 1:18–3:31; Gal 3:6–8 with Rom 4:1–25; and Gal 3:19–4:7 with Rom 5:12–8:39.

Stronger evidence comes from Paul's references to the collection that he aimed to gather in the mid- to late 50s. In 1 Corinthians 16:1 Paul instructs the Corinthians to begin gathering for the collection just as he has instructed the "churches of Galatia." This indicates that, at the beginning of Paul's collection efforts, Paul had positive relations with Galatia and planned for them to be a major contributor to the collection along with Macedonia and Achaia. However, when Paul writes 2 Corinthians 8–9, he has collected in Macedonia and is traveling to Corinth to collect what had been gathered from Achaia. When he finished the collection and prepared to leave and deliver it to Jerusalem, he wrote Romans and reported only Macedonia and Achaia as contributors (Rom 15:23–28). The absence of "Galatia" from this proud report is conspicuous after Paul's confidence that they would contribute when he wrote 1 Corinthians. This fits well with a later date, suggesting that Paul's relations with the Galatians became complicated between his writing positively of them in 1 Corinthians (ca. 53/54 CE) and his writing Romans (ca. 57 CE).

Any more detail on the date requires imagination. Galatia is not mentioned in the collection report in 2 Cor 9:1–5 either, where Paul uses the Macedonians' generosity as an example for the Corinthians. Galatians may, then, have been written in Macedonia at about the same time as 2 Corinthians (or, at least, 2 Cor 1–9), which we estimated to about 56 CE. One also notes one of the letter's odder features: Paul expresses no hope or promise to visit Galatia again. Indeed, he seems unable to return (4:20) and signs off brusquely, "From now on, let no one trouble me" (6:17). This could simply be due to his exasperation, but it may suggest an apostle whose plans are already set in another direction. We know that this was the case in his final movements to deliver the collection: Paul collected in Macedonia and Corinth with his sights already set on what he had planned to do after delivering the collection. He has completed his ministry in the eastern Mediterranean. The collection will put a seal on his work in this region, and thereafter he feels called to begin a new ministry in the far west, in Spain (Rom 15:18–29). Perhaps Paul heard of the troubles in Galatia, maybe from the emissary he sent to collect their funds, but felt compelled to go ahead to Corinth and finish the collection without Galatia, writing this letter as his only response as he proceeded toward the next phase of his ministry?

This scenario is possible, though others are imaginable in view of the data. In any case, we see in this letter a distant apostle arguing fiercely to call the Galatian churches back to "the truth of the gospel" (2:5, 14). Countering the message of the interlopers, Paul defends his gospel and explains the purposes of the Mosaic law within the history of God's promises and plan of salvation. He reminds the Galatians of their own reception of God's Spirit and calls them to heed that Spirit against the impulse to seek life in the law, which is tantamount to rejecting the grace they have received.

OVERVIEW

I. **Letter Opening (1:1–5)**
   A. Paul to all the churches of Galatia (1:1–2)
   B. Grace to you from God, in whose plan Christ gave himself to deliver us (1:3–5).

II. **One Apostolic Gospel (1:6–10)**
   A. I am amazed that you are deserting God's grace in Christ for another "gospel" preached by these troublemakers (1:6–7).
   B. There is only one gospel—the one you received from us. A curse upon anyone who preaches another. I do not (1:8–10)!

III. **Paul, the Apostolic Gospel, and the Gentiles (1:11–2:21)**
   A. This gospel comes from Christ. I received it from Christ, and I preach it at Christ's command (1:11–12).
   B. You know my reception of God's grace in Christ.
      1. So advanced was my zeal for Jewish custom that I persecuted the church (1:13–14).
      2. When God called me to preach Christ to the gentiles, I stayed in Syria and did not confer with Jerusalem until three years later (1:15–20).
      3. But, hearing of my ministry, the Judean Christians still glorified God for turning this persecutor into a preacher of Christ (1:21–24).
   C. Fourteen years later, Barnabas and I presented what we preach to the Jerusalem apostles, to ensure that our ministry had not been in vain (2:1–2).
      1. We had to contend against some false brethren there. But the so-called pillars—Peter, James, and John—added nothing to our gospel. They recognized us as fellows entrusted with the same charge for the gentiles that Peter had been given for the

Jews, and they did not demand that our Greek companion Titus be circumcised (2:3–10).

D. But once, at Antioch, I opposed Peter directly, when he was not acting in accord with the gospel (2:11).

1. Though he regularly ate with gentiles there, he withdrew from them because of some visitors from James. And all the believing Jews there, including Barnabas, followed him (2:12–13).

2. But I rebuked him publicly. How can you suddenly separate from the gentiles out of Jewish concerns, thus compelling them to follow Jewish concerns (2:14)?

3. We, Jews, have put our faith in Christ for justification, because we know that none can be justified by works of the law (2:15–16).

   a. Pursuing this justification is hardly blameworthy (2:17).

   b. Rather, I sin against Christ if I rebuild the law's wall between us and gentiles. I have life by Christ living in me, apart from the law. To act as though justification and life come by the law is to disregard God's grace in Christ (2:18–21).

IV. **The Gospel and the Place of the Law (3:1–4:7)**

A. How then can you Galatians consider getting circumcised? You have already received the Spirit apart from the law when you believed the gospel (3:1–5)!

B. Scripture says Abraham was justified by faith and already foretold that God would justify the gentiles in the same way. It is faith that makes one part of Abraham's family and an heir of the promised blessing (3:6–9).

1. The law's own text curses any disobedience, and the prophets point us to faith for blessing. Christ was crucified to take on the curse that fell on us and to redeem us from it, so that we might receive the Spirit and the blessings of Abraham (3:10–14).

2. If God promised this to Abraham 430 years before the law was given, the later law of Moses can in no way nullify God's original promise (3:15–18).

B. Why then was the law given?

1. This does not mean the law was against God's promise; it was never meant to give eternal life, but was given because of sin. The law puts all under sin, so that blessing in Christ might come by faith (3:19–22).

2. The law was thus preparing us for Christ's coming. But now Christ is here, and we are no longer enslaved under the law. For all—Jews or gentiles—who are baptized are in Christ and counted among Abraham's family (3:23–29).

3. With Christ's coming we are freed from the law's slavery, and God's Spirit dwelling in us makes us God's children and heirs (4:1–7).

V. **Call to Freedom in Christ (4:8–5:12)**

A. How can you gentiles think to turn from Christ to such slavery? Has your conversion been in vain (4:8–11)?

1. What happened to your love for me when I first presented the gospel? I suffered to give birth to you! Will you now stand against me when these troublemakers compete for your affections (4:12–20)?

B. The law—which you want to be enslaved to—speaks of this allegorically. Abraham had two sons by two wives, one free (Sarah, mother of Isaac) and one a slave (Hagar, mother of Ishmael) (4:21–23).

1. Hagar, the slave, is the law-covenant at Mt. Sinai, a figure of today's Jerusalem, whose children are enslaved to this day (4:24–25).

2. The freewoman, Sarah, is our mother, a figure of the heavenly Jerusalem, mother of many nations born to Abraham (4:26–27).

3. Hagar's offspring persecute Sarah's, now as then. But scripture says the promised inheritance is for us, the freewoman's children. In this covenant you are free; do not submit to such slavery (4:28–5:1)!

4. If you seek justification in the law, you are turning your back on the grace you received, and Christ will be of no benefit to you! But we pursue righteousness in the Spirit by faith. For what counts is faith working through love, regardless of circumcision (5:2–6).

C. What has happened to your faith? You were doing well, and I am confident you will again. Those who impose circumcision on you will bear God's judgment (5:7–12)!

VI. **The Meaning of Freedom in Christ (5:13–6:10)**

A. You are free, but you must not use freedom from the law for evil. Freedom in Christ fulfills the law, for it is a freedom to serve one another in love (5:13–14).

1. The sinful flesh desires your destruction, but the Spirit wars against it. Walk by the Spirit in this freedom (5:15–17).

2. The works of the flesh are obvious, and I have warned you before of the judgment coming against them. But avoiding them is a matter not of law but the Spirit, who produces good fruit in those joined to Christ. So live by the Spirit (5:18–26).

   a. Fulfill the law of Christ by bearing each other's burdens (6:1–2).

   b. Do not be haughty or boast against others—at the judgment each will bear his own burden. And show gratitude toward your teachers in Christ (6:3–6).

B. We will reap what we sow. Life lived for the flesh will reap destruction, while living for the Spirit will produce eternal life. So let us progress in good deeds, for we will reap a harvest if we persevere (6:7–10).

VII. **Final Appeal and Letter Closing (6:11–18)**

A. I, Paul, write now in my own hand. These circumcision preachers do not truly serve our crucified Lord; they are motivated by selfish boasting (6:11–13).

B. But my boast must always be in Christ, by whose cross I live. What counts is Christ's work to make us new, not circumcision. Peace upon all God's people who follow this rule (6:14–16).

C. Let no one trouble me about this anymore. Grace be with you (6:17–18).

KEY FEATURES

Galatians skips over the thanksgiving Paul usually expresses at the opening of his letters and dives into polemics. Paul's arguments, sometimes quick and dense, aim to persuade the Galatian gentiles not to undergo circumcision or seek life in the law of Moses but to stand in the power of the Spirit and live in the righteousness of Christ.

Paul and "the Law"

Many Christ-believing Jews in Paul's day were understandably uneasy when he proclaimed freedom from being "under" the law, a state he characterizes as slavery (5:1, 18). Was it not virtue—not slavery—that made Daniel refuse Nebuchadnezzar's impure foods? Does "freedom" from the law of Moses mean freedom from its moral standards too? Indeed, antinomians of every stripe have claimed Pauline "freedom" as their slogan. However, while Paul speaks seriously about the law being a temporary measure, like a tutor or nanny, until the time Christ should come and pour out his Spirit (3:15–4:7), he still quotes the text of the law positively and insists that "freedom" in Christ is a freedom to serve, not a license to sin, and in this way fulfills the law's central command of love for God and neighbor. "For you were called to freedom, brothers [and sisters]—only do not use your freedom as an opportunity for the flesh, rather serve one another through love. For the whole law is fulfilled in one statement: 'You shall love your neighbor as yourself'" (5:13–14).

All this has led to numerous interpretive arguments about Paul's view of the law.[16] To approach the topic, we may pose a few key questions and sketch answers from Galatians and the rest of Paul's letters.

When Paul speaks of "the law," is he talking about all of it or only certain statutes? The phrase "works of the law" (ἔργα νόμου, *erga nomou*; e.g., 2:16; Rom 3:20) has been a frequent point of debate, as it seems to narrow Paul's focus only to certain "works."[17] Since the phrase is used in discussions about whether gentiles should observe certain practices, such as circumcision, food laws, or Sabbaths, it is clear that these are the prototypical "works" at issue. Gentile converts can, Paul asserts, know the core moral statutes

---

16 For patristic readings of the law in Paul, see Wiles 1967, 49–72.

17 Many Church Fathers understood this as indicating only particular Jewish observances. Embroiled in controversy against Pelagius, who taught that humans could earn their salvation apart from grace, Augustine saw in the phrase any human "working" which tried to achieve salvation without the Spirit's empowering grace. (Most Reformers followed Augustine, but without his view of meritorious working *by* the Spirit's grace.) Recent debates are reflected in several essays in Dunn 2005.

naturally (Gal 5:19–21; Rom 2:12–16), and they likely did not receive the prohibition of murder as a matter of adopting the Mosaic law specifically. In saying that these converts are "free" from the law, then, Paul is not removing such moral standards from the church. Even so, Paul's discussion of specific works draws him to speak about "the law" (νόμος, nomos) as a whole (Gal 2:14–16, 21; 3:10, 19; 5:3). When he says that "the law" was given temporarily until Christ came and that in Christ one is "not under the law" (3:23–25; Rom 6:14), he is speaking of the body of code delivered to Israel through Moses. It is something that Israel received and that gentiles do not have by nature (cf. Rom 2:12–16; 9:4; 1 Cor 9:20–21), and it was given at a particular time—specifically 430 years after Abraham in the mid-second millennium BCE (Gal 3:15–18). And it is a package deal: according to Paul, for a gentile to submit to circumcision or food laws is to oblige oneself to this entire legal code (5:3).

What about Paul's calls to "freedom" in the gospel as opposed to taking up the law's yoke of "slavery"? Again, the issue seems to be particularly with gentiles adopting the law given to Israel specifically, not with rules or commands themselves. Paul speaks of Christians following the "law of Christ" in their behavior (6:2; 1 Cor 9:21).[18] He has no qualms about outlining what is and is not Christian behavior or upholding the consequences of one's behavior for the final judgment (see Gal 5:19–21; 6:7–10; Rom 2:1–29; 1 Cor 3:5–10; 6:9–11). In other words, he does not proclaim freedom from "the law" as if Christ has done away with all codes of behavior or with God's judgment of Christian sin.

Paul elucidates his views about the Mosaic law-code in several ways. A key argument in Galatians is salvation-historical. Paul looks back from his current vantage point in Christ to consider God's original purpose in giving the law. The law, he maintains, is not against God's promise that through Abraham's descendants—particularly one descendant, Jesus—the gentiles, too, would receive the blessing of righteousness and life by faith (3:6–21). But this means that, despite the law's own promise of life for those who obeyed it (3:10–12; Lev 18:5), the law must not have been given with that purpose (Gal 3:21). Indeed, God "justified" Abraham when Abraham believed, long before the law was given (3:6; Gen 15:6). And God promised that this blessing Abraham received would be shared among the gentiles (Gal 3:6–9). The

---

18 Thomas 2018 shows the importance of the conviction that Christ gave a law among the second-century Church Fathers, putting it into helpful dialogue with modern views on Paul and the law.

law, which came 430 years later, cannot amend or override God's covenant with Abraham (3:15–18). Paul also points to prophets like Habakkuk, who lamented to God that, despite King Josiah's attempts to enforce the law, "the law is stunted and justice never goes forth" (Hab 1:4). Paul quotes God's later reply to Habakkuk that God's righteous ones will live through the coming distress "by faith" (Gal 3:11; Hab 2:4). The prophet confirms that, even after the law was given, the primary key to life with God remains faith, just as with Abraham. In another line of argument, instead of insisting that the Christ-covenant was the *older* covenant, Paul draws in 2 Corinthians 3:6–18 on God's promises to make a *new* covenant, one "not like the covenant I made with their fathers . . . which they broke" (Jer 31:31–32). God would send out his Spirit to renew the hearts of his people so that they would know him intimately and walk in his ways (cf. Jer 31:33–34; Ezek 36:25–27). The legal code was from God and could legislate and instruct, but it could not transform the heart and was not purposed to give life. In Christ, God does what the law "could not do" (Rom 8:3–4) by the gift of his purifying and transforming Spirit.[19]

But if God's law was not meant to give life, why was it given? It was added "because of transgressions" (Gal 3:19); it was a disciplinarian or "pedagogue" (παιδαγωγός, *paidagōgos*) that trained and disciplined Israel until the coming of Christ (3:24–25; cf. 4:1–2).[20] Through it, Israel learned the liturgical patterns of friendship with God in confession and reparation, praise and thanksgiving. They learned the character of God in statutes that reflected his holiness, justice, and mercy. And in their sin they learned again the depth of their need for God's deliverance (see Rom 3:20; 7:7–12). Indeed, the law's testimony showed sin for what it was, and its curse on disobedience "locked up" everything under sin to prepare it for Christ's redemption (see Gal 3:10–14, 21; 4:4–5; Rom 7:7–13). Yet its statutes, though "good" and "holy" (Rom 7:12–13), were conditioned by Israel's circumstance and God's intent for Israel as a national body different from the nations around them (see Lev 20:22–26; Deut 4:5–8). Not all its specific statutes were meant to

---

19 In Augustine's words: "For what the law commands, faith completes. For without the gift of God—that is, without the Holy Spirit through whom love is poured out in our hearts—the law has power to command, not to help, and moreover can make a transgressor one who cannot excuse himself by pleading ignorance" (*Enchiridion on Faith, Hope, and Love* 31.117).

20 See Lull 1986. Some take this reference quite negatively, seeing the law only as a cruel nanny. But Paul insists that the law was not against God's promises, and the law's pedagogy "unto (εἰς, *eis*) Christ" (3:24) suggests a positive function in God's purposes.

govern God's people eternally or even expressed the fullness of God's will for human behavior. One could point to Jesus's logic in Mark 10:5–6: many laws accommodated the people's "hardness of heart."[21] Those like Daniel who followed and upheld this law were not misguided. Indeed, Paul clarifies in Romans that circumcision is beneficial (though not salvific) for Jews (Rom 2:25–3:4); he even defends those whose private pieties are sensitive to purity concerns (Rom 14–15). But the purpose of this body of legislation, Paul argues, is fulfilled in Christ and does not govern God's multinational people in Christ (Gal 3:21–26; Rom 7:1–6; 10:4).

Following the law of Christ, God's people are led by the Spirit, and in them the Spirit fulfills and completes the good and holy commands of the law (Gal 5:13–25; Rom 3:31; 8:4). Jews, already circumcised, receive the Spirit through faith and baptism into Christ; gentiles, though not previously incorporated into Israel, receive the same Spirit through faith and baptism (Gal 2:15–21; 3:1–5, 27–29; 4:1–7). Though circumcision is a negative focus of Paul's arguments when it is imposed on gentiles, the positive point at issue is the pursuit of Christian life in the Spirit:

> For in Christ Jesus neither circumcision nor uncircumcision has power, but faith working through love. (Gal 5:6)

> For neither circumcision nor uncircumcision is anything, but new creation. (Gal 6:15)

> Circumcision is nothing and uncircumcision is nothing, but keeping God's commandments. (1 Cor 7:19)

Paul's goal is to call all to persevere and deepen their participation in Christ. As he says in Philippians, his life of faith presses always forward, seeking to be more and more conformed to Christ, and he calls his churches to do the same (Phil 3:9–16). He does not cease quoting or reading the Mosaic law (see 5:14; 1 Cor 5:8, 13; 9:9), but he interprets it in ways that aid people's

---

21 Many patristic authors focused on the statement in Ezek 20:25 that some laws were simply "not good," given to discipline the people after the golden calf apostasy, and thus distinguished the earlier commands in Exodus from those given after this event—usually holding the Decalogue as unaffected by Paul's arguments (e.g., *Didascalia Apostolorum* 26.6.10–22; Irenaeus, *Against Heresies* 4.12–18). Even here, however, the Sabbath commandment is explicitly about resting on the seventh day (Saturday), not worship generally. Theologically, Christ's new law takes priority: Christ's change in priesthood brings about a change in law (Heb 7:12), and Christ, who is "Lord over the Sabbath" (Matt 12:1–8), can clarify the purpose of the law and direct the church in new fulfillments of its purpose.

pursuit of life in Christ, as preparation for Christ or as expressing principles of God's will for human conduct. Paul directs believers to receive and pursue the graces given in Christ through the Spirit. When Jews can do this and keep their ancestral piety, Paul does not prohibit it—so long as they do not reject gentile believers as impure or as though Christ's same grace had not made them their brothers (see Gal 2:11–14). But to seek justification in the law apart from the Spirit is to seek life from something that cannot give life—for anyone. And for gentiles who have received the Spirit to then seek justification in the law is to go backward, tantamount to rejecting the grace they received (3:1–5; 5:1–5).

The Spirit and the Life of Faith

To dissuade the Galatians from heeding the interlopers, Paul employs a variety of arguments—from apostolic precedent (2:1–14), from the Galatians' own experience (3:1–5), simple warnings (5:2–4), and especially from scripture itself (chaps. 3–4). The grace of justification and the gift of the Spirit come through Christ, crucified and risen. In him, not in the law, one is made an adopted child of God the Father and, indeed, of Abraham. Throughout his arguments, Paul returns again and again to the theme of "faith."

Paul counterposes the law with "faith" as the means by which one is justified. A central verse comes right after Paul's rebuke of Peter one day when Peter withdrew from gentiles at Antioch: "We are by nature Jews and not gentile sinners. Yet, knowing that a person is not justified through works of the law but only through faith in Jesus Christ, we too believed in Jesus Christ, that we might be justified by faith in Christ and not by works of the law, for by works of the law 'no one will be justified'" (2:15–16, referencing Ps 143:2). Applied to the gentiles in Galatia, if Jews like Paul and Peter—or the interlopers!—put their faith in Christ rather than in their circumcision to be justified, why should gentiles (to whom the Mosaic law was not given) turn to circumcision? He points to the Galatians' own experience as well: they have already received the Holy Spirit, and they, like Peter and Paul, received this grace when they *believed* the gospel (3:1–5).

Paul uses a particular phrasing in this passage and elsewhere, in Greek πίστις Χριστοῦ or πίστις Ἰησοῦ Χριστοῦ (*pistis Christou* or *pistis Iēsou Christou*).[22] The phrase is usually translated as meaning the believer's act

---

22 See Rom 3:22, 26; Gal 2:16; 3:22; Phil 3:9.

of "faith in Christ" (e.g., ESV, NABRE). It is, however, possible to interpret this as referring to Jesus's act of faithfulness—particularly his faithfulness to endure the cross.[23] Many thus translate the phrase not as human "faith *in* Christ" but as the "faith(fulness) *of* Christ," arguing that this makes better sense of Paul's theology of grace: believers are not justified simply by their own acts of faith but by Christ's act to give himself for their salvation (1:4; 2:20). The source of one's standing with God and reception of divine grace certainly flows from the Christ event, a point indisputable across Paul's letters. Paul contrasts the law's inability to justify with the divine source of justification achieved through Christ's death and resurrection and mediated by the Spirit. If one reads Paul's argument as making that point, "faithfulness of Christ" surely fits. On the other hand, when Paul attacks the circumcision of Christian gentiles, the question seems to be not whether grace comes through Christ but what is necessary to participate in Christ and receive that grace. The gentiles and the interloping preachers already believe in Christ; Paul's response is that this faith, by which one receives the Spirit, is sufficient where circumcision is ineffective. Paul's appeal to scripture likewise emphasizes that Abraham, before he was circumcised, actively "believed God, and it was counted to him for righteousness," which he offers as a paradigm and promise that in Christ the uncircumcised would receive the blessing of justification in the same way (3:6–9).

This faith receives the promises of God and clings to the crucified and risen Christ. On the one hand, it is an entry requirement contrasted with circumcision. By faith and baptism one receives the Spirit and is made a child of God and an heir to Abraham's blessings (3:26–29). On the other, it is participatory, the ongoing mode of possessing life in Christ.[24] The Spirit sent to dwell in believers' hearts is the "Spirit of [God's] Son" (4:6). The Spirit unites believers to the reality of Christ's death and resurrection and pours divine love into their very hearts (2:20; Rom 5:5–8; 8:9–11; Eph 3:17; Col 3:3–4). Participation in Christ not only gives the status of being God's children and members of Abraham's family but makes one a new person conformed to the image of the suffering, loving, holy Son of God (see Gal 6:15; 2 Cor 5:17;

---

23 See esp. Hays 2002. Downs and Lappenga 2019 argue, differently, that Christ's "faithfulness" refers less to his earthly obedience than to his current, exalted faithfulness toward his people at the Father's right hand.

24 See Pifer 2019. In the tradition, the statement in Heb 11:1 that faith is the "substance" or reality of what one hopes for plays a role in theological connections between the act of faith and participation in Christ by which what is believed "takes root" in the believer. See Pope Benedict XVI, Encyclical Letter *Spe Salvi* (November 30, 2007), §7.

Eph 2:10; 4:24). Faith is thus "filial existence" before God—a life of hopeful and repentant dependence and love toward the Father.[25]

This "faith," though beginning with the initial act of faith at hearing the gospel, thus endures and grows beyond that first moment of surrender to God. Paul speaks of himself and all the baptized as "co-crucified with Christ"—their old selves who belonged to sin are dead and buried, and their new life is lived by the power of the Spirit (Gal 2:19–20; 5:24; 6:14). They have received the Spirit, and the risen Christ thus lives "in" them (2:20). Those crucified with Christ, who live and endure by faith, work to resist sinful impulses that remain in them, as the Spirit in them contends against the flesh (5:13–17; Rom 8:5–8, 13). Positively, faith endures when it is "active in love" (Gal 5:6). Faith heeds the Spirit in imitating the forgiving and restorative love of God for sinners, for the church, and quite simply for all—fulfilling the "law of Christ" (6:2, 10). The law of Moses was not bad: it expressed God's will for Israel as they entered the land, and it called for a conversion of heart (e.g., Deut 4:29; 6:5–6; 9:4–7; 10:12; 15:7). But the law's statutes were not all intended to be eternal or universal, and the law itself could not transform. In Christ, one not only has instruction and a supreme model of divine love—Christ himself—but receives the Spirit's transformative power to obey God. And faith takes root in the heart, so that believers obey not as slaves but as sons and daughters who freely serve their Father in love (Gal 4:6–7; Rom 10:9–10).[26]

The believer bears the Spirit's fruits of "love, joy, peace, patience, kindness, goodness, faith, gentleness, self-control—against these there is no law" (Gal 5:22–23). Human faith can, of course, fade and fail to bear fruit, as Paul's warnings make clear. One who receives the Spirit but sinks his life into sin without repentance will reap what he has sown (5:19–21; 6:7–9). But the Spirit continually intercedes and beckons through moving the heart and through the church, including the apostle's fiery letter, to call all to endurance and continued repentance in love, suffering, and hope in Christ—in a word, to "faith." Having warned those who received the Spirit but now contemplate turning to the law, Paul counters with a model of enduring faith and life in Christ: "in the Spirit, by faith, we await the hope of righteousness. For in Christ Jesus neither circumcision nor uncircumcision has power, but rather faith working through love" (5:5–6).

---

25 Pope Francis, Encyclical Letter *Lumen Fidei* (June 29, 2013), §19.

26 The contrast between filial and servile obedience is a key distinction between life under the law and life in Christ in Irenaeus, *Against Heresies* 4.13.

FURTHER READING

Cohen, Shaye J. D. 1989. "Crossing the Boundary and Becoming a Jew." *HTR* 82 (1): 13–33.

de Boer, Martinus C. 2011. *Galatians*. NTL. Louisville, KY: Westminster John Knox.

Dunn, James D. G. 2005. *The New Perspective on Paul*. Revised edition. Grand Rapids: Eerdmans.

Hansen, G. Walter. 1989. *Abraham in Galatians: Epistolary and Rhetorical Contexts*. JSNTSup 29. Sheffield: JSOT Press.

Keener, Craig S. 2019b. *Galatians: A Commentary*. Grand Rapids: Baker Academic.

Matera, Frank J. 1992. *Galatians*. SP 9. Collegeville, MN: Liturgical Press.

Moo, Douglas J. 2013. *Galatians*. BECNT. Grand Rapids: Baker Academic.

Nanos, Mark D., ed. 2002. *The Galatians Debate: Contemporary Issues in Rhetorical and Historical Interpretation*. Peabody, MA: Hendrickson.

Pifer, Jeanette Hagen. 2019. *Faith as Participation: An Exegetical Study of Some Key Pauline Texts*. WUNT 2/486. Tübingen: Mohr Siebeck.

Rosner, Brian S. 2013. *Paul and the Law: Keeping the Commandments of God*. New Studies in Biblical Theology 31. Downers Grove, IL: InterVarsity.

Smiles, Vincent M. 1998. *The Gospel and the Law in Galatia: Paul's Response to Jewish-Christian Separatism and the Threat of Galatian Apostasy*. Collegeville, MN: Liturgical Press.

Thomas, Matthew J. 2018. *Paul's "Works of the Law" in the Perspective of Second-Century Reception*. WUNT 2/468. Tübingen: Mohr Siebeck.

Tolmie, D. Francois. 2005. *Persuading the Galatians: A Text-Centred Rhetorical Analysis of a Pauline Letter*. WUNT 2/190. Tübingen: Mohr Siebeck.

Vanhoye, Cardinal Albert, and Peter S. Williamson. 2019. *Galatians*. CCSS. Grand Rapids: Baker Academic.

Williams, Sam K. 1987. "Justification and the Spirit in Galatians." *JSNT* 29 (9):91–100.

CHAPTER TEN

Ephesians

A long with Philippians, Colossians, Philemon, and sometimes 2 Timothy, Ephesians is traditionally classed as one of Paul's "Captivity Epistles." He writes as a "prisoner" in "chains" for the sake of Christ and the church (3:1; 4:1; 6:20). Though its Pauline authorship is doubted by many, the letter presents a moving theological exhortation to believers to know the power of the risen Lord in God's plan of salvation and to grow in unity, love, and holiness as members of Christ's body.

BACKGROUND

Ephesians stands out among Paul's letters in several ways. It has a general character overall, not naming any specific occasion for its writing. Indeed, for a letter apparently written to people Paul is said to have known well, it is bereft of specific references to people or to his own past interactions with them, stating only that he has "heard" of their faith and that they might ("if") know the ministry God gave to him for the gentiles (1:15; 3:2). Its literary style is likewise distinct, with uncommonly long sentences and the piling up of prepositional phrases to describe a single action or thing.[1] Likewise, it is incredibly rich in its theology of participation in Christ and the church—stating, for example, that the baptized are not merely joined to Christ's life and death (as in the undisputed Paulines) but also now seated with Christ in heaven (2:6). Factors like these have caused many scholars to argue that Ephesians was not written by Paul, but more likely by a disciple of his in

---

1 Though English (and some Greek) Bibles insert periods for convenience, the repeated phrase "in whom" (ἐν ᾧ, *en hō*) at the beginnings of 1:7, 11, and 13 links these verses syntactically, making 1:3–14 all one sentence in Greek.

the years after Paul's death to hand on an interpretation or encapsulation of his message. Some even suggest that it was composed as a sort of cover letter written to summarize Paul's theology at the head of the Pauline letter collection when it was being published, in the generation after Paul's death or perhaps later.

Others, however, point to the possibility that Paul himself might have composed a more general letter intentionally. Its rich theology of the church and of Paul's place as God's apostle might be uniquely expressed simply because of Paul's situation, because he has had more time to reflect on the mystery of Christ and develop his own theology, or perhaps because Paul told a trusted colleague or scribe his message and authorized them to write in his name using their own words (see chapter 3). Here we will look for the letter's own hints about its occasion and purpose. Its close affinity to Colossians is also important in considering its background.

The General Character of Ephesians

In contrast to, say, 1 Corinthians or Galatians, Paul does not name specific "problems" in the church that he wants to correct. Paul mentions hearing good reports about them (1:15–16), but the letter remains generally reflective and didactic, teaching and exhorting the audience in their life of faith.

If Paul wrote the letter, this generality is surprising. Paul did significant work in Ephesus, the capital of the province of Asia, and was quite successful despite opposition (1 Cor 16:8–9, 19; 2 Cor 1:8–10; Acts 19:1–30). Acts claims he was there for about three years (Acts 19:10, 22; 20:31). Yet the letter neither mentions nor greets any individual Ephesians, and there are few references to Paul's personal ministry there as in other letters (e.g., 2 Cor 12:12; 1 Thess 1:5). Indeed, two little asides seem to suggest he is unfamiliar with the audience or that he expects many to be unfamiliar with him. In Ephesians 3:2, when referring to himself and his imprisonment, he adds: "if indeed you heard of the stewardship of that grace of God which was given to me for you." And again, in 4:21, having called the Ephesians to obey the truth of Christ, he qualifies: "if indeed you heard of him and were taught in him." Did he not teach them himself?

This could suggest that the letter was written by a disciple after Paul's death, speaking in Paul's voice and passing on the author's understanding of his legacy. On the other hand, Paul does not have to greet his addressees by name—there are no named greetings in 1 Thessalonians or Galatians. The apparent unfamiliarity could instead be due to distance and time. If the letter were written from a late imprisonment, we can imagine that the burgeoning mission in Ephesus had grown during the years since Paul last visited. He may expect many new converts have heard of but not met him (explaining the "if" in 3:2) or that some insufficiently catechized neophytes will hear the letter (which explains 4:21). If the letter was written a few years after Paul's last visit to Ephesus, perhaps from far away, this might also account for the lack of mention of specific problems in the Ephesian church, since Paul may not have known them, though he would know the *kinds* of challenges they faced in this city in which he had once lived.

Some have suggested that the letter was intentionally general because it was not in fact addressed to Ephesus. A few early copies of the letter do not include the phrase "in Ephesus" in 1:1 (omitted in the RSV and NJB), and some think the author intentionally omitted any mention of its addressees to allow the letter to be read aloud to many churches regardless of their location. On the other hand, the author names Tychicus, the letter carrier, and says that he was sent to deliver news of Paul to the addressees (6:21–22), so the letter is not void of all specificity. Moreover, virtually every early Christian writer agrees that the letter was sent "to the Ephesians," apparently even ones who did not have the city's name in their copy of 1:1.[2] So, even if the letter was written with no city name in the *letter* opening so that it could be shared around, it still was likely *sent* to the city of Ephesus and perhaps then copied for use in nearby churches or circulated by Tychicus.

The Specific Character of Ephesians

Overall, the letter is general, offering teaching and exhortation that are not tied to one specific problem. Nevertheless, there are aspects of the letter that are reflective of the circumstances of the Ephesian Christians. Likewise, some of the statements about Paul's imprisonment can help us understand the letter's purpose and character. They are surely significant if Paul is the

---

2 The sole exception is Marcion (ca. 140 CE), who identified this letter as written to the nearby town of Laodicea (see Col 4:16). Tertullian responded: "We have it on the truth of the church that this letter was dispatched to the Ephesians. But at some point Marcion eagerly added a false title, as if he had been the most diligent investigator in this matter" (*Against Marcion* 5.17.1). Already Ignatius of Antioch (ca. 110 CE) says that Paul "remembered" the Ephesians "in an entire epistle" (Ignatius, *Ephesians* 12.2). For the patristic data, see Winger 2015, 28–32. For details about "in Ephesus" in 1:1, see Best 1997, 1–24.

letter's author, but are also important if one views the letter as a product of one of Paul's disciples perpetuating or renewing his legacy in Asia, since it tells us something of how he wanted Paul to be remembered as Christ's "ambassador in chains" (6:20).

Paul's Apostolate and Imprisonment

Paul speaks a lot about himself in this letter, particularly in two ways. First, he fits himself into the life of God's church as an apostle. After expounding the mystery of God's glory and revelation of himself in Christ as savior of both Jews and gentiles, Paul tells of God's work to reveal this mystery through the church (chap. 3). God reveals this mystery to the apostles, who saw the risen Jesus, and through them God communicates it to others. Paul states that he is the least of these apostles, but nevertheless fully an apostle by God's will and purpose (1:1; 3:1–4, 7–11; cf. Gal 1:1, 11–24; 2:7).

The way chapter 3 highlights Paul at the center of God's work may seem boastful to some if written by Paul (or, if by his disciple, as quite high praise of the man). Yet it is worth recalling what happened in Corinth: many were inclined to turn away from Paul when he seemed unimpressive or when his suffering appeared to contradict the divine power and blessing he claimed in his apostleship. Ephesians does not mention specific false teachings to which the audience is being drawn, but it is concerned to address one thing about Paul's ministry that could have seemed very unimpressive: his imprisonment (3:1; 4:1; 6:20). If Paul's personal ministry in Ephesus was accompanied by impressive "signs of an apostle" that drew people to see the almighty God working in him (cf. 2 Cor 12:12; Acts 19:11–12), he is in jail now, and some may have begun to doubt whether God still granted his authority and approval to this man. Ephesians chapter 3 sets Paul at the center of God's power in the church not merely to aggrandize Paul. Rather, this discussion concludes: "Therefore, I ask that you not lose heart at my sufferings for you, which is your glory" (3:13). Paul emphasizes that "the surpassing greatness" of God's power (1:19) is active now in the church to empower and guard his people—even when, as in Paul's case, Christ's power works to keep him *through* suffering instead of simply delivering him *from* it. Instead, the letter reframes his apostolate as providential, moving toward an opportunity for further evangelization: he is in chains, but is "an ambassador in chains" (6:19–20), a prisoner by Christ's—not his enemies'—design "for the sake of you gentiles" (3:1).

Ephesus and the "Powers"

Ephesus was a big, bustling provincial capital. The nearby Roman roads and its seaport brought a large influx of business and people. There were many deities worshipped there, but most especially Ephesian Artemis. This goddess was hailed as a "lord" (κυρία, *kyria*, "lady") and "savior" (σώτειρα, *sōteira*), with power over other gods. Often depicted with the signs of the zodiac, she was believed to have power even over fate itself. This powerful patroness was a significant part of the city's life. Her temple just outside the city was larger than the Parthenon in Athens, and her cultic celebrations and idols played a large role in the city's economic prosperity (see Acts 19:23–41). Two annual festivals to Artemis set the rhythm of the city's heartbeat: people competed in games, played music, danced, worshipped, paraded, and couples got engaged under her blessing. Being an Ephesian and honoring Artemis went hand in hand.[3]

The letter does not name this goddess outright, but its words speak directly to the Ephesians' situation.[4] The letter is addressed—at least predominantly—to former pagans in Ephesus (2:1–2, 11; 3:1, 8), who had surely worshipped Artemis and other gods or astral deities as part of who they were and how their world worked.[5] One can imagine what effects on their business, family relationships, and civic standing could have come from their turning to call a crucified Jew from Nazareth the only divine "Lord" and "savior." Temptations to mix Christ with these other deities would abound. And it may have been tempting to suspect that Christ was, actually, not so powerful as Artemis—especially when Christ's apostle was suffering and in prison.

The letter counteracts this by emphasizing Christ's status as ascended and victorious Lord. Christ has been raised from the dead and ascended to God's right hand, "high above every rule and authority and power and lordship and every name that is named, not only in this age but also in the one to come" (1:21). Christ has triumphed, and every so-called power or authority, every "lordship"—whether earthly or heavenly—is subject to him. Nothing is greater than he. And his great, eternal power is now at work in

---

3 Trebilco (2004, 27) notes that when people became citizens of the city, their names were etched into Artemis's temple.

4 See Immendörfer 2017.

5 Many Jews also lived in Ephesus and were allowed to practice their religion (see Josephus, *Jewish Antiquities* 14.223–27, 262–64; 16.167–68; cf. 12.125), although some gentiles also bore ill will toward the Jews there (Josephus, *Jewish Antiquities* 16.45, 160). It is possible that some of Paul's addressees were ethnically Jewish, but the letter does not address them as such (2:12).

the apostolic church (1:19; 3:7, 16, 20) and empowers believers by his presence and strength (1:19; 3:16–18; 4:16–17; 6:10). The ascended almighty Lord gave divine gifts to his people (4:7–16) so that their life and work might announce the mystery of God's saving plan to the "rulers and authorities in the heavenly places" (3:10). There are spiritual forces and powers that war against God's church—most notably the devil (2:2; 4:27; 6:11–12)—but Christ has conquered, and Christ works his power through and in his church for victory. The Ephesians should have no reason to fear Artemis or the fates or anything if they remain in the Lord Jesus.

The Relationship of Ephesians to Colossians

One final feature to note is the letter's close similarity to Colossians. There are similarities in *audience*, as Colossae was less than 120 miles from Ephesus, and Ephesian Artemis was popular with the Colossians as well. Relatedly, with similar *emphasis*, Colossians also highlights the supremacy and power of Christ in the face of any competing "powers" (see chapter 12 of this volume). Regarding *Paul's situation*, both letters are addressed from prison (see Col 4:3, 18), and both seem to be looking ahead toward Paul's giving a defense of the gospel, asking the audience to pray that Paul would speak well (Eph 6:18–20; Col 4:2–4). Both letters were also sent with the same carrier, Tychicus (Eph 6:21–22; Col 4:7–9).

More intriguing are the similarities in *wording* between the letters. Given in the table is a wooden translation that conveys the similarity in just a few passages.[6] Agreements in vocabulary are underlined. Continuous underlining indicates continuous agreement.

Eph 6:21–22	Col 4:7–9
But so that you also may know of my affairs and what I am doing, Tychicus the beloved brother and faithful minister in the Lord will make everything clear to you, whom I send to you for just this purpose, so that you might know about us and he might encourage your hearts.	My affairs, Tychicus the beloved brother and faithful minister and co-slave in the Lord will make everything clear to you, whom I send to you for just this purpose, so that you might know about us and he might encourage your hearts, with Onesimus the faithful and beloved brother, who is from among you; they will make known to you the things here.

6 Cf. also Eph 1:4/Col 1:22; Eph 1:7/Col 1:14; Eph 2:5/Col 2:13; Eph 3:2/Col 1:25; Eph 4:2/Col 3:12; Eph 4:22–24/Col 3:8–10. See Mitton 1951, 55–74.

Eph 4:16	Col 2:19
[The head, Christ,] from whom the whole body, being joined together and knit together through every ligament of God's supply given powerfully in the measure of each individual member, effects the growth of the body for its own up-building in love.	And not holding fast to the head, from whom the whole body, through the ligaments and ties being supplied and knit together, grows with the growth of God.

Eph 5:19–20	Col 3:16–17
Speaking to yourselves with psalms and hymns and spiritual songs, singing and making song in your heart to the Lord, giving thanks always for all things in the name of our Lord Jesus Christ to God the Father.	Let the word of Christ dwell in you richly, with all wisdom teaching and admonishing yourselves, with psalms, hymns, spiritual songs, singing with thanks in your hearts to God; and whatever you may do in word or deed, do it all in the name of the Lord Jesus, giving thanks to God the Father through him

The commendations of Tychicus show complete agreement for twenty-nine straight words, with the sole exception of "and co-slave" in Colossians. The other parallels are less exact but nevertheless striking. Now, it is not odd for one person to express himself in similar ways about similar topics. What makes these odd is that their shared vocabulary is *not* found in Paul's other letters (e.g., "knit together," "ligament," "hymns") where he addresses the same topics (the body of Christ's many members). Likewise, due to Greek's incredible variety in word order, use of the definite article, and vocabulary, it is highly unlikely that one would say the same thing the *exact* same way for so many words.

What might have caused these similarities? They suggest that one letter was written with the other close to hand, though overall neither is a slavish copy of the other. Most today view Ephesians as dependent on the more specific Colossians. If Ephesians is not Pauline, it makes sense that a later writer wrote with Colossians as a kind of template. But this is not unimaginable if the letter comes from Paul. If he wrote Ephesians quickly after Colossians as a similar but more general exhortation to Christians in the nearby capital, many similarities can be explained by his having Colossians fresh on his mind. He could have consulted his copy or allowed his scribe to reproduce certain parts entirely (like the commendation of Tychicus). Perhaps more likely, the imprisoned Paul may have authorized a trusted companion to do most of the wording and composition of the letter, directing him to adapt and circulate the message of Colossians more broadly in the capital to a church he loved but that he had not visited in some time.

The Purpose(s) of Ephesians

If one views Colossians as written after Paul's death, the same would then obtain for Ephesians. If both Colossians and Ephesians are from Paul, their similarities in situation, location, and letter carrier suggest that they were written from the same mindset. As discussed in chapter 12 of this volume, the most likely date for a Pauline writing of Colossians is during his Roman imprisonment in 60–62 CE. The same date range would also, then, fit Ephesians. This later date, if correct, may explain some of its general nature and Paul's expectation that many in the audience do not know him, since he had not been in the city for about five years when he wrote (or authorized a colleague to write) Ephesians.[7]

How can we characterize the letter's purpose? Whether directly written by Paul or a disciple, the letter probably has no single purpose other than to reach out to these believers with a message of encouragement. Yes, it means to reframe Paul's imprisonment as God's work through him as an apostle, and he asks their intercessory prayer for his ministry, but this is only an accent of the letter, not its main theme. The letter teaches particularly gentiles in Ephesus about the plan of God (1:3–23) and their place in it as co-heirs of his promises in Christ (2:1–10), calling them to know and stand in the power of the risen Christ by walking in the Spirit. The closest thing to a purpose statement in the letter is expressed in Paul's prayers for them (1:16–21; 3:14–21): that they be drawn into deeper knowledge of God in Christ and be strengthened against adversity to grow together in unity and love. Paul waxes eloquent, with a poetic or liturgical flair at several points, inviting the audience to reflect deeply on the eternal plan of God and the wondrous ways of God's grace. And, being so enlightened, the Ephesians are called to

---

7 Some place this letter (and Colossians) in 58–60 during Paul's imprisonment in Caesarea. A few countenance the possibility that Colossians was written earlier in an Ephesian imprisonment (Bormann 2012, 46–52), which might allow one to argue that Ephesians, too, was written from Ephesus as a circular letter, but the letter's features and implied audience seem better suited to composition from a Roman imprisonment or later.

mature individually and together, that the church might "grow in every way into him who is the head, Christ" (4:15).

OVERVIEW

I. **Opening (1:1–2)**
   A. Paul to the Ephesians (1:1–2).

II. **Praise of God's Work in Christ (1:3–3:21)**
   A. Blessed be God for his wondrous plan of salvation (1:3–14).
      1. He planned the grace of adoption and inheritance for us in Christ from the beginning of time (1:3–12)!
      2. And you, too, by the word of his gospel, have been made his own treasured children and sealed with his Holy Spirit (1:13–14).
   B. I thank God for his work in you (1:15–2:22).
      1. I pray you would know more and more deeply the wonder of his work and the majesty of Christ (1:15–23).
      2. While we were dead in sin, our merciful God brought us to share by grace in the heavenly life of the risen Lord Jesus (2:1–10).
         a. Remember that you gentiles, formerly alienated from God's blessings, have now been brought into communion with God through Christ (2:11–13).
         b. He has made us one, Jew and gentile both, and re-created us as one family in whom God's Spirit dwells, a temple built on the cornerstone of Christ and the foundation of the apostles and prophets (2:13–22).
   C. It is for this gospel that I have been made an apostle for you gentiles (3:1–21).
      1. God's saving mystery has now been revealed to the apostles, through whom God powerfully makes it known (3:1–7).
         a. I, Paul, am the least of these apostles, but God has chosen me to preach his gospel to the gentiles. My chains will not hinder God's work (3:8–13).

b. And I pray now for you, that God would bring you to know the wonderful mystery of his love and live faithfully in it (3:14–21).

III. **Exhortation to Grow Together in Christ's Love and Power (4:1–6:20)**

A. So let your life be shaped by God's grace and calling (4:1–6:9).

1. The ascended Christ has made us one and has given gifts to all members of his body, that the whole church might grow and be built up in faith, hope, and love (4:1–16).

2. Do not keep living like the pagans. Let your thinking and values be transformed by Christ, in whom God has created you anew for a life of righteousness and holiness (4:17–24).

3. So put off lying, stealing, and bitterness; direct your mouth, hands, and heart to building up your fellow Christians (4:25–32).

4. Do not take part in the wickedness of the pagan world. Walk together as God's children, embodying his self-giving love in your praise and kindness toward others (5:1–20).

a. This applies also in your household relationships, each acting for the good of the other. Let wives submit to their husbands as the church to Christ, and let husbands love their wives sacrificially as Christ loved the church (5:21–33).

b. Children and slaves, as subordinates, should be obedient in fear of the Lord and hope of reward. Parents should not anger their children but nourish and admonish them. Masters should not be threatening and must remember that their Master in heaven will judge their deeds (6:1–9).

B. Finally, stand fast in Christ (6:10–20).

1. Take up Christ's armor of truth and righteousness to defend against the attacks of evil powers against which we struggle (6:10–17).

2. And be steadfast in prayer for God's church and for our work to speak his gospel to the world (6:18–20).

IV. **Letter Closing (6:21–24)**

A. Receive Tychicus well. He will update you about our affairs (6:21–22).

B. Grace be with all who love the Lord (6:23–24).

KEY FEATURES

A main division in the letter can be seen between 1:3–3:21 (God's saving work for the church, the church's place within God's plan) and 4:1–6:20 (the church's growth in love, unity, and holiness). These sections reinforce each other and repeat the themes of knowledge, grace, love, unity, and Christ's power in the church.[8] Paul draws readers into the mystery of Christ, reflecting on Christ as the realization of the eternal divine plan, and from there Paul prays that the risen Lord's power in his church would strengthen them so that they may stand against evil by the power of the ascended and almighty Lord Jesus.

The Majesty and Mystery of God in Christ

Ephesians is somewhat liturgical and meditative, almost ceaselessly piling up phrases that both laud and teach the power and grace of God in Christ—their "length and breadth" and "unsurpassed wealth" (1:7, 18; 2:7; 3:8, 16, 18). The language of adoration invites the audience to reflect and engage more the "mystery" of God's gracious plan. The letter begins by reflecting on the great plan of God in history and even before history and then leads more specifically into the Ephesians' own reception of the gospel (1:13) to invite them to wisdom and wonder as they ponder the salvation of God.

The letter begins by "blessing" the God who has blessed the church (1:3; cf. 2 Cor 1:3) and traces the present salvation of the church back to God's plan "before the foundation of the world" (Eph 1:4). Strikingly, even when looking back to a time before the incarnate Christ, the letter's picture remains Christocentric. For the blessing of the church and the predestining of both Jews and gentiles to salvation occurs "in Christ" even before the foundation of the world. Paul blesses the God who sent Christ to mediate the grace of adoption "in love" and "in the Beloved"—namely, Christ (1:4, 6). In 1:3–14 Paul uses the phrases "in Christ" or "in him" ten times, driving home again and again that Christ is the sphere "in" which the Lord's saving work is accomplished. Salvation is worked through the Son both before history and

---

8 Heil 2007 identifies in the larger and smaller sections of the letter an intricate chiastic structure (in which, beginning from both ends of the letter and progressing toward the middle, the two halves of the letter correspond in theme).

in history as the ascended Christ lavishes forgiveness and divine graces on the church and seals them in baptism with the Holy Spirit as an "advance" or "down payment" (ἀρραβών, *arrabōn*, 1:14; cf. 2 Cor 1:22; 5:5) of the future inheritance of God's children (Eph 1:11–14; 2:22; 3:17; 4:30).

Paul lauds this plan of God as a deep "mystery" now revealed (1:9; 3:4, 9; 6:19). It is a mystery reaching back to the Father's plan before time but revealed in its fullness now in time in Christ and the church. If God's love for his creation through the Son can be called timeless because it was perfect already before God created anything, the working of God's loving plan occurs in Christ and in time. Christ's death and resurrection turn the wheel of the ages, and in the Christ-event one sees the fullness of a mystery that indeed was not fully revealed before the apostolic age. Israel's prophets and sages knew God's mercy and even foretold God's promise that gentiles would benefit from God's blessings to Israel. But the depths of divine love and mercy are revealed most clearly in the cross (Rom 5:6–8), and the *way* the gentiles would be brought to Zion through Christ and the gift of the Spirit is fully manifest in the church.[9] This connects the Ephesians directly to God's eternal plan as well and to the history of Israel: these gentiles, who were once dead in sin and alienated from the life and promises of God (Eph 2:1–2, 11–12; 4:18), have been made "one body" with Israel and share the inheritance of God's children (3:6; cf. 2:19), receiving the adoption preordained for them through Christ. God has "made the two one" by Christ's blood (2:14), uniting all nations in time and uniting this time to eternity, "summing up all things" in Christ (1:10).[10]

The mystery of salvation is the work of the eternal creator to bring about his "new creation" (2 Cor 5:17; Gal 6:15). God, by his grace, joins sinners to Christ and "creates" them anew for good works (Eph 2:10; 4:24), just as God "creates" the two historical groups of Jews and gentiles to be "one new person" in Christ (2:15), one universal church of believers in whose hearts God dwells (2:22; 3:17). This is God's eternal plan, one worked out within history to bring salvation to the world and, by the apostolic ministry (3:1–10), given in faith and baptism to these Ephesians (1:13; 2:8–9; 5:26). They are invited to meditate and take refuge in this plan of the all-powerful God and to let his new creation have its full effect in their fidelity and charity.[11]

9 See Grindheim 2003.

10 On Jew-gentile issues in Ephesians, see Yee 2005.

11 The logical coherence of Ephesians, moving from the eternal plan of God to Christ, to the church, and to the liturgical and ethical lives of the Ephesians, is drawn out well in Covington 2018.

God's Victory of Love and the Church's Life

The Ascended Lord and His Power in the Church

Paul often appeals to Christ's death and resurrection as the twin poles of the Christ-event in which the baptized participate (see Rom 6:3–11). Ephesians adds another accent by emphasizing the ascension of Jesus to glory and his heavenly seat at the right hand of the Father. In many NT writings, borrowing from Psalm 110:1–2, the ascension marks the moment in which Christ, in his glorified human nature, takes his seat as Lord and judge to rule over all God's enemies (Acts 2:33–36; 1 Cor 15:24–27; Heb 10:12–13; 1 Pet 3:21–22). Raising and exalting Jesus, the Father put "all things under his feet" (Eph 1:22; cf. Ps 8:7 [KJV 8:6]). Christ has triumphed and is infinitely superior to any power that stands against God's plan, "far above all rule and authority and power and lordship and every name that is named" (Eph 1:20–21; cf. Col 2:14–15). The "spiritual forces of evil" still exist in the present age (6:11–12), but Christ the victor reigns now, drawing all things toward their consummation and his final defeat of sin, death, and the devil (cf. 1 Cor 15:24–27, 54–57).

This ascension-driven Christology also informs how Ephesians speaks of the church's salvation and the power of God at work within it. Christ has been exalted, and those who believe are governed and strengthened unto salvation by his universe-ruling power. For if Christ rules over "all things," the God who exalted him also "gave him as head over all to the church, which is his body" (1:22–23). The ascended Christ sends forth the Spirit, and his heavenly power to sanctify and save becomes operative through baptism and in the lives of individuals (4:1–6; 5:26; cf. 1 Pet 3:21–22). Believers, even now, participate in Christ's heavenly exaltation according to Ephesians just as they participate in Christ's new life by his resurrection (Eph 2:5–7; cf. Rom 6:4). And their life in Christ is furthered by the gifts sent forth by the exalted Christ. Quoting Psalm 68:19 (KJV 68:18), Paul speaks of Christ's ascension as a victory in which he "ascended on high" and from his exalted state shared out the spoils, giving "gifts" or graces to empower and sanctify his people (4:7–10).

If any Ephesians were tempted to fear the power of Artemis, they are here reminded of the mighty fortress that God has given them in the church and that the power of the eternal Son who conquered death is theirs to protect and lead them to salvation. Indeed, God's graced saints are not merely protected but are themselves like a monument commemorating the saving victory of Christ, to make known God's "manifold wisdom . . . to the powers and authorities in the heavenly places" (3:10) and demonstrate the "wealth of his grace by his kindness toward us in Christ Jesus" (2:7).[12] If human wars and gods were commemorated by monuments and temples, God's victory monument is his people, whose life together shows forth Christ's infinite power to redeem and reclaim his world.[13]

Growing in Unity and Love

The ethical exhortations in Ephesians are grounded in the church's redemption and its place within God's saving plan as believers are renewed by the Spirit and grow in knowledge. Demonic powers darken the mind, foment enmity, and encourage people to use God's creation and their bodies for hatred and destructive self-interest (2:2-3; 4:17-19, 27). But Christ has triumphed over these to set free those in thrall to the devil (2:1-5). Christ is himself the embodiment of divine love, and he has lavished mercy upon his people (1:4-6; 2:4; 5:2, 25). And the power of the eternal and limitless Lord now "empowers" and "strengthens" his people through the ministry of the church. The ascended Lord "supplies" the Spirit to illuminate believers' minds and strengthen them in fortitude (4:6; cf. Gal 3:5; Phil 1:19; Col 2:19), so that they may no longer live like "the gentiles"—that is, like pagans (Eph 4:17-24).[14] The ways they once followed in darkness—sexual immorality, greed, hurtful or vain speech—are to be rebuked and reformed by the light of Jesus Christ (5:3-14).

Knowing Christ, believers are to discern the will of God and imitate the one from whom they have learned love (5:1-2, 17). Christ has conquered enmity by redeeming all by the same divine mercy, so enmity and division must be undone (2:11-21; 4:1-6). All must be done in love that builds up others in the church. Those who steal should instead work honestly so that they have a legitimate gift to share with the needy (4:28). Mouths should be used to build up those in need rather than for malice and deprecation

---

12 Paul speaks of these powers as being "in the heavenly places" (3:10; 6:12), making the point that these powers are not merely earthly realities. See Brannon 2011, 194-97.

13 See Gombis 2010.

14 Interestingly, while gentile Christians remain gentiles *ethnically*, being in Christ means that they must not be gentiles *ethically*—"you must no longer walk as the gentiles walk" (4:17; cf. 2:11). In the second century, Christians would begin to speak of themselves as a sort of alternative "race," determined not by ancestral bloodlines but by the blood of Christ (e.g., *Martyrdom of Polycarp* 3.2; 14.1; 17.1; Aristides, *Apology* 2.2).

(4:29). Wrath must give way to forgiveness (4:30–32). Household relationships, too, must be grounded in and directed toward the love of God and neighbor, and so should become a sign of God's covenantal love and care for his "bride" and "household" (5:21–6:9; cf. 2:19).[15] Indeed, while the household instructions here parallel those in Roman society, the mode and motivations are centered in Christ: they call for self-giving love for the other within the relational networks of the Greco-Roman household. Wives are called to submit to their husbands as to representatives of Christ, the church's "head" (5:22–25), who like Christ are to provide and care for them.[16] Husbands are not to view their wives as instruments but to care for them as for their own bodies (5:28–30), imitating Christ's self-giving love for their wives' good and sanctification (5:25–27, 31–33). Children and slaves are called to obey, not because they are lesser beings, but because of God's esteem and reward of their goodwill (6:2, 7–8). Parents must work for their children's growth and not provoke them (6:4); masters must treat their slaves with the kind of fidelity and service commanded of slaves in the Lord ("do the same things toward them"), and they must remember God's reward and judgment for their actions toward slaves (6:9).

Paul envisions the whole church growing together into Christ and, thereby, growing closer together. The letter's vision is "Christ-agogical," leading believers deeper into the mystery of Christ, for in clinging to him and knowing him each is reformed in mind, action, and purpose and indeed "created" anew in the one body of Christ (see 2:10, 15; 4:24).[17] The whole church is described as a body or single person, as a building or temple, founded on Christ and the apostles and growing as new believers are joined to Christ and in him become one (2:19–22; 4:13–16). And God's new creation in Christ, already sharing his heavenly life with him, is to grow and mature

---

15 It is Christologically notable that, while "God" is the *paterfamilias* over the "household" (2:19) and the prophets consistently depict God as the groom of Israel, the bride (e.g., Isa 54:5; Jer 3:1–5; Hos 2:4 [KJV 2:2]), Christ as Son is identified as the bridegroom in the NT (e.g., Matt 22:1; Mark 2:19–20; John 3:29; Rev 21:9).

16 "Headship" has connotations of source or authority, but the authority of the "head" also bore obligations toward those under that authority, in this context specified as Christlike love and provision (see Cohick 2020, 356–58). Interpretations of headship stressing only authority and prerogative, or depicting wives' submission as the antithesis of freedom or of independent contribution to society, are unfortunately one-sided. For magisterial clarifications, see Pope Pius XI, Encyclical Letter *Casti Connubii* (December 31, 1930), §27; Pope John Paul II, Apostolic Letter *Mulieris Dignitatem* (August 15, 1988), §24–25.

17 Usami 1983, 71.

by each part living and contributing to the stability and flourishing of the whole by the varied gifts given to them (4:7). Those in apostolic office are especially given to instruct and guide the faithful in this (4:11–14). By admonishing each other, speaking in love to each other, and using their hands and tongues to build each other up, each member contributes to the maturity and growth of the body (4:13–16). This is how individuals grow in sanctity and how the whole church grows and matures together. It is how God proclaims through the church that the powers of darkness have lost the war. And, in the end, this is how the church grows into full and perfect union with her head, Christ Jesus.

FURTHER READING

Best, Ernest. 1997. *Essays on Ephesians*. London: T&T Clark.

Brinks, C. L. 2009. "'Great Is Artemis of the Ephesians': Acts 19:23–41 in Light of Goddess Worship in Ephesus." *CBQ* 71 (4): 776–94.

Cohick, Lynn H. 2020. *The Letter to the Ephesians*. NICNT. Grand Rapids: Eerdmans.

Gombis, Timothy G. 2010. *The Drama of Ephesians: Participating in the Triumph of God*. Downers Grove, IL: IVP Academic.

Grindheim, Sigurd. 2003. "What the OT Prophets Did Not Know: The Mystery of the Church in Eph 3,2–13." *Bib* 84 (4): 531–53.

Heil, John Paul. 2007. *Ephesians: Empowerment to Walk in Love for the Unity of All in Christ*. SBLStBL 13. Atlanta: SBL Press.

Lincoln, Andrew T. 1990. *Ephesians*. WBC 42. Dallas: Word Books.

Lincoln, Andrew T., and A. J. M. Wedderburn. 1993. *The Theology of the Later Pauline Letters*. Cambridge: Cambridge University Press.

MacDonald, Margaret Y. 2000. *Colossians and Ephesians*. SP 17. Collegeville, MN: Liturgical Press.

_____. 2004. "The Politics of Identity in Ephesians." *JSNT* 26 (4): 94–113.

Oster, Richard E. 1992. "Ephesus." *ABD* 2:542–49.

Schnackenburg, Rudolf. 1991. *The Epistle to the Ephesians: A Commentary*. Translated by Helen Heron. Edinburgh: T&T Clark.

Thielman, Frank. 2010. *Ephesians*. BECNT. Grand Rapids: Baker Academic.

Trebilco, Paul. 2004. *The Early Christians in Ephesus from Paul to Ignatius*. WUNT 166. Tübingen: Mohr Siebeck.

CHAPTER ELEVEN

Philippians

hilippians, like Ephesians, Colossians, and Philemon, is another letter Paul sends from prison. Paul writes in part to thank the Philippians for a gift they sent him. But the letter is more than a mere "thank-you." Writing in the face of his possible death, Paul exhorts the Philippians to rejoice in all circumstances because of God's grace and calls them to practice a humility and sacrificial love that are learned from none other than the crucified Christ.

BACKGROUND

Philippi

A major city in the province of Macedonia, Philippi lay along an important Roman road, the Via Egnatia, and near the port city of Neapolis. Among the other locations to which Paul wrote (other than Rome itself), Philippi is distinct for its Roman-ness. After Julius Caesar was assassinated, his supporters Mark Antony and Octavian (who would become the emperor Caesar Augustus) defeated the rebels just outside Philippi in 42 BCE, cementing it in the new and growing story of the Roman Empire. Italians and Roman soldiers were settled in this historically Greek city in the following years, and in 30 BCE Augustus made it a Roman colony.

Philippi came to mirror the city of Rome in many respects. It had its own forum, similar political organization and law codes, and, though there were many Greeks in the city and the Greek language remained spoken, Latin predominated in public inscriptions.[1] The story of the Roman Empire had put Philippi on the map, historically, and the city was growing into its Roman

---

1 See Oakes 2001, 35–54; Hellerman 2005, 64–87.

identity.[2] Roman flavor was present in the culture of social climbing and in the cult of praise and sacrifice to the emperor as a sort of divine benefactor of the Roman world—something that would create tension with steadfast Christians who would not sacrifice to this so-called Lord.[3] This background puts into sharp relief Paul's exhortation to imitate Christ's humility and self-emptying (2:1–11), as well as his call for the Philippian Christians to put stock in their heavenly "citizenship" (3:20).

The Philippian Christians

Paul founded the congregation around 49 CE.[4] According to Acts, he made inroads there both with worshippers of Abraham's God at a small prayer gathering and with pagans, exemplified by the conversion narratives of the God-fearing merchant Lydia, who began supporting the church and Paul specifically, and of a Philippian jailer who guarded Paul and Silas when they were imprisoned for exorcising a fortune-teller (Acts 16:11–40). In 1 Thessalonians 2:2, Paul recalls that he was "treated insolently" in Philippi by the authorities, but this did not stop his evangelical work there. When he was released, Paul left to evangelize Thessalonica (see Phil 4:15–16; Acts 16–17).

The Philippians became a major source of support for Paul and his missionary work. They offered aid when he left Philippi for Thessalonica and thereafter remained "partners" with him through financial and material contributions (1:5; 4:15–16). In fact, when Paul (for strategic reasons) refused contributions from the Corinthians, the Macedonian Christians and particularly those in Philippi sustained him by their gifts (2 Cor 11:9). Paul also acclaims the Macedonian Christians as exemplary for their contributions to the collection for Jerusalem (2 Cor 8:1–5). Paul cherishes the Philippians for their open love and sacrificial support for the gospel mission. And they have now renewed this support by sending a gift with Epaphroditus, whom Paul lauds as an example of self-giving service to God. He gave up his health

---

2 In Acts 16:20–21, Paul's accusers appeal to their identity as "Romans" (not Macedonians or Greeks) to persuade the people against them.

3 When Polycarp of Smyrna (70–156 CE) was being taken to his martyrdom, his sympathetic guards pleaded: "Why is it wrong to say, 'Caesar is Lord,' and to make the sacrifice, etc. and save yourself?" (*Martyrdom of Polycarp* 8.2). He refused.

4 This is a reasonable estimate. Paul's "insolent treatment" in Philippi occurred not long before traveling to Thessalonica (cf. 4:15–16; 1 Thess 2:2), and he left Thessalonica not too many months before writing that letter in 50/51 (see chapter 13).

to bring Paul their gift, which Paul calls a "sacrifice acceptable and pleasing to God" (4:18).

Where and When Was Philippians Written?

This epistle does not explicitly name where it was written other than the fact that Paul is writing from prison (1:7, 13–14, 17). Paul was, however, imprisoned in several places, so we are left looking for other data to help form an educated guess. The letter is obviously written after he founded the church in Philippi (around 49 CE), and probably a few years after he left Macedonia. When Paul comments on the Philippians' financial partnership with him from his founding visit to Thessalonica and to a later period in which they desired to but could not send a gift (4:10, 14–16), he seems to recap a period of at least a few years' worth of partnership with the Philippians. Additionally, several communications must have occurred between Paul and Philippi between their last gift and this letter. After or while delivering the gift Epaphroditus became deathly ill, then recovered, and Paul now sends Epaphroditus back with the letter to comfort the Philippians because they were concerned when they heard of his illness. Several trips are thus necessary to cover the data: the Philippians have to get word that Paul is in prison (1:7, 14; 4:10); they send a gift and Paul receives it (4:18); Epaphroditus gets sick and someone brings news of it to Philippi (2:26); he recovers, and then Paul and Timothy write this letter (1:1). Each of these trips takes time. So, with the previous time period in which they supported him and these trips since his arrest, this letter is surely written at least a few years after Paul's founding visit around 49 CE.

The letter also gives some hints about Paul's own situation. There seems to be a good bit of evangelical activity around the imprisoned Paul: he says that his chains have encouraged many to preach Christ, some out of good motives and others trying to compete with Paul (1:14–18). This makes his location likely one in which a significant ministry has been built up. Paul describes some around him in particularly Roman or at least Latinate terms, saying that his chains have had an evangelical effect on "the whole *praetorium*" (Greek πραιτώριον, *praitōrion*; 1:13) and sending greetings from "Caesar's household" (4:22). As to his own situation, a major feature of this captivity epistle is that Paul seems to be facing a real possibility of execution (1:19–26): he consoles them that he "hopes" to be released and visit them

(1:24–26; 2:24), yet he does not know how things will turn out and encourages them to keep the faith even if he should die where he is (2:17, 23).

Which Imprisonment?

Scholars interpret and combine these data in different ways to locate this letter within different Pauline imprisonments. The three major options are *Rome, Caesarea,* and *Ephesus.*

Paul's imprisonment in Rome is the latest of the three options, dating about 60–62 CE on the testimony of Acts. The last chapters of Acts recount Paul's long imprisonment in Caesarea, after which he is transferred to Rome and awaits his hearing before the emperor. Acts at least indicates that Paul enjoyed considerable freedom during this two-year imprisonment (a sort of house arrest), which would account for his ability to send and receive emissaries such as Timothy or Epaphroditus (Acts 28:30). Rome already had an established church, which can fit with Paul's comments about other preachers in the area. Advocates of a Roman imprisonment especially note Paul's sending greetings from "Caesar's household" and his reference to the *praetorium.* A "household" was an economic unit, involving blood relatives, slaves, and others. The "household of Caesar" thus often referred to the network of slaves, former slaves, soldiers, and others employed in imperial service, which existed in major cities but especially the capital in Rome. The word *praetorium* could refer to the praetorian guard, an elite unit of soldiers tasked with protecting the emperor and keeping the peace in Rome and

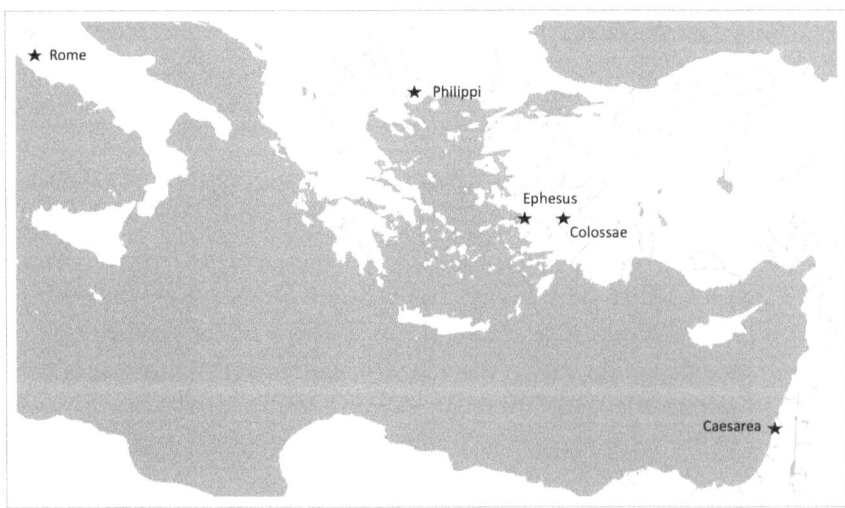

nearby towns, though it was also used of the governors' headquarters in the imperial provinces.

Rome has long been the traditional location for Paul's writing of Philippians. However, none of these data fit Rome only; Caesar's "household" would exist in provincial capitals such as Caesarea or Ephesus, which also had a governor's headquarters called a *praetorium*.[5] And other factors in the letter are less fitting to a Roman provenance. One is the distance between Rome and Philippi combined with the trips and communications required between Paul's being jailed and writing the letter, with the shortest trek crossing Macedonia, sailing across the sea, and then traveling westward across Italy (probably a month each way). One may also question how well the letter's acknowledgment of an unexpectedly close execution fits the picture of Paul being on house arrest in Rome, protected by his citizen's rights and awaiting an audience with Caesar. More significant, his words to the Philippians suggest that he has not been there since his founding visit (cf. 1:26, 30; 4:15–16), but he definitely visited Philippi to gather the collection before his imprisonments in Caesarea and Rome (2 Cor 2:13; 7:5; 8:1–5; 9:4; cf. Acts 20:1–6).

Others locate the writing of Philippians slightly earlier during Paul's imprisonment in Caesarea under Felix and Festus, around 58–60 CE (Acts 23:23 26:32). Our only source for this imprisonment is Acts, which indicates that he had freedom to receive visitors here, too, and Acts explicitly says he was held in the provincial *praetorium* in Caesarea (Acts 23:35). However, if Rome is far from Philippi, Caesarea is even farther, about twelve hundred miles away. Assuming the picture painted in Acts has not left out any serious threats of execution, Paul's imprisonment there is secure—indeed, its whole purpose is Paul's security: Paul is transferred there to protect him as a citizen from being murdered in Jerusalem (Acts 23:12–35), and then he is held by politicking governors until he appeals to be transferred to Rome (Acts 24:26–27; 25:9–12, 21). Further, as above, the letter seems to speak to the Philippians as though he has not visited them since founding the church, which suggests that the letter was written before even his Caesarean imprisonment.

---

5 Actually, in the rest of the NT, the Greek word πραιτώριον is *only* used for provincial governors' headquarters: e.g., Acts 23:35 (Caesarea); Matt 27:27 (Jerusalem). Some claim Paul is choosing his words improperly if not writing from Rome, but this is inaccurate: even the fine Roman orator Cicero uses the Latin *praetorium* to refer to provincial headquarters (*Against Verres* 2.4.65; 2.5.92). See Thielman 2003, 222; Hawthorne 2004, xliii.

Another possibility is that Paul wrote while imprisoned in Ephesus. The main objection many raise is that Acts reports no imprisonment in Ephesus. But Acts clearly omits many imprisonments, reporting those in Caesarea, Rome, and before that only a very brief jailing in Philippi (Acts 16:19–40), whereas already around 56 CE Paul reports that he had been imprisoned numerous times (2 Cor 6:5; 11:23).[6] And an Ephesian imprisonment is incredibly likely.[7] Ephesus was the capital of the province of Asia, where both Paul and Acts indicate that the Christian movement grew and spread around Paul despite challenges and opponents (1 Cor 15:32; 16:8–9; Acts 19:8–10). Particularly, 2 Corinthians 1:8–10 reports that he suffered an "affliction in Asia" and even "despaired of life itself" because of the prospect of receiving "the sentence of death" (τὸ ἀπόκριμα τοῦ θανάτου, *to apokrima tou thanatou*).[8] Paul's words bespeak an arrest and imprisonment for a hostile trial, which leads him to reflect on the prospect of his own death in 2 Corinthians (4:7–5:15) more personally than in other letters except, intriguingly, for Philippians 1:19–26.[9]

If we had to guess the location of one imprisonment that Acts omits, it would be Ephesus, sometime during his ministry there in the mid-50s (most estimate it around 52–55 CE). And Ephesus fits this letter well. As a provincial capital, Ephesus surely would have been a place in which Paul would have found many members of "Caesar's household" and a *praetorium*. If these terms sound particularly Roman, Paul's vocabulary may be owed not to where he is but to whom he is writing, since Philippi prided itself on its colonial status as a kind of "Rome away from Rome." Indeed, he does the same with the very name of the Philippians, not using the normal Greek designation Φιλιππεῖς (*Philippeis*) but calling them Φιλιππήσιοι (*Philippēsioi*), which mimics the Latin *Philippenses*.[10] Paul's fear of a death sentence in Asia fits an Ephesian imprisonment and the possibility of execution he faced when writing Philippians. The success of his ministry there and the spread

6 Writing around 95 CE, Clement of Rome opines that Paul was imprisoned seven times (*1 Clement* 5.5–6).

7 Cf. Trebilco 2004, 83–87.

8 The statement that he "fought wild beasts in Ephesus" (1 Cor 15:32) is likely metaphorical, or at least an exaggeration.

9 On the connection between this event and Paul's reflection on death in 2 Corinthians, see Deibert 2017, 182–211.

10 Thielman 2003, 222–23; cf. Oakes 2001, 65–66.

of the gospel in the area, though not only by people who were under Paul's authority, fits Paul's comments in 1:14–18. Likewise, an Ephesian provenance would allow for Paul to have written Philippians a few years after evangelizing Philippi, fitting his descriptions of their many gifts and communications since he left Macedonia (4:15–16), and before he had made the subsequent visits to Philippi reported in 2 Corinthians before being held in Caesarea or Rome. Ephesus lies only 401 miles from Philippi; each trip would still have taken roughly a week by sea, which fits if one grants that Paul's imprisonment was not incredibly brief.

More Than One Letter?

Another theory should be noted as we consider the letter's composition and background. Several scholars believe that the book of Philippians, as we have it now, is actually a compilation of more than one letter. Suspicion of this comes partly from a statement from Polycarp of Smyrna (70–156 CE) that Paul wrote "letters" (plural) to Philippi (Polycarp, *Philippians* 3.2), but largely from apparent disjunctions detected in the letter's flow. Some see a break at 3:1, where what looks like a closing statement ("finally," λοιπόν, *loipon*) is followed by a shift in tone at 3:2. Some argue for a break after 4:8–9 ("finally") and understand 4:10–20 as a separate, self-contained thank-you note. These and other considerations lead many to see either two or three original Pauline letters to Philippi that have been patched together, though there is little agreement on how many letters or precisely where each begins and ends. Naturally, if the letter was originally two or three letters, it would complicate decisions about its place and time of writing.

However, most commentators see no need to doubt the letter's integrity. The Greek term λοιπόν (*loipon*), often translated "finally" (3:1; 4:8), need not signal a letter's conclusion (see 1 Thess 4:1; 2 Thess 3:1; Ignatius, *Smyrneans* 9.1). Likewise, the various parts of the letter are connected by specific themes and even rare vocabulary that are particular to Philippians, and it has been argued that the letter exhibits an artful and persuasive flow as a single letter.[11] Importantly, too, the alleged break in tone in 3:1–2 depends entirely on how one reads 3:2. Though often translated as "watch out for the dogs"—a sudden, imminent warning—Paul merely says to "look at" them as an example, which

11 See Garland 1985; D. Watson 1988.

fits with the other examples the letter presents throughout for the Philippians to imitate or avoid.[12]

If one treats Philippians as one letter, it can be posited to have been written during a period of captivity in Ephesus. If we assume Paul would not have stayed terribly long after being released from his chains, that would put the letter toward the end of his Ephesian ministry, approximately 54/55 CE.

Why Was Philippians Written?

The Philippians are not a "problem congregation." Like all churches, they need continued encouragement in Christ, and they face internal and external difficulties. There is some kind of conflict between two prominent women in the church (4:2–3) that could lead to fractures. And the enemies of the gospel will likely put pressure on them to compromise their faith (see 1:27–28; 3:18–21). But they are not apparently in the grip of flagrant immorality or running after false teaching.

Paul's most immediate purpose for sending this letter is to thankfully acknowledge a gift that the Philippians have sent him (4:18). There was apparently a period when they did not send a gift, and his letter acknowledges their partnership in his mission and encourages them to continue it despite his imprisonment.[13] But the letter is no mere thank-you note. Paul takes this opportunity to exhort them to abound "more and more" in the faith and love they already exhibit (1:9–11).

One thing that colors Paul's exhortation particularly is his uncertainty about his own fate. This brings him to emphasize God's work and grace through Christian suffering. His reflections on "joy" in suffering pepper the letter (1:4, 18, 25; 2:2, 17, 18, 28, 29; 3:1; 4:1, 4, 10), as he shows by his own example that Christ's power and grace are enough in every circumstance (1:12–26; 4:10–13). Paul's potential fate and the suffering lot of Christians also color his exhortations to faithfulness. The Philippians must be ready to imitate Christ's own humility and the example of leaders like Paul himself, fixing their hope on Christ as they await his return to judge and save (1:10, 27; 2:12–13, 14–17; 3:4–21; 4:4–9).

---

12 See Reed 1996. Paul's βλέπετε (blepete) here merely commands them to "see" or "consider" (as in 1 Cor 1:26), rather than adding other Greek particles that would imply danger or warning (as in, e.g., Mark 8:15).

13 This is a main point of Jennings's analysis, though his argument overreaches itself when he claims that this is the letter's "sole purpose" (2018, 4).

OVERVIEW

I. **Letter Opening (1:1–11)**

A. Paul and Timothy to the saints in Philippi with their bishops and deacons (1:1–2).

B. I thank God for your partnership in the gospel (1:3–11).

II. **Paul's Imprisonment and the Proclamation of Christ (1:12–26)**

A. My imprisonment is no accident: through it God spreads his gospel and inspires bold preaching in others (1:12–18).

B. I may die, and Christ will be magnified, but I believe I will live and continue my ministry for you and others (1:19–26).

III. **Stand Firm, United in Christlike Humility until Christ's Return (1:27–4:9)**

A. But whether I am with you or gone, stand firm in the face of the gospel's opponents—even in suffering for Christ's sake, as I am (1:27–30).

1. Do not look only to your own gain, but look to the interests of others, just as Christ did for us (2:1–5).

   a. Christ humbled himself for us in his incarnation and crucifixion (2:6–8).

   b. Therefore God exalted him highly, and all creation will confess him as Lord (2:9–11).

2. So follow Christ in this way, whether I am present or absent, and remain steadfast in Christ until the judgment day (2:12–18).

   a. In my absence, I hope to send Timothy, who looks to others' interests (2:19–24).

   b. I've sent Epaphroditus, instead, who has suffered greatly for the gospel, that you may be comforted (2:25–30).

B. Imitate me, and watch out for those people who put confidence in circumcision and worldly status rather than Christ (3:1–21).

1. Indeed, I have greater honors and reason for confidence than they (3:4–6).

2. But I consider everything junk when compared with being joined to Christ—his suffering and his resurrection (3:7–11).

　　3. Let us press on to be faithful until that day of resurrection (3:12–17).

　　　　a. The gospel's opponents are headed for destruction (3:18–19).

　　　　b. But those in Christ will be exalted in glory, as he was (3:20–21).

　C. So stand firm! The Lord is near (4:1–9)!

　　　　1. No more squabbles (Euodia and Syntyche, that means you) (4:2–3).

　　　　2. Be joyful through prayer and faith (4:4–7).

　　　　3. Set your mind on what is good, and hold fast what we taught you (4:8–9).

IV. **Paul's Gratitude to God and the Philippians' Gift (4:10–20)**

　A. Your support gladdens me—though my strength and contentment are in Christ (4:10–13).

　B. Your faith is shown by your history of aid for my ministry (4:14–17).

　C. Your gift to me pleases God, who will repay you in Christ (4:18–20).

V. **Letter Closing (4:21–23)**

　A. Receive and pass on our greetings in Christ (4:21–22).

　B. Grace be with you (4:23).

KEY FEATURES

Philippians is shot through with joyful confidence in Christ's care and grace as well as encouragement to follow his self-sacrificial way. Repeated are the themes of Christ's own self-giving humility and examples of others whom the Philippians should imitate against any inclination to pride or quarrelsomeness.

The Christ Hymn (2:6–11): Jesus, the Suffering and Exalted Lord

One of the most significant passages in Philippians comes in 2:6–11. Paul calls the Philippians to stand together in the face of opposition and especially notes that they should be ready to suffer faithfully for Christ (1:27–30). He then calls them to be united with one another in love and compassion, not looking to their own interests—which only breeds competition and strife—but humbling themselves to look to the interests of others (2:1–4).

This leads Paul in 2:5 to call them to the "mind" or mentality exemplified by Christ, which is laid out in 2:6–11. Christ's willing death on the cross is not only the greatest act of self-giving love for others (Rom 5:8; Gal 2:20) but also the very charter of the Philippians' salvation as God's redeemed people. Paul calls the Philippians to live as the people of this self-giving Lord, who set aside the glory that was rightfully his as God's eternal Son and humbly gave himself for others. The passage is important to understanding both NT theology about the person of Christ and the early history of the church's faith in him.

"Jesus Is Lord"

One of the questions that people have asked about Jesus from his own lifetime until today is this: Who is he?[14] This is the disciples' question when they see him calm a storm with his words (Mark 4:41) and the Pharisees' question when he absolves the paralytic's sins (Mark 2:7). He was clearly a human being—he had a mother, ate and drank, and died. But the way he spoke of himself and the preaching of his earliest followers said that he was also more.

Philippians 2:6–8 proclaims that the person who died on the cross existed even before his birth—in other words, that he was *preexistent*.[15] More than merely preexistent, he existed "in the form of God" and in "equality with God" (2:6). This is a very high—so to speak—view of the person of Christ. But this one who held the prerogative of equality with God did not treat it as something to be used to his own advantage, to be clutched at or asserted or manipulated.[16] Instead, the glorious one submitted himself in obedience to the divine plan of salvation (2:7–8)—and, Paul adds elsewhere,

---

14 Compare, e.g., Ehrman 2014 (*How Jesus Became God)* and the response volume, published the same day, in Bird et al. 2014 (*How God Became Jesus).*

15 See Fee 1995, 202–4.

16 Woodenly, 2:6 reads: "He did not consider being equal to God as a ἁρπαγμός (*harpagmos*)." This Greek word indicates a "seizing" or "grasping" and is rare in writings before Paul. For an influential treatment, see Hoover 1971. Readers of French will benefit from Focant 2016 on the significance of Christ's self-emptying within a culture of social climbing.

out of love for fallen humanity (Gal 2:20). The one who was in the form of God "emptied himself" and assumed "the form of a servant" (Phil 2:7). He took on existence "in the likeness" of humanity, and in that state he humbled himself even further to the point of crucifixion (2:8). Though he is clearly a human, who experienced birth and burial, to worship Jesus as divine is to worship him as he has always been.

Equally significant, verses 9–11 give Jesus the name *kyrios* (κύριος), "Lord." In Greek, *kyrios* could be used of people in various positions of authority over something or someone. It could mean "owner" (e.g., "the lords" of a colt, Luke 19:33) or a servant's "master" (as in Col 4:1). It was a title that Caesar held as supreme benefactor of the empire. But it was especially a title of the God of Abraham, *kyrios*, "the Lord," used by Greek-speaking Jews and Christians as a cipher for the divine name YHWH. It is, therefore, very significant that one of the earliest Christian confessions was "Jesus is Lord."[17] The earliest Christians remained committed monotheists and at the same time included the person of Christ within the identity of the one God (see John 1:1–3, 14, 18; 1 Cor 8:5–6; Col 1:19; 2:9; Heb 1:2–3). Indeed, after seeing and coming to know the risen Jesus, Paul could read OT references to the "Lord," the God of Israel, and apply them specifically to Christ (e.g., Joel 3:5 [KJV 2:32] / Rom 10:13; Exod 34:34 / 2 Cor 3:16).[18]

In Philippians 2:9–11 we see the same, using a prophecy from Isaiah where God is specifically calling all to worship him alone as the only God and savior (see Isa 45:5–7, 18, 21–22). The Lord proclaims that to himself alone "every knee will bow and every tongue will confess" (Isa 45:23). Philippians 2:9–11 agrees that on the final day of judgment, every knee will bow and confess to the glory of the Father (cf. also Rom 14:10–11), but *what* they confess to God's glory is that "Jesus is Lord." The world's ultimate acknowledgment of God as God at the judgment day is an acknowledgment of the supreme Lordship of Christ. If Christ is not divine, then calling him "Lord" of all would surely detract from God's glory—since God will share his glory with no other (Isa 42:8). But as this passage uses Isaiah, Christ shares the identity—more specifically, later Christians would use the term "substance"—of

---

17 See Hurtado 2003, 108–18. It was apparently used by some of the earliest Aramaic-speaking congregations, as in the Aramaic prayer *maranatha*, "Our Lord, come!" or "The Lord has come!" (1 Cor 16:22; *Didache* 10.6).

18 See Capes 2018.

the one true God, and the Father is pleased to receive creation's prayer and praise "through" and "in the name of" the Son.

"Hymns" in the Earliest Church

If 2:6–11 is significant for its Christology of divine preexistence, it is also significant that these verses themselves may have been literarily "preexistent"—that is, composed already before the time Philippians was written. Many scholars believe that in writing this passage Paul and Timothy are in fact *quoting* a hymn or creed about Christ that was already being memorized and used by believers. What leads to this view?

Historically, while they might have had access to Israel's scriptures by memory or in writing, the first generation of Christians was short on material to teach and learn their distinctive faith about Jesus. The basics of the faith were therefore put forth in different communities in the forms of pithy sayings, credos to be learned and recited at baptism, and hymns. Occasionally the NT letters give evidence of these. Paul, for instance, recites the words of Christ at the Lord's Supper and hands them down to his congregations (1 Cor 11:23–26). Other formulas crop up in, for example, Ephesians 5:14, 1 Timothy 3:16, and 2 Timothy 2:11–12. These "pre-formed traditions" are identified especially by *style* or *content*. Their style may exhibit elevated prose, poetic rhythm or structure, or vocabulary that is unusual to the author in whose writing we find them. Their content is usually marked by Christological praise, compressed statements about salvation, or something pertinent to core liturgical rites such as baptism or the eucharist. Preformed Christological material is often marked formally, as well, set off by relative clauses ("who . . .") enumerating Christ's qualities or actions.

Many suspect that Philippians 2:6–11 is just such a passage. Its content is certainly what we might expect the earliest Christians would want to memorize and repeat about Christ. It has vocabulary and concepts that Paul does not usually use when describing Christ elsewhere (e.g., "form" rather than "image" of God, as in 2 Cor 4:4), and a poetic structure can be discerned, though scholars debate the details.[19] Of course, Paul could simply be speaking in artful, creative ways to make his point, as some maintain, but most find it likely that he is deploying a formula already in use and using it to illustrate the humility and love the Philippians must imitate. This laudatory and edu-

---

19 See R. Martin 1997, 24–41.

cational poem is similar in form to the ancient ὕμνος (hymnos), not dissimi-
lar from the genre of biblical psalms, and is often called the "Christ Hymn."[20]
If this passage is such a pre-formed hymn, we encounter an impressive fact
about the history of Christian theology: the "high" Christology in this passage was already common currency among at least some Christians even
before Paul wrote Philippians. Belief in Christ's divine preexistence came
early, and not only in the occasional statements of theological luminaries
such as Paul or John, but in communal worship within two decades of Jesus's
crucifixion.

Christ and His Imitators

The Christ Hymn is not injected into the letter simply to exalt Jesus. The
"humility" and "obedience" of Christ that it recalls give specific shape to the
"humility" and "obedience" to which Paul exhorts the Philippians (2:3, 12).
Christ's self-giving on the cross creates the church and is the reason each
individual can be reconciled to God through him. But friendship with God
and the hope of future glory means, in the present life, having "fellowship
with his sufferings" and "being transformed into the likeness of his death"
(3:10). The path of salvation through Christ must give a cruciform shape to
the Christian life. This was counter-cultural in the Roman Empire and especially in Philippi. Social climbing was built into Roman clothing (citizens of
age wore the toga, and those of higher status wore rings and other accesso-
ries to show it), shown in honorary inscriptions that publicly immortalized
one's accomplishments on statues or monuments, and reflected in religious
associations and clubs even among non-elites.[21] It was a basic part of life:
magnify your own name, and advance over others.

But those whose names are written in the book of life (4:3) are called
to a different way. They already have a different "citizenship," a different
community with its own culture and values defined by the crucified Lord
(1:27; 3:20). In baptism they have been joined to Christ's death and life (Rom
6:3–11), which means both suffering with Christ now and being glorified with
him at his return (Rom 8:17; cf. Phil 1:29; 3:10–11, 20–21). For it is the crucified
and risen Christ in whose image they are being renewed (see Rom 8:29; 1

---

20 Some object that it cannot be a "hymn" because we do not find ancient musical tradition
of singing these verses. But see M. Martin 2015, who notes that a hymnos was not necessarily
sung.

21 Hellerman 2005, 12–19, 89–108.

Cor 15:49; 2 Cor 3:18; Col 3:10).[22] Paul calls them to live in self-sacrifice and Christian suffering, and so to pursue their own salvation as God completes his work in them (Phil 1:6; 2:12–13). Throughout Philippians, Paul not only "tells" with commands but also "shows" by giving examples of how the cruciform life takes shape. The fundamental example is given in the Christ Hymn. But Paul also provides examples from his own life and the lives of other ministers such as Timothy and Epaphroditus, since the life of an apostle is a "theater" (θέατρον, *theatron*) in which God's work can be seen on display (1 Cor 4:9). As Paul says in 1 Corinthians 11:1, "Become imitators of me, just as I am an imitator of Christ," so in Philippians 3:17 he commands, "Become imitators of me, brothers [and sisters], and set your sights on those who walk in the pattern that we set for you." Indeed, cruciform imitation runs like a red thread throughout the letter:

1:12–26 Paul emphasizes that his own suffering manifests God's work. His imprisonment serves the mission of the gospel, both because the suffering love of Christ is embodied in his own chains and because it drives others to preach (1:12–18). And even in his imprisonment, Paul rejoices. Paul hopes for release, but he will rejoice even if he must die, and he hopes the Philippians will too (2:17–18). Why? Because Paul's life—and the life of any believer—consists of being in Christ. Paul is joined to Christ and Christ lives in him by the Spirit, and Christ's life in him cannot be threatened by sword or starvation or mobs. From this comes his enduring joy: "for me, to live is Christ, and to die is gain" (1:21). If Paul lives on in the body, Christ's life still abides in him and drives him on in mission. If Paul dies in grace, his soul will depart but will still be with Christ, and in a "far better" state (1:22–23). Paul does not merely bare his soul here but offers an example of how Christians undergo suffering in faith. Christ is the life of his faithful now and at the final day of resurrection (1:20; 3:20–21), and this confidence brings Paul—and should bring all believers—to rejoice in any circumstance.

22 See Gorman 2001.

2:19–30 In what might otherwise look like simple news updates, Paul holds up Timothy and Epaphroditus as examples of the cruciform life taking shape in God's servants. Paul reminds the Philippians of Timothy's faithful character as one who does not seek his "own interests" but obediently serves for the sake of the gospel (2:21–22), offering Timothy as an example of the behavior he commanded when introducing the Christ hymn (2:3–4). Paul also notes the recent example of Epaphroditus, who brought the Philippians' gift to Paul at the expense of his own health and drew near "even to the point of death" ($\mu\acute{\epsilon}\chi\rho\iota\ \theta\alpha\nu\acute{\alpha}\tau\sigma\upsilon$, *mechri thanatou*, 2:30), using the same phrase as he did of Christ's self-sacrifice (2:8). Paul calls the Philippians to honor such exemplary servants of Christ (2:29).

3:2–16 Being ready to lose one's life is a kind of Christian self-emptying in imitation of Christ. We see another kind of self-emptying in 3:2–16. Paul notes those who boast about their circumcision and place confidence in it before God, to which Paul offers himself as a counterexample. As a Pharisee, his zeal and blameless pursuit of the law accorded him just such status, more even than the "dogs" who boast in circumcision. But when Christ encountered him and took hold of him (3:12), he did not grasp at his status or pedigree as a "gain" but rather counted it "loss" (3:7) compared to the true gain of righteousness and life in Christ. Indeed, he goes on to say that he counts *everything* loss outside the sphere of Christ (3:8). For anything that is not Christ cannot truly give him life, and so he now, though not yet perfected, strives forward toward the goal of glory and resurrection with Jesus (3:9–14). Paul's brief praise of himself and his pedigree in the law turns to an example that he calls others to follow in seizing Christ and pressing on to Christian maturity (3:15–16).[23]

---

23 Paul here employs a form of self-praise (in Greek περιαυτολογία, *periautologia*), not merely to indulge in bragging, but to lead them to reevaluate everything in Christ as he has. His presentation, while acknowledging that he is yet imperfect, gives the reader a model of humble perseverance and defends his gospel. See Smit 2014.

4:10–20 This same thinking resurfaces in 4:10–20, where Paul acknowledges the Philippians' gift to him (cf. 1:5, 7). Paul appreciates the gift (4:10, 18), but he is quick to direct all gratitude to the God who inspired the giving and who will repay the Philippians' generosity.[24] Paul's peace does not consist in economic means but in the saving economy of God. Paul knows how to live with nothing because Christ gave everything and now strengthens him to be self-sufficient in all circumstances (4:13). Their gift is helpful to Paul, of course; but even more than meeting his needs, it is an offering to God pure and acceptable, and their heavenly "account" will be filled when God repays them by God's own "wealth," the glory of eternal life (4:17–19; cf. Matt 6:1–4, 20; Luke 14:13–14). Paul's God-oriented perspective on need and wealth both models and reframes the significance of gift-giving for the Philippians.

FURTHER READING

Briones, David. 2011. "Paul's Intentional 'Thankless Thanks' in Philippians 4.10–20." *JSNT* 34 (1): 47–69.

Capes, David B. 2018. *The Divine Christ: Paul, the Lord Jesus, and the Scriptures of Israel.* Grand Rapids: Baker Academic.

DeSilva, David A. 2000. "Ruler Cult." *DNTB* 1026–1030.

Gathercole, Simon J. 2011. "Paul's Christology." In *The Blackwell Companion to Paul,* edited by Stephen Westerholm, 172–87. Chichester: Wiley-Blackwell.

Hawthorne, Gerald F. 2004. *Philippians.* Revised edition by Ralph P. Martin. WBC 43. Nashville: Thomas Nelson.

Hellerman, Joseph H. 2005. *Reconstructing Honor in Roman Philippi: Carmen Christi as Cursus Pudorum.* SNTSMS 132. Cambridge: Cambridge University Press.

Holloway, Paul A. 2017. *Philippians.* Hermeneia. Minneapolis: Fortress.

---

24 See Briones 2011.

Hurtado, Larry W. 2003. *Lord Jesus Christ: Devotion to Jesus in Earliest Christianity.* Grand Rapids: Eerdmans.

Martin, Michael Wade. 2015. "Philippians 2:6–11 as Subversive *Hymnos*: A Study in the Light of Ancient Rhetorical Theory." *JTS* n.s. 66 (1): 90–138.

Martin, Ralph P. 1997. *A Hymn of Christ: Philippians 2:5–11 in Recent Interpretation and in the Setting of Early Christian Worship.* Downers Grove, IL: InterVarsity.

Oakes, Peter. 2001. *Philippians: From People to Letter.* SNTSMS 110. Cambridge: Cambridge University Press.

Osiek, Carolyn. 2000. *Philippians, Philemon.* ANTC. Nashville: Abingdon.

Peterman, G. W. 1997. *Paul's Gift from Philippi: Conventions of Gift-Exchange and Christian Giving.* SNTSMS 9. Cambridge: Cambridge University Press.

Silva, Moisés. 2005. *Philippians.* 2nd ed. BECNT. Grand Rapids: Baker Academic.

Smit, Peter-Ben. 2013. *Paradigms of Being in Christ: A Study of the Epistle to the Philippians.* LNTS 476. London: Bloomsbury T&T Clark.

Thielman, Frank. 2003. "Ephesus and the Literary Setting of Philippians." In *New Testament Greek and Exegesis: Essays in Honor of Gerald F. Hawthorne,* edited by A. M. Donaldson and T. B. Sailors, 205–23. Grand Rapids: Eerdmans.

Watson, Duane F. 1988. "A Rhetorical Analysis of Philippians and its Implications for the Unity Question." *NovT* 30 (1): 57–88.

CHAPTER TWELVE

Colossians

Colossians, like Philippians and Philemon, is a letter written by Paul and Timothy from prison. In it, Paul encourages believers to stay strong and grow in faith and love—avoiding any false worship or thinking that does not accord with the truth in Christ. He extols Christ as Lord over all and calls the Colossians to let their lives and thinking be shaped by the truth of Christ in their homes, work, and worship.

BACKGROUND

Colossae

Colossae was located in the Lycus valley. It was in the Roman province of Asia, whose capital city, Ephesus, lay less than 120 miles away. In previous centuries, Colossae appears to have been well known and prosperous, but in the first century it had fallen somewhat behind its neighbors Laodicea and Hierapolis (both less than twenty miles away).[1]

The region seems to have been a melting pot of religious and cultural practices. Evidence from coinage indicates that there was special worship of the Ephesian Artemis, patronal goddess of the nearby capital (see chapter 10). The Egyptian gods Isis and Sarapis were worshipped there, too, in addition to the Greek pantheon. The area appears to have held a sizeable Jewish population, given reports of the revenue for the Jerusalem temple tax taken from Colossae's neighboring cities in 62 BCE (see Cicero, *For Flaccus*

---

1 There are ancient references to an earthquake in the region around 60 CE, and some have taken this as a significant factor in deciding Colossians' date and authorship. However, some evidence (especially coins) suggests that Colossae remained stable despite any effects of the earthquake, so it should probably not guide our decisions. See the essays in Cadwallader and Trainor 2011.

28.68). Josephus reports that in 45 BCE the rulers in Laodicea called for official tolerance of Jewish customs (*Jewish Antiquities* 14.241–43). The area was rife with religions and ideas about God that sometimes competed and sometimes combined. What influence might they have on people who had recently converted to worshipping "Jesus the Christ"?

The Colossian Christians

The church at Colossae was not founded by Paul, but by Epaphras (1:5–7; cf. 2:1), who was from Colossae (4:12). Epaphras is only mentioned here and in Philemon 23, but he appears to be the key to understanding the birth of the Colossian congregation and how it came into Paul's sights. Since he is from Colossae, it is reasonable to assume that he was converted in the wake of Paul's long and successful ministry in Ephesus, which Acts claims resulted in the gospel's spread throughout the province of Asia (Acts 19:10, 26; 20:31; cf. Col 1:6).

How did he come to evangelize Colossae, and what was his relationship to Paul? One clue comes from Paul's description of him: he is a "slave of Christ" with Paul (Col 1:7; 4:12), a "faithful minister of Christ for your sake" (1:7), who "fights in prayer" for believers in Colossae, Laodicea, and Hierapolis (4:12–13). These descriptions, common in Paul as commendations of ministerial coworkers, suggest that Epaphras was not just a convert who happened to go home and informally evangelize his kin, but that he converted and became involved with the *Pauline mission team*, with authorization to serve in his hometown and its neighboring cities. This may explain why he does not return home with the letter; Tychicus delivers the letter with Onesimus (4:7–9), while Epaphras sends greetings (4:12) and stays on to help Paul.[2]

If this is correct, we reach the following sketch of the events leading up to the letter: through the work of Paul and his team in Ephesus in the early to mid-50s, a Colossian named Epaphras was converted to Christianity. He became a junior member of Paul's team and later returned to evangelize in his home. Afterward, he brought Paul news of the Lycus valley churches

---

2 Some suggest that Epaphras does not return because he too has been imprisoned with Paul, since in Phlm 23 Paul calls him a "co-captive" (συναιχμάλωτος, *synaichmalōtos*). But this descriptor does not necessarily mean he is imprisoned currently (one might expect more of an update about this to Colossae if he were), and in any case might be metaphorical. In Rom 16:7, Paul is not currently imprisoned but still calls Andronicus and Junia his "co-captives."

(2:1; 4:13, 16). Paul then penned Colossians and another letter to Laodicea (4:16) and sent them with Tychicus and Onesimus while Epaphras stayed on to assist Paul.

Where and When Was Colossians Written?

The authenticity of this letter has been questioned in the last two centuries and today remains doubted by many (though not by so many as Ephesians or the Pastoral Epistles). This doubt is owed largely to the letter's style, with long sentences and some vocabulary not found in the undisputed Paulines—although the style is not nearly as distinct as that of Ephesians, and many distinct terms occur in 1:15–20, which was likely not composed by the author but reflects a preexisting "hymn" or poem about Christ (see below). Its theology of the universal church and its statement that one is already "raised with Christ" in baptism (2:12) also strike many as too developed for Paul. On the other hand, one might expect Paul to reflect more universally on the church and his authority within it when writing to people he has not evangelized. Likewise, the resurrection statement in 2:12 is not terribly distant from Galatians 2:19–20, where the reality of Christ's life in him leads Paul to say that he presently "lives to God," describing his present life in Christ just as he describes Christ's resurrected existence, as "living to God" (Rom 6:10). Some also see un-Pauline features in the letter's presentation of false teaching, but, as we will see, the nature of the "Colossian heresy" is debated. Many see these data as indications of an author who was not Paul but who thought in authentically Pauline ways, handing on Paul's teaching in a new key to a church Paul had not visited while alive. However, the same evidence is leading more and more scholars—perhaps even the majority—to hold that the letter is genuine, composed by Paul and Timothy.

If the letter is genuine, it locates Paul in prison as he writes (Col 4:3, 18). However, Paul was imprisoned numerous times (see 2 Cor 6:5; 11:23), so other data in the letter have to be used to deduce the place and date of this imprisonment. If Epaphras was evangelized by Paul's Ephesian mission, the letter must have been written some time after that. More specific data come from the people mentioned in Colossians: Paul names several people with him in his imprisonment (Col 4:10–14), and he sends Tychicus and Onesimus to Colossae with this letter and, it seems, before Colossae to Laodicea (4:7–9, 15–16). In fact, these data appear to correlate Paul's writing of Colossians with his writing of Philemon, which he also sent from prison with the slave Onesimus. If the two letters were dispatched from the same imprisonment, then we can use data from Philemon and Colossians together to locate them within Paul's ministry.

The Relation of Colossians to Philemon

In a letter we will address fully later (chapter 15), Paul wrote to Philemon about Philemon's slave Onesimus. An imprisoned Paul has come into contact with Onesimus—who has either simply run away or gone to seek mediation in a conflict with his master—and Onesimus has converted. Paul sends Onesimus back with a letter exhorting Philemon to treat him mercifully as his own brother in Christ (Phlm 10–20).

Traditionally, Colossians and Philemon are understood to have been written at a similar time and to the same or almost the same place. The strongest evidence revolves around three references. First, Colossians 4:9 indicates that Paul has sent Onesimus with Tychicus and that Onesimus is from Colossae. That Paul introduces Onesimus—a slave in Philemon's household—very briefly, as though the Colossians know him, as well as the fact that Onesimus is from Colossae, suggests that Philemon's household is near enough to Colossae for the two congregations to know each other. Second is the character Archippus: in Philemon 2 this "co-soldier" of Paul's is addressed as though he is part of Philemon's congregation, while in Colossians 4:17 Paul instructs the Colossians to tell him to "fulfill his ministry." So, again, Paul expects the Colossians to have regular and available contact with people in Philemon's congregation. This makes the most sense if Philemon's church is nearby. Third, when Paul wrote Philemon, he was currently with Timothy, Aristarchus, Epaphras, Mark, Luke, and Demas (Phlm 1, 23–24), persons who are also with Paul when writing Colossians (Col 1:1; 4:10–14). That these persons—some hardly mentioned elsewhere—are with Paul at the writing of both letters suggests that both were written near the same time.[3]

---

3 Differently, Balabanski 2015 argues that Philemon's congregation was not near Colossae but close to Rome: Onesimus is only *originally* from Colossae, but as a slave he was taken from his hometown to Philemon's service, and Archippus was a part of Paul's mission team who moved from Philemon's church to Colossae between the two letters. This solution resolves some oddities but creates others: Why then does Paul not do more to commend Onesimus to the Colossians (as he does with other delegates), since they could hardly be expected to recognize a slave who was sold off long ago and, having only converted after being taken away, had never been part of their church?

It is possible Philemon's church was in nearby Laodicea and that the letter to Philemon was the letter to the Laodiceans mentioned in Colossians 4:16. On the other hand, if Paul's imprisonment lasted a while, it may be that Onesimus was released after returning to Philemon, returned to Paul, and then was sent with Tychicus to Colossae later. There are many unknowns. Nevertheless, all this appears to be face-value evidence that both letters were written to the same region and from the same imprisonment.

Which Imprisonment?

As with Philippians, there are three major options held by scholars regarding the location of Paul's writing Colossians and Philemon: *Rome* (ca. 60–62 CE), *Caesarea* (ca. 58–60 CE), and *Ephesus* (ca. 52–55 CE).[4] Weighing each in turn, commentators regularly consider which is more probable in terms of locations and the situations of the audience, and which best fits Paul's descriptions of himself and his own situation at the time of writing.

Perhaps the least accepted is Caesarea, though it has its defenders.[5] It is an odd place for Onesimus to flee from Philemon, no matter whether he was a fugitive slave or going to seek Paul's intercession. Some also point to Paul's request for a guestroom in Philemon's house, suggesting an intent to check up on Philemon's treatment of Onesimus when Paul is released (Phlm 22):

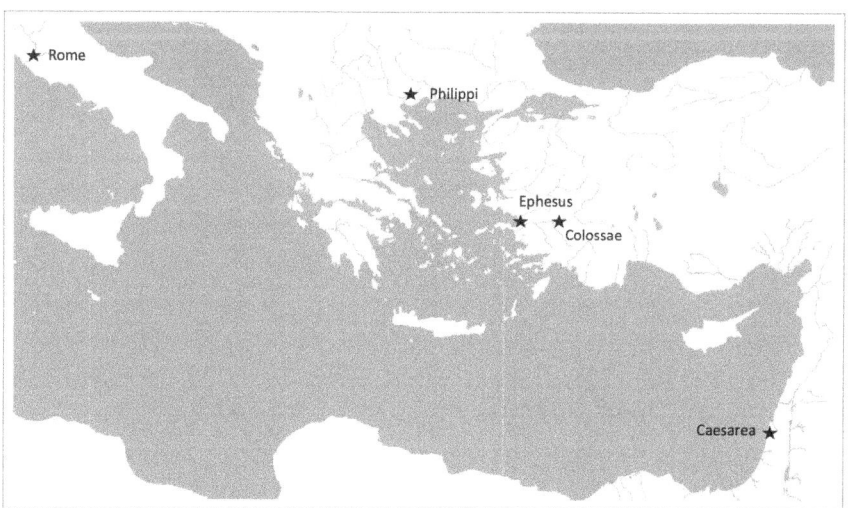

4 An alternative to an Ephesian imprisonment, Campbell (2014, 274–83) argues that Paul wrote from nearby Apamea.

5 See Reicke 1970.

the only source we have for a Caesarean imprisonment paints it as aimed entirely at Paul's being transferred to further custody in Rome to defend himself before Caesar (Acts 25:11–12, 21; 26:32). Caesarea is an option Acts provides for an imprisonment from which Paul may have sent this letter, but there is little positive in its favor.

Scholars studying Philemon frequently favor Ephesus for its place of writing. As noted in our discussion of Philippians, it is very likely that Paul's near sentence of death in Asia (2 Cor 1:8–10) occurred in its provincial capital, Ephesus, and that Paul likely spent some of his long stay in Ephesus in prison (see chapter 11 of this volume). The short distance between Ephesus and the Lycus Valley makes this especially attractive if Onesimus does not run away as a fugitive but only leaves to seek Paul's intercession with his master, converts, and then returns. Ephesus is also possible if Onesimus were a fugitive, running to the nearby big city and then encountering Paul and his team unintentionally. An Ephesian imprisonment is slightly less plausible if one considers Colossians and Philemon together, however. It would have taken some time for Epaphras to (1) be converted during Paul's Ephesian ministry, then (2) evangelize his hometown, and (3) serve the surrounding towns as a minister, all of which has to have happened before the letter for Paul to describe Epaphras and the Lycus Valley churches as he does. It is possible, if Paul spent more than two years in Ephesus as Acts claims (Acts 19:10; 20:31), but it makes Ephesus a less secure location for the writing of both letters together.

The traditional view is that Paul wrote these letters from Rome. Paul's later imprisonment there in the early 60s allows Epaphras time to have done his work to establish the churches in the Lycus Valley and indeed for Paul to be able to claim hyperbolically that the gospel has been preached throughout the (known) world (Col 1:6, 23). It also fits some of the more developed theological statements about the universal church or baptism that many believe reflect a more mature Pauline theology. This time frame also befits Paul's self-description in Philemon 9 as an "old man" (πρεσβύτης, *presbytēs*).[6] Many find that Rome fits less well with the situation of Philemon. For one, Rome is very far from Onesimus's home, and while there are many reports of slaves running away to Rome from all over the empire to gain anonymity and start a new life in the capital, it seems less likely that Onesimus would

---

6 A few have argued this should read "ambassador" (πρεσβευτής, *presbeutēs*). But see Wilson 2005, 347–48.

risk such a long journey if he were only seeking Paul's intercession. Likewise, as with Caesarea, Paul's stated intent to visit Philemon upon his release may seem implausible at this distance and because, before the imprisonments in Caesraea and Rome, Paul's sights were set westward to begin a new ministry in Spain (Rom 15:23–28). However, there are several uncertainties about what precisely was in Onesimus's mind when he left his master (see chapter 15 of this volume). If Onesimus only sought Paul's intercession, he may still have risked the distance and time away if his conflict with Philemon was bad enough, thinking that if he could not find a solution, he would simply flee. As to Paul's request for a guest room, Paul's westward plans may have changed while in prison or required that he first revisit his churches in Greece and Asia Minor to gather funds. In Philemon 22, he merely "hopes" to be released and visit Philemon. Likewise, the request for a guest room puts subtle rhetorical pressure on Philemon to treat Onesimus well, and it may not reflect realistic travel planning. All this makes Rome a good option, perhaps the best of these three, despite some lingering questions.

Why Was Colossians Written?

Paul's purpose in writing the letter is best summarized in 1:9–14 and 2:1–5: as an apostle, he wants to address these Christians whom he has not met to encourage them in love and faithfulness to the gospel. He does this by hailing Christ Jesus, the Lord of all and their redeemer by his cross and resurrection, so that by a deeper knowledge of Christ they might grow strong and endure in their life of faith and love, with both general and specific instructions (esp. chaps. 3–4) about how to live with one another, in their households, and toward "outsiders."

Encouraging them in the "truth of the gospel" (1:5) naturally brings Paul to steer them away from false teachings or temptations that would lead them astray. These concerns surface especially in 2:6–23. The false teaching and its source has been the topic on which perhaps the most ink has been spilled in Colossians scholarship (alongside debates about its authorship). Three points summarize concerns that emerge and how Paul handles them:

(a) Paul is concerned that someone might seduce the Colossians by philosophy and human thinking in line with the "elemental spirits of the world" and not in line with Christ (2:8; cf. 2:4). The term "elemental powers" or "spirits" (στοιχεῖα, *stoicheia*) is one way of speaking of spiritual powers or personalities, often associated with the stars, that many believed held sway in the universe.[7] Paul responds that Christ is the incarnation of the almighty God, ruler of all, and that the Colossians are "complete" and lack nothing when they are in Christ (2:9–10). All the treasures of wisdom and knowledge are found in Christ (2:3–4). Through their baptism they are forgiven and granted new life and eternal hope (2:11–15). How can one seek after the powers of the zodiac when one is already under the Lord, who controls all things?

(b) Therefore, Paul says, they should not let anyone condemn them regarding what they eat, drink, or whether they keep certain festivals or "Sabbaths" (2:16). Such things were "a shadow of things to come," but Christ is the reality (2:17). This kind of dogmatism about eating and drinking is, like the "philosophy" of 2:8, merely "human" (2:20–22). It may sound enlightened or pious, but these observances, if they are outside Christ, do not really do anything to tame one's sinful inclinations (2:23; cf. 2:20; 3:1).

(c) Paul also says they should not let anyone boast over them because of visionary experiences and the "worship of angels" (2:18), presumably claiming to have had a mystical experience of worshipping in heaven with angels.[8] Paul responds that such a one is boastful, "puffed up," and following fleshly thinking rather than holding fast to Christ as the head of his body, the universal church (2:18–19).

Many have tried to read all of Paul's concerns as reflecting a single group of false teachers with a particular "Colossian heresy"—perhaps stemming from Jewish groups, from different philosophical schools, and so on. Some see the references to "Sabbaths" and holy days as indicating that a single Jewish group, perhaps with mystical leanings, was behind all Paul's concerns

---

7 These powers were sometimes also associated with good or bad angels. See Pitre, Barber, and Kincaid 2019, 73–82.

8 "Worship of angels" has also been understood to refer to people worshipping angels as divinities, which was a problem encountered in early Christianity (Rev 19:10; 22:8–9; see Wilson 2005, 6). However, mystics and those who boasted of being mystics often held that they saw heaven and joined with the heavenly choirs, which seems to fit well here. See Sumney 1993 and Rowland and Morray-Jones 2009.

and warnings.[9] Others see a group influenced by a mix of pagan magic and philosophy, who perhaps had drawn on elements of Judaism for their ascetic practices.[10] There is probably truth to all of these suggestions, but one should be cautious about reconstructing a single group with a single set of beliefs. Indeed, while Paul clearly has particular concerns, his argument in Colossians does not necessarily indicate that there is one particular group or one particular heresy.[11] Nor does he claim that the Colossians have succumbed to such a heresy the way he does in, say, Galatians. The way he writes only betrays that he *expects* all these pressures and temptations may exist and that he means to keep the Colossians from falling prey to them. His main argument calls them to cling to Christ, and he names both Christless philosophy and an ascetic kind of mysticism as things that do not align with the truth (2:8, 19). Colossae was home to a great many views about God, and the Colossians probably faced temptations and pressures from more than just one angle. Pagans who had just converted to worship the Jewish God in Christ may have wanted to draw closer to the rites and customs of Judaism, may have simply fit Christ into their old view of the universe's powers rather than rethink it based on Christ, or may have been influenced by mystical philosophies to see asceticism as more powerful than baptism as a way to ascend to God. Paul, aware of the dangers they would face, reminds the Colossians that Christ is Lord of all and that, because they are baptized into him, he is their Lord.

OVERVIEW

I. **Letter Opening** (1:1–14)

A. Paul and Timothy to the Colossians (1:1–2).

B. I have not ceased giving thanks since I heard of your faith, hope, and love from Epaphras (1:3–8).

C. I pray you will continue to grow and remain steadfast in your faith, love, and knowledge of Christ, our savior (1:9–14).

II. **The Lord Christ and His Church** (1:15–2:5)

A. Christ is Lord over all things and all powers and authorities. All things were made through him and for him (1:15–17).

9 See Stettler 2005.

10 See Demaris 1994 and Arnold 1996.

11 See Copenhaver 2018.

B. And he is the head of his body, the church, which he redeemed when he reconciled all things to God by the blood of his cross (1:18–20).

    1. You, too, were reconciled to him and will be saved if you remain steadfast in the gospel (1:21–23).

    2. My sufferings are part of Christ's work, for he has made me a minister of the gospel for you gentiles as God enlightens and trains his people for salvation through us (1:24–29).

    3. I have great love and concern for you in the Lycus Valley and for all who have not seen me in person, that you may know Christ, in whom all the treasures of wisdom are hidden (2:1–5).

III. **Exhortation to Faithful Life in Christ (2:6–4:6)**

A. Hold fast, then. Let none deceive you by arguments and wisdom that do not accord with Christ (2:6–8).

    1. You are baptized, forgiven, joined to Christ's death to sin and his resurrection to new life (2:9–15)!

    2. So do not let anyone hinder your pursuit of this new life by philosophies or observances that are not in accord with Christ and do not contribute to your sanctification (2:16–23).

B. Hold fast and live as the baptized body of Christ.

    1. You have been raised with Christ. Your life is in him, so seek him in thought and action (3:1–4).

    2. Put off your old self and its evil ways of living (3:5–11).

    3. Put on Christ in all you do:

        a. With humility, charity, and unity with fellow believers (3:12–17).

        b. With patience and service toward others at work and at home (3:18–4:1).

        c. With prayer, thanksgiving, and wisdom toward nonbelievers (4:2–6).

IV. **Letter Closing (4:7–18)**

A. Receive Tychicus and Onesimus well (4:7–9). Those with me greet you, and Epaphras prays mightily for you (4:10–13).

B. Greet those in Laodicea. Make sure to let them read a copy of this letter, and you must also read a copy of theirs. Tell Archippus to fulfill his ministry (4:14–17).

C. I, Paul, write this greeting. Grace be with you (4:18).

KEY FEATURES

Paul's exhortation to the Colossians centers on Christ's person, salvation, and how believers should direct their thoughts and actions as they await Christ's return. A significant passage about the person and preeminence of Christ comes in 1:15–20, and the exhortations that follow in 2:6–4:6 develop the connection of the cosmic Lord to the Colossians by his reconciling death, the church, and baptism.

The Christ Poem (1:15–20): Christ First in Creation and Redemption

In discussing Philippians 2:6–11, we saw that some passages in Paul's letters may reproduce poems, hymns, or brief creedal formulae that were already being used in worship. Many believe that the passage extolling Christ in Colossians 1:15–20 is just such a text. It is poetic, with repetition, parallelism, and unique vocabulary, and its Christological content is the kind of thing one can imagine early Christians composing and reciting to hold and pass on the faith. (A few translations even print it in stanza form.)

Since many of its terms do not have easy equivalents in Hebrew or Aramaic, the poem was probably composed in Greek. Nevertheless, the *thought* has deep connections to the OT and Jewish belief. In fact, it appears to have been written by someone who was deeply familiar with the Greek translation of the OT, particularly the Psalms. It is not quite the model of a classical Greek poem (no conventional meter of long and short syllables), but it is the kind of thing a person who had read the Greek Psalms would write if they wanted to extol Christ in the language and style of the Bible.[12] I offer a translation so the reader can see it in somewhat poetic form:

---

12 An important—in my view the best—book on this passage is only accessible in German: Stettler 2000.

[15] He is the image of the invisible God,
The firstborn of all creation.
[16] For in him all things were created
In the heavens and on the earth,
Things visible and invisible,
Whether thrones or dominions,
Whether powers or authorities.
All things were created
Through him and unto him.
[17] And he is before all things
And all things hold together in him.

[18] And he is the head of the body, the church.
He is the beginning,
The firstborn from among the dead,
So that he might be sovereign among all things.
[19] For in him all the Fullness was pleased to dwell
[20] And to reconcile all things
Through him and unto him
By making peace through the blood of his cross,
Whether things on the earth or things in the heavens.

Christ—God's Wisdom and More

Verses 15–17 extol Christ over all things. Christ is the "image of the invisible God." He is the direct revelation of God's own character in a unique way (cf. John 1:18; 14:8–9; 2 Cor 4:4; Phil 2:6; Heb 1:3). Christ is also said to have existed before creation and to have been an active agent of creation. Indeed, "all things" were created "in" (ἐν, *en*) Christ, "through" (διά, *dia*) Christ, and even *for* Christ (εἰς, *eis*) (Col 1:16; cf. John 1:1–3; 1 Cor 8:6; Heb 1:2–3). This poetic pileup of prepositions draws readers into something profound—not only was Christ personally present and involved in the Father's creation of all things, but all creation was made for Christ and is under his authority. And, the poem adds, Christ remains involved now as the one in whom all creation continues to subsist (1:17). He was at the head of all things before they came to be and is still over them even now as the ruler of the universe.

This depiction of Christ has significant OT connections. One often noted is the connection of Christ with personified Wisdom. Proverbs 3:19 states that God established the earth "by wisdom." In Proverbs 8:22–31, God's wisdom speaks as a sort of distinct person—Wisdom—and claims to have existed with God before creation and to have been involved in God's work of creation. This notion was carried on in different ways by Jews closer to Paul's time. Wisdom existed before creation (Sir 1:4; 24:9; Philo, *Drunkenness* 30–31) and was viewed as the agent of God's creative activity (Wis 8:5; Philo, *Who is the Heir of Divine Things* 199). Wisdom was also said to be the unique image of God's character: "For she is the emanation of infinite light, and a spotless mirror of God's power and an image of his goodness" (Wis 7:26), using the same language for "emanation" and "image" that are applied to Christ's relation to the Father in Colossians 1:15. The Jewish teacher Philo of Alexandria calls Wisdom "the Power and Image and Vision of God" (*Allegorical Interpretation* 1.43), even God's "firstborn" (*Confusion* 62–63). Very similar things are said of the divine Word or "Logos," which some identified with Wisdom.[13]

The Christology here is appreciably high. Noteworthy too is that the hymn's author(s), in searching for language to describe the Christ they revered, drew not from descriptions of demigods but from the scriptures of Israel in order to develop the language of their nascent Christian monotheism. Even so, while scripture's prophecies and figures—like Wisdom—all pointed forward to Christ, elements of his identity were "hidden" until the full revelation was given (Col 1:26). Many understood Wisdom as a creature made before the creation of all else, whereas the church was led to see Christ as uncreated because he is the eternally generated Son rather than simply a personified attribute or emanation of God.[14] If divine Wisdom came to dwell specifically in Israel's law (Sir 24:8–12, 23), in Christ one sees this cocreator with the Father in fact take on flesh. Colossians 2:9 states that "the whole fullness of Deity"—all of God's God-ness—dwells in Christ "in bodily form," in a body that hungered, grew, and died. This reality is something the "divine pedagogy" prepared the people to see in Christ, but which could only be confessed once God revealed himself in Jesus of Nazareth as the incarnate and eternal Son.[15]

---

13 See Davies 1980, 147–76. Cf. Ps 33:6; Sir 43:26; Wis 9:1; Philo, *Who Is the Heir of Divine Things* 188; *Confusion of Tongues* 97, 147; *Flight and Finding* 101, 112; John 1:1.

14 See, famously, Athanasius, *On the Incarnation*.

15 Vatican II, Dogmatic Constitution *Dei Verbum* (November 18, 1965), §15.

Lord of the Church, Lord of the Colossians

Verses 18–20 transition from Christ's supremacy as creator and sustainer with the Father to his supremacy in redemption as "head" of the church. He is Lord over all things not simply as the glorious firstborn Son but indeed as the one who brought salvation by the "blood of his cross." He is "firstborn from among the dead," so that his resurrection brings the promise of eternal life to all in Christ (cf. also Acts 26:23; Rom 8:29; 1 Cor 15:20–23; Rev 1:5). His resurrection has brought him a special preeminence, since in it he was publicly vindicated as the unique and righteous Son of God and ruler over all things (cf. also Acts 2:32–36; Rom 1:3–4; Eph 1:20–21; Phil 2:6–11; 1 Tim 3:16; Heb 1:4; 2:9; Rev 1:18). He is not simply supreme over all, but he is the head of his body, the church.

If the Colossians are in any way being tempted to fear, appease, or follow any cosmic or worldly power apart from Christ, then Paul's placement of the Christ Poem is powerful. Before even addressing the concerns he has for their faithfulness and growth, he begins by telling them that Christ is cosmic Lord and master over everything—including all invisible powers or earthly dominions—and that this all-powerful Lord is the deliverer and protector of the church.[16] And then, in Colossians 1:21–23, Paul applies the poem to the Colossians directly to include them in this church under Christ if they hold fast to him. This is a comfort to those afraid that faithfulness to Christ might incur the wrath of gods, emperors, or neighbors, and it challenges any who are tempted to seek help for their souls outside Christ. And this introduction, based around the Christ Poem, grounds Paul's further exhortation to behave in a way that befits their baptismal union with Christ.

Baptism and New Life in Christ (2:6–4:6)

Christ is hailed as preeminent Lord and savior over all, with the power and authority to judge, rule, and bless. And the Colossians' baptism *into* Christ, by which they are "*in* Christ," is what forms the center and even structure of Paul's ethical exhortation to Christian living in 2:6–4:6.

Paul calls the Colossians to remain in the faith as they had received it (2:6). To any who would depart from it for some other philosophy or way of living, he first responds that Christ is the incarnation of the fullness of God's

---

16 There is debate about whether the thrones and powers listed in 1:16 are all earthly, all supernatural, or a mix: contrast Foster's commentary (2016, 184–89) with Moses 2014, 169.

self (2:9). As a close second with this, he reminds them that they have been baptized: "in baptism" they, formerly lifeless because of sin, have died to sin and been raised with Christ to new life (2:11–13; cf. Rom 6:3–4). The rite of baptism "into" Christ makes them partakers of Christ's own death and new life "with" Christ.

This way of understanding baptism not only points to their salvation and the promise that all who remain in Christ will, like him, be raised from the dead to glory (see Rom 6:8–10; 8:29–30; 1 Cor 15:20–23; Phil 3:21). It also indicates that they have a new life and new identity in Christ even now. The new creation has already begun in them by God's saving work (2 Cor 3:18; 4:16; 5:17; Gal 6:15), because, joined to Christ in baptism, Christ himself lives and abides "in" them by the Spirit (Rom 8:10–11; Gal 2:19–20), just as they are "in" Christ (Rom 6:11; 8:1; 1 Cor 1:30; 2 Cor 5:17). The baptized receive the Spirit of God by whom Christ was raised to new life, and so Christ's divine life lives in them (Rom 8:11; Gal 2:20; 1 Cor 12:13). By the power of the Spirit in the water, baptism sanctifies and "regenerates" (Titus 3:5).[17]

For this reason, Paul can point to baptism not only to give believers assurance but also to exhort them to Christian living. He uses different language to call them to this. He speaks of *putting on and putting off.* Baptism means that they have "put on" Christ's person and his ways like new clothing (Gal 3:27). Putting on Christ's life, then, also means "putting off" their old sinful ways (Col 2:11; 3:9). When calling Christians to be who they have been made to be in Christ, Paul can command them to "put on" new life, virtues, even their "new self," and to "put off" evil ways and their old self (3:12; cf. Rom 13:12, 14; Eph 4:22, 25). This putting on/off will be complete on the last day, when all that they are is clothed and transformed to be like Christ (1 Cor 15:53–54; 2 Cor 5:2–3). Paul speaks of baptismal existence also with contrasts of *death and life,* as these are the twin poles of the Christ-event in which the baptized participate. They have been crucified with Christ and, thereby, have died to the powers and influence of all that is outside Christ (Rom 6:6; Gal 2:19–20; 5:24; 6:14). When calling believers to Christian morality, therefore, Paul can call them to "crucify" or "put to death" their old selves and desires

17 The doctrine of baptismal regeneration is clear in the earliest postbiblical tradition as well (e.g., Justin Martyr, *First Apology* 41; Cyril of Jerusalem, *Mystagogical Lectures* 2). According to Tertullian, Christians are fish; our life is conferred in the water (*On Baptism* 1). Like Paul, too, the Church Fathers encouraged Christians to endure by drawing on the ongoing effects of their baptism: "Let your baptism be your continual armor!" (Ignatius, *Polycarp* 6.2).

(Rom 8:13; Col 3:5) and to live and act in the new life that will be complete on the last day (Rom 6:10–11; Col 3:3–4).

This baptismal reality, repeated in Colossians 2:11–12, provides a frame for the rest of the letter's exhortations. Note how Paul takes the Colossians back to the reality of their baptism with repeated language of this reality in his statements and admonitions:

2:11–19 Because they have been baptized into Christ and been forgiven their sins, they should "therefore" let no one pass judgment on them based on ideas that are neither aligned with Christ nor actually useful in the fight against sin.

2:20–23 They have "died with Christ" to this sinful world and so must not let it and its ways control them.

3:1–4 They have been "raised with Christ" and so must direct their attention and energy to following him and his ways. They have died and now have life in Christ, so they must fix their hopes on his reward and his heavenly life.

3:5–11 So they must "put off" all the evil of this world.

3:12–17 And they must "put on" the ways of Christ and imitate him in forgiveness, patience, love, and faithfulness.

3:18–4:1 Commonly called a "household code" (scholars regularly use the German *Haustafel*; cf. Eph 5:22–6:9), this passage includes no explicit baptismal language. But it is still part of the ethics of new baptismal identity: wives, children, husbands, slaves, and masters are called to do right by one another because of "the Lord" and his promised reward. Though they may suffer in these power structures, they are encouraged to endure in doing good as Christ did and to live in hope that "the Lord" will repay every good deed and every wrongdoing. Those in power are reminded that they are accountable to their own master, Christ: societal pressure might encourage a man to abuse his family or slaves, but this has no place among members of the body "bound" together by love in Christ (Col 3:14). All are directed to their new identity in one hope and one calling—to put Christ first in all their thoughts and actions, and in all things to emulate Christ in forgiveness and charity (3:11–17).

FURTHER READING

Arnold, Clinton E. 1996. *The Colossian Syncretism.* WUNT 2/77. Tübingen: Mohr Siebeck.

Barth, Markus, and Helmut Blanke. 1994. *Colossians: A New Translation with Introduction and Commentary.* Translated by Astrid B. Beck. AB 34B. New York: Doubleday.

Beale, G. K. 2019. *Colossians and Philemon.* BECNT. Grand Rapids: Baker Academic.

Copenhaver, Adam. 2018. *Reconstructing the Historical Background of Paul's Rhetoric in the Letter to the Colossians.* LNTS 585. London: Bloomsbury.

DeMaris, Richard E. 1994. *The Colossian Controversy: Wisdom in Dispute at Colossae.* JSNTSup 96. Sheffield: JSOT Press.

Dunn, James D. G. 1996. *The Epistles to the Colossians and to Philemon: A Commentary on the Greek Text.* NIGTC. Grand Rapids: Eerdmans.

Foster, Paul. 2016. *Colossians.* BNTC. London: Bloomsbury T&T Clark.

Francis, F. O. and Wayne A. Meeks, eds. 1973. *Conflict at Colossae: Illustrated by Selected Modern Studies.* SBLSBS 4. Missoula, MT: SBL Press.

Hartman, Lars. 1997. *"Into the Name of the Lord Jesus": Baptism in the Early Church.* SNTW. Edinburgh: T&T Clark.

Stettler, Christian. 2005. "The Opponents at Colossae." In *Paul and His Opponents*, edited by Stanley E. Porter, 169–200. Pauline Studies 2. Leiden: Brill.

Sumney, Jerry L. 2008. *Colossians: A Commentary.* NTL. Louisville, KY: Westminster John Knox.

Wilson, Robert M. 2005. *A Critical and Exegetical Commentary on Colossians and Philemon.* ICC. Edinburgh: T&T Clark.

Wright, N. T. 1991. "Poetry and Theology in Col 1.15–20." In *Climax of the Covenant: Christ and the Law in Pauline Theology*, 99–119. Edinburgh: T&T Clark.

CHAPTER THIRTEEN

1–2 Thessalonians

First and Second Thessalonians are probably the earliest letters of Paul in the NT. The backstory to these letters shows the struggle of Christians to understand Paul's preaching, their calling in holiness, and their current persecution. Paul's responses reveal his heart and concern for a young community and point them especially to Christ's future return as an encouragement to persevere in faith, love, and hope.

INTRODUCTION

Thessalonica

Thessalonica was an important city in the Roman province of Macedonia. It was located not only on a major Roman road but also at an important harbor on the Aegean Sea. Acts locates Paul's initial work in Macedonia within his second journey, evangelizing Philippi and then Thessalonica (Acts 16:6–10; cf. 1 Thess 2:2; Phil 4:15–16).

Two features of Thessalonica are worth noting here. First is its commitment to the empire. Unlike Philippi, Thessalonica was not a Roman colony, and almost all the inscriptions found there from Paul's time are in Greek, not Latin. Nevertheless, it was a committed city of the empire.[1] Caesar Augustus, hailed as the one who organized the empire and by his power brought "peace" to the world (the famous *pax Romana*), had been honored with statuary and a temple in Thessalonica. Obeying the decrees of the emperor was easily viewed as the way to keep peace in the world. Indeed, there is evidence from other cities that local rulers would take oaths to support the emperor and to oppose anything against him.[2] Loyalty to the empire was paramount.

1 See Witherington 2006, 2–9.

2 See Donfried 2002, 31–34.

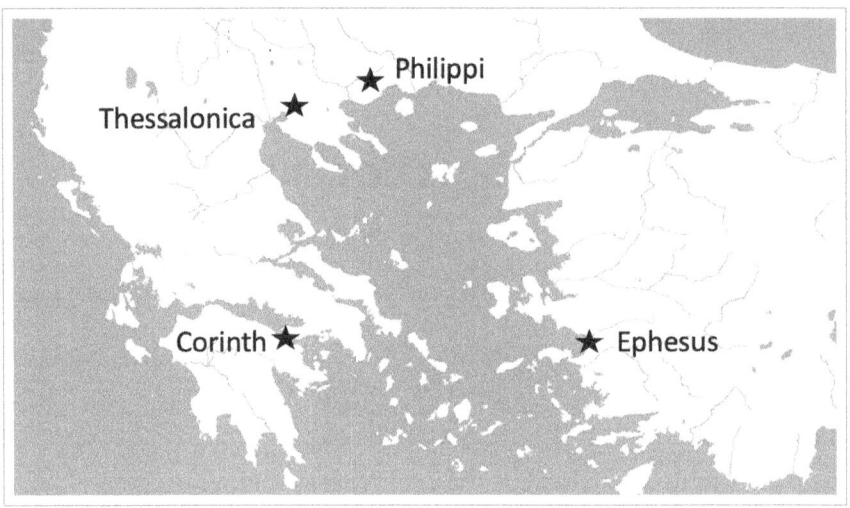

Second is the city's religious diversity. Acts 17:1–3 claims that Paul went to a synagogue on his visit, and we have evidence of synagogues in Thessalonica from the second century (though not the first).[3] Overall, however, the city was pagan, and Paul describes at least most of his audience as pagans converted "from idols" to serve God in Christ (1 Thess 1:9–10). There is evidence of worship of Egyptian deities in addition to the standard Greek pantheon. There was a strong worship of Dionysus (or Bacchus), a god of ecstasy, worship of whom was often marked by drunkenness, frenzy, and sexuality—the latter frequently symbolized by the phallus, a symbol paraded and even carried on worshippers' heads in festivals.[4] This religious environment would prove a hotbed of difficulties and questions for former pagans now converted to the living God in Jesus Christ.

Paul and the Thessalonian Christians

Paul first came to Thessalonica after being harshly treated in Philippi (1 Thess 2:2; cf. Acts 16:16–40), bringing along his companions Silvanus and Timothy (note the plural "we" in 1 Thess 1:1; 2:1–2, etc.; cf. Acts 17:1, 14). Paul and his companions lived among the Thessalonians as they evangelized, working for their sustenance rather than demanding pay, and leading the

3 See Levinskaya 1996, 154–57.
4 Donfried 2002, 22–25.

new believers by example in faith and work (1 Thess 1:5; 2:5–10; 2 Thess 3:7–10). The Thessalonians received the gospel with sincerity and gratitude (1 Thess 2:13).

However, it appears that this founding visit in Thessalonica ended somewhat abruptly and perforce. Paul describes the missionaries as "bereft" or "orphaned" from the Thessalonians and claims that they modeled for the Thessalonians how to endure persecution (1 Thess 1:6; 2:17). According to Acts, some non-Christian Jews and pagan rabble-rousers attacked the young church and accused them of violating "the decrees of Caesar" (Acts 17:5–9), effectively running Paul out of town. We are not told precisely how long Paul and company were in Thessalonica on this initial visit—it had to be long enough for the Philippians to send him aid (Phil 4:16)—but Acts and 1 Thessalonians suggest it was short, perhaps a few months.

With the missionaries gone, the town appears to have continued to persecute or put pressure on this new community of believers. But despite their youth in faith, the Thessalonians held fast their confession of Christ even in the face of affliction (1 Thess 3:1–10; 2 Thess 1:4–10). News of their response to the gospel spread throughout not only Macedonia but also the rest of Greece (1 Thess 1:6–10). As we see in these letters, Paul treasures the faith of the Thessalonian church with particular emotion (see 1 Thess 2:7–8, 11–12, 17–20; 2 Thess 1:4). Later in his travels he revisited Macedonia and apparently kept contact with the Thessalonians. Paul visited the area again on the way to his final visit to Jerusalem, receiving aid for the collection and even taking along missionary travel companions from Thessalonica (2 Cor 1:16; 2:13; 8:1–5; cf. Acts 20:1–6; 27:2).

1 THESSALONIANS
Situation and Date

When did Paul write 1 Thessalonians, and what was going on? The letter itself indicates that Paul wrote it not too long after being run out of Thessalonica. The first three chapters tell the story of the Thessalonians and the missionaries' founding visit, emphasizing Paul's concern for their fate after they left. Any church, no matter how old, needs continued encouragement and instruction. But the Thessalonians' catechesis was relatively short. Paul and his cohort do seem to have had time, as was their custom, to appoint some leaders in Thessalonica (1 Thess 5:12, 27; cf. Acts 14:23), but they had little experience, and the faith of the young church was under fire (1 Thess 2:14; 3:3). How would they respond? Would they endure, or would they abandon the faith (1 Thess 3:5)? Would they resent Paul as a fly-by-night huckster preaching his message and then leaving them to face the hardship it caused?

The letter's first three chapters recount this story from Paul's perspective, appealing to his upright character (*ethos*) with them in the past and his ongoing emotional concern (*pathos*). Paul reminds them of his and the other missionaries' sincerity in dealing with them, how he not only refused pay but also forewarned them of persecution (1 Thess 2:5–8; 3:3–4). And he emphasizes his love for them, describing his care and concern with intimate and emotive images: though he was like a parent to them while present (1 Thess 2:7, 11), he describes himself vulnerably as being "orphaned" when he was driven away (1 Thess 2:17).[5] He attempted to see them but could not (1 Thess 2:17–18), and, having gotten as far as Athens, he finally dispatched Timothy to Thessalonica to encourage them and find out how they were faring (1 Thess 3:1–5).

As Paul relates with elation, Timothy returned with good news (1 Thess 3:6)! They were holding up despite their sufferings, and they still harbored affection and loyalty to Paul and his team. Of course, they still had questions, apparently including questions about the fate of the dead and the living when Christ returned (1 Thess 4:13). And, naturally, they faced continued temptations from their culture—not least in the matters of sexuality and holy living (see 1 Thess 4:3–8). Paul wrote 1 Thessalonians in response to Timothy's report, thanking God for their endurance, telling of his love for them, and instructing them in holiness and hope in the salvation of Christ Jesus (1 Thess 3:10, 12–13).

How much longer after Timothy's report was this written, and can we be more specific about a date and location? 1 Thessalonians and Acts agree on Paul's overall movements from Philippi to Thessalonica, then Thessalonica to Athens (Acts 16–17; 1 Thess 2:2; 3:1). We do not know how long he stayed in Athens, but, according to Acts 18:5, Timothy rejoined Paul in his next major evangelistic locale, Corinth. Paul stayed in Corinth for quite some time, and it makes good sense for him to have written the letter there, where he was again able to earn funds as a laborer (1 Cor 9:6–14; Acts 18:1–3, 11) and would have had time to receive Timothy's report and compose this letter with his colleagues. This also allows us to be more specific about the date of

5 See Aasgaard 2007, 142–43.

the letter, if we trust the datum in Acts that Paul was arraigned before the proconsul Gallio in Corinth.[6] Gallio was proconsul from the summer of 51 to the summer of 52. If Paul had been there a year or more already when arraigned (see Acts 18:11), we may estimate that he arrived in Corinth in 50 CE, perhaps in the middle of the year, or at the latest the winter of 50–51. If he began writing the letter toward the beginning of his time there, we can guess conservatively that 1 Thessalonians was written in Corinth in 50/51.

Overview: 1 Thessalonians

I. **Letter Opening (1:1-10)**

A. Paul, Silvanus, and Timothy to the Thessalonians (1:1).

B. Thanks be to God! You received the gospel in much affliction and yet have remained true—and the story of your faith has spread throughout Greece (1:2–10)!

II. **Paul and the Thessalonians: A Recap (2:1–3:13)**

A. You know our character and the power of the gospel.

  1. We preached to you with no trickery or selfish motives (2:1–6).

  2. We were gentle with you out of love, as you know, and we encouraged you by our example to live uprightly (2:7–12).

  3. You received the gospel from us as God's own word and even saw persecution similar to that in Judea (2:13–16).

B. We have longed to see you since we left.

  1. We were bereft of you and longed to see you, but could not (2:17–20).

  2. So we sent Timothy to strengthen you and report back (3:1–5).

  3. We have heard from Timothy of your continued faith and your love for us, and thank God for this comfort (3:6–10)!

C. We pray we may see you again, and that you might abound in brotherly love and holiness until the day when Christ returns with his holy ones (3:11–13).

---

6 Scholars who do not admit any data from Acts sometimes date the letter earlier, in the 40s CE. But Acts often speaks generally of Paul being tried before "leaders" or "magistrates," so it is unlikely that the author made up the detail about Gallio simply to lend vividness to his story.

III. **Reminders and Instructions for Faith, Love, and Hope (4:1–5:24)**

A. We encourage you now to grow in what you are already doing: holding to what we taught you and living in holiness (4:1–2).

   1. Holy living means self-control and sanctity. No sexual immorality or covetousness. God's wrath is coming, as we taught you (4:3–8).

   2. Continue and grow in your love for one another in the church, and strive as a group to live peaceably and in an exemplary way toward outsiders, as we taught you (4:9–12).

B. Some have died in Christ, but do not despair (4:13).

   1. When the Lord returns, those who have died in faith will come with him. The dead will rise first, and then our triumphant Lord will gather his people (4:14–18).

   2. The Lord will come, and it will be sudden. Arm yourselves now by living in the redemption you have received, and wait in hope for that day together (5:1–11).

C. Honor each other in peacefulness and goodness.

   1. Honor and follow those who work for the gospel among you (5:12–13).

   2. Admonish, encourage, and be patiently good to each other and to all (5:14–15).

   3. Be steadfast in prayer and thankfulness, and heed the guiding of the Holy Spirit (5:16–22).

D. May God make you holy and keep you blameless for the day of Christ's return. God is faithful and will keep his promises (5:23–24).

IV. **Letter Closing (5:25–28)**

A. Pray for us, greet one another, and ensure that this letter is read publicly to all (5:25–27).

B. Grace be with you (5:28).

2 THESSALONIANS
Situation and Date

Second Thessalonians states that it was also written by Paul with Silvanus and Timothy (2 Thess 1:1). The letter's authenticity is questioned by many, though not as many as doubt Ephesians or the Pastoral Epistles (see chapter 3). Its discussion of a "man of lawlessness" who must appear before Christ's return is unparalleled in other Pauline letters, and Paul elsewhere seems to expect Christ's return within his lifetime (note "we who are alive" in 1 Thess 4:15, 17). So some think it was written a generation after Paul to explain why Christ had not yet returned or, as it claims (2 Thess 2:1–2), to counter an eschatology that taught that the Lord had already returned. On the other hand, the historical Paul could have expected this antichrist figure to come in his own lifetime and simply not have mentioned it elsewhere. The expectation of increased wickedness before the final day was a regular feature of Jewish and, therefore, early Christian expectation (see below).

Among those who take this letter as Pauline, the precise situation in which it was written is debated, particularly as it relates to 1 Thessalonians. Paul's opening thanksgiving assures persecuted Christians that there is a day when the Lord will make right all the wrongs done to them. This leads into the main issue to be treated: a rumor that the day of the Lord is already at hand. Paul calls them to be steadfast in faith and, particularly, to avoid idleness. How we understand each feature affects how we read the letter's situation.

(a) *Persecutions.* It is clear from the letter's opening thanksgiving that the Thessalonians are enduring persecution (2 Thess 1:3–12). Paul not only thanks God that they are enduring but also comforts them with the promise that God is not overlooking their suffering and that on the final day all things will be set right: their afflicters will be afflicted, and they will be given rest.

(b) *Is the day already here?* Second Thessalonians 2:1–12 addresses the question of the timing of the day of judgment. Someone or something—Paul does not say (and may not know) exactly— has unsettled the Thessalonians with the message that the "day of the Lord has come" or "is now upon us" (v. 2).[7] It is difficult to know precisely what the Thessalonians were being told. If

---

7 This probably means that the day has come and is now present or that it is currently beginning, rather than that the day came and is now over. Paul uses a perfect tense-form of ἐνίστημι (*enistēmi,* "be present"), which frequently refers to things in the current temporal situation: Paul speaks of "things that ἐνίστημι" as "things present" as opposed to "things future" (Rom 8:38; 1 Cor 3:22; 7:26; Gal 1:4).

they were already taught that the day of the Lord involves the resurrection of the dead and meeting Christ in the clouds (1 Thess 4:13–18), they were also told it would come like a thief in the night (1 Thess 5:2). They may think that the day had come, but that their church was not deemed worthy to be gathered to the Lord. It is possible that someone taught them that the resurrection was spiritual, not bodily, and that they had already experienced it (see 2 Tim 2:18), though if they believed 1 Thessalonians 4:13–18, this seems unlikely to have ensnared them. The "day of the Lord" in the biblical prophets is a day of distress and destruction of God's enemies (e.g., Isa 13:9; Joel 1:15; Amos 5:18). It may be that someone—perhaps an anxious insider or an outsider taunting them—has said that their persecution was a sign that the day was now at hand and that they were on the wrong side.

(c) *Idleness.* Finally, there are apparently "idle" or "unruly" Christians who are not earning their keep (2 Thess 3:6–16). Many understand this idleness to be related to the issue of eschatology: people were so convinced that the day was at hand that they gave up everyday pursuits. Others suggest they were putting off work for the sake of forging connections and social climbing. Another possibility is that some are simply taking advantage of the church. Congregations engaged in sharing possessions with needy believers in their midst (see Acts 2:44–45; 4:32–37; Rom 12:13), and some may simply have been satisfied with this and failed to pursue labor.

All of these elements—persecution, misinformation, idle members—could have happened at any point in time. One notes, however, that they also match up with the situation of 1 Thessalonians: the Thessalonians endure distress at the hands of others (1 Thess 2:14; 3:3), they are troubled by eschatological curiosities (1 Thess 4:13–18), and they are admonished not to be idle but to work so that the whole church may be self-sufficient (1 Thess 4:11–12; 5:14). Most suspect, therefore, that 1 and 2 Thessalonians were written within a short time period, perhaps within a few months of each other. The situation is largely the same, though different developments bring up different questions to which Paul's two letters respond.

If they are written near in time to one another, the biggest question is the order in which they were written. Some have argued that 2 Thessalonians was in fact written first.[8] In this view, 2 Thessalonians was written and dispatched with Timothy while Paul was in Athens, in the wake of the persecution occurring when Paul left. Having left the Thessalonians in persecution, Paul wrote 2 Thessalonians to assure them that their persecutors would be judged and to clarify a false understanding about the day of the Lord. Then, when Timothy returned with good news, Paul wrote 1 Thessalonians thanking God for their endurance and further correcting their understanding about the last day.

However, it is more likely that 1 Thessalonians was written first. That letter indicates that he did not know how the Thessalonians fared at all until he heard Timothy's report, upon receiving which he wrote 1 Thessalonians. If he was anxious about whether they had remained in the faith until he received Timothy's report (1 Thess 3:1–5), it seems odd that he should praise their endurance in 2 Thessalonians 1:3–4 when he did not know whether they had endured. Further, if he had not communicated with them until receiving Timothy's report, how would he have heard that they were being told that the day of the Lord had come? Rather, in 2 Thessalonians 2:15 he asks them to hold to what they had been taught about hope and Christian living through prior traditions and "our letter," which seems to indicate the content of 1 Thessalonians 4–5. So it is most probable that 1 Thessalonians was written first and 2 Thessalonians after, but probably not long after. We can then estimate that 2 Thessalonians was written in 50–52, likely still from Corinth.

Overview: 2 Thessalonians

I. **Letter Opening (1:1–2)**

A. Paul, Silvanus, and Timothy to the Thessalonians (1:1–2).

II. **Thanksgiving and Encouragement (1:3–12)**

A. We thank God that you are enduring in the face of persecutions (1:3–4).

1. At the coming of the Lord, your endurance in faith will be met with eternal life. For those who persecute the church, God's justice will bring destruction when Christ returns (1:5–10).

---

8 See Reicke 2001, 41–43.

2. We pray that God would keep you in faith and love, so that Christ's name may be glorified in you and you will be glorified in Christ on that day (1:11–12).

III. **Remember Our Teaching—the End Is Not Yet (2:1–17)**

A. Don't let anyone tell you that the final day is already here (2:1–3a)!

B. The day of the Lord will not come until after the Lawless One, who will boast that he is God (2:3b-4).

1. I've told you this before (2:5).

2. You know that his rebellion is already at work, but he is being restrained for a time now. Afterward, he will come, but the Lord Jesus will destroy him utterly on the last day (2:6–8).

3. The Lawless One will do many signs by Satan's power, and those who have rejected the truth will follow after him to their own destruction (2:9–12).

4. But we know that God has called you by the gospel to be saved through faith and in holiness. Hold on to the truth we taught you (2:13–15).

C. May God who loved us in Christ give you comfort and fortitude (2:16–17)!

IV. **Call to Faithfulness and Honest Work (3:1–15)**

A. Pray for us and the success of the gospel. God is faithful and he will guard you against Satan, and we are sure you will continue in our teachings (3:1–5).

B. We did not shirk laboring when we were with you and did not simply live off of the church's goods (even though we had that right as ministers). Follow our example (3:6–10).

C. We hear some in your church are not working but just being busybodies. We command them to labor diligently and earn a living (3:11–12).

D. You should not grow weary of doing good. If anyone is disobedient to our teaching, shun him so that he might realize his error—but do it in love, correcting him as your brother rather than treating him as an enemy (3:13–15).

V. **Letter Closing (3:16–18)**

A. The God of peace be with you all (3:16).

B. I, Paul, write this greeting. Grace be with you all (3:17–18).

KEY FEATURES

By far the most fascinating feature of 1 and 2 Thessalonians is their eschatology (teaching about the end times). Grounded in Christ's crucifixion and resurrection, Paul's teaching on the church's future—indeed, the future of all creation (see Rom 8:18–25)—gives a hopeful, forward-looking posture to all his theology. In 1–2 Thessalonians, eschatology gives comfort and hope to churches in crisis and mitigates troubling misinformation about the timing of the Lord's return or *parousia* (παρουσία, "coming").

Hope for the Living and the Dead in Christ (1 Thess 4:13–18)

In 1 Thessalonians 4:13–18, Paul begins: "We do not want you to be ignorant, brothers, about those who sleep, so that you might not grieve like everyone else who has no hope" (4:13). Apparently, there is some question among the Thessalonians about the status of believers who have died before Christ's return. Some suggest that Paul had not preached about the possibility of believers dying before Christ's return—perhaps because he had been run off too quickly, or perhaps because he expected Christ to return before any died—so the Thessalonians were wondering whether the dead would be saved at all. But this is unlikely. Paul would have had years of preaching under his belt before arriving in Thessalonica. He surely knew of Christians dying (note Stephen's martyrdom, Acts 7:54–8:3); his audiences would surely have asked about it, as teaching about death was a common feature of philosophies new and old.[9] While it seems that Paul expected the Lord to return soon, even within his generation (note "we who are alive" in 1 Thess 4:15), we should expect that the resurrection of the dead—believers included—was part of his initial preaching in Thessalonica.[10]

Rather than wondering if the dead would be saved at all, the Thessalonians may have worried that the dead would somehow be "worse off" than those

---

9 See Malherbe 2000, 283–84.

10 Paul's theology seems untroubled by the possibility of Christians dying (cf. Rom 14:9; 1 Cor 15:51–53; 2 Cor 5:1–3; Phil 1:23; 1 Thess 5:10). Even if he expected the Lord's return soon, the necessity of being alive at Christ's return was surely not part of his early preaching (see Luckensmeyer 2009, 224, 233–34).

still alive at the Lord's return.[11] Perhaps they thought that the dead would be raised but have a second-rank or separate share in the blessings of eternity. This appears to be suggested by Paul's dual emphasis on the unity of the dead with the living in Christ and on the order of things: the dead will not only rise but rise *first* (v. 16); the living "will not come in ahead of those who have fallen asleep" (v. 15); the living and the no-longer-dead will be with the Lord together (v. 17).

Paul's is a word of assurance to the Thessalonians regarding their deceased brethren. The dead will not be left out. Both the living and the dead will on that day and for eternity be "with the Lord" together. Indeed, being "with" the Lord is the point, in death or life (see also Phil 1:23; 1 Thess 5:10). So much appears clear. However, the content of Paul's comfort for them in 1 Thessalonians 4:17 is debated: Paul says that those alive at Christ's return will "be caught up together with" the dead Christians "in the clouds to meet the Lord in the air." This verse has caused a number of speculations.[12] We can simplify the core question thus: Is the eschatological event here primarily an *upward* or *downward* movement?

One possibility is that the hope Paul gives here is one of *upward* movement for believers. The Lord is coming to bring the dead (and the living) "with him" (v. 14) toward a heavenly destination (note the language of "air" and "clouds," v. 17). The movement is one of ascending to meet the Lord and be in his presence—think of biblical visions of assumption (Gen 5:24; 2 Kgs 2:11–12) or Moses ascending Mt. Sinai in the "cloud" of God's presence (Exod 24:16–18). Paul details that the dead will be raised first and then, with the living, will be "snatched up" to meet the Lord and remain there and share in the divine life.[13]

Another interpretation focuses instead on the Lord's "descent" (1 Thess 4:16). In this view, while believers do ascend above the earth to meet the Lord, they do not stay there. This largely turns on an analogy from civic life:

---

11 Some Jewish eschatologies seem to address this, e.g., *4 Ezra* 13.24 (ca. 100 CE): "those who are left are more blessed than those who have died" (translation in *OTP* 1, 552). But *2 Baruch* 30.1–3 (ca. 100 CE) states, like Paul, that when the messiah comes the dead will rise and share equal joy with the living.

12 For a survey of interpretations old and new, see Thiselton 2011, 115–45.

13 See Plevnik 2000; 1999. Plevnik argues that this is not irreconcilable with 1 Cor 15:51–53: the image of ascent to divine life here (for living and dead believers) lines up with Paul's insistence that both the dead and the living will be "changed" and come into a mode of incorruptible existence.

it was common for a city to send people to meet a coming king or dignitary with fanfare outside the city and lead him back into the city. Josephus, for instance, relates that when the emperor approached Antioch, the people "would not bear to wait inside the walls because of their joy, but hastened to meet him," with many men and women leaving the city to greet him with acclamations and petitions (Josephus, *Jewish War* 7.100–103). The term Paul uses for "meeting" Christ here (ἀπάντησις, *apantēsis*, 1 Thess 4:17) was frequently used for such receptions.[14] So, on this reading, once all the dead are raised, the dead and living will *ascend* to meet the Lord and accompany him in his *descent* to the world.

Both interpretations are possible, and both emphasize that living and dead believers will be eschatologically united to be "with the Lord" as their life. Neither reading necessarily leads to the end-times speculations that have become popular in some circles.[15] Both, of course, leave us wrestling to fit the passage into what Paul says elsewhere about the end times (e.g., does the judgment happen before or after this?). Overall, the second interpretation is probably correct. It has historical plausibility in the way people received visiting—in Christ's case, conquering and liberating—rulers. It also fits more easily with Paul's eschatological vision expressed in other letters, where the Lord's return is not intended to provide an escape from but a restoration of the created world (Rom 8.18–25) through the cosmic purge of God's judgment (see Rom 2:5–11; 1 Cor 3:10–15; 2 Cor 5:10, etc.). Resurrected believers do ascend, Paul affirms, but they ascend to meet a Lord who is *descending* to judge and rule over this world, putting all created things in subjection to himself (1 Cor 15:20–28).

The Day of Vindication and the Increase of Lawlessness (2 Thess 2:1–12)

The hope of Christ's return also provides comfort to the Thessalonians regarding their persecution. While Paul is adamant that, in the present age, Christians are to exact no retribution for personal vendettas or persecutions (Rom 12:9–21), he does maintain that there will be a day of divine retribution

---

14 Peterson 1964 shows that the term was so regularized that it became a loanword in Hebrew for such meetings. Cf. also Chrysostom, *Homilies on 1 Thessalonians* 8.

15 A common "rapture" view holds that the ascent happens *before* the last day, so that believers escape from this world and the time of tribulation. However, believers clearly suffer during the tribulation (see below).

and wrath, when God will right all wrongs. It is a message that he can proclaim as a warning and a call to repentance (1 Thess 4:5), but for those experiencing persecution it is a message of hope. The Thessalonians are enduring in faith, but their neighbors are apparently hostile toward Christianity, and some are actively opposing the church (1 Thess 2:13–16; 3:3; 2 Thess 1:4, 6; cf. Acts 17:8). Paul makes no promise that this will cease during their lifetime, but he does point them toward the promised "righteous judgment of God" on the final day: "It is righteous in God's sight to repay with affliction those who afflict you" (2 Thess 1:5–6). God's justice is not asleep. There will be a day on which all persecution will end, all evil will end, when the Lord appears in power to judge each according to their works (2 Thess 1:9–10; cf. Rom 2:5–11; 1 Cor 3:16–18; Gal 6:7–10; Phil 3:18–21). He will be received and "glorified among his saints" (2 Thess 1:10), and they will be glorified in him (see also Rom 2:10; 5:2; 8:17–18, 30).

But if that day is not yet, when will it come? The day and the hour are not known. In 1 Thessalonians 5:1–2 Paul reiterates what he, Silvanus, and Timothy preached in Thessalonica, which itself is a reiteration of Jesus's teaching: the day will come suddenly "like a thief in the night" (cf. Matt 24:42–44; Luke 12:35–40), jarring the empire's sense of "peace and security" (1 Thess 5:3). He also likens it to labor pains coming upon a pregnant woman (1 Thess 5:3; cf. Matt 24:8; Mark 13:8).

However, the proclamation that the day will come suddenly does not imply that it will come without preamble. As with a natural childbirth, although no one can predict an absolute date or hour when labor will begin (naturally, at least), its approach is heralded by months of increasing discomfort for the mother.[16] So too with the coming of the Lord. A regular feature of NT eschatology is the expectation of suffering before Christ's return—especially the suffering of God's faithful (Matt 24:24; Rev 7:14; 12:17; 13:7; cf. Dan 7:21). Transgression, lawlessness, and persecution will reach a peak, a divinely ordained fulfillment at which the day of judgment and salvation will come (Dan 8:13, 23; 9:24; 11:36; Rev 6:9–11). Believers are called to endure in faith and hope: for, as in childbirth, increasing distress will give way to new life and joy (Matt 10:22; Luke 21:28; John 16:21; Rev 13:10; 14:12).

This increase in wickedness before Christ's return is detailed in 2 Thessalonians 2:1–12. In response to some notion that the day of the Lord

---

16 Every pregnancy is different—but "increasing discomfort" certainly describes my wife's experiences!

was already present, Paul instructs the Thessalonians that it clearly was not. They must not be deceived: a "rebellion" or "apostasy" will come first (v. 3). Paul's description centers around the "Lawless One" or "Man of Lawlessness." This person will oppose the true God and proclaim himself divine (v. 4). He will manifest deceitful signs and wonders, and those who have rejected God will follow him (vv. 9–12). Christ will then return in power to destroy the Lawless One and judge those who reject and oppose the truth. This "mystery of lawlessness" is already at work, but at present there is a "Restrainer," some entity or person who hinders the coming of this rebellion (vv. 6–7).

This teaching is meant to assure the Thessalonians that the day has not yet come: the rebellion must come first, and it has not. The message of increased persecution of God's people also comforts the Thessalonians by reframing their present affliction: it is not a sign that God despises them, but rather part and parcel of being God's beloved children in the last days (see 2 Thess 1:5). However, the details of this passage leave a lot of room for speculation. Who did Paul think was the Lawless One? A political leader? An apostate churchman? And who or what is the Restrainer? Is it the whole church? Is it Paul himself? Is it a political or social entity? Paul is not terribly specific, and some scholars have simply given up trying to pin down what he has in mind here.[17] Without trying to answer all the questions, two considerations can aid in interpretation.

First, if the letter is by Paul, we should take seriously his claim to have said something about this "rebellion" while in Thessalonica (2 Thess 2:5). Even if it was brief, his prior teaching means that he need not be as specific as we would like. It is also possible that his views were not incredibly defined as to exactly what persons or entities would be involved in this apocalyptic scenario. Indeed, when discussing the Restrainer, Paul speaks of it as an "it" and as a "him," in the space of a few verses.[18]

Second, Paul's discussion is clearly informed by the OT. The description of the Lawless One performing signs, leading others astray, and divinizing himself represents a pattern of biblical figures (usually rulers) who oppress God's people only to be defeated when God steps in to save (e.g., Pharaoh). Indeed, it is the epitome of the sin of Adam and Eve who were tempted to

---

17 For a history of interpretations, see Thiselton 2011, 231–44.

18 In Greek, Paul uses two different grammatical genders: the neuter τὸ κατέχον (*to katechon*, 2 Thess 2:6), "the thing that restrains"; and the masculine ὁ κατέχων (*ho katechōn*, 2 Thess 2:7), "the one who restrains."

be "like God" (Gen 3:5).[19] The pattern takes a sharply apocalyptic shape in Daniel, where it is prophesied that a future ruler will exalt himself as divine, desecrate the temple, lead away the unfaithful, make war on God's saints, and finally be defeated by heaven (see Dan 9:27; 11:31–32, 36–37). In Daniel, too, a kind of "restrainer" figure can be seen in the archangel Michael.[20] Daniel's prophecy is usually taken to refer to the Greek ruler Antiochus IV Epiphanes (e.g., by Josephus, *Jewish Antiquities* 10.276), but Paul and other Jews at the time were quite capable of seeing in this prophecy a still future and greater apocalyptic fulfillment that would fit the same pattern (cf. Matt 24:15). Indeed, rulers had done things like this even in Paul's lifetime: the emperor Gaius Caligula (reigned 37–41 CE) not only claimed divinity but tried to have a statue of himself erected in the Jewish temple (see Josephus, *Jewish Antiquities* 18.261–309; Philo, *Embassy* 203–346).

Any interpretation should take seriously that Paul's hope and expectation are biblically patterned. Unlike Daniel, Paul has not received a detailed revelation from an angel. He speaks out of conviction that in Christ God's promises are confirmed and approaching their final end (see Rom 4:16; 15:8; 2 Cor 1:20). He himself may not have any one specific person in mind when he preaches of this coming "rebellion." Reading Paul with Daniel and Revelation, we may expect the Lawless One to be a political leader, but the fulfillment of prophecy frequently takes unexpected forms. If Christians mean to think with Paul today, our task is not so much to identify a specific person as "the" Lawless One (or Restrainer), but instead to think in biblical patterns with Paul and learn to see them in the world, respond with faithful endurance, and keep the hope that Jesus, Paul, and the books of Daniel and Revelation proclaim: God will return, heaven will conquer, and all will be put right.

---

19 Cf. A. Johnson 2014, 133–37.

20 See Nicholl 2000.

FURTHER READING

Burnett, D. Clint. 2020. "Imperial Divine Honors in Julio-Claudian Thessalonica and the Thessalonian Correspondence." *JBL* 139 (3):567–89.

Donfried, Karl Paul. 2002. *Paul, Thessalonica, and Early Christianity.* London: T&T Clark.

Fee, Gordon. 2009. *The First and Second Letters to the Thessalonians.* NICNT. Grand Rapids: Eerdmans.

Johnson, Andy. 2014. "Paul's 'Anti-Christology' in 2 Thessalonians 2:3–12 in Canonical Context." *Journal of Theological Interpretation* 8 (1): 125–43.

Luckensmeyer, David. 2009. *The Eschatology of First Thessalonians.* NTOA 71. Göttingen: Vandenhoeck & Ruprecht.

Malherbe, Abraham J. 2000. *The Letters to the Thessalonians: A New Translation with Introduction and Commentary.* AB 32B. New York: Doubleday.

McNeel, Jennifer Houston. 2014. *Paul as Infant and Nursing Mother: Metaphor, Rhetoric, and Identity in 1 Thessalonians 2:5–8.* ECL 12. Atlanta: SBL Press.

Nicholl, Colin R. 2000. "Michael, the Restrainer Removed (2 Thess. 2:6–7)." *JTS* n.s. 51 (1): 27–53.

_____. 2004. *From Hope to Despair in Thessalonica: Situating 1 and 2 Thessalonians.* SNTSMS 126. Cambridge: Cambridge University Press.

Plevnik, Joseph, SJ. 1997. *Paul and the Parousia: An Exegetical and Theological Investigation.* Peabody, MA: Hendrickson.

Reicke, Bo. 2001. *Re-Examining Paul's Letters: The History of the Pauline Correspondence.* Edited by David P. Moessner and Ingalisa Reicke. Harrisburg, PA: Trinity.

Thiselton, Anthony C. 2011. *1 and 2 Thessalonians Through the Centuries.* Blackwell Bible Commentaries. Chichester: Wiley-Blackwell.

Weima, Jeffrey A. D. 2014. *1–2 Thessalonians.* BECNT. Grand Rapids: Baker Academic.

Witherington, Ben, III. 2006. *1 and 2 Thessalonians: A Socio-Rhetorical Commentary.* Grand Rapids: Eerdmans.

CHAPTER FOURTEEN

The Pastoral Epistles: 1–2 Timothy and Titus

First and Second Timothy and Titus are, together, often called the Pastoral Epistles (PE) because they address ministers in the Pauline mission—Timothy in Ephesus, Titus in Crete. They treat matters of ecclesial organization and encourage Timothy and Titus to follow Paul's example as an apostolic minister. Their theology, style, and setting within Paul's life have caused the vast majority of scholars to doubt their Pauline authorship. In any case, however, they remain a witness to the life of the church in its early generations and offer canonical encouragement and commands about the apostolic ministry and the work of the church.

INTRODUCTION
The Pastorals within Paul's Life and Letters

The letters addressed to Timothy and Titus are distinct within the Pauline corpus especially by their address and focus: all three are addressed to an individual minister and speak to this singular addressee throughout.[1] Their apparently private character sets them apart from other Pauline letters. Likewise, all three treat the minister's task and conduct as a churchman and administrator. Though the name "Pastoral Epistles" appears to have caught on in the eighteenth century, these distinctive features were noted already in antiquity. Tertullian, *Against Marcion* 5.21, summarized these letters as treating "ecclesiastical institution" (*de ecclesiastico statu*). According to the

---

1 Second-person verbs and pronouns in these letters are singular except in their closing benedictions, "Grace be with you all" (1 Tim 6:21; 2 Tim 4:22; Titus 3:15).

Muratorian Canon, the church esteems these letters for "the regulation of ecclesiastical discipline."[2]

They are also distinct for other reasons, for some of which the majority of scholars—more ardently than with the other disputed Paulines—have judged them pseudonymous. The three letters share numerous vocabulary that are otherwise not attested in Paul's letters. This includes distinct theological language; for instance, in the PE the term "savior" is used frequently of God the Father (1 Tim 1:1; 2:3; 4:10; Titus 1:3; 2:10; 3:4), whereas Paul's other letters use it rarely and always of Christ (Phil 3:20). Many question the consistency of the PE with Paul's thought evidenced in other letters: Would the Paul who said there was "no male and female" in Christ (Gal 3:28) and esteemed women as his benefactors and helpers in the gospel (e.g., Rom 16:1–3, 6–7) also prohibit women from any exercise of authority, as 1 Timothy 2:11–15 appears to do? Scholars especially question whether these writings evince a more developed church structure than what we can infer from other Pauline letters or whether they have lost the more fervent eschatological expectation of the earliest believers, seeing in them a reflection of Christian life and hope in a generation later than Paul's.

Nonetheless, there remain advocates of these letters' authenticity. Linguistic differences may be owed to Paul's use of different secretaries or collaborators in composition (see chapter 3). Likewise, one must reckon with the virtual certainty that Paul's thinking, terminology, and institutional management of his churches developed over time, or that Paul may have altered his way of speaking in these more private letters to trusted ministers, taking his audiences into account.[3] Advocates for authenticity can also insist that the other letters are not consistent or similar enough to judge the PE against them.[4] Note, for example, the lack of OT quotations in Philippians versus the constant stream of them in Romans, or Paul's vehement opposition to imposing the Mosaic law in Galatians versus his authoritative citation of its moral and civil-cultic commands in 1 Corinthians. Likewise, while Paul praised women's contributions to his mission and saw no difference between men and women in their salvation or created dignity, he was not necessarily

---

2 Text in the Pontifical Biblical Commission's revised *Enchiridion Biblicum* (1954, 2–3).

3 According to Prior 1989, the PE may show the *most* authentic Paul, while the other letters are different because of the influence of collaborators and secretaries.

4 Cf. L. Johnson 2001, 60, 68–72.

an egalitarian when it came to roles in the home or public liturgy (see 1 Cor 11:1–16; 14:33b–36).

The PE's authenticity has been debated for more than two centuries now. Many recent scholars emphasize the need to read and evaluate each individually rather than lump all three together, which has provided a haven for mediating positions—that only one (or two) may be inauthentic, or that one or all contain fragments of genuine Pauline letters that were later edited or incorporated into our PE. Ultimately, every argument against authenticity can be deconstructed, but the distinctive features of these letters do beg for explanation, and there is no way to "prove" them authentic other than to argue that Paul *could* have written them in his lifetime. Canonically, uncertainties about authorship should not diminish the PE's religious authority, but authorship is significant for our understanding of Paul's thought historically and likewise for the interpretation of these epistles' intent and purpose. Most significant, therefore, is the question of what these letters are meant to be and where they fit within the life of Paul or, if after Paul's life, the early church.

The Pastorals and Their Purposes

What unites the letters, other than some distinctive vocabulary and disputed authorship, is the voice of Paul to his delegates regarding their own faithfulness and administration of the churches. Second Timothy purports to be a letter from Paul in prison and preparing to be executed, exhorting Timothy to take heart in the face of Paul's peril, hold fast the gospel, and serve God well by following Paul's example. It has a more personal tone. First Timothy and Titus are marked by directives about specific behaviors that should be encouraged to maintain order in the church and to avoid scandalizing outsiders, reinforced by theological statements and Paul's example.

If these letters are pseudonymous, what are they and why were they written? Some see these as a rather tendentious power grab in the third Christian generation or later, deceptively claiming Paul's authority to refute heretics such as Marcion, who rejected the OT, or to enforce patriarchal social norms. Patristic heresiologists certainly *quoted* the PE's exhortations to hold fast the apostolic faith.[5] But if this were the primary purpose of their composition, we should expect apologetic arguments refuting something

---

5 On Irenaeus and the PE, see White 2011.

like Marcion's position, but find none. Likewise, the discussion of women and men in authority is explicit only in a few verses.

If pseudonymous, it is better to think of these as written within a generation of Paul's death (ca. 70–100 CE) by some of his disciples.[6] Their apparently private address to "Timothy" or "Titus" is, then, a literary device by which Paul's disciples addressed perhaps several churches in Paul's name and after his memory. The farewell discourse exhorting Timothy to remember Paul's example and remain faithful is something of a literary monument recalling Paul's legacy and encouraging the churches he left behind. In some ways (though only some), 1 Timothy and Titus parallel "church orders" from the first through third centuries, giving models of faithful management and practice for the growing body of Christ. Their references to Crete or Ephesus may be fictive, a literary vehicle to instruct churches in several places. Their interest in seemly behavior and respect for societal norms would have been crucial in the late first century as the church gained the notice of an empire that was always ready to crush new movements that appeared to subvert imperial and societal order.[7] From this perspective, the PE together would have much in common with the pseudonymous Socratic letters and other works in which later disciples offered exhortation to their community in the name and by the example of their founding figures, often filling in plausible but not necessarily factual details.[8]

However, if the letters are Pauline, their purposes are fairly transparent. Rather than a remembrance of Paul for many churches, 2 Timothy is a real letter to Timothy composed as Paul approaches death, exhorting Timothy to keep the faith, set his hope in Christ, and visit Paul if possible. First Timothy and Titus were written to Paul's representatives as reminders and instructions about how they should manage their particular churches. Timothy and Titus may have read these letters out to their churches—perhaps showing everyone that their policies were not merely theirs but bore Paul's apostolic authority—but the letters are specific missives addressed to these ministers about their temporary assignments. If they are genuine letters, they would be similar to Greco-Roman letters to one's subordinates, giving orders, advice, updates, or encouragement related to their assignments.[9] In this case, each

---

6 See Quinn 1990: 17–21.

7 See Hoklotubbe 2017.

8 See Fiore 1986.

9 See L. Johnson 2001, 91–97, who calls them in English "letters to Paul's delegates."

must be read according to its specific location in Paul's life and his way of managing churches under his apostolate.

Locating the Pastorals

If the PE are pseudonymous, it is possible that they were all written at once as a single corpus by a single author or group of authors. On the other hand, it may be that one was written first by one author—whether Paul or a later disciple—and then was used as a template for the other letters by later authors. There are many theories here, but the more distant one views the letters to be from the historical Paul, the less certain one can be about how and when they were composed.

If the PE are all authentic, where are they located within Paul's life and ministry? Do they belong together or separate? While they do appear to be a distinct set within the Pauline corpus, they indicate different situations.

The simplest place to begin is 2 Timothy. Paul speaks of himself as currently in chains, imprisoned, and apparently in Rome (2 Tim 1:8, 16–17; 2:9). One might then reason that this letter was written in the Roman imprisonment with which Acts ends, around 60–62 CE. However, early tradition uniformly claims that Paul was imprisoned twice in Rome: he was freed from the imprisonment mentioned in Acts, engaged in further ministry in the 60s CE, and then was imprisoned again and martyred under Nero Caesar (ca. 65–67). Most who accept 2 Timothy's authenticity hold that it was composed during this second Roman imprisonment, and data within the letter fit this view. Paul indicates that he has already undergone one legal "defense" of himself, at which he was abandoned by many companions and later released (2 Tim 4:16–17). This letter is also written with a very real expectation of execution: Paul hopes Timothy will come soon, but his "departure" (i.e., his death) is very near (2 Tim 4:6–9). In earlier letters from prison, Paul holds out hope of release—even in Philippians, where he faces the real prospect of execution (see Phil 1:19–26; Phlm 22). Here, however, while he praises God for granting earthly deliverance after his previous defense, he has hope only of eternal deliverance through martyrdom (2 Tim 4:7–8, 16–18).[10] That would put this letter written from Rome in the mid-60s.

In 1 Timothy and Titus, however, Paul does not appear to be in prison. He writes to Titus after leaving him in Crete, apparently not long after evan-

---

10 The passage was interpreted thus already in Eusebius, *Ecclesiastical History* 2.22.

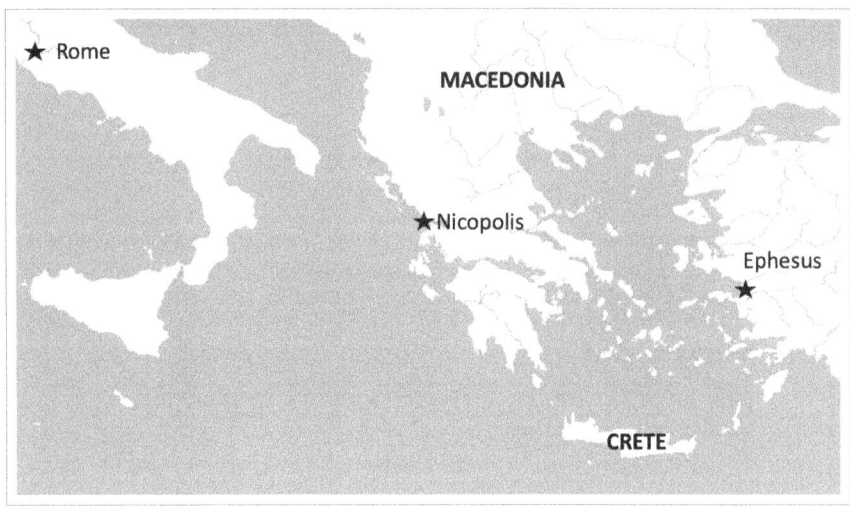

gelizing the island. Titus's job is to appoint presbyters or bishops throughout the island's churches for the sake of Crete's long-term growth in the gospel (Titus 1:5–9), despite some dangerous influences and Crete's reputation for degeneracy (Titus 1:10–12). Paul has since left Crete and traveled north through Greece, and he plans to spend the winter along Greece's west coast in Nicopolis, where he hopes Titus will meet him when his work is done (Titus 3:12).[11] On the other hand, 1 Timothy is addressed to Timothy as Paul's delegate overseeing the more established church in Ephesus, with exhortations about faithful ministry and proper conduct in "God's household" (1 Tim 3:15). Paul instructs Timothy to remain there while he travels ahead to Macedonia, that Timothy might tighten the administration and catechesis in a large community in which false teachings and other troubles were arising (1 Tim 1:3).

The question with 1 Timothy and Titus, if authentic, is whether they too should be dated after Paul's first Roman imprisonment or earlier, within the time frame covered in Acts. Since 1 Timothy gives few concrete details other than that Paul left Ephesus for Macedonia and that the church in Ephesus was established, it could have been written at almost any time since Paul's

---

11 The name "Nicopolis" (woodenly, "Victory Town") was given to several cities in commemoration of a great victory, from Egypt to Greece and elsewhere. One was the capital of the province of Epirus on the north-central west coast of Greece. Given Paul's preference for evangelizing urban centers and his known work in Greece, this is the most likely reference in Titus 3:12.

Ephesian ministry (ca. 52–55). Perhaps we should imagine Paul leaving Timothy to begin his task at that time (cf. Acts 20:1; 1 Tim 1:3). Titus is more difficult, since we have no other evidence of a time at which Paul would have evangelized Crete and then moved northward through Greece. It is not impossible to posit that he did so before his first Roman imprisonment, but accepting this scenario requires that one either rearrange the itinerary in Acts to squeeze Crete in or simply acknowledge that Acts is incomplete and remain agnostic about specifics.[12]

However, the majority of those who see 1 Timothy and Titus as authentic date these also to the period after Paul's first Roman imprisonment, outside the narrative of Acts. A few factors tip the scales in this direction. Paul's evangelizing Crete, at least, seems to make more sense after his first Roman imprisonment. Before his imprisonment, he had set his sights on heading west to Spain via Rome (Rom 15:20–28), but the intervening years of captivity surely interrupted his plans for immediate departure. Early tradition holds that Paul did undertake his western campaign (*1 Clement* 5.6–7), but the years between his release (ca. 62) and martyrdom (ca. 66?) allow for a good deal of travel to Crete and northward through Greece in the meantime.[13] And if Titus was written in this period, it is likely that 1 Timothy was as well. The letters both have similar purposes, and both reference similar situations despite their different destinations: the danger of false teaching—sometimes motivated by greed—including an asceticism that denies God's created gifts and a preoccupation with "myths," "genealogies," apparently involving disputes about Jewish law and custom (see 1 Tim 1:4–7; 4:1–3, 6; 6:3–5; Titus 1:10–16; 3:9). Likewise, all three Pastoral Epistles share a concern that false teachings have infiltrated Christian households through susceptible or idle women (1 Tim 5:11–16; 2 Tim 3:6–7; Titus 1:11). Perhaps such troubles arose in both Ephesus and Crete, but it is simpler to imagine that the characterizations of these dangers are similar because they all reflect Paul's wor-

---

12 Paul's time in Crete in Acts 27:7–20 has him under guard, being transferred by ship from Caesarea to his first Roman imprisonment, with no need to go through Nicopolis. If this account is Luke's way of tipping his hat to a Pauline church in Crete, it is of no help in reconstructing our letter's background. One might think Paul's journey north from Crete included one of his visits to Corinth, but these all have a southward trajectory from Macedonia to Corinth (see 1 Cor 16:1–8; 2 Cor 9:1–5).

13 Paul's plan to winter in Nicopolis (Titus 3:12), a western seaport, could mean he was positioning himself to move toward Spain afterward. However, he could also have traveled west (perhaps with a less-than-successful mission) already before evangelizing Crete. There simply are too few data to say what happened first or last in this period.

ries, experiences, and ways of speaking at a single, late stage of his ministry. Finally, 1 Timothy shares with 2 Timothy the names of opponents who have recently taught some of the falsehoods these letters denounce—particularly Hymenaeus and Alexander (1 Tim 1:20; 2 Tim 1:15; 4:14)—and this seems to put 1 Timothy's situation also in this later period after Paul's first release. If authentic, these three are separate letters, yet they seem to reflect a common outlook and a common stage in Paul's ministry, between 62 and 66 after his first defense and release in Rome.

1 TIMOTHY

Timothy collaborated with Paul on several of his letters (2 Cor 1:1; Phil 1:1; Col 1:1; 1 Thess 1:1; 2 Thess 1:1; Phlm 1) and frequently served as Paul's envoy to teach and administer Paul's churches. Paul commended Timothy as his "coworker," as a "brother," as a fellow "slave of Christ" (Rom 16:21; 2 Cor 1:1; Phil 1:1), and also as a dutiful disciple to Paul, his "beloved and faithful son in the Lord" (1 Cor 4:17).

In this epistle, Timothy has stayed behind in Ephesus and is tending the church there. Paul hopes to be able to visit him in Ephesus soon, but, until he can, Timothy is to continue preaching and teaching (1 Tim 4:11–16). The church is the "pillar and foundation of truth" on earth, and it must be strengthened and defended against the threats of disorder and falsehood (3:14–16). The letter is especially concerned with behavior that befits the gospel, both in the liturgical assembly and outside of it—"that you may know how one ought to conduct oneself in God's household" (3:15). Paul's instructions relate to all but focus particularly on those who lead and influence others within the church. Paul laments that many pursue position or simply their own passions, not following the tradition Paul has handed down, and he warns that those who cannot live with self-control are easily corruptible and will corrupt others (1:19–20; 6:3–10, 21). He urges Timothy to set an example of good conduct and lists qualifications Timothy should require before ordaining ("laying hands on") new presbyters, bishops, or deacons (2:1–3:13; 4:6–16; 5:22; 6:11–16, 20). Paul's concern that God's servants be content with the reward of godliness reaches from bishops also to widows, whom he encourages to serve Christ by remarrying or by remaining single and committed to charity, but in either case avoiding wantonness and serving Christ and the church (5:9–16). He is likewise concerned about false teaching and an asceticism that rejects certain foods and forbids marriage (4:1–5; contrast Paul's prudential preference for celibacy in 1 Cor 7).

The letter's content and structure appear to fit its private, minister-to-minister address. It denounces but rarely describes particular false teachings or explains why they are wrong (excepting 1:6–11; 4:1–5). If it is a real letter from Paul to Timothy, Paul presumably felt no need to explain. The letter gives various directives, not always with a smooth rhetorical flow. The instructions about worship and church office are more clearly organized (2:1–3:13), counterbalanced elsewhere by abrupt transitions (5:1, 23) and an informal conclusion (6:20–21). This, again, befits a more personal letter from administrator to administrator.[14] Nevertheless, the letter maintains a clear focus throughout on the purpose of Timothy's work and its eternal importance: Christ has died and risen to save, and he has entrusted Paul and, through Paul, Timothy with the task of bringing people to this promise of salvation (4:16) and training other ministers to carry on the work.

Overview: 1 Timothy

I. **Letter Opening** (1:1–20)

  A. To Timothy, my spiritual son (1:1–2).

  B. As I urged you before, rebuke those who teach contrary to the truth, for the sake of conscience and love (1:3–5).

   1. Some have veered off into speculation and debate about the law (1:6–7).

   2. The law is good, but it should be used for its purpose: to constrain immorality (1:8–11).

  C. Thanks be to God for his mercy upon me, a sinner, to serve him in this gospel (1:12–17)!

  D. In this service, Timothy, I charge you to fight the good fight and keep a clean conscience as you serve (1:18–20).

II. **Order and Harmony in the House-Church** (2:1–3:13)

  A. Therefore, all must pray that we may lead a gentle and quiet life in the name of God, who desires all to be saved by the gospel we preach (2:1–7).

---

14 Quinn and Wacker (2000, 170–71) argue that 2:1–3:13 borrows from an older "church order" document.

1. So I want men to pray in holiness, not in competition or wrath (2:8).

2. Likewise, women should adorn themselves with modesty and piety. Let women learn, peaceably and under authority rather than striving to dominate; just as Eve was created separately and after Adam (2:9–15).

B. Any who desire to lead should be examined.

1. Those who desire the office of bishop should be pious, gentle, orderly, upright teachers, respectable in the eyes of outsiders (3:1–7).

2. Deacons should be upright beyond reproach, not greedy or wanton. The women should be upright and faithful, and deacons should be able to manage their own households well (3:8–13).

III. **Timothy's Task (3:14–4:16)**

A. I hope to come to you, but if I cannot, I write that you may know how God's household should be managed, for the church is the pillar of truth (3:14–15).

1. The mystery of our faith is great—the resurrected Christ, ascended to heaven and proclaimed in the world (3:16).

2. But the Spirit foretold false teachers would come, denying God's created goods like marriage and foods (4:1–5).

B. If you put my instructions before the believers and cling to the truth, you will be a good minister (4:6).

1. But keep yourself in the truth and train yourself in piety (4:7–10).

2. Be bold. Do not neglect your ordination, but remain devoted to public reading, preaching, and teaching. Be an example of godliness until I come (4:11–16).

IV. **Orderly and Respectful Conduct in the Church (5:1–6:2a)**

A. Honor the old as fathers and mothers, and the young like brothers and sisters in God's household (5:1–2).

B. Regarding widows:

1. They should first be cared for by their own kin, and should not live wantonly but be steadfast in prayer (5:3–8).

2. Genuine widows should be enrolled for the church's care (5:9–10). But younger, idle widows should marry—for they are susceptible to falsehoods, and some have already been led astray (5:11–16).

C. Regarding presbyters:

1. Those who preside well are worthy of honor and payment, and they should not be accused frivolously (5:17–19).

2. Reprove publicly those who sin. You must do nothing out of prejudice, and ordain no one hastily! (Have a little wine, not just water, due to your stomach issues.) Not all sins are obvious at first, just as good deeds cannot remain entirely hidden (5:20–25).

D. Regarding slaves, they should honor their masters—especially Christian masters, since they are their brothers and sisters—lest Christ be blasphemed (6:1–2a).

V. **Final Exhortation: Steadfastness and Contentment (6:2b-21)**

A. Teach these things, which befit the truth and godliness in Christ. Do not, like others, veer from the truth out of arrogance or greed (6:2b–10).

B. You must flee vanity. Pursue godliness and the promises of Christ, following his example of steadfastness until he returns (6:11–16). And urge the rich to set their hope in Christ, not earthly treasure (6:17–19).

C. O Timothy, keep the faith—so many have gone astray (6:20–21a)!

D. Grace be with you (6:21b).

2 TIMOTHY

In 2 Timothy, Paul encourages Timothy as Paul prepares for his death. Imprisoned in Rome, Paul expects martyrdom soon, and he is left almost entirely alone (4:10–16; cf. 1:15). Timothy's current whereabouts are not entirely clear. Timothy is expected to know people who used to be in Ephesus (1:15, 18) and is charged to greet Prisca and Aquila, who were in Rome when Paul wrote Romans, though they might now be elsewhere (4:19; cf. Rom 16:3). It is usually assumed that he is still on assignment in Ephesus (as in

1 Timothy). He is probably at least somewhere in Asia Minor, since he is expected to travel to Rome via Troas, a little north of Ephesus (2 Tim 4:13). The letter has a more personal feel than the other PE. Its opening grounds Paul's relationship to Timothy in personal more than functional terms, and it is the only PE to include a thanksgiving (1:3–7).[15] The troubles affecting God's church are the same as in the other PE: vain controversies and "myths" (2:14, 23; 4:4), immorality and false teaching (3:1–9; 4:3–4)— though 2 Timothy 2:17–18 adds specifically that some opponents have taught that the resurrection has already occurred. Yet while these troubles form a backdrop to the letter, they are not its primary focus or occasion. Its focus remains on Paul's relationship to Timothy as "father" and apostle in light of Paul's impending death.

Timothy has shed "tears" over Paul's imprisonment and impending fate (1:4, 8). Paul comforts Timothy and exhorts him to remain faithful in ministry, ready to follow Paul's same path for the sake of Christ. The letter is peppered with reminders of hope in the midst of suffering: persecutions must come, but the faithful God will sort out evildoers and crown those who endure with life (1:1; 2:10–13, 19; 3:9, 12; 4:1, 8). Paul offers himself as an exhibit of God's grace and a model of fidelity and hope (1:9–14; 3:10–12; 4:6–8). In the short term, Paul hopes that Timothy will come visit him soon—before winter, when travel was difficult—as he awaits deliverance through martyrdom into the life Christ has won for his people (4:9–18, 21).

Overview: 2 Timothy

I. **Letter Opening (1:1–2:7)**

   A. To Timothy, from Paul, apostle of Christ (1:1–2).

   B. I thank God for you and long to see you, remembering your tears on my account and your steadfastness in the faith (1:3–5).

   C. Take heart, now, and grow in the strength of your faith and in the work for which I ordained you (1:6–7).

      1. Do not be ashamed of me or of suffering for Christ, our savior (1:8–10).

      2. This is the gospel entrusted to me, which I have taught you, and for which I am not ashamed to suffer. Follow my teaching and example (1:11–14).

---

15 For these and other reasons, 2 Timothy is often regarded as having the best claim to Pauline authorship among the PE.

  a. I have been abandoned by many, but not all are ashamed of my chains (1:15–18).

  b. You must remain strong in Christ, ready to suffer as a soldier of the Lord. Heed my words and entrust them to more ministers (2:1–7).

II. **Exhortations to Faithful Ministry amid Opposition (2:8–4:8)**

 A. Remember Christ. For him I suffer in chains, but God's word is not chained. I can endure everything for the sake of God's church, because I know God is faithful (2:8–13).

 B. Remind your people to hold fast to Christ, and present yourself to God as a faithful minister (2:14–15).

  1. Stay away from useless teaching—many do not, but God knows who are his (2:16–19).

  2. Strive to be a pure vessel, to be used for good things in God's house. Flee youthful passions and useless controversies, but pursue what is right and restore the errant (2:20–26).

  3. Remember that in the last days wickedness will increase; many treacherous persons have arisen and disrupt Christian households with falsehood and immorality. Avoid them (3:1–9).

   a. But you have followed me in all my teaching and my persecutions, from which God saved me. Persecution comes to all the upright, while the wicked get worse and worse (3:10–13).

   b. Remain steadfast in what you have learned from me and through the scriptures, God's word to train you and ready his people for service (3:14–17).

 C. I adjure you: preach, be faithful, and exhort the people with patient fervor (4:1–2).

  1. For times will come when people will detest sound teaching (4:3–4).

  2. You must be ready to teach and to suffer, and stay faithful (4:5).

  3. My own death is near, but I have finished my race. And God will award me the crown of life, as he will all those who remain in him (4:6–8).

III. **Letter Closing (4:9–22)**

   A. Only Luke is with me now. Come soon, and please bring my cloak and books (4:9–13). Beware our false friend Alexander. He opposes the gospel (4:14–15).

   B. God has kept me as his minister and delivered me at my first defense—and I know he will now deliver me to his heavenly kingdom (4:16–18).

   C. Receive and pass on our greetings. Please come before winter (4:19–21).

   D. Grace be with you (4:22).

TITUS

As noted above, this letter bears much in common with 1 Timothy. Both are letters to Paul's delegates instructing them on their ministerial tasks. Yet there are differences. Timothy's Ephesian church appears more established, and the instructions about ministerial qualifications make it seem as though this is a matter of course in the growing church at Ephesus. Titus's church in Crete seems only recently evangelized, and appointing presbyters and bishops throughout the towns on the island is his most urgent task before he leaves (1:5; 3:12). He is also to "rectify" or "set straight" the other unfinished tasks in establishing the church at Crete (1:5).

Beyond leadership and stability, this letter also has a frequent focus on "good works" (2:14; 3:8, 14). Against the moral disorder for which Crete was infamous (1:12), Paul is concerned that all behave in such a way that the church will be respectable to outsiders (2:5, 8, 10; 3:1–2). Christ saved his people for good works, not for inane controversies or disputations, and Christians' behavior should show forth the Spirit's gift of transformation that they received in baptism and their justification (3:1–11). Christ has redeemed his people to be "zealous" for good works, and he trains his people to pursue pious and upright lives for others as they await his return (2:11–14). Paul calls Titus to insist on this in his own preaching as he attends to the church's leadership and administration, appointing ministers who will exemplify such a life and call others to do the same.

Overview: Titus

I. **Letter Opening (1:1–4)**

A. To Titus, my spiritual son, partner in faith and ministry (1:1–4).

II. **Titus's Task (1:5–3:11)**

A. I left you in Crete to complete our work and establish presbyters in every town (1:5)

1. They must be above reproach. A bishop is God's steward and must be holy and prudent, maintaining true doctrine, that he may be able to exhort and rebuke (1:6–9).

2. For many teach out of greed or promulgate Jewish myths and merely human traditions about purity. They must be corrected (1:10–16).

B. But you must teach conduct that befits sound doctrine (2:1).

1. Elder men should be respectable and sound in faith. Elder women should likewise be respectable in life and conversation and train the younger women, lest God's word be blasphemed because of Christians' behavior (2:2–5).

2. Encourage younger men to be prudent, following your example, that none might have cause to slander us (2:6–8).

3. Slaves should be submissive, not contrary, adorning sound doctrine with faithfulness in their current station (2:9–10).

C. For Christ has taught us to live prudently, justly, and piously in the present age, having given himself to redeem a people zealous for good works (2:11–14).

1. Teach these things. Remind the people to be submissive to civil authorities, not rebellious, but decent and gentle toward all (2:15–3:2).

a. For we once were ignorant and hateful, slaves to our passions (3:3).

b. But by God's mercy, Christ delivered us through the grace of the Spirit and baptism, making us his righteous heirs of eternal life (3:4–7).

2. I want you to insist on these things, that believers may set their minds to excel in good works profitable for all (3:8).

a. But avoid vain disputes and arguments about the law, which profit no one (3:9).

b. And avoid anyone who opposes you in this and refuses to repent (3:10–11).

III. Letter Closing (3:12–15)

A. When I send Artemas or Tychicus, come to me in Nicopolis, where I plan to stay the winter (3:12).

B. Send Zenas and Apollos off with ample provisions. Let all who are with us learn to excel in good works (3:13–14).

C. Receive and pass on our greetings (3:15a).

D. Grace be with you (3:15b).

KEY FEATURES
The "Quiet" Life and the Church's Mission

The PE's concern for order and upright leadership can appear less than thrilling, perhaps lacking the theological fervor of other epistles. If they are Pauline and truly letters to individuals, their purpose and their administrator-to-administrator perspective goes a long way to explain this. But, more importantly, these administrative concerns have a practical and theological end. Upright and skilled leaders are integral to the church's *mission of salvation*. These letters frequently support their practical directives with theological convictions about Christ and salvation.[16] Leaders who hold fast to the faith and teach it can "save" their hearers (1 Tim 4:16), while false teaching and scandal can do the opposite. Paul's apostolic suffering is for the sake of others' salvation, and he calls Timothy to imitate the same (2 Tim 2:10). Scripture must be read and taught because it makes one "wise unto salvation" (2 Tim 3:15). Christ, the mediator between God and humanity, has died to save sinners through the ministry of the church (1 Tim 1:15; 2:5–6; 2 Tim 1:8–12; Titus 3:3–7). To leave this ministry unguarded is to leave God's beloved sheep in the care of wolves.

The mission of salvation also affects other parts of the vision of the PE, specifically with regard to outsiders and the government. This becomes visible in

---

16 These often come in the form of "faithful sayings" (e.g., 1 Tim 2:5–6; 3:16; 2 Tim 2:11–13; Titus 3:4–8a), which appear to be pre-formed traditions repeated and incorporated into the PE. See Yarbrough 2009.

the PE's instructions on respectable behavior. Though they decry immorality as do other NT documents, the PE's specific injunctions focus on how individual believers should treat each other according to their societal stations—being respectful of the old, caring for the young, slaves not being rebellious, as well as a command to pray for the emperor and civil authorities (1 Tim 5:1–8; 6:1–2; Titus 2:1–10; 3:1). One may compare Paul's injunctions to Philemon about how he runs his household and treats his slave Onesimus, as well as the codes for household relations, in Colossians 3:18–4:6; Ephesians 5:22–6:9.

These injunctions do not make up the whole of morality or even the primary part of it. They are part of what these letters call the "quiet" life. At the outset of the instructions in 1 Timothy, Paul urges that the church offer prayers for all people, including civil authorities, "that we might lead a peaceable and quiet life in all piety and probity" (1 Tim 2:2). The term "quiet" here (ἡσύχιος, hēsychios) does not mean muzzled and in a corner—the church always has a prophetic and evangelical task within the world—but indicates a lack of turmoil, tumult, oppression, or antagonism. In 1 Thessalonians 4:11–12, the congregation seeks this quiet when insiders work honorably with their own hands, take care of each other's needs, and live in a way that is respectable or "seemly" to outsiders. Following Jeremiah 29:4–7, Paul, like other Jews at the time, encourages honoring the state and societal fabric, though not following the pagan state as a moral authority (Rom 13:1–7; cf. Mishnah, tractate ʾAbot 3.2). The PE want ministers and all believers to be as above reproach as possible in the eyes of outsiders, that the church might be seen as a respectable movement rather than a new philosophy promoting social anarchy (1 Tim 3:7; 5:7; Titus 2:5, 8; 3:2). Practically, it would hardly be expedient to feed into outsiders' fears that this new religious movement upended all decency and threw society into chaos, that it nurtured contention and hypocrisy. The empire loved to quell with violence any group that even smelled as though it bred dissent or turmoil.[17] This does not mean that the gospel is not subversive of societal evil or injustice. But in the PE's vision, the church's "quiet" life operates *within* a culture in order to affect it. According to Titus 2:12, Christ himself has "trained us, that we, denying impiety and worldly desires, might live prudently, justly, and piously in

---

17 This concern is clearly visible in the century after Paul's death, but it surely existed earlier. If Paul wrote 1 Tim and Titus after a narrow release from an unsympathetic Nero (2 Tim 4:16–17), it is quite imaginable that he would devote space to behaviors that might forestall persecutions he feared would come.

the present age." The church's imitation of Christ, who was crucified by the imperial engine of violence, is not one of open rebellion but one of subversive suffering and enduring patience in evangelization by word and deed. Representing Christ for the salvation of souls, this vision asks the church to keep its head down for the sake of the world. For God "desires that all people be saved and come to knowledge of the truth" (1 Tim 2:4).

Pastoral Ministers: Stewards and Representatives of Christ

The mission of salvation is also the goal of the PE's perspective on the qualifications and tasks of ecclesiastical ministers. Ministers guard and hand down the "deposit" of truth Christ gave his apostles (2 Tim 1:12, 14). They rebuke, teach, preach, and administer to this end. Timothy is called to steep himself in devotion and charity and to encourage the same in others, "for by doing so you will save both yourself and your hearers" (1 Tim 4:16).

The church is the "pillar and foundation of truth" on earth (1 Tim 3:15), and it must not be left unguarded and subject to the will of the masses or of overzealous upstarts, or to a few elites who expect that they will have the same sway in the church as in society (1 Tim 3:1–13). Christ has given apostolic ministers for the edification and sanctification of all (Eph 4:11–16). We see Paul's view of this vocation in his own ministry here and in other letters. He speaks of himself both as a priestly minister and as a father (see Rom 1:9; 15:16; 1 Cor 4:15; Phil 2:17; 2 Tim 1:3). He teaches, counsels, rebukes, and even protects God's household by casting out the obstinate who harm his family (1 Cor 5:1–5; 1 Tim 1:20). He is an administrator and works for order within the liturgical assembly, ensuring that everything serves to edify the worshippers and that particular churches keep in line with the traditions maintained elsewhere (see 1 Cor 11:2, 16, 23; 14:1–36). Timothy and Titus are called to continue Paul's work and to appoint others to do the same.

The concept of ministers as "stewards" is frequent throughout the NT, especially where ministers are being reminded of the great authority Christ gives them and their accountability to use it for Christ's purposes (e.g., Matt 25:14–30; Luke 12:35–48; Col 1:25). The metaphor of "stewardship" depicts the church as a Greco-Roman household (οἶκος, *oikos*), an economic and societal entity consisting of several ordered interrelations of the *paterfamilias* to family, employees, slaves, children, and others. God is the *paterfamilias* at the top, and apostolic ministers are the managers commanded to use God's property and wealth for the good of God's dependents. Bishops and presbyters are such "stewards" managing God's estate (Titus 1:7), and the PE accordingly insist that those who receive this office be well qualified (1 Tim 3:1–13; Titus 1:5–9). The PE and other documents from the period show the church beginning to develop titles that would later become standard or replaced by others. Borrowing from the synagogue, it was only natural that congregations developed governance by "elders" or "presbyters."[18] Other texts speak of "prophets" or "pastors/shepherds" in local churches (see Eph 4:11; *Didache* 11.1–6; 15.1). The title "bishop" occurs in the PE and earlier in Philippians 1:3; literally meaning "overseer" or "visitor" (ἐπίσκοπος, *episkopos*), it suggests someone with jurisdiction over several churches.[19] Deacons, literally indicating a "server" (διάκονος, *diakonos*), were introduced as helpers to the apostles (Acts 6:1–6), though how they helped probably differed from place to place.

Presbyters and bishops were quickly understood in priestly and cultic terms, especially in the service of the eucharist (e.g., *Didache* 13.3; 14.1–3; cf. 1 Cor 10:16–22). By the end of the first century, apostolic ministers were understood to represent Christ to those in their charge, with deacons and priests under the bishop, and the bishops under Christ governing the universal church (see *1 Clement* 40–44; Ignatius, *Ephesians* 3–6; *Magnesians* 6–7). This is an exclusive office; only some have it (1 Cor 12:29–30). Yet not all of its duties are exclusive. The whole church represents Christ to the world (Phil 2:14–16). And all believers are tasked with evangelizing, admonishing, and serving (Gal 6:1–2; Eph 4:15–16; Col 3:12–16; 1 Thess 4:9, 18). But the PE and the NT indicate that ministers represent Christ among Christians in a singular and concentrated way, and they do it "with all authority" (Titus 2:15). If the whole church is to exemplify holiness and love *within the world*, ministers are to be singular examples of sanctity *within the church*—presbyters and then, representing Christ over the presbyters, the bishops. If all believers teach in small ways, ministers are entrusted with a particular charism and teaching office. If all offer their own bodies as sacrifices to Christ, apostolic

---

18 Note, for instance, that Jas 2:2 calls the local church a "synagogue" (συναγωγή, *synagōgē*). Paul's more common term for the "church," ἐκκλησία (*ekklēsia*), is a borrowed term designating an acting or voting assembly, but it too had already been used in the Greek OT to translate the "assembly" of God's people. See Trebilco 2011.

19 However, in Titus 1:5–7 presbyter and bishop seem almost the same office. Jerome, a little unhappy with his own rank, used this to argue that there is no difference between presbyter (priest) and bishop excepting that only bishops could ordain (*Letter* 146).

ministers are "stewards of the mysteries of God" (1 Cor 4:1), offering Christ's own body for the rest of the faithful in the eucharist.

In a controversial passage, 1 Timothy 2:8–15 peers into the liturgical assembly and, first, calls men not to be contentious when offering public prayer; second, it calls women not to wear gaudy garb but to adorn themselves with wisdom and good deeds.[20] The passage then addresses women's role with regard to the teaching office: women are to learn "in quiet" and neither to "teach" with independent authority nor to "dominate" over men in the assembly (vv. 11–12).[21] The argument grounds the distinction and complementarity between male and female in God's creative act to "form" two distinct sexes in Adam and Eve (v. 13). The submission of women regarding the teaching office in the assembly also corresponds to the fall into sin (v. 14; cf. 1 Cor 14:34), perhaps recalling sin's curse of male-female competition in Genesis 3:16.[22] But the emphasis on Eve's deception is balanced by the proclamation that "she" will be saved "through childbearing," perhaps recalling that Eve's fall is matched by the saving birth of Christ through a woman (Gen 3:15; Gal 4:4), and reminding the audience that women, like men, are saved if they hold fast the faith (1 Tim 2:15).[23]

Canonically, the implementation of this passage in the life of today's church is subject to the church's discernment as it hands on the deposit of faith. Traditionally it is understood to indicate that the office of bishop and presbyter/priest is restricted to males. (In the OT, one may compare the male-only priesthood with the role of prophet, which was held by males and females.) Exegetically, we may offer some points to understand the text. First, two views of women may lay in the background. In parts of the empire at this time, women were receiving new rights, and many encouraged emancipation from one's husband both economically and sexually—with promiscuity

---

20 Some argue that the passage is about husbands and wives at home, not in the liturgy. But churches met in the homes of men and women; the lines cannot be so cleanly divided.

21 The term for women learning "in quiet" (ἐν ἡσυχίᾳ, en hēsychia, 1 Tim 2:11–12) is the same as that used in 1 Tim 2:2 for the church's "quiet life." The verb αὐθεντέω (authenteō) is often translated as "have authority," but this rare term usually has a negative connotation, indicating domination or usurpation (occasionally referring to murder). Chrysostom, hardly a proto-feminist, warned Christian husbands *not* to think they could "dominate" (αὐθεντέω) over their wives just because wives were to be submissive (*Homilies on Colossians* 10.1).

22 If the PE's details accurately reflect their historical situation, emphasis on Eve's deception may be a dig against the current trouble of false teachings infiltrating Christian homes through particular women (see 1 Tim 5:11–15; 2 Tim 3:6–7; Titus 1:11).

23 See Wieland 2006, 69–84.

signaled often by dress and hairstyle—which some philosophers, and apparently Jews and Christians, thought broke down society's basic element, the family.[24] On the other hand, some religious opinions taught that women were simply unsavable: some pagan associations banned women entirely, and Gnostics in the second century believed women could only be saved by becoming male and casting off femininity.[25] This passage vitiates against both; it encourages women's religious learning, valuing the feminine as distinct from male, yet condemns trends that flouted the family. Second, the Pauline churches esteemed women as patrons and hosts of liturgical gatherings (Rom 16:1–5; Col 4:15); they offered prayer in the Corinthian assembly (1 Cor 11:5, 13) and, like male laity, could teach in some cases (Col 3:16; Titus 2:3).[26] The present passage does not appear to vitiate against these practices or command that women as women do nothing but learn.[27]

The text may be operating with the concentric circles of representation mentioned above. Christ is imitated by women and men in their love and self-giving for others (at home and elsewhere). Within the male-female dynamic, women imitate Christ as he submits to the Father (1 Cor 11:3), and wives imitate the church in receiving his love and working productively for mission and under his authority (see Eph 5:22–33). Men represent Christ in their own spheres and, within marriage, imitate him by sacrificially loving their wives. Within the liturgical body, all of these representations occur in the various vocations of men and women. But among them stands the presbyter or bishop as one who represents Christ for the others' sake, the servant of God's servants, standing in for Christ directly in teaching authority, in

---

24 See B. Winter 2003, 17–74.

25 Compare the Gnostic *Gospel of Thomas* 114: "Peter" says women are unworthy of eternal life, and Jesus responds that he will "make her male" so that she may receive salvation.

26 See MacDonald 2011. For women's hosting duties, see Osiek and MacDonald 2006, 144–63. Phoebe is also called a "deacon" in Rom 16:1 (cf. 1 Tim 3:11), though this office of "service" is underdefined in the NT period. As the office of deacon developed and the church sought to maintain this passage's teaching and the tradition of male priesthood, the feminine term "deaconess" came to be used of female deacons, whose role was acknowledged but designated as lay (see Council of Nicaea I, canon 19). A similar ambiguity surrounds Rom 16:7, where Paul may be calling Junia an "apostle" (or perhaps one esteemed *by* the apostles), since Paul sometimes uses "apostle" for those who saw the risen Christ and evangelized (1 Cor 15:5–8; 2 Cor 8:23) but did not necessarily hold the authoritative office that he and the Twelve did.

27 One's view of authorship plays a role here. Viewing 1 Timothy as authentic, some read these instructions as particular to Ephesus in light of temporary, local problems (see Westfall 2016, 300–311). Judging it pseudonymous, others see this as a later author's attempt to rei' egalitarianism in Paul's name for the universal church (see Verner 1983).

exemplary holiness, and in sacramental service as the steward of Christ's "mysteries" (1 Cor 4:1). And this image of Christ to whom other Christians (male and female) submit is male, representing the bridegroom for the sake of the bride.[28] Yet the sexes bear equal dignity in nature and grace and are complementary: Eve came from Adam, but new humans are born through women (1 Cor 11:7–12); Eve was tempted first, but it is only by a woman that the world received its savior (1 Tim 2:15). The two are complementary and equally necessary, and, in the Pauline letters, each is to represent Christ and the church by embodying the love of God within their created and ecclesial interrelations.

FURTHER READING

Fiore, Benjamin, SJ. 1986. *The Function of Personal Example in the Socratic and Pastoral Epistles.* AnBib 105. Rome: Biblical Institute Press.

_____. 2007. *The Pastoral Epistles: First Timothy, Second Timothy, Titus.* SP 12. Collegeville, MN: Liturgical Press.

Hoklotubbe, T. Christopher. 2017. *Civilized Piety: The Rhetoric of Pietas in the Pastoral Epistles and the Roman Empire.* Waco, TX: Baylor University Press.

Horrell, David G. 2001. "From ἀδελφοί to οἶκος θεοῦ: Social Transformation in Pauline Christianity." *JBL* 120 (2): 293–311.

Johnson, Luke Timothy. 2001. *The First and Second Letters to Timothy: A New Translation with Introduction and Commentary.* AB 35A. New York: Doubleday.

MacDonald, Margaret Y. 2011. "Women in the Pauline Churches." In *The Blackwell Companion to Paul,* edited by Stephen Westerholm, 268–84. Chichester: Wiley-Blackwell.

Marshall, I. Howard. 1999. *A Critical and Exegetical Commentary on the Pastoral Epistles.* With Philip H. Towner. ICC. London: T&T Clark.

Quinn, Jerome D. 1990. *The Letter to Titus: A New Translation with Notes and Commentary.* AB 35. New York: Doubleday.

28 See John Paul II, Apostolic Letter *Mulieris Dignitatem* (August 15, 1988), esp. §10, 25–27.

Quinn, Jerome D., and William C. Wacker. 2000. *The First and Second Letters to Timothy: A New Translation with Notes and Commentary.* ECC. Grand Rapids: Eerdmans.

Towner, Philip H. 2006. *The Letters to Timothy and Titus.* NICNT. Grand Rapids: Eerdmans.

Van Zyl, Hermie C. 1998. "The Evolution of Church Leadership in the New Testament—A New Consensus?" *Neot* 32 (2): 585–604.

Westfall, Cynthia Long. 2016. *Paul and Gender: Reclaiming the Apostle's Vision for Men and Women in Christ.* Grand Rapids: Baker Academic.

Winter, Bruce W. 2003. *Roman Wives, Roman Widows: The Appearance of New Women and the Pauline Communities.* Grand Rapids: Eerdmans.

Young, Frances Margaret. 1994. *The Theology of the Pastoral Letters.* Cambridge: Cambridge University Press.

CHAPTER FIFTEEN

Philemon

Philemon is Paul's shortest extant letter. Philemon's slave, Onesimus, has gone missing, met Paul, and converted to Christianity. Paul, currently in prison, sends Onesimus back with a letter asking Philemon to be forgiving and receive him well, expressing a desire that Onesimus might be released to aid Paul. The letter, naturally, is significant in Christian discussions of slavery. But we also must not miss the theological rationale that motivates Paul's appeal: Onesimus is now a Christian and is, therefore, Philemon's brother. This letter applies Paul's view of the church as family to a real-life situation of slaves and masters.

BACKGROUND

The letter's background is highly important to its interpretation, but Paul assumed that the original audience already knew the details. This leaves us, as modern readers, to do some guessing based on what Paul does say. We may focus on the two main characters: Philemon and Onesimus, with a glance at the institution of slavery in the Roman Empire of Paul's day.

Philemon and His Congregation

Paul esteems Philemon with the title "coworker," and it appears that he hosts a congregation in his home (vv. 1, 2), one served also by Apphia "the sister" and Archippus (v. 2; cf. Col 4:17). To host a church, Philemon is likely at least middle-class, using his resources to aid the ministry of the gospel (vv. 4–7). As we saw in chapter 12, Philemon's congregation appears to have been relatively near to Colossae. But, different from most Colossians, Philemon has apparently met Paul and was converted through Paul (perhaps visiting Ephesus?), since Paul emphasizes that Philemon "owes" him his very life in Christ (v. 19).

Onesimus the Slave and Roman Slavery

Onesimus was a slave in Philemon's household (v. 16).[1] He was, legally, Philemon's property. Slavery in ancient Rome differed from slavery in the nineteenth-century American South, and not only because it was not based on race or skin color.[2] Slaves in Paul's world often lived in the same house as their masters and were only more rarely housed in separate, poorer quarters. Slaves did not legally own money or property, but the head of a household (the *paterfamilias*) could allot them money or property. Slaves could use and amass money or property from their master to eventually purchase their freedom. Likewise, educated and skilled slaves were prized—not feared—and could be employed as tutors, scribes, money managers, or authoritative ambassadors, and some slaves were even philosophers. Some ancient examples show loyal slaves being held as close confidants and advisors to their masters. In fact, one could gain a good deal of status and upward social mobility by being a beloved slave of a good master, especially if the master was successful or powerful in the community.[3] Masters who wanted to be seen as generous and upright by others were more likely to free ("manumit") loyal slaves after a term of service and were discouraged by philosophers from being overly harsh (see Seneca, *Epistle* 47). Manumitted slaves ("freedpersons") were usually then obliged to be loyal supporters or employees of their former master, still part of his household, and it could benefit masters to treat loyal slaves well so that they would later become faithful supporters in business and public life. For the slave or freedperson, the more honor or success your *paterfamilias* had, the more you stood to gain from his success. Some slaves attained a relatively high level of social standing and even boasted about it on their tombstones. There are even examples of free women marrying slaves because they were marrying "up."[4]

---

1 This is based on Onesimus being received by Philemon "no longer as a slave but more than a slave, a beloved brother, certainly to me, but how much more to you a brother in the flesh and also in the Lord" (v. 16). Differently, Callahan (1993) proposes that Philemon and Onesimus are simply brothers, and Paul is asking Philemon to reconcile and stop treating his brother *like* a slave.

2 It is also worth recalling here that race and skin color in antiquity have a complex relationship. See, e.g., Junior 2019.

3 See D. Martin 1990, 1–49.

4 Meeks 1983, 23.

So Roman slavery as an institution offered more possible benefits than American antebellum slavery. However, it was still slavery. Slaves, like Onesimus, were still legally property. This means that *all the benefits mentioned above were at the discretion of the master.* A master might simply choose to be cruel. A master might reward loyal slaves with good treatment, but only consider a slave "loyal" who gave his or her body to the master's sexual desires. A master might never free a slave. Some masters freed a slave but kept the children the slave begat or birthed, since the child born to a slave was also considered the master's property. Likewise, some generous masters were simply not very wealthy and so could promise little upward mobility. A slave's fate depended on the master, in terms of both the master's whim and the master's situation.

The Backstory: Onesimus's Departure

What went on between this master and slave that occasioned Paul's letter? The primary data are these:

(a) Onesimus, a slave in Philemon's household, has left Philemon, and Paul expects Philemon feels wronged by Onesimus (vv. 15, 18–19).

(b) Paul is in prison (vv. 1, 9–10, 13), probably in Rome (see chapter 12 of this volume). Onesimus has been with Paul there and converted to Christ (v. 10).

(c) Paul would like Onesimus to serve him in ministry, but sends him back and leaves this to Philemon's decision (vv. 12–14).

(d) Paul seems nervous that Philemon will not receive Onesimus kindly, since he says he is concerned about him and repeatedly asks Philemon to receive him well and not hold any previous wrong against him (vv. 12, 16, 17, 19–20).

Onesimus is with Paul, not Philemon, and Paul expects Philemon is unhappy about this. It also appears that Philemon did not know where Onesimus was or why. In his letter, Paul offers an explanation for Onesimus's absence and suggests that God's providence led him away to Paul so that he could be converted and become Philemon's brother in Christ (vv. 15–16). If Paul needs to do this kind of explaining to make Philemon see Onesimus's departure as a good thing, it probably means that Onesimus has gone "absent without leave." Further, one assumes that Paul would not have such concern for

Philemon to receive Onesimus well if he did not expect Philemon felt wronged by Onesimus; this matches up with verses 18–19a, where Paul exclaims that he will compensate for any "wrong" or "injury" Onesimus has done.[5]

These factors have led readers since the early church to assume that Onesimus is a *runaway* (Latin *fugitivus*; Greek δραπέτης, *drapetēs*). There are many reports about slaves, even some who were (at least according to the masters who wrote the reports) well treated, stealing from their master and running to get lost in larger cities or joining gangs of bandits. The penalties for this could be severe, and honor prescribed that masters who caught runaways punish such an affront. This makes sense overall with Onesimus's apparently unauthorized absence, his location in a big city—perhaps Ephesus or, as argued above in chapter 12, faraway Rome—with Paul, and with Paul's worry that Philemon will not be charitable to him when he returns.[6]

Why might Onesimus have run? Perhaps Philemon, for all his support of the church, was a cruel master. Perhaps Onesimus was a troublesome or lazy slave (Paul thinks Philemon thought so, v. 11). Perhaps Onesimus was in charge of Philemon's accounts, and Philemon blamed him for some failed business transaction that was not actually Onesimus's fault, and he ran in fear of punishment (Paul only says "*if* he has wronged you," v. 18). We do not know. We also do not know how he encountered Paul. According to Acts 28:30, Paul's Roman imprisonment was more like house arrest than being chained in a secluded cell, so there are several ways Onesimus might have chanced to meet him (through employment he got in the city, by meeting a Christian who brought him to the apostle, etc.).

Another possibility, advocated by several recent scholars, is that Onesimus *intended to seek Paul's intercession*. There are examples of slaves (or freedpersons) taking unauthorized leave to seek out their master's friend or superior to ask for help in a conflict with their master. Indeed, some Roman jurists did not consider such a person technically as a runaway but as a "truant" or "wanderer" (Latin *erro*; Greek ῥέμβος, *rhembos*), since the slave's intention was ultimately to return and be reconciled with the master.[7] Onesimus and Philemon were in some sort of conflict, and Onesimus—

---

5 Some argue that Onesimus was sent to Paul, e.g., S. Winter 1987. Philemon's lack of knowledge about Onesimus's whereabouts suggests that, if he was sent, it was not to Paul directly but to somewhere near Paul and that Onesimus stayed away too long after encountering Paul or, if he *was* sent to Paul, that he stayed longer than Philemon authorized.

6 See Nordling 1991.

7 The influential essay here is available only in German: Lampe 1985.

perhaps because he had heard Paul spoken of highly in Philemon's house-church?—sought Paul's help. On this reading, Onesimus might not have stolen anything from Philemon; Paul's mention of "wrong" done might just refer to the work Onesimus "owed" Philemon while he was away with Paul.

Was Onesimus a stereotypical runaway? Did he only run to seek mediation? Perhaps he originally meant to run away, then encountered Paul somehow, and after his conversion Paul asked him to return and offered mediation. Perhaps he was away at Philemon's order, near to Paul, but stayed without leave to be evangelized or to seek Paul's support because he feared a falling-out with his master. From our perspective as modern readers, certainty is difficult. And we must, moreover, remember that Philemon and Onesimus may have seen the issue from different perspectives even as these events were unfolding. For instance, if *Onesimus* thought he was only seeking mediation, *Philemon* would probably not have seen it this way when he realized his slave had been missing for a few days.[8] Even the Roman jurists who distinguished "runaways" from "truants" acknowledged that most people (presumably including Philemon) thought any slave who was absent one night longer than authorized was punishable as a runaway.[9] The travel alone would have taken longer than that: Onesimus's conversion likely took more than just an hour's conversation, and it would have taken longer for Paul to compose this letter with a scribe.[10] Whatever Onesimus intended, it is likely that Philemon had been thinking of Onesimus as a runaway ever since he turned up missing—and that he was preparing to treat him accordingly if he met him again. His honor demanded it. Roman law provided for it. But, as we see in Paul's letter, the gospel demanded something different.

OVERVIEW

I. **Letter Opening (Phlm 1–7)**
   A. Paul and Timothy to Philemon and the whole congregation (1–3).
   B. I thank God, Philemon, because you show kindness to all fellow Christians (4–7).

---

8 A recent reconstruction of the situation from Onesimus's perspective is given in Beavis 2021.

9 See Harrill 1999, 137.

10 If Paul was imprisoned in Ephesus and not Rome (see chapter 12), the time required for the journey and for Onesimus's time with Paul would still not have been brief.

II. **Paul's Appeal for Onesimus (Phlm 8–22)**

   A. Onesimus is with me and is now a Christian; I am concerned for him (8–10).

      1. I would like him to assist my ministry here in prison, but I am sending him back to put everything at your discretion (11–14).

      2. Perhaps he was separated from you so that when he returned you would get him back not as a slave but as a brother (15–16).

   B. For my sake, receive him back as you would me (17).

      1. If he owes you anything, I'll repay it (18–19a)!

      2. Don't forget what you owe *me*, brother Philemon—your very life (19b–20).

      3. I'm sure you'll do even more than I ask. In any case, ready a guest room for me, so that I can visit if I am released (21–22).

III. **Letter Closing (Phlm 23–25)**

   A. Those with me greet you (23–24).

   B. Grace be with you all (25).

KEY FEATURES

Paul's Persuasive Power

If Paul wants Philemon to be forgiving to his returned slave, he is fighting an uphill battle against legal custom and Philemon's indignation and honor. One impressive feature of this letter is how forceful and yet subtle Paul's persuasive technique is as he makes his appeal. Note these four features:

(a) *Philemon's Christian Track Record*. In verses 4–7, Paul begins by praising Philemon's love "for all the saints." Philemon has used his means to "refresh" (ἀναπαύω, *anapauō*) the "hearts" (σπλάγχνα, *splanchna*) of the saints. Paul prays Philemon's "partnership" (κοινωνία, *koinōnia*) in the faith might continue to mature in doing what is "good" (ἀγαθόν, *agathon*). Paul is not necessarily fibbing, but he is definitely buttering Philemon up: Philemon's track record gives Paul, he says, reason to be confident of Philemon's obedience (note the "therefore" in v. 8). For as he intercedes for Onesimus, who is now also a saint, he appeals to all these aspects of Philemon's Christian behavior. Paul does not force Philemon's hand, because he would rather allow him the opportunity to do "good" (ἀγαθόν, *agathon*) by sending Onesimus to aid Paul's ministry (v. 14). He appeals to Philemon's "partnership" in the faith: "if you regard me as a partner (κοινωνός, *koinōnos*), receive him as you would receive me" (v. 17). Paul calls Onesimus his very own "heart" (σπλάγχνα, *splanchna*, v. 12) and, in verse 20, calls Philemon to "refresh" (ἀναπαύω, *anapauō*) Paul's "heart" (σπλάγχνα, *splanchna*) by receiving Onesimus well. All that Paul has praised in Philemon now becomes persuasive pressure: Will you now, in this situation, be the magnanimous Christian I have just described?

(b) *Who Owes Whom? And Who Is in Charge Here?* Paul appeals to Philemon's Christian character, but he is also not above telling Philemon who is in charge. Paul reminds him frequently that he is an apostle—one in chains, for that matter—and that, as one who wields Christ's authority, he could just *command* him to forgive Onesimus (vv. 8–9). In fact, in verse 21, he lets slip that he wants Philemon to "obey" him. When he mentions the loss Onesimus may have caused Philemon, Paul not only offers to pay it himself; he also says that, whatever Onesimus may owe Philemon, Philemon owes *Paul* his own self (v. 19). These appeals essentially turn the tables and place Paul over Philemon in the chain of power. Philemon is the *paterfamilias* with legal power over this slave who owes him, but in God's household—the church—Philemon is the beggar who owes Paul his salvation and the servant who must obey the Lord. Philemon the master once judged Onesimus "useless," but Paul the apostle now demands that Philemon be of "use" to him (vv. 11, 20). Paul prefers to appeal to Philemon's love and Christian character, but he is not above stepping into the power game.

(c) *"I'll Drop by Sometime."* A curious note at the end is Paul's request that Philemon ready a guest room for him (v. 22). While this may sound like a simple travel announcement, if Philemon had up to this point harbored any hope that he could get away with dismissing Paul's exhortation, this request puts Philemon on notice that Paul may check up on things. Philemon has no clue when Paul might be released, nor presumably does Paul. But an indefinitely reserved guest room would be a constant reminder of his command to reconcile with Onesimus.

(d) *Peer Pressure.* Lastly, this letter, though mostly talking to Philemon directly, is not a "private" letter. The letter is addressed to Philemon *and Apphia and Archippus and the church that meets in Philemon's house* (v. 2). The grace-wishes at the beginning and end of the letter are to "you" plural— that is, to the whole assembly (vv. 3, 25; also "your" in v. 22). That means that all of Paul's appeals are not just being read privately by Philemon, who might decide to follow them or not, but are being read aloud to the whole congregation![11] This puts perhaps the greatest pressure on Philemon, because his standing as a Christian is at stake in the eyes of his whole church—slaves and freepersons alike—who now know what Paul has asked him to do and could keep Philemon accountable.[12] If Philemon felt that keeping his societal honor required punishing Onesimus, his honor among believers calls for the opposite.

"Neither Slave nor Free": The Church as Family

With all this persuasive pressure, what does Paul ask of Philemon? Paul clearly wants him to receive Onesimus well and not punish him for any offense (vv. 18–19), and he expresses confidence that Philemon will "do more than I say" (v. 21). Verses 13–14 invite Philemon to send Onesimus back to Paul to aid his ministry, though this appears somewhat indirect, and the threat of a visit later (v. 22) suggests that immediate release is not the letter's sole intent. By giving Philemon no explicit command, he gives him no

11 A few, surprisingly, insist that this is a private letter because Paul would not air Philemon's "private business" before the church. But what we see here is that the fate of a human life or the relation between two believers in Christ is not, to Paul, private business, but involves the whole body of Christ in behalf of its members.

12 The close relationship of the people in Colossians and Philemon adds another pressure because of their contact with each other (see chapter 12). If, as some have argued, Philemon's congregation is in Laodicea and Paul wants this letter to be read in Colossae as well (Col 4:16), then Paul craftily apprises another congregation and its leaders of the situation.

one thing that he can grudgingly do and then say he has fulfilled his duty. Instead, Paul seems to obligate Philemon indefinitely to a new, positive way of relating to and treating Onesimus.[13]

What is interesting theologically is the *reason* Paul has for asking such things of Philemon. What does Paul think is a good reason to intervene in this master's treatment of a slave he believes has done him wrong? Paul and other NT writers were certainly aware that slaves suffered injustices at the hands of their masters, but Paul does not base his argument here on the inhumanity of slavery. When Paul speaks to slaves directly elsewhere, although he encourages them to seek freedom where possible (1 Cor 7:21), he chooses to *dignify slaves as slaves* even if they are not freed.[14] While others considered slaves human "tools," Paul esteems them as active moral agents choosing—not simply being coerced—to serve God and others (Col 3:22–24; cf. 1 Pet 2:18–21). While some might have expected that God valued slaves' work as less important, Paul says that God will judge and reward slave and free equally (Eph 6:5–8). And he reminds masters that regardless of what secular law allows, God will judge them for cruelty to those under their charge (Eph 6:9; Col 4:1). In God's judgment, the distinction between "slave and free" dissolves when both are sinners receiving equal mercy at the foot of the cross (Gal 3:28; Col 3:11).

So why does Paul ask Philemon to receive Onesimus well? Simply this: *Onesimus is now a Christian.* Paul has given "birth" to Onesimus (Phlm 10), an image that indicates Onesimus's conversion (see 1 Cor 4:15; Gal 4:19). This is where Paul stakes his case because, in his view of the world, it is here that Onesimus and Philemon share the most radical unity. The church is a family, and everyone "born" into this family is therefore "brother" or "sister" to every other Christian (e.g., Rom 14:10; 1 Cor 6:5–6; 7:15; cf. Mark 3:31–35; Jas 2:15). And this is not just churchy talk that ends when people leave the

---

13 See Prothro 2020.

14 Paul's encouragement for slaves to obtain freedom where possible is matched by the Christ-like self-giving of believers later in the first century who, in Christian charity, sold themselves into slavery "that they might ransom others" or to use the money they received to feed the poor (*1 Clement* 55.2). Jews and Christians had always opposed kidnapping people to enslave or sell them ("man-stealing," 1 Tim 1:10). With Paul, the church values the moral agency and dignity of enslaved humans and, speaking beyond Paul with its global political voice, denounces as a "crime" against that dignity "any systematic deprivation of individual freedom for the purposes of personal or commercial exploitation." Pope Francis, "Declaration on International Day for the Abolition of Slavery" (December 2, 2014). See *CCC* §2414; Vatican Council II, Dogmatic Constitution *Gaudium et Spes* (December 7, 1965), §27.

worship assembly. Note Philemon 15–16: "For perhaps this is the reason he was separated from you for a time: so that you might receive him back eternally, no longer as a slave but more than a slave, as a beloved brother . . . both in the flesh and in the Lord." The relationship that exists between them because of Christ is one that extends to daily life "in the flesh," and it obliges them to treat one another with peace, forgiveness, honor, and unpretentious "brotherly love" (Rom 12:9–12; Col 3:12–17).

Simply because Onesimus has converted, Paul can claim that Onesimus and Philemon are now *eternally* related to each other as brothers in Christ.[15] Are they currently related to each other economically, functionally, and legally as master-slave? Yes, but such structures are part of the present age that is passing away (1 Cor 7:31). God's household transcends the structures of the present world and makes its own demands of how Christians treat each other within and despite these structures. Some might have thought, in a worldly way, that cruelty to Onesimus is no more serious than misusing a tool. But in Christ, cruelty to this slave is actually closer to Cain murdering Abel, and it represents a stifling of divine grace (cf. Col 3:13; Matt 6:14–15; 18:23–35).

Paul changes Philemon's perspective from a world of the master's rights and privileges to a world of familial obligation—not "What am I allowed to do to this piece of human property?" but "How should I treat my brother or sister, who happens to be my slave?" Despite the laws, Onesimus cannot be treated as property. Even as a slave, he is a beloved and valued servant of God, and he is—and so must be treated as—nothing less than Philemon's brother.

15 The ecclesial character of Paul's intervention is a part of Onesimus's later legacy, as he has often been identified with an Onesimus who became a bishop in the late first century (mentioned in Ignatius, *Ephesians* 1.3; 2.1; 6.2).

FURTHER READING

Bartchy, S. Scott. 1992. "Slavery: New Testament." *ABD* 6:65–73.

Barth, Markus, and Helmut Blanke. 2000. *The Letter to Philemon: A New Translation with Notes and Commentary.* ECC. Grand Rapids: Eerdmans.

Beavis, Mary Anne. 2021. *The First Christian Slave: Onesimus in Context.* Eugene, OR: Cascade.

Brookins, Timothy A. 2015. "'I Rather Appeal to *Auctoritas*': Roman Conceptualizations of Power and Paul's Appeal to Philemon." *CBQ* 77 (2): 302–21.

Frilingos, Chris. 2000. "'For My Child, Onesimus': Paul and Domestic Power in Philemon." *JBL* 119 (1): 91–104.

Glancy, Jennifer A. 2006. *Slavery in Early Christianity.* Minneapolis: Fortress.

Harrill, J. Albert. 2006. *Slaves in the New Testament: Literary, Social, and Moral Dimensions.* Minneapolis: Fortress.

_____. 2016. "Paul and Slavery." In *Paul in the Greco-Roman World: A Handbook*, volume 2, edited by J. Paul Sampley, 301–45. 2nd edition. London: Bloomsbury T&T Clark.

Keener, Craig S. 2000. "Family and Household." *DNTB* 353–67.

Martin, Dale B. 1990. *Slavery as Salvation: The Metaphor of Slavery in Pauline Christianity.* New Haven, CT: Yale University Press.

McKnight, Scott. 2017. *The Letter to Philemon.* NICNT. Grand Rapids: Eerdmans.

Nordling, John G. 1991. "Onesimus Fugitivus: A Defense of the Runaway Slave Hypothesis in Philemon." *JSNT* 41:97–119.

Thompson, James W., and Bruce W. Longenecker. 2016. *Philippians and Philemon.* Paideia Commentaries on the New Testament. Grand Rapids: Baker Academic.

Paul's Faith and Hope for Today

Paul's letters are historically important and theologically inspiring. There are, as we have seen throughout, debates and questions about his exact meaning and thought, as well as about his biography. And some questions may, because of the limitations of the evidence and our methods of study, never be answered with the full certainty one might desire. But that does not mean they are not worth researching, pondering, or debating for the sake of either history or theology.

We see in Paul one who was prepared to consider "all things" loss in order to gain Christ, whose life was marked by constant conversion and seeking the Lord, "straining forward to what lies ahead" in the "upward calling of God in Christ Jesus" (Phil 3:8, 13–14). His own life and his teaching impress hope upon us, confident in the promises of God, all of which are "yes and amen" as God gives every spiritual good in Christ to the church (2 Cor 1:20). Coming to the conviction that the crucified Jesus was in truth the risen and vindicated Son of God, seated now at the right hand of the Father, Paul put all stock in Christ and the task given to him as an apostle for the salvation of others, ready to suffer for the sake of his promised reward (Rom 8:17; 1 Cor 9:26–27). If Christ is raised from the dead, neither our faith nor our labor nor our suffering is in vain (1 Cor 15:17–19, 58).

We see also one whose hope in the future was grounded in the past, in Jesus's death and resurrection and his own baptism into the Triune God. Fundamentally, the Father shows his love for the world in not sparing his Son Jesus—with even greater faithfulness than was exemplified by Abraham when Isaac was demanded of him (Rom 5:8; 8:32). The Son likewise gave himself for sinners not out of grudging obedience or obligation, but because "he loved me" (Gal 2:20). Paul lives by this knowledge, by his awareness of the gift and grace of God in Christ. "By the grace of God I am what I am"

(1 Cor 15:10). He knows the Lord's love personally in the forgiveness he received for his persecutions and in the gift and task laid upon him as an apostle. He is marked by this love in his soul and in his suffering body (Gal 6:17). And he urges all to know and cling to the one who makes meager and broken human beings sufficient for eternal perfection through his righteousness, allowing themselves to be broken pots of clay through which the light of God's love shines for the world (2 Cor 4:6–12). Moreover, Paul is moved knowing not merely that God *has* loved him, but that God continues to pour the grace of his love into believers' hearts through the Holy Spirit (Rom 5:5), transforming their minds and guiding their actions to conform them to God's will and his self-giving love (Rom 12:1–2; Phil 2:12–13).

We see in Paul a faith that orders life constantly around Christ and the "treasures of wisdom" hidden in him (Col 2:3). Faith reorients his perspective on earthly, legal realities to value God's rule over Rome's, though he will gladly use and affirm what is good in the broken world that yet remains under God's care. It brings him to see in a slave like Onesimus the image of Christ who took on the form of a slave (Phil 2:7) and to call his master to value Onesimus as a brother, an equal sharer in the Spirit of God. It brings Paul to a new perspective on honor in humility and on suffering when offered for the good of others (Phil 2:1–11; Col 1:24). It brings Paul to reframe the notion of freedom as freedom truly to love and serve God in one's neighbor, freedom in Christ from the structures and compulsions of a world that neither gives real forgiveness nor enables one to rise above one's sinful inclinations (Gal 5:13–26).

What we see in Paul's life and letters not only teaches but also sets precedents and trajectories for those who follow him. Grounded neither in a vision of utopian progress nor in a traditionalism that resisted development, Paul pursued the goal that he might take hold of the one who already had taken hold of him, to know him by whom he was always known (Phil 3:12; Gal 4:9). He knew his Lord, yet continually sought more deeply to know, understand, and live the truth. This is a faith and a life worth imitating for all who seek to know Christ through the words and example of the apostle: to speak as we believe (2 Cor 4:13), to seek always a deeper understanding of the mysteries revealed (Eph 3:14–19), and to "walk in a manner worthy of the God who calls you into his own kingdom and glory" (1 Thess 2:12).

Bibliography

Aasgaard, Reider. 2007. "Paul as Child: Children and Childhood in the Letters of the Apostle." *JBL* 126 (1): 129–59.

Adams, Dickinson W. 1983. *Jefferson's Extracts from the Gospels: The Philosophy of Jesus and the Life and Morals of Jesus.* Princeton: Princeton University Press.

Aletti, Jean-Noël, SJ. 2011. "Rhetoric in the Letters of Paul." In *The Blackwell Companion to Paul*, edited by Stephen Westerholm, 232–47. Chichester: Wiley-Blackwell.

_____. 2015. *Justification by Faith in the Letters of Saint Paul: Keys to Interpretation.* Translated by Peggy Manning Meyer. AnBib Studia 5. Rome: Gregorian and Biblical Press.

Anderson, Garwood P. 2016. *Paul's New Perspective: Charting a Soteriological Journey.* Downers Grove, IL: IVP Academic.

Anderson, Gary A. 2013. *Charity: The Place of the Poor in Biblical Tradition.* New Haven, CT: Yale University Press.

Arnold, Clinton E. 1996. *The Colossian Syncretism.* WUNT 2/77. Tübingen: Mohr Siebeck.

Ashton, John. 2000. *The Religion of the Apostle Paul.* New Haven, CT: Yale University Press.

Aune, David E., ed. 2006. *Rereading Paul Together: Protestant and Catholic Perspectives on Justification.* Grand Rapids: Baker Academic.

Balabanski, Vicky. 2015. "Where Is Philemon? The Case for a Logical Fallacy in the Correlation of the Data in Philemon and Colossians 1.1–2; 4.7–18." *JSNT* 38 (2): 131–50.

Barclay, John M. G. 1987. "Mirror-Reading a Polemical Letter: Galatians as a Test Case." *JSNT* 31: 73–93.

_____. 2020. *Paul and the Power of Grace.* Grand Rapids: Eerdmans.

Bartchy, S. Scott. 1992. "Slavery: New Testament." *ABD* 6:65–73.

Barth, Markus, and Helmut Blanke. 1994. *Colossians: A New Translation with Introduction and Commentary.* Translated by Astrid B. Beck. AB 34B. New York: Doubleday.

_____. 2000. *The Letter to Philemon: A New Translation with Notes and Commentary.* ECC. Grand Rapids: Eerdmans.

Baum, Armin D. 2017. "Content and Form: Authorship Attribution and Pseudonymity in Ancient Speeches, Letters, Lectures, and Translations—A Rejoinder to Bart Ehrman." *JBL* 136 (2): 381–403.

Beale, G. K. 2019. *Colossians and Philemon*. BECNT. Grand Rapids: Baker Academic.

Beavis, Mary Anne. 2021. *The First Christian Slave: Onesimus in Context*. Eugene, OR: Cascade.

Béchard, Dean P. 2002. *The Scripture Documents: An Anthology of Official Catholic Teachings*. Collegeville, MN: Liturgical Press.

Becker, Jürgen. 1993. *Paul: Apostle to the Gentiles*. Translated by O. C. Dean Jr. Louisville, KY: Westminster John Knox.

Beker, J. Christiaan. 1980. *Paul the Apostle: The Triumph of God in Life and Thought*. Edinburgh: T&T Clark.

_____. 1992. *Heirs of Paul: Paul's Legacy in the New Testament and the Church Today*. Edinburgh: T&T Clark.

Benedict XVI (Pope). 2007. *Spe Salvi*. Encyclical Letter. November 30.

_____. 2009. *Saint Paul: General Audiences July 2, 2008–February 4, 2009*. San Francisco: Ignatius.

Best, Ernest. 1997. *Essays on Ephesians*. London: T&T Clark.

Betz, Hans Dieter. 1985. *2 Corinthians 8 and 9: A Commentary on Two Administrative Letters of the Apostle Paul*. Hermeneia. Philadelphia: Fortress.

Bird, Michael F., and Joseph R. Dodson, eds. 2011. *Paul and the Second Century*. LNTS 412. London: T&T Clark.

Bird, Michael F., Craig A. Evans, Simon J. Gathercole, Charles E. Hill, and Chris Tilling. 2014. *How God Became Jesus: The Real Origins of Belief in Jesus's Divine Nature*. Grand Rapids: Zondervan.

Blue, Bradley B. 1993. "Food Offered to Idols and Jewish Food Laws." *DPL* 306–10.

Bormann, Lukas. 2012. *Der Brief des Paulus an die Kolosser*. THKNT 10/1. Leipzig: Evangelische Verlagsanstalt.

Bowens, Lisa M. 2017. *An Apostle in Battle: Paul and Spiritual Warfare in 2 Corinthians 12:1–10*. WUNT 2/433. Tübingen: Mohr Siebeck.

Brannon, M. Jeff. 2011. *The Heavenlies in Ephesians: A Lexical, Exegetical, and Conceptual Analysis*. LNTS 447. London: T&T Clark.

Brinks, C. L. 2009. "'Great Is Artemis of the Ephesians': Acts 19:23–41 in Light of Goddess Worship in Ephesus." *CBQ* 71 (4): 776–94.

Briones, David. 2011. "Paul's Intentional 'Thankless Thanks' in Philippians 4.10–20." *JSNT* 34 (1): 47–69.

Brookins, Timothy A. 2015. "'I Rather Appeal to *Auctoritas*': Roman Conceptualizations of Power and Paul's Appeal to Philemon." *CBQ* 77 (2): 302–21.

Burnett, D. Clint. 2020. "Imperial Divine Honors in Julio-Claudian Thessalonica and the Thessalonian Correspondence." *JBL* 139 (3): 567–89.

Byrne, Brendan, SJ. 1996. *Romans*. SP 6. Collegeville, MN: Liturgical Press.

———. 2021. *Paul and the Economy of Salvation: Reading from the Perspective of the Last Judgment*. Grand Rapids: Baker Academic.

Cadwallader, Alan H., and Michael Trainor. 2011. *Colossae in Space and Time: Linking to an Ancient City*. NTOA 94. Göttingen: Vandenhoeck & Ruprecht.

Callahan, Allen Dwight. 1993. "Paul's Epistle to Philemon: Toward an Alternative Argumentum." *HTR* 86 (4): 357–76.

Campbell, Douglas A. 2014. *Framing Paul: An Epistolary Biography*. Grand Rapids: Eerdmans.

Capes, David B. 2018. *The Divine Christ: Paul, the Lord Jesus, and the Scriptures of Israel*. Grand Rapids: Baker Academic.

Carlson, Stephen C. 2016. "On Paul's Second Visit to Corinth: Πάλιν, Parsing, and Presupposition in 2 Corinthians 2:1." *JBL* 135 (3): 597–615.

Chester, Stephen J. 2017. *Reading Paul with the Reformers: Reconciling Old and New Perspectives*. Grand Rapids: Eerdmans.

Chow, John K. 1992. *Patronage and Power: A Study of Social Networks in Corinth*. JSNTSup 75. Sheffield: Sheffield Academic.

Cohen, Shaye J. D. 1989. "Crossing the Boundary and Becoming a Jew." *HTR* 82 (1): 13–33.

———. 2014. *From the Maccabees to the Mishnah*. 3rd edition. Louisville, KY: Westminster John Knox Press.

Cohick, Lynn H. 2020. *The Letter to the Ephesians*. NICNT. Grand Rapids: Eerdmans.

Collins, John J., and Daniel C. Harlow, eds. 2012. *Early Judaism: A Comprehensive Overview*. Grand Rapids: Eerdmans.

Collins, Raymond F. 1988. *Letters That Paul Did Not Write: The Epistle to the Hebrews and the Pauline Pseudepigrapha*. Collegeville, MN: Michael Glazier.

———. 1999. *First Corinthians*. SP 7. Collegeville, MN: Liturgical Press.

———. 2013. *Second Corinthians*. Paideia Commentaries on the New Testament. Grand Rapids: Baker Academic.

Copenhaver, Adam. 2018. *Reconstructing the Historical Background of Paul's Rhetoric in the Letter to the Colossians*. LNTS 585. London: Bloomsbury.

Cover, Michael. 2015. *Lifting the Veil: 2 Corinthians 3:7–18 in Light of Jewish Homiletic and Commentary Traditions*. BZNW 210. Berlin: de Gruyter.

Covington, Eric. 2018. *Functional Teleology and the Coherence of Ephesians: A Comparative and Reception-Historical Approach*. WUNT 2/470. Tübingen: Mohr Siebeck.

Crossan, John Dominic, and Jonathan L. Reed. 2004. *In Search of Paul: How Jesus's Apostle Opposed Rome's Empire with God's Kingdom*. San Francisco: HarperCollins.

Crowe, Brandon D. 2020. *The Hope of Israel: The Resurrection of Christ in the Acts of the Apostles*. Grand Rapids: Baker Academic.

Davies, W. D. 1980. *Paul and Rabbinic Judaism: Some Rabbinic Elements in Pauline Theology*. 4th ed. Philadelphia: Fortress.

de Boer, Martinus C. 2011. *Galatians*. NTL. Louisville, KY: Westminster John Knox.

_____. 2020. *Paul, Theologian of God's Apocalypse: Essays on Paul and Apocalyptic*. Eugene, OR: Cascade.

Deibert, Richard I. 2017. *Second Corinthians and Paul's Gospel of Human Mortality: How Paul's Experience of Death Authorizes His Apostolic Authority in Corinth*. WUNT 2/430. Tübingen: Mohr Siebeck.

DeMaris, Richard E. 1994. *The Colossian Controversy: Wisdom in Dispute at Colossae*. JSNTSup 96. Sheffield: JSOT Press.

DeSilva, David A. 2000. "Ruler Cult." *DNTB* 1026–1030.

_____. 2018. *The Letter to the Galatians*. NICNT. Grand Rapids: Eerdmans.

Dodson, Joseph R., and David E. Briones, eds. 2019. *Paul and the Giants of Philosophy: Reading the Apostle in Greco-Roman Context*. Downers Grove, IL: InterVarsity.

Donaldson, Terence L. 1997. *Paul and the Gentiles: Remapping the Apostle's Convictional World*. Minneapolis: Fortress.

_____. 2006. "Jewish Christianity, Israel's Stumbling and the *Sonderweg* Reading of Paul." *JSNT* 29 (1): 27–54.

_____. 2007. *Judaism and the Gentiles: Jewish Patterns of Universalism (to 135 CE)*. Waco, TX: Baylor University Press.

Donfried, Karl P., ed. 1991. *The Romans Debate*. Expanded edition. Peabody, MA: Hendrickson.

_____. 2002. *Paul, Thessalonica, and Early Christianity*. London: T&T Clark.

Downs, David J. 2016. *The Offering of the Gentiles: Paul's Collection for Jerusalem in Its Chronological, Cultural, and Cultic Contexts*. Grand Rapids: Eerdmans.

Downs, David J., and Benjamin J. Lappenga. 2019. *The Faithfulness of the Risen Christ: Pistis and the Exalted Lord in the Pauline Letters*. Waco, TX: Baylor University Press.

Dunn, James D. G. 1988. *Romans*. WBC 38. Nashville: Thomas Nelson.

_____. 1996. *The Epistles to the Colossians and to Philemon: A Commentary on the Greek Text*. NIGTC. Grand Rapids: Eerdmans.

_____. 1998. *The Theology of Paul the Apostle*. Grand Rapids: Eerdmans.

_____. 2005. *The New Perspective on Paul: Collected Essays*. Revised edition. Grand Rapids: Eerdmans.

Eastman, Susan Grove. 2017. *Paul and the Person: Reframing Paul's Anthropology*. Grand Rapids: Eerdmans.

Ehrman, Bart D. 2013. *Forgery and Counterforgery: The Use of Literary Deceit in Early Christian Polemics*. New York: Oxford University Press.

_____. 2014. *How Jesus Became God: The Exaltation of a Jewish Preacher from Galilee*. San Francisco: HarperOne.

Elliott, Neil, and Mark Reasoner. 2011. *Documents and Images for the Study of Paul*. Minneapolis: Fortress.

Engberg-Pedersen, Troels. 2000. *Paul and the Stoics*. Edinburgh: T&T Clark.

_____. 2010. *Cosmology and Self in the Apostle Paul: The Material Spirit*. Oxford: Oxford University Press.

Eubank, Nathan. 2015. "Justice Endures Forever: Paul's Grammar of Generosity." *JSPL* 5 (2): 169–87.

Fee, Gordon D. 1995. *Paul's Letter to the Philippians*. NICNT. Grand Rapids: Eerdmans.

_____. 1996. *Paul, the Spirit, and the People of God*. Peabody, MA: Hendrickson.

_____. 2009. *The First and Second Letters to the Thessalonians*. NICNT. Grand Rapids: Eerdmans.

Ferguson, Everett. 2003. *Backgrounds of Early Christianity*. 3rd edition. Grand Rapids: Eerdmans.

Finlan, Stephen. 2004. *The Background and Content of Paul's Cultic Atonement Metaphors*. AcBib 19. Atlanta: SBL Press.

Fiore, Benjamin, SJ. 1986. *The Function of Personal Example in the Socratic and Pastoral Epistles*. AnBib 105. Rome: Biblical Institute Press.

_____. 2007. *The Pastoral Epistles: First Timothy, Second Timothy, Titus*. SP 12. Collegeville, MN: Liturgical Press.

Fitzmyer, Joseph A., SJ. 1993. *Romans: A New Translation with Introduction and Commentary*. AB 33. New York: Doubleday.

_____. 1998. *The Acts of the Apostles: A New Translation with Introduction and Commentary*. AB 31. New York: Doubleday.

_____. 2000. *First Corinthians: A New Translation with Introduction and Commentary*. AB 32. New Haven, CT: Yale University Press.

Focant, Camille. 2016. "La portée de la formule τὸ εἶναι ἴσα θεῷ en Ph 2.6." *NTS* 62 (2): 278–88.

Foster, Paul. 2016. *Colossians*. BNTC. London: Bloomsbury T&T Clark.

Francis (Pope). 2013. *Lumen Fidei*. Encyclical Letter. June 29.

_____. 2014. "Declaration on International Day for the Abolition of Slavery." December 2.

Francis, F. O., and Wayne A. Meeks, eds. 1973. *Conflict at Colossae: Illustrated by Selected Modern Studies*. SBLSBS 4. Missoula, MT: SBL Press.

Fredriksen, Paula. 2017. *Paul, the Pagans' Apostle*. New Haven, CT: Yale University Press.

Frilingos, Chris. 2000. "'For My Child, Onesimus': Paul and Domestic Power in Philemon." *JBL* 119 (1): 91–104.

Furnish, Victor Paul. 1984. *II Corinthians: A New Translation with Introduction and Commentary.* AB 32A. New York: Doubleday.

Gadenz, Pablo T. 2009. *Called from the Jews and from the Gentiles: Pauline Ecclesiology in Romans 9–11.* WUNT 2/267. Tübingen: Mohr Siebeck.

Garland, David E. 1985. "The Composition and Unity of Philippians: Some Neglected Literary Factors." *NovT* 27 (2): 141–73.

_____. 2003. *1 Corinthians.* BECNT. Grand Rapids: Baker Academic.

Gathercole, Simon J. 2011. "Paul's Christology." In *The Blackwell Companion to Paul*, edited by Stephen Westerholm, 172–87. Chichester: Wiley-Blackwell.

Gaventa, Beverly Roberts. 2016. *When in Romans: An Invitation to Linger with the Gospel according to Paul.* Grand Rapids: Baker Academic.

Glancy, Jennifer A. 2006. *Slavery in Early Christianity.* Minneapolis: Fortress.

Glinert, Lewis. 2017. *The Story of Hebrew.* Library of Jewish Ideas. Princeton, NJ: Princeton University Press.

Gombis, Timothy G. 2010. *The Drama of Ephesians: Participating in the Triumph of God.* Downers Grove, IL: IVP Academic.

Goodrich, John K. 2016. "Until the Fullness of the Gentiles Comes In: A Critical Review of Recent Scholarship on the Salvation of 'All Israel' (Romans 11:26)." *JSPL* 6 (1): 5–32.

Gorman, Michael J. 2001. *Cruciformity: Paul's Narrative Spirituality of the Cross.* Grand Rapids: Eerdmans.

_____. 2009. *Inhabiting the Cruciform God: Kenosis, Justification, and Theosis in Paul's Narrative Soteriology.* Grand Rapids: Eerdmans.

_____. 2015. *Becoming the Gospel: Paul, Participation, and Mission.* Grand Rapids: Eerdmans.

Gray, Patrick. 2016. *Paul as a Problem in History and Culture: The Apostle and His Critics through the Centuries.* Grand Rapids: Baker Academic.

Grindheim, Sigurd. 2003. "What the OT Prophets Did Not Know: The Mystery of the Church in Eph 3,2–13." *Bib* 84 (4): 531–53.

Guthrie, George H. 2015. *2 Corinthians.* BECNT. Grand Rapids: Baker Academic.

Haacker, Klaus. 1992. "Gallio." *ABD* 2 :901–3.

Hafemann, Scott J. 1990. *Suffering and Ministry in the Spirit: Paul's Defense of His Ministry in II Corinthians 2:14–3:3.* Grand Rapids: Eerdmans.

_____. 2015. "Paul and His Interpreters since F. C. Baur." In *Paul's Message and Ministry in Covenant Perspective: Selected Essays*, 3–28. Eugene, OR: Cascade.

Hahn, Ferdinand. 1993. "Gibt es eine Entwicklung in den Aussagen über der Rechtfertigungslehre bei Paulus?" *Evangelische Theologie* 53 (4): 342–66.

Hansen, G. Walter. 1989. *Abraham in Galatians: Epistolary and Rhetorical Contexts.* JSNTSup 29. Sheffield: JSOT Press.

Harrill, J. Albert. 1999. "Using the Roman Jurists to Interpret Philemon: A Response to Peter Lampe." *ZNW* 90 (1): 135–38.

_____. 2006. *Slaves in the New Testament: Literary, Social, and Moral Dimensions.* Minneapolis: Fortress.

_____. 2016. "Paul and Slavery." In *Paul in the Greco Roman World: A Handbook,* volume 2, edited by J. Paul Sampley, 301–45. 2nd edition. London: Bloomsbury T&T Clark.

Hartman, Lars. 1997. *"Into the Name of the Lord Jesus": Baptism in the Early Church.* SNTW. Edinburgh: T&T Clark.

Hawthorne, Gerald F. 2004. *Philippians.* Revised edition by Ralph P. Martin. WBC 43. Nashville: Thomas Nelson.

Hays, Richard B. 1989. *Echoes of Scripture in the Letters of Paul.* New Haven, CT: Yale University Press.

_____. 2002. *The Faith of Jesus Christ: The Narrative Substructure of Galatians 3:1–4:11.* 2nd edition. Grand Rapids: Eerdmans.

Heil, John Paul. 2007. *Ephesians: Empowerment to Walk in Love for the Unity of All in Christ.* SBL Studies in Biblical Literature 13. Atlanta: SBL Press.

Hellerman, Joseph H. 2005. *Reconstructing Honor in Roman Philippi: Carmen Christi as Cursus Pudorum.* SNTSMS 132. Cambridge: Cambridge University Press.

Hengel, Martin. 1991. *The Pre-Christian Paul.* With Roland Deines. Translated by John Bowden. Philadelphia: Trinity Press International.

Hoklotubbe, T. Christopher. 2017. *Civilized Piety: The Rhetoric of Pietas in the Pastoral Epistles and the Roman Empire.* Waco, TX: Baylor University Press.

Holladay, Carl R. 2016. *Acts: A Commentary.* NTL. Louisville, KY: Westminster John Knox.

Holloway, Paul A. 2017. *Philippians.* Hermeneia. Minneapolis: Fortress.

Hoover, Roy W. 1971. "The HARPAGMOS Enigma: A Philological Solution." *HTR* 64 (1): 95–119.

Horrell, David G. 2001. "From ἀδελφοί to οἶκος θεοῦ: Social Transformation in Pauline Christianity." *JBL* 120 (2): 293–311.

Hughes, Frank W. 2010. "Pseudonymy as Rhetoric: A Prolegomenon to the Study of Pauline Pseudepigrapha." In *Rhetorics in the New Millennium: Promise and Fulfillment,* edited by James D. Hester and J. David Hester, 216–34. Studies in Antiquity and Christianity. London: T&T Clark.

Hurtado, Larry W. 2003. *Lord Jesus Christ: Devotion to Jesus in Earliest Christianity.* Grand Rapids: Eerdmans.

Immendörfer, Michael. 2017. *Ephesians and Artemis: The Cult of the Great Goddess of Ephesus as the Epistle's Context.* WUNT 2/436. Tübingen: Mohr Siebeck.

Inwood, Brad, and L. P. Gerson. 1997. *Hellenistic Philosophy: Introductory Readings.* 2nd edition. Indianapolis: Hackett.

Jennings, Mark A. 2018. *The Price of Partnership in the Letter of Paul to the Philippians: "Make My Joy Complete."* LNTS 578. London: Bloomsbury.

Jewett, Robert. 2007. *Romans.* Hermeneia. Minneapolis: Fortress.

John Paul II (Pope). 1988. *Mulieris Dignitatem.* Apostolic Letter. August 15.

Johnson, Andy. 2014. "Paul's 'Anti-Christology' in 2 Thessalonians 2:3–12 in Canonical Context." *Journal of Theological Interpretation* 8 (1): 125–43.

Johnson, Luke Timothy. 1992. *Acts.* SP 5. Collegeville, MN: Liturgical Press.

_____. 2001. *The First and Second Letters to Timothy: A New Translation with Introduction and Commentary.* AB 35A. New York: Doubleday.

_____. 2013. "The Body in Question: The Social Complexities of Resurrection in 1 Corinthians." In *Contested Issues in Christian Origins and the New Testament: Collected Essays,* 295–315. NovTSup 146. Leiden: Brill.

_____. 2020. *Constructing Paul: The Canonical Paul.* Vol. 1. Grand Rapids: Eerdmans.

Junior, Nyasha. 2019. *Reimagining Hagar: Blackness and Bible.* Biblical Refigurations. Oxford: Oxford University Press.

Kaminsky, Joel and Mark Reasoner. 2019. "The Meaning and Telos of Israel's Election: An Interfaith Response to N. T. Wright's Reading of Paul." *HTR* 112 (4): 421–46.

Käsemann, Ernst. 1971. "Justification and Salvation History in the Epistle to the Romans." In *Perspectives on Paul,* 60–78. Translated by Margaret Kohl. Philadelphia: Fortress.

Keener, Craig S. 2000. "Family and Household." *DNTB* 353–67.

_____. 2012–15. *Acts: An Exegetical Commentary.* 4 vols. Grand Rapids: Baker Academic.

_____. 2019a. *Christobiography: Memory, History, and the Reliability of the Gospels.* Grand Rapids: Eerdmans.

_____. 2019b. *Galatians: A Commentary.* Grand Rapids: Baker Academic.

Kennedy, George A. 1984. *New Testament Interpretation through Rhetorical Criticism.* Chapel Hill: University of North Carolina Press.

Kim, Seyoon. 1982. *The Origin of Paul's Gospel.* Grand Rapids: Eerdmans, 1982.

Klauck, Hans-Josef. 2006. *Ancient Letters and the New Testament: A Guide to Context and Exegesis.* Translated and edited by Daniel P. Bailey. Waco, TX: Baylor University Press.

Kurz, William. 1993. *Reading Luke-Acts: Dynamics of Biblical Narrative.* Louisville, KY: Westminster John Knox.

Lakey, Michael J. 2019. *The Ritual World of Paul the Apostle: Metaphysics, Community and Symbol in 1 Corinthians 10–11.* LNTS 602. London: Bloomsbury.

Lambrecht, Jan, SJ. 1998. "Paul's Boasting about the Corinthians: A Study of 2 Cor. 8:24– 9:5." *NovT* 40 (4): 352–68.

_____. 1999. *Second Corinthians.* SP 8. Collegeville, MN: Liturgical Press.

Lampe, Peter. 1985. "Keine 'Sklavenflucht' des Onesimus." *ZNW* 76 (1): 135–37.

Lanuwabang, Jamir. 2016. *Exclusion and Judgment in Fellowship Meals: The Socio-historical Background of 1 Corinthians 11:17–34.* Eugene, OR: Pickwick.

Lentz, John Clayton, Jr. 1993. *Luke's Portrait of Paul.* SNTSMS 77. Cambridge: Cambridge University Press.

Levering, Matthew. 2014. *Paul in the Summa Theologiae.* Washington, DC: The Catholic University of America Press.

Levinskaya, Irina. 1996. *The Book of Acts in Its Diaspora Setting.* Vol. 5 of *The Book of Acts in its First Century Setting.* Grand Rapids: Eerdmans.

Lincoln, Andrew T. 1990. *Ephesians.* WBC 42. Dallas: Word Books.

Lincoln, Andrew T. and A. J. M. Wedderburn. 1993. *The Theology of the Later Pauline Letters.* Cambridge: Cambridge University Press.

Longenecker, Richard N. 2011. *Introducing Romans: Critical Issues in Paul's Most Famous Letter.* Grand Rapids: Eerdmans.

Luckensmeyer, David. 2009. *The Eschatology of First Thessalonians.* NTOA 71. Göttingen: Vandenhoeck & Ruprecht.

Lull, David J. 1986. "'The Law Was Our Pedagogue': A Study in Galatians 3:19–25." *JBL* 105 (3): 481–98.

MacDonald, Margaret Y. 2000. *Colossians and Ephesians.* SP 17. Collegeville, MN: Liturgical Press.

———. 2004. "The Politics of Identity in Ephesians." *JSNT* 26 (1): 94–113.

———. 2011. "Women in the Pauline Churches." In *The Blackwell Companion to Paul*, edited by Stephen Westerholm, 268–84. Chichester: Wiley-Blackwell.

Malherbe, Abraham J. 2000. *The Letters to the Thessalonians: A New Translation with Introduction and Commentary.* AB 32B. New York: Doubleday.

Marguerat, Daniel. 2013. *Paul in Acts and Paul in his Letters.* WUNT 310. Tübingen: Mohr Siebeck.

Marshall, I. Howard. 1999. *A Critical and Exegetical Commentary on the Pastoral Epistles.* With Philip H. Towner. ICC. London: T&T Clark.

Martin, Dale B. 1990. *Slavery as Salvation: The Metaphor of Slavery in Pauline Christianity.* New Haven, CT: Yale University Press.

———. 1995. *The Corinthian Body.* New Haven, CT: Yale University Press.

Martin, Michael Wade. 2015. "Philippians 2:6–11 as Subversive *Hymnos*: A Study in the Light of Ancient Rhetorical Theory." *JTS* n.s. 66 (1): 90–138.

Martin, Ralph P. 1997. *A Hymn of Christ: Philippians 2:5–11 in Recent Interpretation and in the Setting of Early Christian Worship.* Downers Grove, IL: InterVarsity.

Martyn, J. Louis. 1997. *Theological Issues in the Letters of Paul.* Nashville: Abingdon.

Matera, Frank J. 1992. *Galatians.* SP 9. Collegeville, MN: Liturgical Press.

_____. 2003. *II Corinthians: A Commentary.* NTL. Louisville, KY: Westminster John Knox.

_____. 2010. *Romans.* Paideia Commentaries on the New Testament. Grand Rapids: Baker Academic.

_____. 2012. *God's Saving Grace: A Pauline Theology.* Grand Rapids: Eerdmans.

May, Alistair Scott. 2004. *"The Body for the Lord": Sex and Identity in 1 Corinthians 5–7.* JSNTSup 278. London: T&T Clark.

McGrath, Alister E. 2020. *Iustitia Dei: A History of the Christian Doctrine of Justification.* 4th edition. Cambridge: Cambridge University Press.

McKnight, Scott. 2017. *The Letter to Philemon.* NICNT. Grand Rapids: Eerdmans.

McKnight, Scott, and B. J. Oropeza, eds. 2020. *Perspectives on Paul: Five Views.* Grand Rapids: Baker Academic.

McNeel, Jennifer Houston. 2014. *Paul as Infant and Nursing Mother: Metaphor, Rhetoric, and Identity in 1 Thessalonians 2:5–8.* ECL 12. Atlanta: SBL Press.

Meek, James A. 2008. *The Gentile Mission in Old Testament Citations in Acts: Text, Hermeneutic, and Purpose.* LNTS 385. London: T&T Clark.

Meeks, Wayne A. 1983. *First Urban Christians: The Social World of the Apostle Paul.* New Haven, CT: Yale University Press.

Mihaila, Corin. 2009. *The Paul–Apollos Relationship and Paul's Stance toward Greco-Roman Rhetoric: An Exegetical and Socio-historical Study of 1 Corinthians 1–4.* LNTS 402. London: T&T Clark.

Mitchell, Margaret M. 1991. *The Rhetoric of Reconciliation: An Exegetical Investigation of the Language and Composition of 1 Corinthians.* Louisville, KY: Westminster John Knox.

_____. 2002. *The Heavenly Trumpet: John Chrysostom and the Art of Pauline Interpretation.* Louisville, KY: Westminster John Knox.

Mitton, C. Leslie. 1951. *The Epistle to the Ephesians: Its Authorship, Origin, and Purpose.* Oxford: Clarendon.

Moessner, David Paul. 2016. *Luke the Historian of Israel's Legacy, Theologian of Israel's "Christ": A New Reading of the "Gospel Acts" of Luke.* BZNW 182. Berlin: de Gruyter.

Moo, Douglas J. 2013. *Galatians.* BECNT. Grand Rapids: Baker Academic.

Moses, Robert Ewusie. 2014. *Practices of Power: Revisiting the Principalities and Powers in the Pauline Letters.* Minneapolis: Fortress.

Mullin, Robert Bruce. 2014. *A Short World History of Christianity.* Revised edition. Louisville, KY: Westminster John Knox.

Murphy-O'Connor, Jerome, OP. 1995. *Paul the Letter-Writer: His World, His Options, His Skills.* Good News Studies 41. Collegeville, MN: Michael Glazier.

_____. 1996. *Paul: A Critical Life.* New York: Oxford University Press.

Nanos, Mark D., ed. 2002. *The Galatians Debate: Contemporary Issues in Rhetorical and Historical Interpretation.* Peabody, MA: Hendrickson.

Nanos, Mark, and Magnus Zetterholm, eds. 2015. *Paul within Judaism: Restoring the First-Century Context to the Apostle*. Minneapolis: Fortress.

Nathan, Emmanuel. 2020. *Re-membering the New Covenant at Corinth: A Different Perspective on 2 Corinthians 3*. WUNT 2/514. Tübingen: Mohr Siebeck.

Nicholl, Colin R. 2000. "Michael, the Restrainer Removed (2 Thess. 2:6–7)." *JTS* n.s. 51 (1): 27–53.

———. 2004. *From Hope to Despair in Thessalonica: Situating 1 and 2 Thessalonians*. SNTSMS 126. Cambridge: Cambridge University Press.

Nickelsburg, George W. E., and Michael E. Stone. 1983. *Faith and Piety in Early Judaism: Texts and Documents*. Philadelphia: Fortress.

Noblom, Rodolfo Puigdollers I. "¿Por qué Pablo quería ir a Hispania?" *EstBib* 74 (3): 389–410.

Nordling, John G. 1991. "Onesimus Fugitivus: A Defense of the Runaway Slave Hypothesis in Philemon." *JSNT* 41: 97–119.

Oakes, Peter. 2001. *Philippians: From People to Letter*. SNTSMS 110. Cambridge: Cambridge University Press.

———. 2009. *Reading Romans in Pompeii: Paul's Letter at Ground Level*. Minneapolis: Fortress.

Oropeza, B. J. 2016. *Exploring Second Corinthians: Death and Life, Hardship and Rivalry*. Atlanta: SBL Press.

Osiek, Carolyn. 2000. *Philippians, Philemon*. ANTC. Nashville: Abingdon.

Osiek, Carolyn, and Margaret Y. MacDonald. 2006. *A Woman's Place: House Churches in Earliest Christianity*. With Janet H. Tulloch. Minneapolis: Fortress.

Oster, Richard E. 1992. "Ephesus." *ABD* 2: 542–49.

Penna, A. 1960. *St. Paul the Apostle*. Translated by K. C. Thompson. London: St. Paul Publications.

Perkins, Pheme. 2011. "Adam and Christ in the Pauline Epistles." In *Celebrating Paul: Festschrift in Honor of Jerome Murphy-O'Connor, OP, and Joseph A. Fitzmyer, SJ*, edited by Peter Spitaler, 128–51. CBQMS 48. Washington, DC: Catholic Biblical Association of America.

Peterman, G. W. 1997. *Paul's Gift from Philippi: Conventions of Gift-Exchange and Christian Giving*. SNTSMS 9. Cambridge: Cambridge University Press.

Peterson, Erik. 1964. "ἀπάντησις." *TDNT* 1: 380–81.

Phillips, Thomas E. 2009. *Paul, His Letters, and Acts*. LPS. Grand Rapids: Baker Academic.

Pifer, Jeanette Hagen. 2019. *Faith as Participation: An Exegetical Study of Some Key Pauline Texts*. WUNT 2/486. Tübingen: Mohr Siebeck.

Pitre, Brant, Michael P. Barber, and John A. Kincaid. 2019. *Paul, a New Covenant Jew: Rethinking Pauline Theology*. Grand Rapids: Eerdmans.

Pius XI (Pope). 1930. *Casti Connubii*. Encyclical Letter. December 31.

Plevnik, Joseph, SJ. 1989. "The Center of Pauline Theology." *CBQ* 51 (3): 461–78.

_____. 1997. *Paul and the Parousia: An Exegetical and Theological Investigation*. Peabody, MA: Hendrickson.

_____. 1999. "1 Thessalonians 4:17: The Bringing in of the Lord or the Bringing in of the Faithful?" *Bib* 80 (4): 537–46.

_____. 2000. "The Destination of the Apostle and of the Faithful: Second Corinthians 4:13b–14 and First Thessalonians 4:14." *CBQ* 62 (1): 83–95.

Pontifical Biblical Commission. 1954. *Enchiridion Biblicum: Documenta Ecclesiastica Sacram Scripturam Spectantia*. Revised edition. Rome: Editiones Comm. A. Arnodo.

_____. 1993. *The Interpretation of the Bible in the Church*. In *The Scripture Documents: An Anthology of Official Catholic Teachings*, edited by Dean P. Béchard, 244–315. Collegeville, MN: Liturgical Press.

_____. 2002. *The Jewish People and Their Sacred Scriptures in the Christian Bible*. Rome: Libreria Editrice Vaticana.

_____. 2014. *The Inspiration and Truth of Sacred Scripture: The Word That Comes from God and Speaks of God for the Salvation of the World*. Translated by Thomas Esposito, O.Cist. and Stephen Gregg, O.Cist. Collegeville, MN: Liturgical Press.

Porter, Stanley E. 1999. *The Paul of Acts: Essays in Literary Criticism, Rhetoric, and Theology*. WUNT 115. Tübingen: Mohr Siebeck.

Prior, Michael, CM. 1989. *Paul the Letter-Writer and the Second Letter to Timothy*. JSNTSup 23. Sheffield: Sheffield Academic.

Prothro, James B. 2018. *Both Judge and Justifier: Biblical Legal Language and the Act of Justifying in Paul*. WUNT 2/461. Tübingen: Mohr Siebeck.

_____. 2020. "History, Illocution, and Theological Exegesis: Reading Paul's Letter to Philemon." *Nova et Vetera* English Edition 18 (4): 1341–63.

Quinn, Jerome D. 1990. *The Letter to Titus: A New Translation with Notes and Commentary*. AB 35. New York: Doubleday.

Quinn, Jerome D., and William C. Wacker. 2000. *The First and Second Letters to Timothy: A New Translation with Notes and Commentary*. ECC. Grand Rapids: Eerdmans.

Rabens, Volker. 2010. *The Holy Spirit and Ethics in Paul: Transformation and Empowering for Religious-Ethical Life*. WUNT 2/283. Tübingen: Mohr Siebeck.

Räisänen, Heikki. 1983. *Paul and the Law*. WUNT 29. Tübingen: Mohr Siebeck.

Reasoner, Mark. 1999a. *The Strong and the Weak: Romans 14.1–15.13 in Context*. SNTSMS 103. Cambridge: Cambridge University Press.

_____. 1999b. "The Theme of Acts: Institutional History or Divine Necessity in History?" *JBL* 118 (4): 635–59.

_____. 2005. *Romans in Full Circle: A History of Interpretation*. Louisville, KY: Westminster John Knox.

Reece, Steve. 2017. *Paul's Large Letters: Paul's Autographic Subscriptions in the Light of Ancient Epistolary Conventions*. LNTS 561. London: Bloomsbury.

Reed, Jeffrey T. 1996. "Philippians 3:1 and the Epistolary Hesitation Formulas: The Literary Integrity of Philippians, Again." *JBL* 115 (1): 63–90.

Reicke, Bo. 1970. "Caesarea, Rome, and the Captivity Epistles." In *Apostolic History and the Gospel: Biblical and Historical Essays Presented to F. F. Bruce on His 60th Birthday*, edited by W. Ward Gasque and Ralph P. Martin, 277–86. Grand Rapids: Eerdmans.

_____. 2001. *Re-Examining Paul's Letters: The History of the Pauline Correspondence*. Edited by David P. Moessner and Ingalisa Reicke. Harrisburg, PA: Trinity.

Richards, E. Randolph. 2004. *Paul and First-Century Letter Writing: Secretaries, Composition and Collection*. Downers Grove, IL: IVP Academic.

Riesner, Rainer. 1998. *Paul's Early Period: Chronology, Mission Strategy, Theology*. Translated by Doug Scott. Grand Rapids: Eerdmans.

Rodríguez, Rafael. 2014. *If You Call Yourself a Jew: Reappraising Paul's Letter to the Romans*. Eugene, OR: Cascade.

Rodríguez, Rafael, and Matthew Thiessen, eds. 2016. *The So-Called Jew in Paul's Letter to the Romans*. Minneapolis: Fortress.

Rosenmeyer, Patricia A. 2001. *Ancient Epistolary Fictions: The Letter in Greek Literature*. Cambridge: Cambridge University Press.

Rosner, Brian S. 1993. "Acts and Biblical History." In *The Book of Acts in Its Ancient Literary Setting*, edited by Bruce W. Winter and Andrew D. Clarke, 65–82. Vol. 1 of *The Book of Acts in Its First Century Setting*. Grand Rapids: Eerdmans.

_____. 2013. *Paul and the Law: Keeping the Commandments of God*. New Studies in Biblical Theology 31. Downers Grove, IL: InterVarsity.

Rowe, C. Kavin. 2009. *World Upside Down: Reading Acts in the Graeco-Roman Age*. New York: Oxford University Press.

Rowland, Christopher, and Christopher R. A. Morray-Jones. 2009. *The Mystery of God: Early Jewish Mysticism and the New Testament*. CRINT 3/12. Leiden: Brill, 2009.

Rutgers, Leonard Victor. 1994. "Roman Policy towards the Jews: Expulsions from the City of Rome during the First Century C.E." *Classical Antiquity* 13 (1): 56–74.

Sanders, E. P. 1977. *Paul and Palestinian Judaism: A Comparison of Patterns of Religion*. Minneapolis: Fortress.

_____. 2015. *The Apostle's Life, Letters, and Thought*. Minneapolis: Fortress.

Schnackenburg, Rudolf. 1991. *The Epistle to the Ephesians: A Commentary*. Translated by Helen Heron. Edinburgh: T&T Clark.

Schnelle, Udo. 1991. *The Human Condition: Anthropology in the Teachings of Jesus, Paul, and John*. Translated by O. C. Dean Jr. Edinburgh: T&T Clark.

_____. 2005. *Apostle Paul: His Life and Theology*. Translated by M. Eugene Boring. Grand Rapids: Baker Academic.

Schweitzer, Albert. 1931. *The Mysticism of the Apostle Paul.* Translated by William Montgomery. London: Black.

Scott, Ian. 2006. *Implicit Epistemology in the Letters of Paul: Story, Experience and the Spirit.* WUNT 2/205. Tübingen: Mohr Siebeck.

Segal, Alan F. 1990. *Paul the Convert: The Apostolate and Apostasy of Saul the Pharisee.* New Haven, CT: Yale University Press.

Seifrid, Mark A. 1992. *Justification by Faith: The Origin and Development of a Central Pauline Theme.* NovTSup 68. Leiden: Brill.

_____. 2000. *Christ, Our Righteousness: Paul's Theology of Justification.* New Studies in Biblical Theology 9. Downers Grove, IL: InterVarsity.

Silva, Moisés. 2005. *Philippians.* 2nd edition. BECNT. Grand Rapids: Baker Academic.

Smiles, Vincent M. 1998. *The Gospel and the Law in Galatia: Paul's Response to Jewish-Christian Separatism and the Threat of Galatian Apostasy.* Collegeville, MN: Liturgical Press.

Smit, Peter-Ben. 2013. *Paradigms of Being in Christ: A Study of the Epistle to the Philippians.* LNTS 476. London: Bloomsbury T&T Clark.

_____. 2014. "Paul, Plutarch and the Problematic Practice of Self-Praise (περιαυτολογία): The Case of Phil 3.2–21." *NTS* 60 (3): 341–59.

Smith, Daniel Lynwood, and Zachary Lundin Kostopoulos. 2017. "Biography, History and the Genre of Luke-Acts." *NTS* 63 (3): 390–410.

Staples, Jason A. 2011. "What Do the Gentiles Have to Do with 'All Israel'? A Fresh Look at Romans 11:25–27." *JBL* 130 (2): 371–90.

Stegman, Thomas D., SJ. 2005. *The Character of Jesus: The Linchpin to Paul's Argument in 2 Corinthians.* AnBib 158. Rome: Pontifical Biblical Institute.

_____. 2009. *Second Corinthians.* CCSS. Grand Rapids: Baker Academic.

_____. 2017. "St. Paul on Holiness." *JJT* 24: 60–73.

_____. 2018. "Romans." In *The Paulist Biblical Commentary,* edited by José Enrique Aguilar Chiu, Richard J. Clifford, SJ, Carol J. Dempsey, OP, Eileen M. Schuller, OSU, Thomas D. Stegman, SJ, Ronald D. Witherup, PSS, 1234–88. New York: Paulist Press.

Stettler, Christian. 2000. *Der Kolosserhymnus: Untersuchungen zu Form, traditionsge-schichtlichem Hintergrund und Aussage von Kol 1,15–20.* WUNT 2/131. Tübingen: Mohr Siebeck.

_____. 2005. "The Opponents at Colossae." In *Paul and His Opponents,* edited by Stanley E. Porter, 169–200. Pauline Studies 2. Leiden: Brill.

Stockhausen, Carol Kern. 1989. *Moses's Veil and the Glory of the New Covenant: The Exegetical Substructure of II Cor. 3,1–4,6.* AnBib 116. Rome: Pontifical Biblical Institute.

Sumney, Jerry L. 1990. *Identifying Paul's Opponents: The Question of Method in 2 Corinthians.* JSNTSup 40. Sheffield: Sheffield Academic.

_____. 1993. "Those Who 'Pass Judgment': The Identity of the Opponents in Colossians." *Bib* 74 (3): 366–88.

_____. 2008. *Colossians: A Commentary.* NTL. Louisville, KY: Westminster John Knox.

_____. 2017. *Steward of God's Mysteries: Paul and Early Church Tradition.* Grand Rapids: Eerdmans.

Tatum, Gregory, OP. 2006. *New Chapters in the Life of Paul: The Relative Chronology of His Career.* CBQMS 41. Washington, DC: Catholic Biblical Association of America.

Theissen, Gerd. 1982. *The Social Setting of Pauline Christianity: Essays on Corinth.* Edited by J. H. Schütz. Minneapolis: Fortress.

Thielman, Frank. 2003. "Ephesus and the Literary Setting of Philippians." In *New Testament Greek and Exegesis: Essays in Honor of Gerald F. Hawthorne,* edited by A. M. Donaldson and T. B. Sailors, 205–23. Grand Rapids: Eerdmans.

_____. 2010. *Ephesians.* BECNT. Grand Rapids: Baker Academic, 2010.

Thiselton, Anthony C. 2000. *The First Epistle to the Corinthians: A Commentary on the Greek Text.* NIGTC. Grand Rapids: Eerdmans.

_____. 2011. *1 and 2 Thessalonians Through the Centuries.* Blackwell Bible Commentaries. Chichester: Wiley-Blackwell.

Thomas, Matthew J. 2018. *Paul's "Works of the Law" in the Perspective of Second-Century Reception.* WUNT 2/468. Tübingen: Mohr Siebeck.

Thompson, James W. 2001. "Paul's Argument from *Pathos* in 2 Corinthians." In *Paul and Pathos,* edited by Thomas H. Olbright and Jerry L. Sumney, 127–45. SymS 16. Atlanta: SBL Press.

Thompson, James W., and Bruce W. Longenecker. 2016. *Philippians and Philemon.* Paideia Commentaries on the New Testament. Grand Rapids: Baker Academic.

Thrall, Margaret E. 1994, 2000. *A Critical and Exegetical Commentary on the Second Epistle to the Corinthians.* 2 vols. ICC. Edinburgh: T&T Clark.

Tobin, Thomas H., SJ. 2004. *Paul's Rhetoric in Its Contexts: The Argument of Romans.* Peabody, MA: Hendrickson.

Tolmie, D. Francois. 2005. *Persuading the Galatians: A Text-Centred Rhetorical Analysis of a Pauline Letter.* WUNT 2/190. Tübingen: Mohr Siebeck.

Towner, Philip H. 2006. *The Letters to Timothy and Titus.* NICNT. Grand Rapids: Eerdmans.

Trebilco, Paul. 2004. *The Early Christians in Ephesus from Paul to Ignatius.* WUNT 166. Tübingen: Mohr Siebeck.

_____. 2011. "Why Did the Early Christians Call Themselves ἡ ἐκκλησία?" *NTS* 57 (3): 440–60.

Usami, Kōshi, SJ. 1983. *Somatic Comprehension of Unity: The Church in Ephesus.* AnBib 101. Rome: Pontifical Biblical Institute.

Uytanlet, Samson. 2014. *Luke-Acts and Jewish Historiography: A Study on the Theology, Literature, and Ideology of Luke-Acts*. WUNT 2/366. Tübingen: Mohr Siebeck.

Van Nes, Jermo. 2018. *Pauline Language and the Pastoral Epistles: A Study of Linguistic Variation in the Corpus Paulinum*. Linguistic Biblical Studies 16. Leiden: Brill.

Van Zyl, Hermie C. 1998. "The Evolution of Church Leadership in the New Testament—A New Consensus?" *Neot* 32 (2): 585–604.

Vanhoye, Cardinal Albert, and Peter S. Williamson. 2019. *Galatians*. CCSS. Grand Rapids: Baker Academic.

Vegge, Ivar. 2008. *2 Corinthians—A Letter about Reconciliation: A Psychagogical, Epistolographical and Rhetorical Analysis*. WUNT 2/239. Tübingen: Mohr Siebeck.

Verner, David C. 1983. *The Household of God: The Social World of the Pastoral Epistles*. SBLDS 71. Chico, CA: Scholars.

Ware, James. 2014. "Paul's Understanding of the Resurrection in 1 Corinthians 15:36–54." *JBL* 133 (4): 809–35.

Watson, Duane F. 1988. "A Rhetorical Analysis of Philippians and Its Implications for the Unity Question." *NovT* 30 (1): 57 88.

Watson, Francis. 1984. "2 Cor. x-xiii and Paul's Painful Letter to the Corinthians." *JTS* n.s. 35 (2): 324–46.

Weima, Jeffrey A. D. 2014. *1-2 Thessalonians*. BECNT. Grand Rapids: Baker Academic.

Welborn, L. L. 1995. "The Identification of 2 Corinthians 10–13 with the 'Letter of Tears.'" *NovT* 37 (2): 138–53.

Westfall, Cynthia Long. 2016. *Paul and Gender: Reclaiming the Apostle's Vision for Men and Women in Christ*. Grand Rapids: Baker Academic.

White, Benjamin L. 2011. "How to Read a Book: Irenaeus and the Pastoral Epistles Reconsidered." *VC* 65 (2): 125–49.

Wieland, George M. 2006. *The Significance of Salvation: A Study of Salvation Language in the Pastoral Epistles*. Paternoster Biblical Monographs. Milton Keynes: Paternoster.

Wiles, M. F. 1967. *The Divine Apostle: The Interpretation of St. Paul's Epistles in the Early Church*. Cambridge: Cambridge University Press.

Williams, Sam K. 1987. "Justification and the Spirit in Galatians." *JSNT* 29 (9): 91–100.

Wilson, Robert M. 2005. *A Critical and Exegetical Commentary on Colossians and Philemon*. ICC. Edinburgh: T&T Clark.

Winger, Thomas M. 2015. *Ephesians*. ConcC. St. Louis: Concordia.

Winter, Bruce W. 2001. *After Paul Left Corinth: The Influence of Secular Ethics and Social Change*. Grand Rapids: Eerdmans.

———. 2003. *Roman Wives, Roman Widows: The Appearance of New Women and the Pauline Communities*. Grand Rapids: Eerdmans.

Winter, Sara C. 1987. "Paul's Letter to Philemon." *NTS* 33 (1): 1–15.

Wischmeyer, Oda, ed. 2012. *Paul: Life, Setting, Work, Letters*. Translated by Helen S. Heron. Revisions by Dieter T. Roth. London: T&T Clark.

Witetschek, Stephan. 2018. "Peter in Corinth? A Review of the Evidence from 1 Corinthians." *JTS* n.s. 69 (1): 66–82.

Witherington, Ben, III. 2006. *1 and 2 Thessalonians: A Socio-Rhetorical Commentary*. Grand Rapids: Eerdmans.

Wolf, E. R. 1966. "Kinship, Friendship, and Patron-Client Relations." In *The Social Anthropology of Complex Societies*, edited by M. Banton, 1–22. New York: Praeger.

Wolter, Michael. 2015. *Paul: An Outline of His Theology*. Translated by Robert L. Brawley. Waco, TX: Baylor University Press.

Wrede, William. 1907. *Paul*. Translated by Edward Lummis. London: Philip Green.

Wright, N. T. 1991. "Poetry and Theology in Col 1.15–20." In *Climax of the Covenant: Christ and the Law in Pauline Theology*, 99–119. Edinburgh: T&T Clark.

_____. 2003. *The Resurrection of the Son of God*. Christian Origins and the Question of God 3. Minneapolis: Fortress.

_____. 2005. *Paul: In Fresh Perspective*. Minneapolis: Fortress.

_____. 2009. *Justification: God's Plan and Paul's Vision*. Downers Grove, IL: IVP Academic.

_____. 2013. *Paul and the Faithfulness of God*. Christian Origins and the Question of God 4. Minneapolis: Fortress.

_____. 2015. *Paul and His Recent Interpreters*. Minneapolis: Fortress.

Yarbrough, Mark M. 2009. *Paul's Utilization of Preformed Traditions in 1 Timothy: An Evaluation of the Apostle's Literary, Rhetorical, and Theological Tactics*. LNTS 417. London: T&T Clark.

Yee, Tet-Lim N. 2005. *Jews, Gentiles and Ethnic Reconciliation: Paul's Jewish Identity and Ephesians*. SNTSMS 130. Cambridge: Cambridge University Press.

Young, Frances Margaret. 1994. *The Theology of the Pastoral Letters*. Cambridge: Cambridge University Press.

Zetterholm, Magnus. 2009. *Approaches to Paul: A Student's Guide to Recent Scholarship*. Minneapolis: Fortress.

Scriptural Index

Old Testament

Author Index

Index

A BIBLICAL PATH TO THE TRIUNE GOD
Jesus, Paul, and the Revelation of the Trinity

Denis Farkasfalvy, O. Cist
Foreword by Bruce D. Marshall
Edited by Thomas Esposito, O. Cist

ECCLESIAL EXEGESIS
A Synthesis of Ancient
and Modern Approaches to Scripture

Gregory Vall